A RICHER
LIFE FOR
YOU IN
CHRIST

A RICHER LIFE FOR YOU IN CHRIST

An Exegetical Commentary on
First Corinthians One

SPIROS ZODHIATES, TH.D.

AMG
PUBLISHERS

Chattanooga, TN 37422

A Richer Life for You in Christ

An Exegetical Commentary on
First Corinthians One

©1972 by Spiros Zodhiates
All Rights Reserved.
Revised Edition, 1997

ISBN 0-89957-442-4

Printed in the United States of America
02 01 00 99 98 97 –R– 6 5 4 3 2 1

To Dorothy R. Bryant,
my editorial manager, whose faithful service for twenty-four
years has been of inestimable help in producing my writings

Contents

Preface

In my studies in the Corinthian Epistles I have been struck by the great similarity between their first century society and our own. Corinth was the crossroads for people of a variety of languages and cultures: Jews, Greeks, Romans, and many others. The temple of Apollo stood proudly in the midst of their marketplace. Thought, commerce, intrigue, moral degeneracy were all most evident in the half million inhabitants of Corinth—at that time the capital of Achaia (now superseded by Athens).

To such an environment the Apostle Paul brought the gospel of the saving grace of the Lord Jesus Christ. Although he was rebuffed by the Athenian philosophers, he believed that where sin abounded grace could much more abound. Corinth was the place to test that principle. It succeeded. Souls were saved, among them some of the greatest opponents of the gospel and the most sinful. This is the primary historical evidence we derive from the study of Paul's Corinthian Epistles.

But the emergence of a Christian Church in as sinful an environment as Corinth's created many internal problems of behavior. Each person coming into the Christian Church through regenerating faith in Jesus Christ still remained an individual laden with his cultural and traditional background. The human element in man endeavored to carry these remnants of the old life into the new Christian community: hence, internal problems of conduct—ecclesiastical, communal, and individual. Paul endeavored to solve these problems and set some standards.

But what have the problems of the Corinthian church and its members to do with us? When we study them, we find that man has basically not changed. The problems of Corinth are the problems of our day. In one sentence, the Corinthians were characterized by a propensity to "sanctify evil." For example, they called the prostitutes priestesses. Today we find this same basic tendency in our society—a subtle endeavor to persuade all of us that there is nothing wrong with the generally accepted practice of polarizing believers, of fornication, of premarital relations, of unbelievers occupying positions of prominence in the Christian Church, and so on.

Because of the relevance of the Corinthian problems to our own society, I decided to study these Epistles of Paul exhaustively and delineate the principles that he sets forth as an apostle of Jesus Christ whose word has binding authority. I have endeavored to examine every word, every sentence from the Greek text, and make the meaning as plain as possible for the English reader, who may not be able to conduct such a study on his own. It is not enough to know the Greek language; one must be able to enter into the Greek mind and thought. Through these studies I trust that with the Holy Spirit's help I may have been able to provide at least some food for thought, some guidelines for Christian behavior in an age of confusion.

The chapters have been divided into short studies originally delivered on our radio network as "New Testament Light." The discipline of having to deliver a study each week accounts for the production of volumes such as this.

This study on the first chapter was prepared some time after my studies on the 12th and 14th chapters of 1 Corinthians, the love chapter of 1 Corinthians 13 (in my book *To Love Is to Live*), and the studies on 1 Corinthians 15 (published under the title, *Conquering the Fear of Death*).

I hope to continue these studies in Corinthians as time goes on. If you derive spiritual benefit from them, I would greatly appreciate your prayers that they may continue to bless others.

My deepest gratitude goes to our Editorial Manager, Mrs. Dorothy Bryant, who has worked with me for twenty-four years, producing the final manuscripts from handwritten copy. Also my gratitude to my research consultant, Robert S. Moreland, whose knowledge of the original biblical languages has helped to check the accuracy of the entire study. And finally, but not least, my gratitude to my librarian, Frederick Kronmeyer, who has culled hundreds of books from our 15,000 volume library to assist me in my research. Alone it would have been impossible for me to accomplish this colossal task. With such dedicated help, I hope to produce more of these studies. Above all, I dedicate this book to the glory of God.

Spiros Zodhiates

An Overview of First Corinthians

Author: Paul the Apostle, author of thirteen other epistles to various individuals and congregations.

Date: About A.D. 55.

Recipients: The congregation which Paul established in Corinth.

Place: From Ephesus

Theme: Paul had received news about the Corinthian brethren from several sources (1 Cor. 1:11; 7:1; 16:17). The church was afflicted with many problems that face young churches and new converts. The Apostle, under the inspiration of the Holy Spirit, decided to write this urgent letter to admonish and instruct the church. Among other topics he discussed: the necessity of church discipline (5:1-13); divisions and disputes among Christians (1:10-16; 6:1-11); matters of conscience (8:1-13; 10:19-33); the support of preachers (9:1-27); abuses of the Lord's Supper (10:16-17, 21; 11:17-34); the misuse of spiritual gifts (12:1—14:40); and the importance of the resurrection of Jesus Christ (15:1-58).

An Outline of First Corinthians

In the days of the Apostle Paul, Corinth was the capital city of the Roman province of Achaia and the glory of Greece. Though its great ancient splendor had been destroyed by the Romans in 120 B.C., the city was rebuilt under Julius Caesar and restored to wealth and luxury under Augustus. Among all the cities of the world, however, it was most well known for its lewdness. The Apostle Paul lived in Corinth for eighteen months (Acts 18:11). After his departure, Paul went to Ephesus. During his three-year stay there, he heard reports of wickedness and division within the Corinthian church. In an effort to correct these evils, Paul wrote several letters to them, including the Epistle of First Corinthians.

1 Cor. 1:1 | *Paul's Authority as an Apostle of Christ Jesus*

Paul, called to be an apostle of Jesus Christ through the will of God and Sosthenes our brother.

When you and I write a letter, we wait until the end to sign our names, but this was not the custom in ancient times. The name came first. The writer began the letter by identifying himself, realizing that the importance of what he had to say was in direct relation to his identity. If a stranger writes you, you do not know whether you can believe him or not, but if he is someone whose good character and credentials you know, you are far more receptive to what he has to say.

When Paul wrote his First Epistle to the Christians of Corinth, he was already known to them. He had labored among them. He was their spiritual father (1 Cor. 4:14, 15), for it was through him that they first heard the gospel. He knew that by mentioning his name at the very beginning of his letter, he would ensure their reading it because they would regard it as a letter from a father to his children.

Who Gave Paul the Right to Tell Us What to Do?

Although Paul could run circles around any present-day psychologist, he used no public-relations gimmicks in his greeting. He did not follow the principle of trying to make his readers feel

1

important by starting with the word "you," but immediately started with a reference to himself. Why? He wanted them to know that he was not writing to them as man to man, but as an apostle of Christ to the followers of Christ. He wanted to establish his authority, to impress upon them that his words and his counsel were not to be taken as having relative value but absolute authority. A king does not need public-relations language, nor does a general when he speaks to his soldiers. Neither does God, when He speaks to His people through His chosen messengers. Because Paul is what he is, the Corinthian believers are under obligation to listen to what he has to say.

Of course, we must not consider Paul an egotist, as some have done. He is not blowing his own trumpet here, for immediately after setting down his name he adds the qualifying term, "called apostle" (a.t. *klētós* [2822] *apóstolos* [652]). He is what he is because of a divine call. It was nothing that he sought for himself; in fact, in his sin and unbelief he resisted it and by God's grace had to be arrested on the road to Damascus and made willing to follow Christ.

The Greek word *klētós* comes from the verb *kaléō* (2564), meaning "to call." In this context, however, as well as in others (Rom. 1:6; 1 Cor. 1:24), the *klētoí*, the "called ones," are the Christian believers. It can be used in this manner if a comma is placed after *klētós* "a called one," making it an adjectival noun. Thus, we see that Paul is actually declaring here that he is a believer before he is an apostle. The Corinthians knew this well, but he does not hesitate to repeat it. There were, and still are, too many preachers who are not believers yet claim to speak with authority. If a preacher does not frequently affirm his unequivocal faith in Jesus Christ as the Son of God, through whose atonement alone man can find salvation, we should beware of him. He is not in the tradition of the Apostle Paul. Paul's first declaration is that he is a *klētós*, a "called one," a Christian believer. And a believer speaks with authority about his beliefs: "I know whom I have believed" (2 Tim. 1:12).

If *klētós* is taken as a qualifying adjective, it can be connected with the word *apóstolos*, "apostle," which follows it. With Paul, his call to believe and his call to become an apostle were practically simultaneous. This is often the case. It is a double call—to believe and to preach—and blessed is the person who is so chosen of the Lord. The word *apóstolos* in the New Testament is sometimes used with the general sense of a man who is sent with full authority. At other times it has the meaning of an ambassador, a person legally commissioned to represent a person or cause (John 13:16). And sometimes it means the commissioned representative of a congregation (Phil. 2:25). In the New Testament particularly it means the bearer of the gospel message.

But here and elsewhere in his epistles (2 Cor. 1:1; Eph. 1:1; Col. 1:1, etc.), Paul claims to be an apostle in a more specific sense, as one of that small group of disciples who saw Jesus Christ after His resurrection (1 Cor. 9:1) and who was commissioned to deliver to men once and for all the revelation of God in Christ. These disciples were equivalent in many ways to those Old Testament prophets selected by God to prepare the way for the Messiah (Eph. 2:20; 3:5).

Although you and I are called upon to be apostles of Jesus Christ, it is not in the same restricted sense as Paul and his fellow apostles whose writings establish what God has revealed for us to believe. Paul's words were to be accepted by the Corinthians, therefore, not as the words of a mere man, but as the words of God through a man—Paul. They were a revelation from God, about which there could be no dispute. This is the way you and I should read them. We cannot choose what we like out of his writings and reject what we do not like. True, what he says must be considered within the framework of the times and environment in which he wrote, but the principles established must be adhered to as indisputable.

We have shown that Paul's authority was not arbitrary but delegated. By whom was Paul called? The Lord Jesus Christ. Apostolic authority began with the risen Christ and it cannot exist without Him. Have you ever thought how strange it was that Christ, after His resurrection and before He ascended into heaven, told His disciples, "All power is given unto Me in heaven and in earth" (Matt. 28:18), and then immediately commission them to go into the whole world and proclaim His message? They were the ones who actually needed power and authority as they preached. But Christ did not say, "All power I give unto you," but "All power is given unto Me." He wanted to impress upon them that all authority and power must forever be centered in Him, and that their share in it is directly proportionate to their closeness to Him. Paul never lost this sense of his authority as being derived entirely from the Lord. Because He arose, Christ has the authority to speak as no one else and to give us this same authority.

Do you remember the Roman officer, a centurion, who described himself as "a man *under* authority" (Luke 7:8)? Why is it not stated as "a man *of* authority"? Because he stood in a long line of delegated authority, he could give orders and have them obeyed. He had authority because he was under authority. So it was with the Apostle Paul. Had he not been under the authority of the Lord Jesus Christ, he would not have had authority for the Corinthians, and he would not have had any for us.

Was Paul Authoritative or Authoritarian?

What would happen if mobs were free to demonstrate in the streets without any regulatory authority? In Montreal, when the police and fire departments went on strike for only one day, the city was rapidly becoming a shambles. Without authority, chaos reigns.

The Scriptures tell us that all authority in heaven and earth centers in Jesus Christ. Why? Because He is God incarnate, co-Creator with the Father (John 1:1–3), who "is before all things, and by him all things consist" (Col. 1:17). Now, when God made us, He did not ask us how we wanted to be formed. As Creator He possesses all wisdom and therefore knows what is best for us. Thus, He has the right to tell us how to live to fulfill the purpose for which He created us—a harmonious relation with His divine authority.

Man, under Satan, however, continually sought in his history to usurp that authority. The first man cut the cords of union with Deity, and ever since, men have been exercising their own authority. Whatever discord and catastrophe we are now reaping is not due to the exercise of God's spiritual and moral authority but our own. We have become self-directed relativists instead of accepting God's absolute authority.

Of course, we have to accept God's authority when it comes to the laws of nature that He has established, for if we did not, we would perish. We must eat food, breathe oxygen, and reckon with gravity every day of our lives. But we have rejected His absolute laws in the spiritual and moral realm, acting as if God knows the rightness of one but not the other. That's why we're advancing in science and retrogressing in morals. We have placed our dependence on God's natural laws but have questioned the dependability of His moral laws. Nevertheless, God has all authority, and He expects us to respect and obey it.

This authority was manifested to us in a tangible and unmistakable way in history through the Lord Jesus Christ. Christian faith starts, not with an idea, but with a supernatural Person who can be traced in a historical context. This unique individual lived on this earth; He spoke as no one ever spoke, claimed what no man ever claimed, did what no man ever did, and died as no one ever died—predicting that in three days He would rise again. And, because He did, we can respect His authority. He proved He was what Scripture claims Him to be—the Creator of all things including us. He is therefore entitled to our absolute obedience. Our joy and peace depend on whether we accept or reject what He has to say to us.

Now, because Paul (as Saul) had been a self-satisfied intellectual, he saw no reason to accept such authority. Such pride keeps many a man from examining the evidence for the truth of the gospel. Therefore, the Lord had to bring Paul to the place where he could no longer deny His authority. He spoke to him audibly, knocked him down, and blinded him. Sometimes our stubbornness causes God to take strong measures with us. His actions are often conditioned by our attitude toward His revelation. If we voluntarily reject His authority, it then becomes necessary for Him to impose it forcibly. Now He allows a certain period of time in which we have some latitude in this matter of accepting His authority, but the day will come when our relative and permitted authority to reject His absolute authority will be put "under his feet" (1 Cor. 15:25).

What He is going to do to all earthly authority at the consummation of the age, the Lord does even now in some instances, as in the case of Paul. That is why, at the beginning of his epistles, Paul so consistently says, "Paul, a called apostle of Christ Jesus." He declares his authority as an apostle, but he does so in a way that shows he recognizes it to be derived directly from the Lord. He is under authority and therefore vested with authority. He felt the authority of the Lord Jesus in His risen glory more forcibly than any other disciple. He was not simply wooed by it in a simple command to "Follow Me, and I will make you fishers of men" (Matt. 4:19) as were Peter and Andrew. No, Paul was struck down by it.

PAUL'S AUTHORITY AS AN APOSTLE OF CHRIST JESUS

It is obvious to me that Paul never lost the impact of this authority of the Lord in his entire life. That is why, more than any other apostle, he asserts it every time he writes to believers in various places. He wants them to know that he is truly an apostle under authority and with authority. Consequently, what he says must be received, not with the challenge of human wisdom, but with the obedience of a child toward a father, of a creature toward the creator, in spite of the fact that in himself Paul was neither, but was the servant and ambassador of God the Father and Creator and of His Son Jesus Christ. He spoke with authority derived directly from Christ Himself—something we cannot do because we have not had the same opportunity of seeing the risen Christ.

It is noteworthy that in the original Greek the order of the words here is not the same as in the King James translation. Paul does not say "a called apostle of Jesus Christ" but "of Christ Jesus." He does the same thing in 2 Corinthians 1:1 and at the beginning of Philippians, Colossians, 1 and 2 Timothy, and Philemon. Paul was claiming his apostleship, not from a historical figure called Jesus, but from *Christ* Jesus. He was looking at the Lord first as God and then as man. Christ was the name of the Lord's function of office. It means "the Anointed One." He was the coming One, the pre-existent One, the One who was before the world was made. Christ was to be found in the Old Testament, and Paul, being a Jew, begins there. In the New Testament we have Jesus the man who is the fulfillment of all the Old Testament sayings about Him who was to come. Christ is our authority, not so much as a man, but as God manifest in the flesh. If you think of Him only as man, you will never speak about Him with authority.

Though Paul starts his epistles with his authority as an apostle, he should not be considered authoritarian but authoritative because his authority is based on Christ Jesus, the Christ of eternity and the Jesus of history. An authoritarian is one who demands blind obedience regardless of who or what he is. But an authoritative person is one who has the right to be obeyed because of what he is. Christ was not authoritarian but authoritative. And because Paul's authority and apostleship were derived from Christ, they, too, were authoritative and not authoritarian.

Can You Be Saved in Spite of Yourself?

Have you ever opened a watch or clock and observed the motions of its various wheels? You will notice that, though they move contrary to one another—some one way, and some another—yet all serve the intent of the workman, to show the time or to make the clock strike. This helps us to understand the theological puzzle—the relationship between God's will and man's will. In the world, the providence of God may seem to run contrary to His promises—one man takes this way, another that; good men go one way, wicked men another—yet in the end, all people accomplish the will of God and center in the purpose of God, who is the great Creator of all things.

Saul of Tarsus hated Christianity. He was a Pharisee of the Pharisees who had no intent or desire to be a turncoat to Judaism. He was determined to put an end to the new religion that Christ introduced among the Jews. His will was set against the Galilean teacher. Christ had died and then had risen, but Saul's attitude did not change. And yet this same man became the chief apostle of Christ. He does not hesitate to acknowledge that it was not of his own doing, but all "by the will of God." His wheels were turning against Christ. However, because Jesus Christ was God manifest in the flesh, it was His will which prevailed in the end.

Paul knew from his own personal experience—what he taught throughout his writings—that man of himself never wills to be saved; the initiative always comes from God. He takes this initiative in a variety of ways: sometimes by words, sometimes by His goodness, sometimes by lightning and thunder, sometimes through suffering and pain. God turns the wheels whichever way He wants to accomplish His ultimate purpose. God's purpose is never our eternal loss and punishment but our salvation. This is clearly stated by Christ Himself, who said, "Him that cometh to me I will in no wise cast out" (John 6:37). When God moves the wheels in your life, the motion is meant to bring you to the best possible position for believing. He chooses for you to believe, but He does not put you in a place where you cannot help but reject Him against your will. "All [*pán* {3956}] that the Father giveth me shall come to me" (John 6:37). The Father would not have given them to the Son if they were ultimately going to refuse to come.

Peter tells us, "The Lord . . . is longsuffering to us-ward, not willing that any should perish, but that all should come to repentance." (2 Pet. 3:9). (See also Acts 2:21, Rom. 5:18; 10:13, 1 Tim. 2:4.) No one can ever say that God has predestined him to hell. He has chosen that himself by refusing to come to Him. God does all in His power to attract man, but He gives him the right to refuse, and He is not responsible for that refusal. Hell is simply the consequence that He sets for those who, through their choice, reject His will for their salvation. It is when we give up our will and take His will that we are saved. He knows all who are going to submit their wills to the divine will and all who will not. But God will never permit the contrary wills to hinder the overall execution of His will in the world as a whole. Similarly, the wheels in a watch which turn contrary to what one might expect cannot frustrate the original maker's purpose and design.

Interestingly, the term "will of God" in the New Testament is almost always singular and scarcely ever plural. God does not have a different will for each one, but each individual, whatever motion he chooses to make, is in execution of the overall will of God. It is not "wills of God," therefore, but the will of God. And all things in each individual work together for good, which is the execution of God's eternal plan (Rom. 8:28). Only as we understand this basic doctrine of the nature and work of God, will we have peace in our soul, as we observe all that is going on in the world.

How it must have hurt Paul at first to realize that his stubborn human will did not prevail. It was humiliating to submit to the One he had tried to overthrow. He must have been miserable before his conversion, in spite of the fact that he had been having his own way. Mind you, at the time Paul was writing to the Corinthians, he was at peace because he had made God's will his will. If that does not happen, if your way is not in accord with the way of God's divine revelation in Christ, you are inherently miserable, whether you recognize it or not. If you are a non-Christian, your will is certainly contrary to the will of God, for it is His will that you be saved. If you are a Christian, it is possible that even as a child of God you are somewhat of a rebel, at times following your own stubborn will and considering it better than God's will.

What great joy must have filled Paul's heart when, upon being "called" (that is, being converted and becoming an apostle), he recognized that these two great changes in his life had not occurred because he sought them or wanted them, but were brought about "by the will of God."

The phrase, "by the will of God," "expresses with striking brevity and force the complete subjection of Paul's ministry to his commission," according to Kittel's *Theological Dictionary of the New Testament* (Vol. 3, p. 59). The word "will" in Greek here is *thélēma* (2307). There is another Greek word, *boulē* (1012), which also expresses "will," but more in the realm of resolution, counsel, and decision. Interestingly enough, *boulē* is the name that modern Greeks give to their parliament. A parliament decides, makes resolutions, expresses opinions, but does not execute them. Both of these words occur in Ephesians 1:11, "being predestinated according to the purpose of him who worketh all things after the counsel [*boulēn*] of his own will [*thelēmatos*]." By using the word *thélēma* rather than *boulē*, Paul indicates that both the plan of salvation and the call to apostleship were not only resolved upon by God, but they were also executed and effected by Him. There is an irresistibility to the grace and call of God in my own life, Paul says in effect. And such is the case in God's total plan for the world and its inhabitants. God decides and executes. This is the meaning in the expression *diá* (1223) *thelēmatos* (2307) *theoú* (2316), "by the will of God."

Socrates, the great father of philosophy in the pre-Christian era, had an amazing spiritual insight. When the tyrant threatened him with death, Socrates told him that he was willing. This drove his persecutor mad. "If that is so," he said, "then you will live against your will." "No," said Socrates, "but whatever you do with me, it shall be my will." God is no tyrant, but an all-wise and loving Father, whose will is always for our highest good. Can you really look upon your own life and say it is "by the will of God"? In making decisions has it really been His will that you have followed or your will?

You Have to Believe It Before You Can Preach It

Paul had a rough time of it in Greece. He had landed in Neapolis from Asia Minor, after hearing and obeying the call to "Come over into Macedonia, and help us" (Acts 16:9). He did not stop to think of the cost or the consequences. He was not deterred by the religious fanaticism of his fellow countrymen, or the military might of the Romans, or the rationalism of the Greeks. He had submerged his will to the will of God with regard to his own salvation and life's vocation. He was willing to go anywhere that

the eternal will of God called him. That is the true missionary
spirit, without which no man can serve God acceptably.

Paul might have been discouraged by what happened to him
in Greece. From the port of Neapolis (the present city of Kavala)
he had gone about ten miles to the famous city of Philippi.
There the result of his preaching was imprisonment for himself
and Silas. Yet far from being downhearted, they sang in jail. God
performed a miracle through an earthquake, liberating them and
saving the Philippian jailer at the same time. As Paul was leaving this man and his family, now Christian believers, he must
have reflected that imprisonment was indeed worthwhile. He
may have even praised the Lord for the earthquake. What seem
like calamities to some can be used by God to accomplish His
plan for others—perhaps even you.

Paul then proceeded to the city of Thessalonica, where, as a
result of his witness, he had to escape for his life. From there he
went to Berea, where he rejoiced to find some diligent students of the Old Testament Scriptures. Then he took a boat to
the port city of Athens, Piraeus. He walked up to the very seat
of the world's learning, the Acropolis, where on Mars Hill (the
Areopagus) he delivered his famous address. The philosophers
ridiculed him, but he was undaunted. He proceeded some fifty
miles south to the Roman world's most sinful city, Corinth.
He believed that where sin abounded grace could much more
abound, and now he was going to put his belief to the test in a
city so vile that they called the prostitutes priestesses and even
built a temple in their honor.

Paul was not sent to Corinth by any congregation or missionary society. He went there prompted by the Spirit of God.
He worked for his living and stayed with fellow believers and
craftsmen, Priscilla and Aquila. On Saturdays he went to the
synagogue to preach the gospel. When he declared that Jesus was

the Christ, Crispus, the chief ruler of the synagogue, a Roman convert to Judaism, threw him out.

Next door to the synagogue lived a God-fearing man by the name of Justus, who invited Paul to start preaching in his house. Perhaps while Paul was preaching in the house of Justus, Crispus could hear him next door through the open windows. However that may be, the gospel won out. In each instance it was not because of the will of man but in spite of man's initial opposition that the gospel triumphed. Crispus received Christ. He was baptized and others with him (Acts 18:8). You can well imagine the uproar in Corinth when it was learned that the man who had excommunicated Paul had now become a believer in Christ.

Crispus, too, was excommunicated from the synagogue. Another man, apparently a Greek convert to Judaism by the name of Sosthenes (Acts 18:17), was apparently elected to replace him. A tougher man than Crispus, he vowed to put an end to the preaching of Paul. He haled him to court, to what they called the "judgment seat" (*bēma* [968]), which can be seen in Corinth today. There Sosthenes brought his trumped-up accusations before the Roman governor, Gallio. Gallio, being a just man, rejected these accusations and dismissed the case. But, strangely enough, some Greeks who were present at the trial, though apparently not Christians, were outraged at the injustices heaped upon Paul by his own countrymen. When Sosthenes came out of court, they began beating him unmercifully.

Paul, of course, had nothing to do with this punitive act. That great apostle of love could not have remained indifferent as he witnessed this scene. If we have any understanding of Paul's personality, we know he must have intervened on Sosthenes' behalf, assuring him that he was not the one who instigated the abuse. I can well imagine those loving arms of Paul being thrown around his persecutor and hearing him say to him, "Sosthenes, I love you. I, too, persecuted the Lord Jesus

Christ and His followers, but now I am His apostle, not by my own will but by the will of God; and I would lay down my life for Him. Sosthenes, you, too, can be saved the same way. Even though you are trying to put me in jail, I love you. The day will come when I shall call you my brother in the Lord."

Well, that day did come. When Paul was writing to the Corinthians from Ephesus a few years later, at the very beginning of his letter he called Sosthenes "the brother." By so designating him, it was as if he were saying to them right at the start that love never fails; it can accomplish what nothing else can. Paul wanted the Corinthians to realize that their former persecutor was now "the brother," *ho* (3588) *adelphós* (80), the exact translation of the Greek. (Sosthenes, of course, should not be considered the co-writer of this epistle with Paul. His name is followed by the designation of "brother" merely to demonstrate to the Corinthians the power of the gospel in their midst.) He was "the brother" par excellence to the Corinthians and to Sosthenes, an example of the power of God to save to the uttermost. You must affirm the power of the gospel if you are going to preach it with power. You will only fight on to victory if you believe victory is possible.

Said an archbishop to the manager of an acting group, "Tell me, how is it that you actors hold the attention of your audience so vividly that you cause them to think of things imaginary as if they were real, while we of the church speak of things that are real but our congregations take them as imaginary?"

"The reason is plain," answered the actor. "We actors speak of things imaginary as if they were real, while too many in the pulpit speak of real things as if they were imaginary." No wonder much preaching is both uninteresting and fruitless. It was said of one famous old preacher, "He showed us the fires of hell, and then he swept our souls up to the gates of heaven." When you talk about Christ, you have to believe in the transforming power of the gospel if you expect to convince anyone else of its power to save.

LESSONS:

1. Paul's words to the Corinthians carried authority because Paul was not writing to them as man to man, but as an apostle of Christ to the followers of Christ. Because Paul wrote as an apostle, his words should be beyond dispute.
2. Paul's authority as an apostle was delegated to him by Christ Jesus. Apostolic authority cannot exist without Christ. In fact, all authority in heaven and earth centers in Jesus Christ because He is God incarnate, co-Creator with the Father.
3. We are created to fulfill God's purpose for us—a harmonious relation with divine authority. Under Satan, we have become self-directed relativists instead of accepting God's absolute authority.
4. Christian faith does not start with an idea, but with a supernatural Person who can be traced in a historical context.
5. Man of himself never wills to be saved; the initiative always comes from God.
6. No man can ever say that God has predestined him to hell. He chooses that himself, by refusing to come to Him.
7. God does not have a different will for each individual, but each person's course in life lies within the overall will of God. If our ways are not in accord with the way of God's divine revelation in Christ, we are inherently miserable whether we recognize it or not.
8. As in the cases of Crispus and Sosthenes, the gospel triumphs not because of the will of man but often in spite of man's initial opposition to it.

1 Cor. 1:2 | *The Church of God*

Unto the church of God which is at Corinth, to them that are sanctified in Christ Jesus, called to be saints, with all that in every place call upon the name of Jesus Christ our Lord, both theirs and ours.

Did you ever stop to think that the letters which you write not only reveal a great deal about you, but also about those to whom you are writing. By reading Paul's letters to the Corinthians we not only learn much about Paul but also about Corinth and the Corinthians at that particular period.

However, the New Testament letters, besides having reference to specific people, places, and situations, have a far more general application. It takes spiritual discernment to determine what applied locally and to draw conclusions from this as to the principle that would apply in similar situations. We must keep this in mind as we carefully analyze and interpret First Corinthians, that eminently practical epistle in which Paul touches upon almost every life situation. On one hand, we should not be too hasty to conclude that every place is a Corinth; and, on the other, we should recognize that a principle that applies to Christian conduct in Corinth can and should apply everywhere.

Are There Any Perfect Churches?

Paul declares at the very beginning of chapter one (v. 2) that what he is about to say applies principally to "the church of God which is at Corinth." He is not writing to all the people of Corinth—just to the congregation. The Greek word for "church" is *ekklēsía* (1577), from the preposition *ek* (1537), meaning "from," and the verb *kaléō* (2564), "to call out." A church is a group of people called out of the world, while still living in the world, for a witness to the world for the Lord. This is its general universal meaning (Matt. 16:18; Eph. 1:22; 5:23). In writing this epistle, it is quite evident that Paul was not addressing himself to the entire Church of Christ in the world, but to specific situations in the Corinthian church. What would apply to the Corinthians might not apply in every detail to the rest of the Church.

Should you expect a congregation to be perfect and absolutely pure? That is what God wants it to be, of course. But the Church is made up of individual Christians, and who of us can claim he is all he is supposed to be? The reality of our present condition does not coincide with Christ's idealism. That is why Paul wrote this letter—to urge the Corinthian Christians to move from their present disappointing state to where they should be. This church was a heartache to Paul. "And I, brethren, could not speak unto you as unto spiritual, but as unto carnal, even as unto babes in Christ," he says (1 Cor. 3:1). And yet he had labored among them for a year and a half.

Most probably Paul wrote the Corinthian letters from Ephesus about A.D. 55, three years after he left Corinth because he learned of serious trouble in the Corinthian church. The letters are not merely dissertations on the theory of Christian behavior, but arise from actual life situations which is one reason for their vibrancy.

THE CHURCH OF GOD

One possible reason that the Corinthian church underwent a greater struggle than other congregations Paul dealt with may have been its location, for Corinth was a most sinful city. In 146 B.C. Corinth was taken over by the Romans and reduced to a heap of rubble. Because of its important geographic location as a maritime center, it was completely rebuilt in 46 B.C. by Julius Caesar. It was a Roman colony and the chief city of the region of Achaia. It was also the center of immorality and evil. In those days, when you wanted to call a man immoral, all you needed to say was that he lived like a Corinthian—*Korinthiázetai* (from *Korínthios* [2881]). Atop its Acropolis stood the great temple of Aphrodite, goddess of love, where a thousand "sacred prostitutes" lived. In the evening they sought their prey in the streets of Corinth.

It was a city of abounding wealth, commerce, luxury, drunkenness, debauchery, and filth. It is hardly possible to find a modern counterpart in our society, in spite of the fact that our cities rightly evoke our moral indignation. What was actually happening in Corinth was that, with the passage of time, the congregation was having a decreasing influence over the community precisely because it was allowing the general community to have too much influence over the congregation.

Yet it is possible to have a living Church, an assembly of called-out ones, even in a city like Corinth. Imperfect, yes, but still the Church of God in Corinth. That is where God wants His people to be witnesses. They are meant to be the salt of the earth, the light of the world (Matt. 5:13). Salt is needed to preserve society from corruption; light is needed most in the darkest places. We may learn two valuable lessons from the fact of "the church of God which is at Corinth." First, it is possible for God to call out His own from the most sinful environment and the most fanatical opposition. Second, once a congregation has been established, the grace of God can keep it. In spite of the imperfections of its members, it is still the Church of God.

> I think that I shall never see
> A church that's all it ought to be:
> A church whose members never stray
> Beyond the strait and narrow way;
> A church that has no empty pews,
> Whose pastor never has the blues,
> A church whose deacons always deak,
> And none is proud, and all are meek;
> Where gossips never peddle lies,
> Or make complaints or criticize;
> Where all are always sweet and kind,
> And all to others faults are blind.
> Such perfect churches there may be,
> But none of them are known to me.
> But still, we'll work, and pray, and plan
> To make our own the best we can.
> —Author unknown

Paul was not concerned about the building in which the Corinthian Christians met. The building is not really the Church. God's people are. Yet the Church today spends more money for buildings than for anything else. When an artist was asked to paint a picture of a decaying church, to everyone's astonishment, instead of putting on canvas an old, tottering ruin, the artist painted a stately edifice of modern grandeur. Through the open portals could be seen the richly-carved pulpit, the magnificent organ, and the beautiful, stained-glass windows. To one side was an elaborately-designed offering plate for foreign missions—covered by a cobweb! Paul's concern was not with a building in Corinth but with a group of Christians who were living in, and being contaminated by, a sinful environment.

Paul worked hard to establish the Church of God in Corinth. Yet throughout his Corinthian epistles he never refers to it as "my" church. So many of us have a tendency to speak of the church where we minister in any capacity as "ours." Oh, no, that church is not yours or mine at all. When we recognize it as the Church of God we will treat it as God's property and not ours. Recognize also that the Bible-believing church of which you are not a pastor or a member is just as much the Church of God as yours.

The Apostle Paul always placed great emphasis on the local church; no central church body ever concerned him. Every local church seems to be an entity in God's possession. It is "*the* church which is situated at Corinth." The Greek expression *tē* (3588) *ousē* (5607) means "which being." It is not just a part of God's Church, but it is the Church of God—a whole which possesses the whole of God, not that God *does* not possess other congregations in other localities. The local church where you worship God is His unit. Never think of it as unnecessary. It is the very unit that may cause God to preserve your entire community.

Are There Any Perfect Christians?

A young lawyer, an infidel, boasted that he was going west to locate a place where there were no churches, no Sunday schools, and no Bibles. Before the year had passed in his new location, he wrote to a classmate, a young minister, begging him to come out and start a church. "Be sure to bring plenty of Bibles," he urged. "I have become convinced that a place without Christians or Sunday schools and churches and Bibles is too much like hell for any living man to stay in." He was right. What a hell Corinth would have become without "the church of God which is at Corinth." An imperfect church, yes, but absolutely necessary for the survival of all. Support it in spite of its imperfections and work for its perfection through your own holiness of life.

To demonstrate what he meant by "church" in 1 Corinthians 1:2, Paul adds "to them that are sanctified in Christ Jesus, called to be saints, with all that in every place call upon the name of Jesus Christ our Lord, both theirs and ours." In addressing this letter to "the church of God which is at Corinth," Paul uses the Greek dative *tē ekklēsía*, "to the church." In the second part of the verse he uses the same dative case but this time with a plural participle used here as an adjectival noun, *tois* (3588) *hēgiasménois* (37), "to the sanctified ones." The church means people who are sanctified, not a building set apart for worship, necessary though that may be.

Now what does "sanctified" mean? It comes from the verb *hagiázō* (37), "to sanctify." The substantive adjective *hágios* (40) means "holy one" or "saint." The basic meaning of the word is "to separate." When we say "holy is the name of God," we mean that it is a name that stands apart from all others. A place is holy when it is set apart for a particular sacred use. A city such as Jerusalem was holy when it was set apart for the worship of God. A person is holy when he is separated from the spirit of worldliness and is set apart for God.

Now let us consider two Greek words that can be translated "holy" or "sacred": *hágios*, which is used here in 1 Corinthians 1:2, and *hierós* (2413), as in 2 Timothy 3:15 and 1 Corinthians 9:13. *Hierós* is the adjective from which we get *hiereús* (2409), "priest." The English word "hierarchy" is also derived from it, meaning leadership, the set apart ones who are also the mighty ones. The New Testament would call a thing holy, *hierós*, which was in itself spotlessly clean, like the holy (*hierá* [2413]) Scriptures. But *hágios*, which we render "holy" or "saint" or "set apart," is something or somebody that is now offered to God regardless of what may have been its own nature or past history. Such were the Corinthian Christians. In themselves they were anything but saintly. Their background was evil and sinful.

But they were sanctified by Christ when they welcomed Him into their hearts. Their sanctification was a snatching away from sin, a purification, and a setting apart unto God. It had nothing to do with their merits.

Hēgiasménois is a participle in the perfect tense, which tells us that a certain act has been completed in the past, the results of which are continuing. Furthermore, it is in the passive voice, indicating that this act of sanctification was due to an outside agent. We cannot sanctify ourselves, and neither could the Corinthians. They were sanctified at a certain time in their lives by the Lord Jesus Christ and set apart to Him. Paul applies the concept of sanctification passively, like justification, indicating that God is its author. "Sanctification," according to Kittel's *Theological Dictionary of the New Testament,* "is not moral action on the part of man, but a divinely effected state." "And such [i.e. thieves, covetous, drunkards, revilers, extortioners] were some of you: but ye are washed, but ye are sanctified [*hēgiásthēte* {37}], but ye are justified in the name of the Lord Jesus, and by the Spirit of our God" (1 Cor. 6:10, 11).

Paul wanted these Corinthian believers to realize their position in Christ in spite of their many imperfections. They were purified from sin, and hence lived no more unto sin but unto Christ. This did not mean inherent, once-and-for-all sinlessness. There is constant growth to be attained in the Christian life. Our perfection is in Christ but never in ourselves. That is why the same apostle who called the Corinthian Christians "sanctified" called upon the same Christians to perfect this holiness.

In 2 Corinthians 7:1 Paul wrote, "Having therefore these promises, dearly beloved, let us cleanse ourselves from all filthiness of the flesh and spirit, perfecting holiness in the fear of God." Thus, God does His work through Christ to cleanse us. "By the which will we are sanctified through the offering of the body of Jesus Christ once for all" (Heb. 10:10). He sets us apart. We live no more in the sphere of the devil and the world. We are in the sphere of Christ, "sanctified in Christ Jesus." Paul does not say "sanctified *by* Christ" but "sanctified *in* Christ." He is not emphasizing the agent of our sanctification so much as our position as believers. His whole epistle stresses the realization of our responsibility being in Christ. Though the Christians were imperfect, they were still in Christ. Just as those in the physical world are possessed of various degrees of maturity, so are those in Christ.

Observe again that "Christ" comes before "Jesus"—the divine nature, the redemptive element of the Lord, before His historic manifestation as the human Jesus. As man, the Lord cannot give you a new nature and set you apart from the world while you are still in the world, but as the expected Anointed One, Christ, the eternal Word who became flesh, surely can.

But there is also a work of sanctification for the believer to do. He, too, is to act redemptively in regard to others in introducing them to the Lord Jesus Christ. The believing spouse is urged by Paul to dwell with the unbelieving spouse and children in the hope of sanctifying them (1 Cor. 7:14). Here "to sanctify" means to bring them to the place where the believer is, that is, in Christ.

The Bible speaks of the beauty of holiness. Sometimes, however, what is called holiness by man is not really beautiful. The Pharisees in our Lord's day thought themselves to be holy. They were very exact in keeping the law, but their lives were anything but beautiful. They offered long prayers and spent much time in the synagogue, but they were mean, selfish, critical, and dishonest in their backbiting lives. True saintliness is beautiful.

Saints—Dead or Alive?

A woman who had become a Christian went a distance to visit her worldly sister whom she had not seen for years. When she returned she said to her husband, "I have been much cheered by my visit. While my sister is worldly," she said, 'I do not know what has happened to you, but you're a great deal easier to live with than you used to be.' "

That may be a good yardstick of our sanctification. Do others admire Christ or despise Him as a result of living with us?

A person who is "sanctified in Christ" is like the water spider, which is a very peculiar insect. The water spider lives at the bottom of muddy pools and has the distinctive power of ascending to the surface of the pool and there surrounding itself with a tiny globule of air. Thus enveloped it descends to the sludge and ooze at the bottom of the pool and remains there unsullied by its environment until the air is exhausted. Then it rises again to the surface and the process is repeated.

We also are peculiar to the environment in which we live. Similarly, it is possible to be a saint in Corinth or in whatever unfavorable environment where we are right now. Although we must live in the world, the indwelling Christ can provide us with an enveloping shield. And this shield may be compared to that specially-processed glass which enables a person to see from the inside out but prevents others from seeing from the outside in. We who are sanctified in Christ in "Corinth" are supposed to look on the outside world and affect it for Christ, but not allow the outside world to affect us.

Perhaps the greatest misunderstanding about the word "saint" is that it can only refer to a dead person who is honored by the living because of his or her pure and exemplary life. To the writers of the New Testament, being a saint was a way of life effected by Christ in man while he is living in an environment that is filthy and opposed to Christ. Saints are not persons who are isolated from the world, but those who are laboring for Christ in the world.

A devout Frenchman truthfully said, "Beware of a religion which substitutes itself for everything. That makes monks. Seek a religion which penetrates everything. That makes Christians." Just as the chlorophyll of the green trees is needed so that it may be acted upon by the sun to absorb from the dirty atmosphere the carbon dioxide that poisons us, so the believer in Christ needs the Holy Spirit to purify his environment.

In the gospels the followers of the Lord Jesus are called disciples. A disciple is a scholar, a learner. In Acts they are called believers, which indicates a more intimate relationship than that of discipleship. A disciple may listen to and receive the teachings of a master and yet have little personal relation with him. However Christ demands not only knowledge about Him but also belief in Him. Today believers in Christ are known as "Christians." The term "Christian" occurs only three times in the New Testament (Acts 11:26; 26:28, and 1 Pet. 4:16); unlike today, this term was used by the enemies of the faith, not by fellow believers. During this time no Christian churches or Christian assemblies existed, only churches of the faithful or of the elect, or still more frequently, assemblies of the saints.

Do you realize that you have no place in a Christian church unless you are a saint? Are you one? Would you feel out of place if I were to stand behind the pulpit of your congregation and call you "an assembly of saints"? My words would probably provoke a smile or an expression of surprise. And, if you were to call me a "saint" to my face, it would give me an uneasy feeling, and I would wonder what I had been doing to deserve such an exalted title.

We cannot think of a saint as doing business on the floor of the stock exchange, or contesting for a seat on the town council, or campaigning for the presidency, or even standing behind a counter to serve customers. Even less can we think of him as a shrewd businessman buying in the cheapest and selling in the most expensive market. Such things have become incongruous to us. A saint and a successful businessman, a saint and an alert politician, a saint and a woman shopping for the best bargains for her household—it is hard for us to associate the two.

We imagine that the saint must be altogether or more than half out of this world, and sometimes half out of his mind. We think of a saint as a person far above ordinary affairs, with his or her eyes so constantly fixed on heaven as to be sublimely indifferent to what goes on below, as "a being so heavenly minded as to be no earthly good."

We do not call the members of our Christian churches "saints" now. One branch of the Church does not declare anyone a saint until that person has been dead for at least fifty years. But the people whom Paul was addressing in sinful Corinth were alive. They had believed in Christ as a result of his preaching to them. When they believed, they constituted a separate group in the world, the "called-out" ones, the Church, the *ekklēsía*, the saints. But they stayed in Corinth and continued to work there.

As Joseph A. Vance said of saintliness, "its face [is often] weather-beaten, and its shoulders bowed with burden carrying. Preoccupation with his daily task leaves the saint little time for posing. The real saint is so busy doing the duty set him by his Lord that the devil has no chance to lure him into thinking 'What a great saint am I' "(*The Christian World Pulpit*, Vol. 109, p. 84.).

> Are you sheltered, curled up and content by your world's warm fire?
>   Then I say your soul is in danger.
> The sons of Light, they are down with God in the mire,
>   God in the manger.
> So rouse you from your perilous ease; to your sword and your shield!
>   Your ease is that of the cattle!
> Hark, hark, where the bugles are calling: out to some field!
>   Out to some battle!

THE CHURCH OF GOD

Can You Be a Christian Without Joining a Church?

You have probably heard it said that "the blood of the martyrs is the seed of the Church," and it is true that many churches have been founded as a result of persecution. When Paul, Crispus, and Sosthenes were excommunicated from the synagogue in Corinth because they believed that the historical Jesus was the Messiah, they moved next door to the house of Justus, thus establishing the first assembly of saints in Corinth (Acts 18:7). This was a cohesive group of believers who held a common faith in the Lord Jesus Christ as the eternally Anointed One, the Redeemer of the world. This seems to be a universal pattern. Those who believe in Christ as He is revealed to us in God's Word are almost always ejected from the fellowship of those who do not acknowledge the same faith. The believers then form a band of saints who witness as a group and as individuals.

If you are a believer in Christ, and thus a saint, you most certainly ought to belong to a group of saints, a church. Paul addresses his Corinthian epistle first to the church as a whole (*te ekklēsía*), thus showing its importance for the fellowship of the saints, and then to the sanctified ones, the individuals constituting the church. You hear people say, "Can't I be a Christian without joining the church?" Yes, it is possible, but it is something like being a student who will not go to school, a soldier who will not go to battle, a citizen who refuses to pay taxes or vote, a football player without a team, a scientist who does not share his findings, or a bee without a hive.

Saint of God, do not look down on the local church. Imperfect as it may be, it is still God's primary organizational unit for the benefit of all saints. Seek a local church where there are other saints of God. But just one word of warning. Only saints, that is, those who are in Christ, should be admitted to a Bible-believing church. They are the ones who constitute the Church universal.

But lest anyone think that the saints have earned the right to that title by their own efforts, or have been so constituted by their fellow members, Paul adds two words, *klētoís* (2822) *hagíois* (40), "called to be saints." This actually qualifies "the church" at the beginning of the verse, "to the church of God which is at Corinth, to the sanctified ones in Christ Jesus, to the called saints." It is in the same dative case as "the church" and "the sanctified ones." It refers to the same people.

Throughout the New Testament, the believers in Christ are referred to as "the called ones," those who have received the invitation of Christ to repent and believe, and have obeyed Him. Paul is a "called" apostle, and they are "called" saints. It is the same word in both instances. It refers among other things to their having experienced a radical change. Paul could not have become an apostle without first having believed in Christ; and these saints could not have belonged to the church as saints without first of all becoming believers.

Since the word *klētoís*, "called ones," appears with the word *hagíois*, "saint," it must qualify it. As you read the English translation in the King James Version, you find that the emphasis is placed on "saints," while it should actually be upon "called." (See Kittel, Vol. 1, p. 107.) Romans 1:6 makes this more apparent: "Among whom are ye also the called of Jesus Christ." This is the same word. Because of Christ, we are not only believers, but also saints. Holy life is not achieved by human effort but by the indwelling Christ. As He lives in us, we die unto self. We are not saints by human effort any more than Paul became an apostle by anything he did, but by divine grace in Christ. Our position in the Church of God is not due to merit but to submission to Christ. The emphasis is on the One who effectively calls and shapes us to conform to His will.

THE CHURCH OF GOD

This One who called Corinthian sinners to be saints is the same Lord today. What He did for them He can do for us. If the name "saint" applied to them, why should it not apply to us? The church in Corinth was in no way superior to the average congregation today. We will find this out as we study in detail Paul's two epistles to them. They were saints, not angels. They were distinctly human. They had their failings. They quarreled and split up into factions, and were very fond of having their own way. They had the same passions as we do. And yet they were sanctified in Christ Jesus and "called saints." God called them. And if you believe substantially and fundamentally as they did, you also are His "called saints."

Paul did not write this epistle only for the Corinthian saints. It was meant to meet their particular needs, of course, but its application was to be more general. That is why he adds, "with all that in every place call upon the name of Jesus Christ our Lord." Observe the conjunction he uses. It is not the common *kaí* (2532), "and," but the word *sún* (4862), "with." He was not addressing directly all the saints of God everywhere, but he wanted the Corinthians to realize that they were not the only saints in the Church of God. What a wonderful feeling it should give every local assembly of believers to realize that God's family is larger than their little congregation, that He has His saints everywhere.

Yet in this realization lies an incipient danger—the danger of thinking that, since there are so many belonging to the Church, why not "Let George do it?" I'm reminded of the eastern story of four brothers who decided to have a feast. As wine was rather expensive, they agreed that each one should bring an equal quantity and add it to the common stock. But one of the brothers thought he might escape making his contribution by bringing water instead of wine. "It will not be noticed in the common wine jar," he reasoned. But when, at the feast, the wine was poured out, it turned out not to be wine at all but plain water. All four brothers had thought alike. Each one had said, "Let the other do it." This is a real danger in the Church. We must realize, of course, that there are other brothers and sisters in the Church of God, but we must work as if there were none when it comes to fulfilling our personal responsibility as a saint of God. Yes, work as if there were no one else to do your job, but behave with humility because the grace of God has reached His "called ones" all over the world.

Let's Not Be Church Snobs

The Apostle Peter said, "Whosoever shall call upon the name of the Lord shall be saved" (Acts 2:21). The word for "call on," *epikaléomai* (1941), is the same word used in 1 Corinthians 1:2, where Paul refers to the other believers in Christ "in every place," who do not belong to the church of Corinth. Now why is it that when Paul speaks of the Corinthians, he wants them to think of themselves as "saints," those that are set apart, sanctified, but when he bids them look at others in the Church, he directs them not to look, at their character, but at their confession of faith, as those who "call upon the name of the Lord"? When you look inside yourselves, he implies, I want you to be strict in your judgment. Do not hesitate to judge yourselves. But when it comes to others, all you can do is take them into your consciences as fellow believers on the basis of their calling upon the Lord Jesus Christ for salvation.

Actually the participle *epikalouménois* (1941), describing those who call upon the name of the Lord, comes from the words *klētós* (2822), "called," used to indicate Paul's call as an apostle in verse 1, and *klētoí*, "called," used to indicate the call of the believers in Corinth as saints. These are all from the same root verb *kaleō* (2564). There is a fundamental difference in the voice, however. The adjective *klētós* and the plural form *klētoí*, referring to the calling of Paul as an apostle and to the believers he is addressing as saints, have a passive significance, stressing the One who is calling rather than the ones called. It is as if Paul were saying, "When it comes to my apostleship it is all due to God, the Author of it; and when it comes to your saintliness, that, too, is due to God."

Fellow Christians, when we look into our own lives and see ourselves as saints, let us not become puffed up as though we had achieved this high calling through our own merit and effort. The good that is in us must always be ascribed to God, the Author and Finisher of our faith. But when we look at our fellow believers, we should not judge, but accept them because they call upon the Lord. We are not and cannot be judges of our fellowman.

An old fable tells of a man cursed with the power of seeing other human beings, not in the beauty of flesh and blood, but as skeletons gaunt and grisly. Some saints seem to have taken upon themselves this curse. Do you feel that you are the only one who is right with the Lord—that everybody else is a spiritual skeleton because he is not of the same denominational stripe, or does not have the same scruples of conscience as you? Take him or her into your circle of believers as Paul did, as long as they are calling upon the name of the Lord Jesus Christ.

The Corinthians were both educated and wealthy. Consequently they were proud even after they became Christians. They had a tendency to look upon Christians living elsewhere with a spirit of contempt. That is why, at the very beginning of his letter, Paul seeks to make them conscious of the fact that there were others who held the faith of Christ in common with them. When he reminds them of "all that in every place call upon the name of Jesus Christ our Lord, both theirs and ours," he does not use the definite article "the" before the name of the Lord, but the possessive plural pronoun "our," even as our Lord did when He taught us to pray, "Our Father which art in heaven" (Matt. 6:9).

Whenever you think of your relationship to God, remember that you are not the only child of God. Nevertheless, it is necessary to consider yourself a child of God if you possess the Lord Jesus Christ. Observe that Paul does not indiscriminately call all people everywhere children of God—only those who call upon the name of the Lord Jesus Christ. He wanted the Corinthian saints to realize that all who did so belonged to the same Church of God, the same family of God, as they. The Lord is theirs and ours, he told them. Never consider Him to be yours exclusively. On the other hand, anyone who does not call upon the name of the Lord Jesus Christ can not be counted a member of the Church of God nor as a child of God. Does this seem too harsh? Is it too narrow? Indeed, God has made certain things very narrow and restricted, things that we would never dream of questioning, such as the necessity for air, food, and water to maintain physical life. Why, then, should we question His narrow requirements for spiritual life?

At the close of a missionary's address on universal brotherhood, two professors from a local school claimed to find a flaw in his reasoning. They questioned him, asking if not all individuals of the human race descended from Adam and Eve? And did not God create Adam and Eve? And therefore were not all individuals the children of God? In reply the missionary pointed to the benches in the room and asked, "Who made these benches?" The men answered that they had been made by the local carpenter. "And do you, therefore, call these benches the carpenter's children?" he asked. "Of course not," they answered. "They are not the carpenter's children because they do not have the carpenter's life in them." "And do you have the life of God in you?" asked the missionary, revealing the men's departure from God.

THE CHURCH OF GOD

No one can be called a child of God if he does not have the life of God within him. "They that call upon the name of our Lord Jesus Christ" must have within them the life of God, or they would not be calling on the name of His Son. "As many as received him [Jesus Christ], to them gave he power to become the sons [children] of God" (John 1:12).

Bite Your Tongue!

To listen to the various notions people have about who is going to heaven and who is not would be amusing if it were not tragic. The amusing part is that they place themselves in the position of telling God Himself what He can and cannot do, whom He can and cannot save, without once asking what He has to say about it. "I've done the best I could. I've never robbed or murdered anybody; and I've helped out many people in need. I'm sure God will not be too hard on me," is the gist of their personal creed. The tragic part is that they are so ignorant of one simple qualification set forth in God's Word, "Except a man be born again, he cannot see the kingdom of God" (John 3:3). They do not even have a remote idea of what it means to be born again. How tragic that they seemingly do not care or want to find out the truth.

We must not be deceived by our own ideas as to what makes a person a child of God. "No man cometh unto the Father, but by me," said the Lord Jesus (John 14:6). Either He was mistaken or we are. Certainly we are mistaken if we think that those who call on His name and those who do not are all His children and therefore members of His Church universal. Can we claim to know more about it than the Lord Himself?

It is as if Paul is saying to the Corinthian church as well as to all believers, "Watch out for two things." First that you do not become exclusive. Remember that there are other believers in the universal Church. And second that not everyone is your spiritual brother. The man who does not acknowledge Christ as Savior is your fellow creature, and may even be considered your brother after the flesh, but only those who are in Christ are your spiritual brethren."

The word *epikalouménois* (1941), "the calling ones" (the Greek word for "that call upon," in the phrase "all that in every place call upon the name of Jesus Christ our Lord") is in the middle voice, indicating here an operation of the will of the individual person upon believing. Although God is available to all and desires the salvation of all, man must take this offer of salvation to himself, recognizing it as his very own because Christ purchased this redemption for him. This involves a confident willing dependence on Christ's work. Each individual person must believe, must call upon the name of the Lord, to receive the initial life of God within his or her soul; then, and only then, does God become his or her Father.

The last expression in verse 2, "both theirs and ours," refers to the possession of Christ. Observe Paul's humility in putting others first. He does not say, "He is ours and also theirs," but "He is theirs and also ours." He includes himself with the Corinthians, in spite of the fact that he is about to take them to task for the laxness of their Christian lives, even in their sainthood.

What a lesson we ministers of God can learn from this great apostle. Even though we find much to be desired in our congregations, we must identify with them. We must not place ourselves on a pedestal above them; we must not preach "at" them, but must speak "to" them in the warmth of our common Christian faith. Fellow minister, do not speak to others of "my Lord" but of "our Lord," remembering that they are one with you in Christ.

The Apostle Paul knew the worth of putting others before himself (Rom. 12:10). Try it. You will be the winner, not the loser. At first it may not be easy. You will need to keep watch over yourself and subdue your pride when it threatens to make you want to put yourself ahead of others. You may have sarcastic and cynical tendencies. You can annihilate humbler persons with a word or wither them with a look. But cynicism hurts and sarcasm wounds. It might relieve your own feelings if you could toss off these witty and telling remarks when they occur to you, but for love's sake should you not bite your tongue and remain silent?

As children of God we must cultivate patience with all who call upon the name of the Lord with us. It is not always easy to find common ground with others intellectually or culturally. It is far too easy to see their eccentricities, the ways in which they differ from us, and to ridicule them or even to avoid them at times. We must practice love. We must make a creed of kindness. We must cultivate a family atmosphere in our congregations so that men and women battered and beaten by the world may feel comforted and at home.

All this is not impossible. Love should be easy. We are "called ones" because of God's love. Love has redeemed us. When the love of God is shed abroad in our hearts, we shall have plenty to share with others. We must love the congregation. Honor the congregation. Give our best to the congregation. Pray for its peace and prosperity. Love the brethren as we love our own family. If we are at home with each other in the congregation on earth, we shall feel at home with them when we enter heaven. (See "The Family Church," by J. G. Bowran, in *The Christian World Pulpit*, Vol. 75, p. 55.)

LESSONS:

1. Once a congregation has been established, the grace of God can keep it even in the most sinful environment and through the most fanatical opposition.

2. The Apostle Paul always placed great emphasis on the local church. The local church where we go to worship God is His unit. It is the very unit

that may cause God to preserve our entire community.

3. The church means people who are sanctified, not a building set apart for worship, necessary though that may be. All who are believers in Christ, and thus saints, most certainly ought to belong to a group of saints, a church.

4. To be sanctified (*hágios* [40]) means to be set apart, offered to God regardless of a person's own nature or past history.

5. Sanctification is an act of God by which He calls people to be saints, but the believer, too, must act redemptively in regard to others in introducing them to the Lord Jesus Christ and laboring for Christ in the world.

6. When we look at our fellow believers we should not judge them, but accept them because of they call upon the Lord.

7. As children of God we must cultivate patience with all who call upon the name of the Lord with us. When the love of God is shed abroad in our hearts, we shall have plenty to share with others.

1 Cor. 1:3 | *Grace and Peace*

Grace be unto you, and peace, from God our Father, and from the Lord Jesus Christ

If you were writing to a group of people whom you loved very dearly, what would be the first wish you would make for them? Would it be that old standby of "health, wealth, and happiness"? What you wish for others is oftentimes a good indication of what you consider most important in your own life.

What Do You Want Most in Life?

Consider the Apostle Paul as he was writing to the Corinthians among whom he had labored for a year and a half. He loved them as a father loves his own children, for they were truly his children in the faith. Most of them were presumably well off financially, well-educated, and healthy. If you were writing to people in similar circumstances, what wish would you send? Paul expresses his desire for them in one word, which he used not only in writing to the Corinthians but also when writing to others. It is a fascinating word—grace. How often have you begun a letter to someone by wishing them "grace"? You generally say something like, "I hope you are all in good health, and that everything is going well with you," but you never think of grace as the most important thing in life.

"Grace unto you, and peace, from God our Father, and from the Lord Jesus Christ." This was almost a standard greeting with Paul. The grace of God, or grace from God, was the greatest blessing he could wish for anyone. Do you have it? Before you can answer that, you must know precisely what grace is. The Greek word for "grace," *cháris* (5485), occurs over ninety times in the New Testament. Words are like people in that, if you want to understand them better, you really ought to look up their ancestry. The Greek word *cháris* originally seems to have meant simply "beauty," first in persons and then in things. If you looked at a person who had grace, it gave you pleasure. Later, "grace" came to mean a lovely act revealing beauty of character, loveliness of heart. And since the loveliest act we can perform is to give, the act of grace took on the meaning of giving freely, doing something for someone when he had not earned it or might not even deserve it. The word "grace," therefore, became synonymous with favor. In the New Testament meaning of the word, God's grace is His disposition toward us that shows forth the beauty of His character. That beauty consists in the fact that, instead of bringing upon us the destruction that we deserve because of sin, He shows us favor. He constructs a bridge to unite us with Himself.

However, the only reason that God can show favor toward us as sinful human beings is that the punishment we deserve was imposed upon His Son, the Lord Jesus Christ. Though grace is a favor, there is always a price tag upon it. What makes grace distinctive is that, instead of the price having to be paid by man who owes the debt, it is paid by God Himself, who freely pardons the debtor. You can never earn the favor of God; you may only receive it—and that never because of your own merit.

Human effort can never conquer evil. However, what our will cannot accomplish, the grace of God can. All human work upon our character is negative, bent on eradicating evil, but the grace of God is positive, not only removing evil but also creating good. Even if we could succeed in eradicating some evil traits, we might cut less or more of the cancer that is eating away at our character than is safe. Sin is a malignant growth that has fastened upon some natural function or quality, good and harmless in itself. Slashing away at the sin may be an excellent thing, but we cannot be sure that we will not excise part of the organ that it grows upon.

Our Lord does not desire merely to operate on a man to remove the cancerous growth of sin. Nor does He want us maimed and decimated in His kingdom as a result of our strenuous efforts to remove our own evil tendencies. He does not want us so much to be minus what is evil as to be whole with the evil changed to good. Therefore, He does not cut out the cancer but heals it. His work is not that of a surgeon but of a Creator. He does not simply remove the evil; He changes and transforms it. Thus the grace of God is a positive work. Grace never leaves us lacking something, but always gaining something. Salvation is not a negation, not merely being free from sin; it is being full of light. If we are proud, it is not enough that we get rid of our pride; we must acquire humility. If we are unchaste, we do not want merely to stop our unchaste acts; we want to become pure.

Human nature never tolerates a vacuum. Denying our sexual passion can make us miserable, but sublimating it can bring untold joy. Denying ourselves sinful pleasures is only half of the answer to growth in Christ; we also grow by conforming to His character. That is the mistake so many young Christians make when they give up sinful pursuits and then find life empty and dull because they fail to get busy in the work of the Lord by letting Christ do His works through them. If we give up our sins, we have a right to ask what is going to compensate for them. There is no denying that many sinful pursuits are pleasurable. Sin is all around; it is easy and exciting. There is every inducement to indulge in it. Now why should we give up doing what brings us pleasure at present unless we are offered something beautiful that will make it worth our while to turn to it instead? It is all very well to receive a promise of eternal life, but we also want abundant life here and now.

Grace gives us beauty and abundance in this life. That is why it is Paul's first wish for everyone to whom he writes. It is comprehensive. Money, health, happiness, or whatever else men deem good, constitute only a part of grace. God's favor has various parts. Why wish for part of something when you can have all of it? Grace makes us conscious of an altered sense of values. It creates in us the sense of more pleasure in being pure than in being unclean, in being what God wants us to be than in being what the world, the flesh, and the devil want us to be. Then we will look back upon our previous life and realize how ugly it was. But it takes grace to put beauty into life. (See *Lenten Sermons,* "Grace," T. H. Passmore, Doubleday, Doran & Co., 1928, pp. 115–125.)

When we have God's favor, Paul intimates that we have everything. And it is free! We have open access to God the Creator. He is our Father; we are His children. What more could we want? Which is better—to be children of the King with unlimited resources at our disposal, or to possess only a certain number of stated privileges?

Some people are hard to convince in this matter. A man stood up in a meeting and facing the preacher who had spoken about the sufficiency of God's grace said, "You can talk like that about Christ—that He is dear to you, that He helps you— but if your wife was dead, as my wife is, and you had some babies crying for their mother who would never come back, you could not say what you are saying." A little later the preacher lost his wife in an accident. After others had conducted the funeral service, he stood by the casket, looked down into the face of the silent wife and mother, and said, "The other day when I was preaching, a man said I could not say that Christ was sufficient if my wife were dead and my children were crying for their mother. If that man is here, I want to tell him that Christ is sufficient. My heart is broken, my heart is crushed, my heart is bleeding, but there is a song in my heart, and Christ put it there. And if that man is here, I tell him that, though my wife is gone and my children are motherless, Christ comforts me today." That man was there, and down the aisle he came and stood beside the casket and said, "Truly, if Christ can help us like that, I will surrender to Him!"

Do you know why Paul could say to the Corinthians, "Grace unto you"? Because Christ had said to him, "My grace is sufficient for thee" (2 Cor. 12:9). Paul was not theorizing; he was speaking out of practical experience.

Is Peace on Earth Possible?

Peace is a word that is on every lip in this day of turmoil. Everybody professes to desire peace—even those whose responsibility it is to wage war. Said Napoleon on St. Helena, "The more I study the world, the more I am convinced of the inability of brute force to create anything durable."

Some persons view peace as the total absence of war. They believe that we can achieve this through controlling our environment. But if they will take the trouble to glance through history, they will find that there were very few years in which man was able to enjoy peace on earth.

Of course, men should not kill each other, but the sad fact is that there has always been murder in the human heart since the days of Cain and Abel. Because of a fear of being killed by enemies, known or unknown, men have armed themselves for the purpose of protection. And thus the vicious cycle of war and peace has been perpetuated throughout history. We must view war not idealistically but realistically. If we do not, we will find ourselves at the mercy of predatory individuals and nations sooner than we think. Surely we can serve humanity better if we do not allow ourselves to be killed without a challenge.

We must recognize the fact that war always has been and always will be in the world as we know it because both man and nature are fallen. When God created man with freedom of choice so that man could voluntarily obey Him. But man believed the devil's lie, that he could become omnipotent like God. Man not only did not become omnipotent but, as a result of his rebellion against God, he has been plagued by disease and death ever since. If all people were once again to be reconciled to God, there would be an end to the present state of affairs. But such reconciliation entails the will and action of two, God on one side and man on the other. God has done His part. Because man's sin could not be allowed to go unreckoned with, He sent His Son, the Lord Jesus Christ, to satisfy divine justice. Instead of punishing man, He punished His Son—which actually means that God bore our punishment Himself, for Christ is God the Son.

However, Christ's sacrifice does not automatically reconcile man to his Creator. Man has to accept it on his behalf through faith and repentance. Those who do so become reconciled to God. In their hearts they experience the grace of God, His unmerited favor. They no longer fear God with a sense of dread, but with reverential awe that leads them to obey Him out of love, just as a child obeys his father and tries to please him. Peace of heart is the product of grace. If all men were to experience God's grace, we would have universal peace. But since in their sin and ignorance many men are not willing to accept this grace, there can be no peace, either in this world or in the hearts of individuals who reject Christ. God cannot be unjust in permitting the fruits of a state of grace for all (that is, universal peace), since a great many reject His offer of reconciliation. Hence, we

GRACE AND PEACE

have wars and the absence of individual peace. The only person who has true peace today is he who stands by faith on Christ, the Rock that remains unmoved in the midst of storm.

Paul's salutation to the Corinthians embodies more theology and realistic thinking than is usually realized. "Grace unto you, and peace, from God our Father, and from the Lord Jesus Christ." If we hope for peace in the world or in our heart without the acceptance of God's grace to overcome man's sinful human nature, we are doomed to disappointment. Peace will never come about by the efforts of unregenerate man. We may change environmental factors, but our own sinful heart can only be changed by the Lord Jesus Christ, since He alone paid the penalty for sin. Peace in the universe, both in nature and among men, will be achieved only when two things happen:

First, when this age of grace closes. This will take place when every last man, woman, and child that is to believe, believes.

Second, when those who reject the Lord Jesus are no longer allowed to act against God. They will be forced to submit to His control. Paul tells us this will take place (1 Corinthians 15:24–28) after the Second Coming of the Lord. His First Coming introduced the era of grace. His Second Coming will introduce the era of a changed universe, where peace will be the norm.

At this time, genuine peace exists only in the hearts and lives of those who have voluntarily accepted the grace of God. But their environment, both in man and nature, is full of war, disease, and death. These are the undesirable and inescapable consequences of that one little word that most men do not want to acknowledge—sin. Eliminate sin in the world and you will have universal peace. Subdue the sinful human nature of man through the grace of God, and you will have peace in the individual. The first is impossible, not through any fault of God but because of man's love of sin. The second is possible only on an individual basis, as men here and there respond to God's proffered grace with a wholehearted "yes!"

Paul knew very well that universal peace was impossible in his day, so he made no fanciful and unrealistic wish to the Corinthians for peace in their time. Such peace would entail the absence of evil.

We must be realistic in our thinking about peace. It is impossible to achieve it on a worldwide scale. Nature is fallen and corrupt, and so is mankind. The age of grace is an age of storm, death, war, and destruction. James put it succinctly when he asked, "From whence come wars and fightings among you? come they not hence, even of your lusts that war in your members?" (James 4:1).

But in the midst of it all, Paul says to the Corinthians, there can be peace for those who have accepted the grace of God. Are you one of them?

How to Have Peace

War is the result of man trying to play God. When man runs counter to the natural and spiritual laws of God, and thinks he himself can control nature outside himself and within himself, he produces conflicts. Go back and read the third chapter of Genesis and you will see what I mean. You do not have to be a psychologist to understand why people fight among themselves, both as individuals and as nations. Man fights because his heart is evil as a result of choosing to misuse the freedom which God gave him. We do not like to hear these things, but they are the stark realities that explain the conditions of the world today.

When Paul greeted the Corinthian believers with the wish that they might have grace and peace "from God our Father, and from the Lord Jesus Christ," did they not already possess these blessings? Yes, indeed. But grace and peace are not gifts that one receives once-and-for-all, to last a lifetime. When you receive

Christ, you have an initial experience of grace and peace, but you also experience a day-to-day infilling of these two wonderful gifts of God.

As Christians we know that, as long as we live in a world where sin abounds, we shall encounter any number of circumstances and people that will try to disturb our relationship with God. And whenever this relationship is disturbed we need more grace and peace. The rock on which we stand will not sink, but it can get splashed with the waves that seek to engulf us.

In Robert Louis Stevenson's story of a storm, he describes a ship caught off a rocky coast, threatening death to all on board. When terror among the passengers was at its worst, one man, more daring than the rest, made the perilous passage to the pilot-house and saw the pilot lashed to his post with his hands on the wheel turning the ship little by little into the open sea. When the pilot beheld the ghastly white, terror-stricken face of the man, he smiled, and the man rushed to the deck below shouting, "I have seen the face of the pilot, and he smiled. All is well." A sight of that smiling face averted a panic and converted despair into hope.

So a new sight of the face of Christ every day averts a panic in life and fills the soul with peace and hope. That was actually what Paul wished for the Corinthian believers. If you do not want to be panicky in the daily storms of life, take a good look at the Pilot, the Lord Jesus Christ. Remember this fundamental truth: true peace is not merely absence of war but the presence of God.

Paul was deeply conscious of the fact that these believers in Corinth would have a great deal of fighting to do against their evil environment and their own propensity to sin. In the midst of all this, they could possess the grace and peace of God. Since their initial peace with God had already been made, they could constantly experience His peace, whatever their circumstances.

GRACE AND PEACE

He who has not made peace with God is the victim of his circumstances, but he who has experienced peace with God can have the victory over his circumstances.

Observe that the source of grace and peace is "God our Father." The preposition *apó* (575), translated "from," indicates the source and direction of these two possessions of the believer. They never result from man's efforts. Their origin is in God. When He has forgiven our sin, it is natural that His attitude toward us is not that of wrath but of peace. Grace and peace come as a unit, a package, and one follows the other. Their source is identical, God our Father.

And yet it is not just that the source of grace and peace is God. Paul indicates that both he and the Corinthian believers were related to this God. He was their Father. God stands for omnipotence. Father stands for relationship. What confidence can you have in omnipotence if it is not related to you favorably? When you understand your relationship to omnipotence as a Christian believer, you will understand how you can have peace in a storm.

The only way we or anyone else can have peace in a world such as ours, is by being related to God, by having Him as our Father. As a child, we would have been disturbed had we known the strength of the enemy. But the strength of our earthly father instilled confidence and peace in us. If our father, on the other hand, had been a weakling, we would have shared his fears. But now we have a unique privilege, to have God as our heavenly Father. Refusal to accept Him is spiritual insanity. Remember, we cannot play God and have peace. The circumstances of life are beyond our control. Therefore, we need someone as a Father who is omnipotent. God inspires trust; and knowing Him as our Father helps to cast out fear (Is. 12:2). That is the secret of peace.

Paul always included himself in any declaration concerning the believer's relationship to God. To the Corinthians he spoke of grace and peace from God "our" Father. He was their Father and He was also Paul's. He had as much need of God's grace and peace in his daily life as they had in theirs. Things were not all rosy with the Corinthians. Paul's main purpose in writing to them was to chide and correct them. Yet he claims common possession of God as Father with them. The best way to help people in their trials of faith is to confess that you are just as dependent upon God as they are. He is the same God to whom you are pointing them.

LESSONS:

1. The grace (*cháris* [5485]) of God was Paul's constant wish for fellow Christians everywhere. It is defined as God's free-flowing benevolence toward those who have not earned it.
2. Grace makes us conscious of an altered sense of values. It creates in us the sense of more pleasure in being what God wants us to be than in being what the world, the flesh, and the devil want us to be.
3. True peace is not merely absence of war but the presence of God. The only person who has true peace today is he who stands by faith on Christ, the Rock that remains unmoved in the midst of storm.
4. When we receive Christ, we have an initial experience of grace and peace, but we also experience a day-to-day infilling of these two wonderful gifts of God.

GRACE AND PEACE

1 Cor. 1:4, 5 | *Thanksgiving and Riches*

I thank my God always on your behalf, for the grace of God which is given you by Jesus Christ. That in every thing ye are enriched by him, in all utterance, and in all knowledge.

In greeting the Corinthian Christians, Paul told them that grace and peace came not only from "God our Father" but also from "the Lord Jesus Christ." Scripture clearly teaches that there is only one way in which an omnipotent God can become our Father, and that is through the Lord Jesus Christ. John 1:12 states, "As many as received him [Christ], to them gave he power to become the sons of God, even to them that believe on his name"; and this is confirmed in Galatians 4:7, "Wherefore thou art no more a servant, but a son; and if a son, then an heir of God through Christ." It was through Christ that the grace of God, and therefore peace with God, was made possible for the sinful human race.

Dwight L. Moody commented on that familiar passage of John 14:27 ("Peace I leave with you") as follows:

> Did you ever think that, when Christ was dying, He made a will? Perhaps you have thought that no one ever remembered you in a will, but, if you are in the kingdom, Christ remembered you in His. He willed His body to Joseph of Arimathea, His mother to John, the son of Zebedee,

and He willed His spirit back to His Father. But to His disciples He left His peace (not ours, but His) and His joy.

Christ earned for us that oneness with God that we lost through our disobedience. Therefore, He is our peace with God. He is God who became man to bridge the gap between the sinner and the Father. This gift of peace means the recovery of a healthy fellowship.

But make no mistake about it; the gift of peace does not imply perfection. There may be a general rightness between husband and wife, and yet an occasional misunderstanding arises, even a temporary outburst of temper, while nothing fundamental in their relationship becomes affected by it. A general "rightness" of health in the body is consistent with an occasional twinge of pain.

Peace is a state of the heart, not of outer circumstances. It is stable in spite of conditions. When the world speaks of peace, it speaks of the environment, of material things. But if at all observant we will agree that the most disturbed people are frequently those who possess the most. The world offers to put us into a fine house, beautifully decorated, but the Lord offers to make us a fine tenant. We can have peace of heart no matter what our circumstances. However, this does not mean that we must tolerate unjust circumstances. We should strive to change our environment for the better, but not expect it to result in a peaceful human heart. This peace of which Paul speaks is not the peace that the world gives but as Christ gives. It can be ours, if we come to God in repentance and faith, through receiving Christ as Savior and Lord.

Thank God for the Good in Others

Paul had to write the Corinthians because there was turmoil in the local congregation because of sinful behavior and erro-

neous belief. Nevertheless Paul did not begin his letter by crit-
icizing the Corinthians but began it giving thanks for them. In
everyone there is something for which we should be thankful.
Even in the Corinthians Paul could find something for which
to thank God. "I thank my God always on your behalf, for the
grace of God which is given you by Jesus Christ." Preacher, if you
do not want to discourage your congregation, begin with the
things that you can thank God for, not with the mistakes and
shortcomings of your people. When a person realizes that you
are fair in recognizing what is good in him, he will more readily accept your recognition of what is wrong. Paul was a master
psychologist. He knew instinctively that love should precede correction. Before you criticize, create confidence that you have
20/20 vision.

Never say, "I thank God that I am better than you," either by
word or by attitude. Rather say, "I thank God for what is good
in both of us; and both you and I can be better." Do not be
afraid that you will make people conceited by honest words of
praise. Look how beautifully Paul expresses his approval of what
is good in the Corinthians. He thanks God for what the Lord has
done in them and among them. The verbs that he uses in verses
4 and 5 are in the passive voice, as he speaks of "the grace of God
which is given you [*tē* {3588} *dotheísē* {1325} *humín* {5213}] by
Jesus Christ; that in everything ye are enriched [*eploutísthēte*
{4148}] by Him, in all utterance, and in all knowledge." The Lord
Jesus Christ had performed a good work in the lives of these
Corinthians, and Paul wanted to give it due recognition. When
we have no good word for our brethren, we are denying God's activity in the lives of others. If He is absent from the lives of
others, how can we be so sure that He is present in our own lives?

An officer on the battlefield aimed his cannon toward what
he thought was the distant enemy. Just before he fired, the
commander, looking through his field glasses, shouted, "Your aim

seems perfect, but stop! They are not the enemy; they are our own people." Did you ever think that when you aim criticism at God's people so thoughtlessly, you are actually aiming your cannon at the Lord of your brethren?

The very word with which verse 4 begins contains the word "grace." In Greek it is *eucharistō* (2168), a combination of the adverb *eu* (2095), meaning "well," and the root word *cháris* (5485), "grace." It came to mean "to give thanks for that which man does not necessarily deserve." If we are in the good graces of someone, we are pleased, we give thanks. It is from this word that we derive the English word "eucharist," implying God's favor in communing with us in the Lord's Supper. Actually, Paul does not praise the Corinthians; he praises God for the expression of His good favor toward them.

Some manuscripts say, "I thank my God," and others, "I thank our God," but I believe the preponderance of weight is on the side of "my God." Paul was telling the Corinthians that he included them in his personal prayers of thanksgiving to the Lord. How many times have we thanked the Lord for His grace manifested in the lives of others? At times we may not feel like it because of some dissatisfaction that we may have with them, as Paul had with the Corinthians, but remember that little word "always": "I thank my God always on your behalf." Paul could always find some evidence of God's grace working in their lives. A scolding preacher disheartens his congregation. A flattering preacher blinds them to their need for improvement. But a preacher who praises them for what is good in them and lovingly points out their faults encourages them to "grow in grace."

How to Get Rich

Someday when you are feeling sorry for yourself because you cannot afford something you think would make you a little happier, try a psychological experiment. Go to any of your friends or relatives who are better off than you financially and ask them if they have enough. Almost invariably you will find that they would like "just a little bit more." That is human nature. Most men's definition of "enough" is "just a little bit more" than what they now have. As John Quincy Adams said:

> My wants are many, and, if told,
>   Would muster many a score;
> And were each wish a mint of gold,
>   I still should long for more.

When the Apostle Paul wrote to the believers in the congregation at Corinth, he indicated what true riches are for the Christian. "I thank my God concerning you for the grace of God which was given unto you in Christ Jesus" (1 Cor. 1:4, a.t.). He does not say that they deserved this grace. The participle *dotheísē*, "which was given" (not "is given," as the King James Version has it), is in the passive voice, placing the emphasis more on God's part in giving than on theirs in receiving. This grace was given them by virtue of their position in Christ Jesus. Observe that Paul does not say "given you by Jesus Christ," as the King James Version has it, but "given you in Christ Jesus." The Corinthian believers, despite their many shortcomings, were "in Christ Jesus" and therefore the recipients of the greatest benefit of that position, the constant experience of the grace of God.

In verse 5, Paul goes on to speak of the more concrete manifestations of that grace. He says, "In everything ye are enriched by him, in all utterance, and in all knowledge." The Corinthian Christians, being for the most part educated and well-to-do, may have thought that embracing Christ and His cause would mean loss to them. They may have resented the demand for obedience to a higher standard of life, fearing the insistence upon character as the evidence of creed. Like many in our day, they seemed inclined to limit belief to mental assent rather than to enlarge it to include a changed life.

They were not emancipated from the attractions and fascinations of the old life, and with it all they were given to the infirmity of self-pity. Like Peter, who one day said to the Lord, "Behold, we have forsaken all, and followed thee; what shall we have therefore?" (Matt. 19:27), they were inclined to feel that they had been deprived of something. True, following Christ means forsaking our old ways, but it also means being enriched in everything. How? By possessing Christ. Have you noticed how little emphasis the Lord laid on the material benefits to be gained by following Him? True, He promised that, if we seek God's kingdom and righteousness first, all things needful will be supplied, but this was never in the nature of an inducement, or to encourage hopes of material gain. Having Christ, we have everything! No area of life is impoverished, for the grace of God adds a new dimension that makes it meaningful. All those who are in Christ are rich, for the very possession of Christ is the greatest wealth anyone can enjoy.

> There are no paupers in the kingdom of God. You can be poor in this world's goods and yet be richer than your wealthy neighbor. "Godliness with contentment is great gain," said Paul when writing to Timothy (1 Tim. 6:6). Did you ever stop to think of the paradox in our Lord's statement in Luke 6:20, "Blessed [be ye] poor: for yours is the kingdom of God"? The word "blessed" here describes the man indwelt by God for the sake of the Lord Jesus Christ. When you are "blessed" in this sense, you are fully satisfied. Your blessedness in Christ makes you rich. But your riches do not possess you; you possess them. You are even willing to become poor for the sake of Christ. Yet you do not become less wealthy for being poor because you possess the true riches that cannot be affected by material gains or losses.

When Paul said to the Corinthians, "In everything ye are enriched," he was telling them, "In everything you have found its inherent satisfaction, the fulfillment it was intended to give."

People who leave Christ out of their human relationships do not really find satisfaction in other people. People who leave Christ out of their possessions and pursuits do not realize the full enjoyment of life. He who has Christ within, inherits the earth. Real happiness, blessedness, does not begin with things and work its way into the human heart, but it begins with the human heart as it opens itself to Christ.

Having Christ, as Paul says in Ephesians 3:8, you have "unsearchable riches." Why is that? Because Christ is God, and possessing Him you possess the Creator and Sustainer of all people and all things. Which is better, to have a limited sum of money, or to be the son of a wealthy man; to have access to the limited resources of this world, or to have the limitless God as your Father?

In anticipation of marriage, a young man had saved for many years to build a fine house for his bride. His dream was realized. But on the eve of his honeymoon, as he and his wife were about to sail on an ocean voyage, he received word that their beautiful home had burned to the ground. With tears in his eyes he broke the news to his bride. With that fine instinct of love that was to characterize their whole life together she said, "Never mind, dear, we still have each other."

That is what it means to be a Christian. As Paul so beautifully put it in Philippians 3:8, "I count all things but loss for the excellency of the knowledge of Christ Jesus my Lord; for whom I have suffered the loss of all things, and do count them but refuse, that I may win Christ." When you can say that with all your heart, you know the meaning of true riches.

Wealth That Can Never Be Lost

"Riches have wings," said the poet Cowper. And that is more truth than fiction, as many ruined investors discovered in the stock market crash of 1929. Those whose sole wealth consisted of stocks and bonds were completely demoralized by their losses, and many of them committed suicide.

There are two basic differences between material and spiritual riches. Things satisfy us to a limited extent. They procure for us, or enable us to procure, the satisfaction of some of our desires. But while food may satisfy a person's hunger, it cannot satisfy his total personality. One reason he can never be fully satisfied by material things is that his appetite for them grows a good deal faster than the supply. Man can never have enough money, it seems. When he sets his goal at a certain sum, he will automatically set it higher as soon as he attains it.

But this is not true of the treasures that God gives us. They grow in proportion to the growth of our power of apprehending them. The more we take of them and use them the more we are able to take of them. When our money is spent, it is gone, but here is wealth that is with us, in greater supply than it was before we began to spend it. The more we have, the more we may have; the more we desire, the more we possess; and the more we use, the richer we become.

And yet there is another difference: These riches that Christ gives us, if we will only take them by faith, are inseparable from ourselves. They consist of things that become part of our being and so can never be wrenched from us. We need fear no loss by outward violence, as from force or fraud. They last, and we know that there is no possibility of their being taken from us. The more money a man makes in this world the more trouble he has to know what to do with it, but here is wealth that cannot be parted from us and so brings with it no anxiety. Our riches in Christ need not be left behind at death as our worldly wealth must. To the rich man whose treasures were laid up on earth came the solemn word, "Thou fool, this night thy soul shall be required of thee: then whose shall those things be, which thou hast provided?" (Luke 12:20). (See "The Unsearchable Riches of Christ," by Alexander Maclaren, in *The Contemporary Pulpit*, Vol. 5, pp. 15-25).

In the second century, a Christian was brought before a pagan ruler and told to renounce his faith. "If you don't do it, I will banish you," threatened the king.

The man smiled and answered, "You can not banish me from Christ, for He says 'I will never leave you nor forsake you.'" To which the king angrily retorted, "Then I will confiscate your property and take all your possessions."

Again the man smiled and said, "My treasures are all laid up on high; you cannot get them." The king became furious and shouted, "I will kill you!"

"Why," the man answered, "I have been dead forty years; I have been dead with Christ, dead to the world, and my life is hidden with Christ in God, and you cannot touch it." In desperation the king turned to his advisers and asked, "What can you do with a fanatic like that?"

Yes, we who are in Christ are permanently enriched. This distinctive quality of permanence is borne out by the tense of the verb *eploutísthēte*, "ye were enriched." It is in the first aorist passive, indicating that this enrichment was effected at a definite time in the past and is final as well as continuing. This is the old causative verb from *ploútos* (4149), "wealth," common in Attic writers, which was dropped out for centuries and later reappeared in the Septuagint. In the New Testament it appears only three times (1 Cor. 1:5, 2 Cor. 6:10, 11) and is used by Paul alone.

As recipients of God's grace, we cannot become poor in the way that a person can who stands the chance of losing material wealth. The passive verb "were enriched" indicates that what we are as believers is all due to Christ. When we are in Him, we are in the family, "an heir of God through Christ" (Gal. 4:7). Is there a greater privilege, a greater enrichment, than being children of Him by whom all things were created and all things consist? A true sense of values should lead each of us to prefer that above all else. Is this your experience? Are you enriched in everything because you are in Christ?

There is no area of your life that will not be affected once Christ comes into your heart. Do not be afraid that you stand to lose anything by accepting Him as your Savior and Lord. You have everything to gain. Conversely, without Christ, you have everything to lose.

When a certain wealthy man died, his will could not be found. Since his wife and only son had preceded him in death, his possessions were sold at auction. Everything was disposed of except a picture of the son. Nobody seemed to want it, until an elderly woman approached and pleaded with the auctioneer to let her have it for the few pennies in her possession. When he gave her the picture, she hugged it to her heart because she had been the son's nurse in his infancy and boyhood days.

Attached to the back of the painting she discovered an envelope addressed to an attorney. Taking it to him, she was astonished to hear him exclaim, "Woman, you have a fortune! This is the man's will, and in it he has left a large sum of money to anyone who loved his son enough to buy the picture!"

This is an illustration of what Paul meant when he wrote the Corinthian believers that, the moment they stepped into the family of God through faith in Christ, they were enriched in everything. The moment a person accepts Christ, he acquires a spiritual nature that he did not have before. "Whereby are given unto us exceeding great and precious promises: that by these ye might be partakers of the divine nature, having escaped the corruption that is in the world through lust" (2 Pet. 1:4). He is transferred from the devil's family to the family of God. "For ye are all the children of God by faith in Christ Jesus" (Gal. 3:26). The debt for sin has been paid through the atoning death of Christ upon the cross. And, sad to say, the man who is in hell today is there because he is paying for his own sins, not having availed himself of God's offer of pardon through Christ.

What Happens When You Open Your Mouth?

After telling the Corinthian Christians that they were enriched in everything in Christ, Paul proceeded to mention two areas of life in which they were particularly enriched. The King James Version has it: "in every thing . . . in all utterance, and in all knowledge." The Greek word translated "every" and "all" in this verse is *pánti,* the dative form of *pán* (3956), and would literally read, "that in all [things: this word is understood; it is not in the Greek text] ye are enriched by Him, in all word, in all knowledge."

In the first instance, "all things" does not refer to our being given every material thing that we may wish for, but to Christ's adding the dimension of meaning and purpose to everything that makes up our lives, whether it be food, clothing, human relationships, morality, life, or death. Take this last experience, for instance. All men die, whether in Christ or out of Christ. But what a difference there is in their attitudes toward death.

When Robert Owen, the notorious freethinker, visited Alexander Campbell to arrange the preliminaries for the great debate that was to follow, they walked about the farm until they came to the family burying ground. "There is one advantage I have over the Christian," boasted Mr. Owen. "I am not afraid to die. Most Christians have fear in death, but, if some few items of my business were settled, I should be perfectly willing to die at any moment." "Well," replied Mr. Campbell, "you say you have no fear in death; have you any hope in death?" "No," said Mr. Owen after a thoughtful pause. "Then," said Mr. Campbell, pointing to an ox standing nearby, "you are on a level with that animal. He has fed till he is satisfied, and stands in the shade whisking off the flies, and has neither hope nor fear in death. How true is the saying, 'They that die without dying thoughts shall die without living comforts.'"

A wounded soldier said to his comrades who were carrying him, "Put me down. Do not bother to carry me farther. I am dying." They did as he requested and returned to the battle.

A few minutes later, an officer saw the man wallowing in his blood and said to him, "Can I do anything for you?" "Nothing, thank you." "Shall I get you a little water?" "No, thank you. I am dying." "Is there anything I can do for you?" persisted the kind-hearted officer. "Shall I write to your friends?" "I have no friends that you can write to. But there is one thing for which I would be much obliged. In my pack you will find a New Testament. Will you open it at the 14th chapter of John and, near the end of the chapter, you will find a verse that begins with 'Peace.' Will you read it to me?" The officer did so and read the words, "Peace I leave with you, my peace I give unto you: not as the world giveth, give I unto you. Let not your heart be troubled, neither let it be afraid" (John 14:27). "Thank you, sir," said the dying man. "I have that peace—I am going to that Savior—God is with me—I want no more," and he was gone. Can you say that? If you are in Christ you should be able to. If not, you have neither peace nor hope in the prospect of death.

In every kind of situation we are better off if we are in Christ. Paul, however, singles out two areas in particular in which Christ enriches our lives: in word and knowledge. What is the real meaning of the Corinthians having been enriched "in all word, and in all knowledge"? Let us look at the Greek expressions. First, *pánti*, "all," in reference to these two areas of life, means that the Corinthians were enriched in every kind of word, their total realm of expression, and every kind of knowledge, all knowledge put together.

The word translated "utterance" here is *lógō* (3056) in Greek. I do not believe this translation does justice to what Paul meant.

In Acts 2:4, "as the Spirit gave them utterance," the Greek word is *apophthéngesthai* (669), which is the same word found in its verbal form in 2 Peter 2:16, 18, and in its substantive form in Romans 10:18 and 1 Corinthians 14:7. The noun *phthóngos* (5353) primarily refers to sound or the tone of a musical instrument. It does not necessarily refer to a thoughtful expression of the mind. *Lógos* is the noun that refers to words that have meaning, those which express thought. The Lord in His pre-incarnate spiritual essence is called "the Word" (*ho* [3588] *Lógos*; see John 1:1).

The enrichment that Christ brings to His believers in their "utterance" is not merely a pleasing sound added to the sound produced by their lips but is an enrichment of every word. Everything a Christian says, when enriched in this way, is meaningful; there is thought behind it. Look at Matthew 12:36 to understand the distinction among three Greek words used of men's speech: "But I [Christ] say unto you, That every idle word [*rĕma* {4487} *argón* {692}] that men shall speak [*lalēsousin* {2980}], they shall give account [*lógou*] thereof in the day of judgment." In the expression "idle word" (*rĕma argón*), *rĕma* (word) is more equivalent to "saying," and this "saying" does not necessarily involve its being a product of one's own mind. "That men shall speak," *lalēsousin*, comes from *laliá* (2981), which is more equivalent to the sounds made by animals and persons who have no understanding of what they are saying. And "they shall give account," *lógou*, refers to a logical explanation for the words spoken idly.

It would be incorrect to assume that Paul was saying here that Christ had enriched the Corinthians by enabling them to speak in "unknown tongues." Throughout the 12th and 14th chapters of this epistle, these are never designated by the verb *légō* (3004) (the verb form of *lógos* [3056]) but always by the verb *laléō* (2980). In the 14th chapter, Paul makes two pronouncements: (1) that those who spoke in "unknown tongues" did not understand what they were saying, and therefore, what came out of their mouths was not *lógos* but *laliá* (2981); and (2) that others could not understand them either; so that speaking in an "unknown tongue" in the presence of others could only be tolerated if it were interpreted in an understandable language. Where God is concerned, of course, it would make no difference (v. 2) because He, being omniscient, does not need language to understand the dispositions of our hearts in prayer.

Lógō in 1 Corinthians 1:5 therefore, must mean speech that is the result of thought—purposeful, meaningful expression. This is what Christ enriches when He enters the human heart. Our words cease to be idle, unclean, or meaningless, but instead become "seasoned with salt." How different the world would be if, every time we opened our mouths, God was glorified and men were benefited by our speech. What Paul meant is well expressed by what was said of an aged minister: "The older he grew, the less he spoke, and the more he said." We better understand what is meant by being enriched in every word when we sit in the pew under such a man, in contrast to the preacher who talks to fill up time, giving us no lesson to take with us to change or enrich our lives. Fellow ministers, a few words that are *lógoi*— not rambling, not just talking—are better than a whole flood of sounds that convey nothing to the hearer because there is no real thought behind them. The enrichment of our words is not in their quantity but in their quality. Wise is the man who knows what not to say and remembers not to say it.

> If any little word of mine
>   May make a life the brighter,
> If any little song of mine
>   May make a heart the lighter,
> God help me speak that little word,
>   And take my bit of singing,
> And drop it in some lonely vale
>   To set the echoes ringing.

THANKSGIVING AND RICHES

Enriched in All Knowledge

> What wondrous blessings overflow
> When we can truly say, "I know"—
> I know in whom I have believed,
> I know the One I have received,
> I know His blood avails for me,
> I know that I was blind, but see,
> I know that my Redeemer lives,
> I know the gift He freely gives,
> I know He'll keep me to the end,
> I know He's my unfailing Friend,
> I know He's coming in the sky,
> I know the time is drawing nigh.
> —R. F. Neighbour

How can anyone know all that? Surely man's unaided intelligence cannot give him such assurance of "things not seen." It needs to be enlightened by the One who endowed him with intelligence in the first place, God, the Creator of us all. And this enlightenment comes only as man's disrupted relationship with God, caused by sin, is restored through faith and repentance in Christ as Savior and Lord.

When we thus accept Christ, we do not know everything, but what we do know becomes more meaningful. He enriches our intelligence and the expression of our intelligent thoughts (*lógō*). This is what Paul meant by the expression, "Ye have been enriched in every knowledge." It is not that "Ye have been imparted every knowledge," but everything that you know or come to know, Christ enriches. The Greek words *pánti* (masculine) and *pásē* (feminine), translated "all" in the expressions "in all utterance, and in all knowledge," mean every kind of word and every kind of knowledge. The word "knowledge" itself (*gnōsis* [1108]) here refers to learning in the realms of both physical and spiritual realities. There is no area of learning that Christ does not enrich. Knowledge for its own sake may not always be advantageous. The purpose of knowledge determines its value.

Our greatest enrichment of knowledge is that when we are in Christ, we can see farther than our senses would take us. We can know the naturally unknowable. Where our human discovery stops, Christ begins His revelation. This makes the religion of Christ not a "hope-so" or "guess-so" affair but a "know-so" certainty. Christ is not a mythical figure; He is God incarnate, made manifest in history for the purpose of revealing to us what we could never know about Him through our natural thought processes. We know the unknowable because we know Christ. God can be known in no other way. The Athenians did better than they knew when they dedicated an altar to "The Unknown God." Only if we are in Christ can we say with Paul, "I know whom I have believed" (2 Tim. 1:12). In Christ we can experience God.

But do we all become equally rich the moment we step into the circle of Christ, the family of the redeemed, or are there degrees of spiritual riches? Does Christ pour out upon every new believer all the riches of spiritual enlightenment at once, or is it a matter of growth in varying degrees according to the capacity of the individual?

As in the material world God dispenses His blessings in varied amounts, so He does in the spiritual realm. When we acquire spiritual life in Christ, we begin to exercise our spiritual muscles, so to speak, in working and living for Him. That is our responsibility as His follower. And God also assumes a certain responsibility—that of making available to us all His riches. Our effort to acquire them would result in nothing if it were not for His provision. Very few of us, however, acquire all that God has for us. Let us never blame God for withholding His blessing; let us rather examine ourselves to see whether it is not really our unwillingness to meet the conditions He has set forth for the appropriation of His riches that keeps us so spiritually poor.

LESSONS:

1. Praising believers first for what is good in them, and then lovingly pointing out their faults, encourages them to "grow in grace."
2. Following Christ means forsaking our old ways, but it also means being enriched in everything. We who have Christ within, inherit the earth.
3. Two areas of life in which Christians are particularly enriched are our words and our knowledge.

1 Cor. 1:6 | *A Positive Testimony*

Even as the testimony of Christ was confirmed in you.

What we said regarding 1:5 is preliminary to an understanding of the Greek adverb *kathōs* (2531), with which verse 6 begins. The King James Version translates it "even." The New English Bible leaves it out altogether. Yet it is an important link between verses 5 and 6. In verse 5 we read, "That in everything ye are enriched by Him [Christ], in all utterance [intelligent speaking], and in all knowledge." The questions then arise, "In what measure, and by what criterion?" Verse 6 answers these questions. It begins with the Greek adverb *kathōs,* a compound word made up of *katá* (2596), "according," and *hōs* (3739), "as." *Kathōs,* then, means "according as, in the measure that, to the degree that." The same adverb is used in 1 Corinthians 12:11, where Paul speaks about the distribution of the gifts of the Holy Spirit. "But all these worketh that one and the selfsame Spirit, dividing to every man severally as [*kathōs*] He will"—that is, "to the degree that He pleases."

You have been enriched, Paul tells the Corinthians, through your act of faith in receiving Christ. But you are not all equally rich. Your enrichment is in accordance with certain conditions. What are they? What makes one Christian spiritually richer than another? Two things: first, the measure of spiritual instruction

69

he is able to receive, and, second, the amount of spiritual instruction he is willing to assimilate into his own life. This is what Paul means in verse 6: You have been enriched to the degree that "the testimony of Christ was confirmed in you."

The word translated "testimony" is *martúrion* (3142) in Greek. It is not the more common feminine gender, *marturía* (3141), which means primarily the process of giving a testimony, whether that provides proof or not, but the neuter word used only twenty times in the entire New Testament. This neuter form is used primarily in a negative sense as the proof against someone in judgment, as in James 5:3, Mark 6:11, and Luke 9:5. Note that Matthew 10:18 and Mark 13:9 say, "And ye shall be brought before rulers and kings for my sake, for a testimony [*martúrion:* actually, 'for a proof'] against them and the Gentiles." This does not mean that the persecuted apostles were to give their verbal testimony before these authorities. Instead, the apostles were brought before them to be punished for the testimony they had already given concerning Christ. This would be proof of the persecutors' guilt on the day of judgment. (See also Luke 21:13.) In these instances the neuter word *martúrion* stands with a negative emphasis for guilt or proof of guilt and not for the evangelistic witness that the feminine word *marturía* usually denotes. Are our lives bearing such strong witness to our faith in Christ that they will some day be used as a testimony against those who refuse to believe in Him?

How Effective Is Your Witness for Christ?

A young man got up to give his testimony for Christ in an open air meeting. Not being accustomed to speaking in public, he stammered a good deal at first. An atheist who was present shouted at him, "You ought to be ashamed of yourself standing and talking like that!" "You're right," the young man replied. "I am ashamed of myself, but I'm not ashamed of Christ."

A POSITIVE TESTIMONY

In 1 Corinthians 1:6, we have seen that the word "testimony" (*martúrion*), when used in a negative sense, implied that the preaching of the gospel would one day be a witness against those who heard it and would cause persecution of those who preached it. But in a positive sense *martúrion* should be understood as proof for something or somebody, rather than against something or somebody. It is what we would call "effective witness." The genitive or prepositional phrase used with it is *toú* (3588) *Christoú* (5547), of Christ. Therefore *martúrion toú Christoú* would mean the effective witness of Christ. If we take Christ to be the subject (as Lenski does), then we must paraphrase it as the witness or proof that Christ Himself brought to the Corinthians. However, I tend to agree with A. T. Robertson, who takes Christ as the object, which would make us paraphrase it as the witness concerning Christ.

This witness ultimately, of course, has Christ as its subject, for He is God's proof to man that God is, and what God is. "He that hath seen me hath seen the Father" (John 14:9). We would have no proof that the Almighty God could also be man's loving Father apart from the person of the Lord Jesus Christ. That is what John 1:18 says: "God [eternal, infinite] no one [no created being] has ever seen; the only begotten [*monogenés* (3439), the only one of the same family] Son, who has always been at the bosom of the Father [note the introduction of God as Father], he himself has revealed him" (a.t.).

However, Paul was not referring here primarily to that basic proof of God's love in Christ by Christ Himself, but rather to the effective witnessing concerning Christ that he himself had engaged in among these Corinthians for a year and a half (Acts 18:11). His witness for Christ in Corinth was positive and effective. It was proof that Jesus was the Christ, as Paul had declared in the synagogue (Acts 18:5) before he was excommunicated. He

A Positive Testimony

did not tear down the Jewish religion; he simply gave proof as to who the historical Jesus really was.

In Acts 18:4 two highly significant words are used to show the method of Paul's preaching in Corinth. The first is "reasoned" (*dielégeto* [1256]), from which we get our English word "dialectics," and the second is "persuaded" (*epeíthe* [3982]). Paul did not expect intellectuals like the Corinthians to accept Christ without being fully persuaded that He was indeed God incarnate. Nothing short of that faith and persuasion could suffice for their salvation.

That the Greek word *martúrion* refers to the effective witnessing about Christ is sustained by the main verb used in this 6th verse. It is not the common word "preached" but the Greek verb *ebebaiōthē* (from *bebaióō* [950]), usually translated "confirmed." The verb *bebaióō* means "to make firm, to establish, to make sure." The witness of Paul among these Corinthians never wavered. He did not change it to please his hearers or to avoid persecution. It was firm and therefore took root in their hearts, including such pronounced persecutors as the two chief priests of the synagogue in Corinth. The one thing the Jews of that day, as well as today, would not accept is that Jesus is the Messiah predicted in the Old Testament, the Anointed One, the Christ. Yet that is what Paul preached to them (Acts 18:5). He almost went to prison for it at that time, and finally did, but his preaching of the truth was firm and unwavering, hence effective. If we should wonder why our witness is ineffective, perhaps we should examine ourselves to see if it is firm and unequivocal. If we try to set a heavy pole in loose earth, we will find that it wavers. It will not hold unless firmly set in cement.

Paul does not say that he was the one who brought this message about Christ to them with such effectiveness and certainty. It was he, of course, but he prefers to refer to it in the third person passive instead of the first person active. He does not say,

"You have been made rich in the measure that I have firmly proclaimed the proof of Christ in you or among you," but "in the measure that it was confirmed in you." While he was always careful to establish his apostolic authority among them so that his words would have binding force, he was equally careful to avoid any use of the personal "I" that sounded like bragging. We ought never to say, "I led so and so to Christ," but rather, "He found Christ," or even better, "The Holy Spirit brought him to Christ." Paul would rather leave the impression among the Corinthians that the true agent of effectiveness in making them believe was not he but the Holy Spirit, of whom Jesus said, "He will reprove the world of sin, and of righteousness, and of judgment" (John 16:8).

And yet we must also recognize that the Holy Spirit expects us to proclaim the gospel, just as God expects us to sow the seed in the ground before He causes it to grow. We are to fulfill His conditions, and He will fulfill His promises. As Clarence Tucker Craig so aptly said,

> Though most Protestants prefer to avoid the word "succession" because of the implications with which it has been surrounded, they recognize in fact a "believer's succession." Every believer has come to Christ through some other believer, and so the chain that goes back ultimately links each one of us with the life of our Lord on earth. Men and women, laymen and ministers alike, have served as links in this chain. Rarely does Christian experience begin *de novo* without personal contact with someone who has mediated the Christian witness. Here is a form of horizontal continuity which all may gratefully acknowledge as well as the apostolic function to which they are called [*A Reader's Notebook*, Harper & Bros., p. 306].

One stormy night a man traveling along a dark road met a man coming from the opposite direction who said to him in a hesitant manner, "I think maybe the bridge is out. At least I heard something to that effect." The traveler was not convinced and decided to proceed. A little farther on a man came rushing out of the dark toward him and said, "Stop! Do not go any farther. The bridge is out!" So passionately convincing were his tones that the traveler turned back and his life was saved. That is how we are to witness—with passion and conviction.

Tell It Out and Live It Out

"Christianity is not taught; it is caught." It spreads like fire from one burning heart to another heart prepared to catch the flame. The willingness to share Christ is a definite test of discipleship. We must have something to testify to before we can testify. We must have the fire before we can pass it on. In court a witness does not tell what he thinks or imagines but what he knows. His information must be first-hand or it is of little value. The witness of Christ tells what he knows of Christ as revealed in his own experience of Him. He relates not views but news. This makes his witness one of the most personal things in the world, since he is stating only what is known to himself and God, and that which cannot be known by another unless he makes it known. As John says, "That which we have seen and heard declare we unto you" (1 John 1:3). That is witnessing. To spread the fire, we can begin just where we are. When a converted railroad engineer asked C. H. Spurgeon what work he ought to do for Christ, the preacher asked him if the stoker on the engine were a Christian. When he replied, "No," Spurgeon said, "Then that is your work for Christ. Win him."

Paul tells the Corinthians that "the testimony of Christ was confirmed in you." The Greek verb *ebebaiōthē*, "was confirmed or made certain," intimates a witness that is not merely hearsay but that emanates from a personal, intimate knowledge of Christ. "And ye shall be witnesses unto Me [or, on my behalf]," the risen Lord said to His disciples before His departure from earth (Acts 1:8). They were to speak of Him primarily because they knew Him. They were to speak and live so that those who heard them and observed their lives would have sufficient proof of Christ's deity and the truthfulness of His claims. His disciples were to tell the truth about Him. If they spoke doubtingly, if they failed to be faithful in their witnessing, if they withheld any part of the truth that they were to tell, the mission of Christ would fail.

What the world needs today in order for the gospel to be established is apostolic faithfulness. As J. R. Miller says, "You are to do things which nobody but a Christian would do, and do them in a way that only a Christian would do them." (See *The Garden of the Heart*, Hodder & Stoughton, 1906, p. 164.)

This rooting of Christ's witness was not done in governmental recognition but in human hearts. Christ was not officially recognized in sinful, secular, commercial Corinth. That was not Paul's aim—as it was the Emperor Constantine's later on—to have the Christian religion officially recognized by the state. He was aiming for human hearts to accept Christ in spite of their sinful surroundings. He did not seek primarily to change the status quo of Corinthian society, though it desperately needed to be changed, but to preach the gospel so effectively, so fearlessly, that some lives would be radically changed. "The witness of Christ was confirmed in you," Paul says to the converts from paganism. That was its aim. It succeeded. Paul was not so naive as to think that society could change through a change in the official establishment, as some seem to think today. Only as individual hearts are cleansed from their sinful lusts will society change. A clean house used as a shelter for pigs will not remain clean very long. A pig will mess it up because that is its nature—to wallow in mud. Man needs to be redeemed from sin if the society in which he lives is to become characterized by righteousness and peace. Like Paul, we are to consider our primary

task as Christians that of establishing Christ in human hearts
and lives.

What a responsibility this 6th verse of 1 Corinthians 1 places
on us as Christians. Unbelievers may have the same opportunity
to be spiritually enriched as they hear and see our witness for
Christ. If those around us are spiritually poor, it may be because
of our failure to witness to them. We lament the spiritual bank-
ruptcy of the world, but would not the world be richer spiritually if our witness for Christ were firmer and more faithful?

A wealthy unbeliever who had spent much money on the education of his daughter returned home from a business trip to
be informed by his wife that the girl had gone forward and
accepted Christ at an evangelistic meeting. When she ran to
greet him, he struck her again and again and told her to get out
and never come back. She took shelter in a friend's home and
spent the night in prayer. Early the next morning the father sent
for her to come back. He met her at the gate, saying, "I give you
my heart and hand to go with you to heaven!" The mother followed, and all rejoiced in the saving power of Christ. A firm
stand for Christ did it all. Oh, that Christians would get a
firmer grasp on Christ so that our prayers and love would melt
those around us to embrace the same saving faith in Him.

The main thrust of verse 6 is that the enrichment of the
Corinthian believers was in direct proportion to the fidelity of
apostolic witness—a fidelity of words and works, of speech and
behavior. No amount of wordy witness is enough unless it is obviously backed by the quality of life we profess. Unless there is
reality behind the effort, all our attempts at soul-winning are
justly doomed to failure.

Before we can fully understand the Corinthian letters, we
must analyze and digest Acts 18:1–17, which describes Paul's
ministry in Corinth. When persecuted and excommunicated
from the synagogue, he said to those who were cursing him,

"Your blood be upon your own heads; I am clean" (Acts 18:6). That declaration, "I am clean," is absolutely essential and must be evident before we open our mouths to speak of Christ. It is good to recall Emerson's saying, "What you are speaks so loudly I cannot hear what you say."

A man got up in a testimony meeting and said, "I'm mean; I lie and steal and get drunk, but, praise the Lord, I haven't lost my religion!" "Such a testimony," T. Howard Crago says, "is supposed to produce convulsions rather than conversions." (See *Real Discipleship*, Marshall, Morgan, and Scott, Ltd., p. 62.)

> Only a word, yes, only a word,
> That the Spirit's voice said: "Speak."
> But the soul passed on, unblest and weak,
> That you were meant to have stirred
> To hope and courage and faith anew,
> Because when the message came to you
> You were out of touch with your Lord.

Resisting the Temptation to Spiritual Pride

A missionary approached a native whom he had not seen before and asked, "Have you ever heard the gospel?" "No," he replied, "but I have seen it. I know a man who used to be the terror of the neighborhood. He was a bad opium smoker and as dangerous as a wild beast. But he became completely changed. He is now gentle and good and has quit opium." As Christians we should ask ourselves if we are enriching others in and through Christ by what we say and do. But we cannot do it if we ourselves are spiritual paupers.

The word *ebebaiōthē* means not only confirming our belief in Christ by words, but, as in the case of the Apostle Paul, confirming it by our lives. Paul went to Corinth and stayed with fellow tentmakers. He became a burden to no one. He worked for his living and witnessed in his spare time until he was finally able to devote every bit of his time to the Lord's service. The love he preached to men, he lived and exemplified among them. A non-practicing Christian in word and deed makes a poor witness for his Lord.

Consider the experience of a man who was giving out gospel tracts on a steamship. One gentleman he approached accepted a tract graciously but said, "I have not much faith in that kind of work." The Christian worker replied, "It was through a gospel tract given to me in Glasgow twenty years ago that I was converted." Asking for particulars, the gentleman discovered that it was he who had given him the tract! He had ceased to do this because he saw so little results from his efforts. He added, "But by the grace of God I shall start again."

So many times we become discouraged as we give our witness for Christ. We present objective proof of His deity from the Word of God and practical proof of the transformation that has taken place in our own lives, and yet so often it seems ineffective. To offset this human element of discouragement in witnessing, it is good to recall Paul's experiences in Corinth. It was a most sinful place, and yet the testimony of Christ took root. The sowing of the seed is our duty, but the fruitbearing is God's gracious province. "Ye became rich in the degree that the testimony of Christ was confirmed in you," said Paul. Every time we meet a Christian, we have a confirmation of the effectiveness of the gospel. What farmer would sow seed in the ground if he did not expect it to yield a crop? That is how it must be with us as we witness for Christ. If we are not hopefully expectant of fruitbearing, we will not be faithful in sowing.

God's grace was planted in Corinth in the hearts of sinful men and women. That grace was received. And those who received it, in the measure in which they appropriated it, became enriched in Christ Jesus.

A POSITIVE TESTIMONY

In the next verse (1:7) we see the result of this planting of the grace of God, of Christ's spiritual enrichment. *Hōste* (5620), the Greek conjunction with which this verse begins, means "therefore, so that." It is as though Paul were saying, "As a result of the grace given, of the enrichment effected, and of the testimony confirmed, here is what can be said of you." It is important to note that the three verbs employed here—*dotheísē* (1325), given in verse 4, *eploutísthē* (4148), enriched, in verse 5, and *ebebaiōthē* (950), confirmed, in verse 6—are all in the passive voice, aorist tense, indicating acts that are complete, that were effective, and that were caused by an outside agency—in this case by God the Father, God the Son, or God the Holy Spirit, or by whatever agency God was pleased to use.

In his introduction of the Epistle to the Corinthians, Paul was careful to tell them that being the recipients of God's grace was not because of anything extraordinary they had done. He wanted them, of course, to recognize their position in Christ, but not to become puffed up about it, not to feel they had reached it by climbing to it on the ladder of good works, or that they deserved it, but that it was the result of their receiving the grace of God and submitting to His will for their lives. The basic principle of the Scriptures regarding our position in Christ is to realize who and what we are in Him, but never to make the mistake of thinking that what we are and have is the result of our deserving it or achieving it. We are children of God because we have allowed ourselves to be molded into a new creation (2 Cor. 5:17), something we could never have become on our own, coming only through the supernatural power of God.

A subtle temptation that comes to the new believer in Christ is to become proud of his position. He finds it all too easy to take the lead and to assign to Christ a position of lesser importance. Thomas Aquinas was a true saint of God whose crown of glory never faded because he never polished it himself.

A POSITIVE TESTIMONY

One day when he was walking in the cloisters of a monastery in Bologna where he was lecturing, a monk came hurrying up to him and told him to come with him on an errand to the city. The monk had been ordered by his superior to bring with him the first brother monk he saw; and, not knowing Thomas by sight, he told him to come.

The great teacher never said a word but followed the monk as well as he could, though a bit slowly, for he was rather lame. "Hurry up, can't you?" the monk said impatiently, and Thomas did his best. After a while, the monk noticed that all the people in the street were looking at his companion, and many of them were saluting him with great respect. Presently one of them asked, "Isn't that the great teacher, Thomas Aquinas, who is with you?" The monk was horror-stricken! He had disturbed one of the most important men in the city and then treated him with scant courtesy. With tears in his eyes he begged the master's pardon.

Paul was scrupulously careful lest any human being, whether the Corinthians or he himself, shine brighter than Christ in the wonderful work accomplished in Corinth. God has done it all; therefore give Him all the glory. That was the tenor of his message.

> Not I, but Christ, be honored, loved, exalted,
> Not I, but Christ, be seen, be known, be heard;
> Not I, but Christ, in ev'ry look and action,
> Not I, but Christ, in ev'ry thought and word.
> —A. A. Whiddington

LESSONS:

1. Christians are enriched (1:5) to the degree that they receive the witness concerning Christ and assimilate it in their own lives.
2. The main thrust of 1 Corinthians 1:6 is that the enrichment of the Corinthian believers was in direct proportion to the fidelity of apostolic witness—a fidelity of words and works, of speech and behavior.
3. The Greek word *martúrion* (3142) refers to the effective witnessing about Christ. Paul's effective witness for Christ in Corinth was proof that Jesus was the Christ as Paul had declared.

A POSITIVE TESTIMONY

4. The true agent of effectiveness in making the Corinthian Christians believe was not Paul but the Holy Spirit. As we witness, we must remember that the sowing of the seed is our duty, but the fruit-bearing is God's gracious province.

5. Only as individual hearts are cleansed from their sinful lusts will society change. Man needs to be redeemed from sin if the society in which he lives is to become characterized by righteousness and peace. Like Paul, we are to consider our primary task as Christians that of establishing Christ in human hearts and lives.

A Positive Testimony

1 Cor. 1:7 | *Present and Future Gifts*

So that ye come behind in no gift; waiting for the coming of our Lord Jesus Christ.

The purpose of God's activity in this world is people. Glorious though the beauties of our environment may be, God does not center His interest upon them. Pascal, that great thinker, was right when he wrote: "Man is but a reed, the feeblest thing in nature, but he is a reed that thinks. It needs not that the universe arm itself to crush him. An exhalation, a drop of water, suffices to destroy him. But, were the universe to crush him, man is yet nobler than the universe, for he knows that he dies; and the universe, even in prevailing against him, knows not its power."

All that God does has one aim—mankind. His grace is for you. His love is not so much for the mountains and the multicolored birds, as it is for man, whom He originally made in His own image. Although the thought of this truth exalts a man, it really ought to humble him as well.

Being Satisfied With God's Gifts

As we consider 1 Corinthians 1:7, we note the little word "ye." "The testimony of Christ was confirmed in you," Paul has just told the Corinthians in verse 6. "Therefore [the contextual meaning of *hóste* {5620}, translated in the King James Version as 'so that'] you come behind in no gift." The purpose of God's activity in Corinth was people. That is why the second Greek word in this verse is *humás* (5209), "you." He enriched these Corinthians in Christ so that they might receive every spiritual gift from His hand.

A wealthy Englishman had added to his valuable collection a rare violin which Fritz Kreisler, the celebrated virtuoso, greatly longed to possess. When the owner persisted in refusing to part with it, Kreisler begged permission to play it just once. That was granted. With trembling hands the artist tuned the instrument and then played. He played as only a genius can play. He forgot himself. He poured his soul into his music. The Englishman stood as one transfixed until the playing had ceased, and he did not speak until Kreisler had tenderly returned the instrument to the antique box, as a mother puts her baby to bed.

"Take the violin," he burst out. "It is yours. I have no right to keep it. It ought to belong to the man who can play it as you did!" Although the reasoning in this story seems odd, it is representative of the attitude Paul wanted to arouse in the Corinthians who were made rich in Christ. In a sense, ought not an instrument belong to the master who can draw the finest music from it? And ought not your life and mine belong to the Master who can draw the noblest harmonies from them?

In verses 4 and 5 of this chapter, Paul told the Corinthians that the grace of God had been added to them as a result of their position in Christ. They were enriched in everything, and particularly in their intelligence, expression, and knowledge. In verse 7 he expresses this same truth to them by stating, "You do not lack anything." Some people seem to have the attitude, "I'll admit I have many blessings, but on the other hand, look at all the things I don't have." Paul was aware of the human heart's condition in which we desire to have what we cannot have.

PRESENT AND FUTURE GIFTS

Consider man when he was first created. He was placed in a beautiful garden, a paradise on earth. He had everything except omnipresence, omniscience, and omnipotence, which God reserved for Himself. There was only one tree of which God told man not to eat of its fruit. He could eat of all the others. Man would not have suffered hunger by being deprived of the fruit of this one tree. God's provision for his need was not only sufficient but abundant. But man fixed his eyes on the one thing that God told him he could not have. An uncontrollable curiosity took possession of him. He set his will against God's and determined to have what had been forbidden. Man had his own way, but along with it suffered the consequence of his disobedience. And, he has never, of himself, been satisfied since.

We can never be satisfied by grabbing more than God intends for us. We cannot escape from this eternal principle. How often in prayer, when thanking God for what He has given us, we spoil it all by saying, "But look at what I don't have," further spoiling things by then striving to get it regardless of whether it is His will for us to have it or not. When we who have so much, let it bother us that there is one little thing that God has not given us and reach out for it, we should remember the acts of Adam and Eve and the consequence of their disobedience.

That great Spartan lawgiver Lycurgus, who flourished in the 9th century B.C., was asked why in his laws he had set down no punishment for ingratitude. His answer, "I have left it to the gods to punish," was only partly right. Indeed, in a sense the punishment is built in for the ungrateful person is unsatisfied and always longing for more or something better.

Actually, Paul says to the Corinthians, when you are in Christ you lack nothing. How many times have we actually confessed that in Psalm 23 when repeating, "The Lord is my shepherd; I shall not want"? Do what a little child did when, after quoting the first verse, explained it by saying, "The Lord is my shepherd; I don't need anything else." Or better yet, say as another child did, "The Lord is my shepherd; that's all I want." When we have the grace of God, we have everything.

Listen to Paul: "Therefore you do not lack in any gift or grace." The Greek word *hustereisthai* (5302) in verse 7 has been translated "ye come behind" in the King James Version: "So that ye come behind in no gift." This translation implies that the Corinthians ought to be blamed for falling behind in anything because they were refusing to do certain things. If I fall behind as I walk or as I work, it is usually because of a willful or an inherent inability to keep up with others. But that is not what Paul meant here. He wanted to impress on the Corinthians that they should have a spirit of complete satisfaction for all that God had given them, not to complain over what He had not given them or try to attain the impossible. Paul expressed it beautifully to these believers in 2 Corinthians 3:5 when he said, "Not that we are sufficient of ourselves, but our sufficiency is of God."

Loving the Giver More Than the Gift

You are not like anyone else in the world. Just as God makes no two mountains, trees, leaves, or even snowflakes the same, He makes no two people exactly alike. Equality excites man much more than it impresses God. God knows best why this is so. Would our world be any better, or man any happier, if all people and things were exactly the same? I wonder. One thing is certain—God does not equally distribute His blessings to everyone. Yet there seems to be in God's provision, whether it is physical or spiritual, a sufficiency even in inequality.

Describing the varying gifts of the Spirit, the Apostle Paul says in 1 Corinthians 12:11, "But all these worketh that one and the selfsame Spirit, dividing to every man severally as He will." Just as it does not take the same amount of food to satisfy every individual, but depends on the constitution of each, so it is in spiritual matters. God's provision is according to our need, determined not by our own limited knowledge of ourselves but by His omniscience.

A poor woman who had struggled hard to make ends meet and knew what it meant to go without food was taken on an outing to the seaside. Delighted with the scene, she looked out over the vast expanse of waters with tear-filled eyes and exclaimed, "Thank God for a sight of something there is enough of!" The soul experiences such delight when it gets its first vision of the infinite fullness of God's grace in Christ. His grace is quite enough for the soul's every need. Seeing Him, we say with the hymn-writer:

> Thou, O Christ, art all I want;
> More than all in Thee I find.

Charles H. Spurgeon once said, "God is satisfied with Himself, and sufficient to His own happiness. Therefore, surely, there is enough in Him to fill the creature. That which fills an ocean will fill a bucket; that which will fill a gallon will fill a pint; those revenues which will defray an emperor's expenses are enough for a beggar or poor man." Didn't Paul say, "My God shall supply all your need according to his riches in glory by Christ Jesus" (Phil. 4:19)? And He sees fit to bestow these riches on us as an inherent gift. Thus all believers possess Christ, but not everyone has all His gifts, for He gives them as it pleases Him, and His pleasure is according to His knowledge.

The word *hustereísthai*, "lacking" or "wanting," is not used here in an absolute sense but in a relative one, "therefore you come behind in no gift." Notice that we are not promised that we will not lack in any "thing" because there are many things which we as Christians may lack. But we are promised that when we are in Christ, we will not lack in the gifts that God bestows. Having Christ, we have all that is His.

The word used in the Greek text translated "gift" is *charísmati*, the dative singular form of *chárisma* (5486), from which we derive the English adjective "charismatic." We hear of the charismatic movement composed of those who emphasize special gifts that some people are said to possess. Let us carefully study this word. *Chárisma*, "gift," and *cháris* (5485), "grace," have a common root, the verb *chaírō* (5463), which means "to rejoice." *Cháris*, or grace, is what affords joy, that is, someone else's good will, lovingkindness, and favor toward us. *Chárisma*, coming more directly from *charízomai* (5483)—which means "to give freely or graciously as a favor"—is a gift of grace. It is bestowed by God according to His grace. It is used of His free bestowments upon sinners (Rom. 5:15, 16; 6:23; 11:29), of His endowments upon believers by the operation of the Holy Spirit in the congregations (Rom. 12:6; 1 Cor. 1:7; 12:4, 9, 28, 30, 31; 1 Tim. 4:14; 2 Tim. 1:6; 1 Pet. 4:10), of what is imparted through human instruction (Rom. 1:11), of the natural gift of self-control, consequent upon the grace of God as Creator (1 Cor. 7:7), and of gracious deliverances granted in answer to the prayers of fellow believers (2 Cor. 1:11).

Man is always the recipient of *charísmata* (gifts). God has *cháris* (grace) but not *charísmata* (gifts). A *chárisma* or gift is the product of *cháris*, grace. It is not achieved by self. In the Scriptures, God the Father, God the Son, and God the Holy Spirit are all the dispensers of *cháris* and *charísmata*. God does not need either, but we need both. *Cháris* is part of God's nature, like truth and love. Because He has done no wrong, He does not need favor from anyone. When this happens, our guilt from sin disappears and He gives us His *charísmata* or gifts. *Cháris*, grace, can be called the mother of individual *charísmata*, or gifts.

PRESENT AND FUTURE GIFTS

Perhaps Paul tells the Corinthian Christians they were not lacking in any gift (*chárisma*). They had placed such great importance upon gifts, seeking them instead of the Giver (see 12:4, "Now there are diversities of gifts, but the same Spirit"). It is for the Giver to seek out the recipients of His gifts, not for the recipients to choose which gifts they prefer to have. As humans we are most likely to seek the gifts that tend to puff us up and place us in the public eye. However, God alone knows which gifts are best for us.

Apparently, Paul believed that the Corinthians were seeking the gifts of least importance, and saw danger in this. After discussing the various gifts in chapter 12, he concludes with the admonition, "But covet earnestly the best gifts" (12:31). Then he adds in the second part of the verse, "And yet show I unto you a more excellent way," which was in seeking love, *agápē* (26), the very nature of God, for "God is love" (1 John 4:16). No Scripture states that God is any of the other gifts or *charísmata* of the 12th chapter, whether it be tongues, or prophecy, or knowledge, or anything else. Love is His character. Christ is life, the Giver of all gifts; and having Him one lacks no gifts because He is grace, *cháris*, from whom all *charísmata* or gifts spring. We ought to prefer to have Him and speak of Him than to boast of any gifts.

Ask yourself this question: Is my sufficiency in Christ or in what Christ gives me? If it is in the second, you will feel the lack of many gifts. If it is the first, you will never feel that you lack anything important.

The Christian's Present and Future Riches

Nobody likes to see a little child rush out to greet someone with the question, "What did you bring me?" Still less becoming is it for supposedly mature Christians to feel a rush of affection for God only when He bestows some gift upon them.

The Christians in the church of Corinth in Paul's day had a weakness that is all too prevalent today—that of emphasizing the gift rather than the Giver. They also showed a tendency to become more attached to the preacher than to the One he preached about. This explains the various factions that sprang up in the congregation, Christians who proclaimed themselves to be followers of Peter, of Apollos, or of Paul, instead of being united followers of Jesus Christ. Paul reminds them to watch out for this tendency. Seek the Giver rather than the gift. Seek grace (*cháris*) rather than gifts (*charísmata*), Christ rather than the preacher of Christ.

Let us strive to be known as Christians rather than as charismatics. *Charísmata* or gifts are something of which you can never seem to have enough. Only Christ can fully satisfy you. If you are in Him, you will never find yourself lacking anything. Being rich in and through Christ is not conditioned by what you have but by what you are.

Of course, this enrichment in Christ was not just for the Corinthians. Indeed, even as they experienced the fulfillment of Christ, we too can know that it is not limited to His work in the past, but it also rests upon His future work. He came to this world, He died, He rose, to give us the hope of our own resurrection, and He is coming back for us.

Paul's testimony about Christ did two things for the Corinthians. First, it made them rich in His grace. They lacked no gift because they had the Giver. Today, believers cannot become all that Christ intends us to become since we cannot, in our present condition, attain to what we will become in our ultimate eternal state. Although we have been sanctified, the world is still sinful, while we have been made pure in and through Christ. We still have a corruptible body, still get sick, and still live in the prospect of death. Environmental limitations also hinder us. In order for us to attain the ultimate state of perfection, an event must take place—the Second Coming of Christ. We are saved and sanctified because of His first coming. We shall be perfect, incorruptible, glorious, and strong as a result of His Second Coming.

Secondly, Paul's testimony about Christ caused all believers to look forward to His Second Coming. This would bring about the complete and radical transformation of both believers and nonbelievers, of both the dead and the living, and of the whole creation.

"Therefore you lack in no gift, waiting for the revelation of our Lord Jesus Christ." By paraphrasing this to read, "Therefore, the sense of lacking anything is fully compensated for by the hope you as Christians have of the coming of the Lord," we will see what Paul was emphasizing here. If we look for the revelation of our Lord Jesus Christ, we lack in no gift. The inadequacies of this life are made up for by the expectation of what is to come.

People will endure almost anything as long as they have hope. Cyrus Field said that he was nearly in despair on many occasions as he sought to make his vision of the Atlantic cable a reality. Some called it a "mad freak of stubborn ignorance," that a man should endure all that he and his co-workers went through to make this feat possible. "Many times," he confessed, "when wandering in the forests of Newfoundland in the pelting rains, on the deck of ships on dark, stormy nights, alone, far from home, I have almost accused myself of madness and folly to sacrifice the peace of family, and all the hope of life, for what might prove, after all, but a dream. And yet one hope has led me on; and I have prayed that I might not taste death till this work was accomplished. That prayer is answered. And now, beyond all acknowledgments to men, is the feeling of gratitude to God."

Christians of all ages have endured because of the hope of Christ's return and a future life with Him: "waiting for the coming of our Lord Jesus Christ." The participle "waiting" in Greek is *apekdechoménous* (553), "awaiting eagerly." Paul uses it to express eager expectation of the end. Christians stand in this attitude of eager expectation. It is used in Romans 8:23 in reference to the burning expectation of the redemption of our bodies, that is, their resurrection. The redemption of our souls has already taken place, but the redemption of our bodies is yet to come. "Waiting" is also used in relation to the redemption of the whole creation, of our environment, in Romans 8:19. Unfortunately, the King James Version gives a most inadequate rendering of the Greek here. It should read, "For the eager expectation of the creation [not 'the creature'] waiteth [*apekdéchetai* {553}] for the manifestation [*apokálupsin* {602}, the same word as in 1 Cor. 1:7] of the sons of God." The work of Christ has begun already in our hearts. But His Second Coming will consummate the work of redemption in creation and in us. The word is used particularly with reference to the Second Coming, as in Philippians 3:20, "For our conversation is in heaven; from whence also we look [*apekdechómetha* {553}] for the Savior, the Lord Jesus Christ."

The etymology of this word is most interesting. The basic verb is *déchomai* (1209), which means "to receive." It expresses "the reaction to action on the other side." The verb is prefixed by two prepositions, *apó* (575), meaning "from," indicating more specifically the starting point, and *ek* (1537), meaning "from within." *Ekdéchomai* (1551) means "to wait for someone." This waiting for Christ is a hope that springs from within. The preposition *apó*, which is basically Pauline, may very well indicate that the starting point is outside oneself. We are anxiously waiting for Him who will come from heaven.

The participle *apekdechoménous is* in the present tense, "waiting anxiously or eagerly" for the revelation of our Lord Jesus Christ. Its significant meaning is "looking forward to." Although this was a future event, it had a present impact upon the believers. If we are looking forward to the coming of the Lord,

PRESENT AND FUTURE GIFTS

we will be inclined to overlook anything we may be lacking at present. Our riches are not counted merely in terms of our present possessions but in terms of what we will possess when the Lord reveals Himself from heaven.

The Church is often referred to as the Bride of Christ. At present she is looking forward to her marriage day when the Bridegroom will come to receive her to Himself. She may be poor in this world's goods, but she feels the lack of nothing. After all, her Bridegroom is the King of Glory to whom all the kingdoms of the world belong, and she knows she will reign with Him forever and ever.

When Will Jesus Christ Return?

Let us now examine what is meant by the expression, "the coming [or revelation] of our Lord Jesus Christ." The Greek word translated "coming" in the King James Version is *apokálupsin*—one of three Greek words used in Scripture that refer primarily (but not exclusively) to the Second Coming of Christ. The other two words are *epiphaneía* (2015), literally "appearing" or "shining upon," and *parousía* (3952), "presence" or "arrival."

Christ's coming will take place in two stages. The first stage is the coming of the Lord for His saints which will constitute what is commonly known as the rapture of the Church described in 1 Thessalonians 4:16, 17: "For the Lord himself shall descend from heaven with a shout, with the voice of the archangel, and with the trump of God: and the dead in Christ shall rise first: then we which are alive and remain shall be caught up together with them in the clouds, to meet the Lord in the air: and so shall we ever be with the Lord." This is the hope and comfort of God's people.

Note that the coming of the Lord for His saints is sometimes indicated by the word *parousía*, "presence" or "arrival" (as in 15:23; 1 Thess. 2:19; 4:15; 5:23; 2 Thess. 2:1; James 5:7, 8;

2 Pet. 3:4; 1 John 2:28), sometimes by the word *apokálupsis*, "revelation" (as in 1 Cor. 1:7, which we are now examining, and in 1 Pet. 1:7, 13), and sometimes by the word *epiphaneía*, (His) "shining forth" (as in 1 Tim. 6:14; 2 Tim. 4:8).

The second stage of His coming is with His saints. And again all three words are used to indicate this event. Listen to this undeniable truth as set forth in the following passages of Scripture: In 1 Thessalonians 3:13: "To the end he may establish your hearts unblameable in holiness before God, even our Father, at the coming [*parousía* {3952}] of our Lord Jesus Christ with all his saints." Yes, here the Greek decidedly says "with" (*metá* [3326]). The word *parousía* used for this coming of the Lord with His saints, commonly called the Second Coming, is also used in Matthew 24:3, 27, 37, 39; 2 Thessalonians 2:8; and 2 Peter 1:16. The word *apokálupsis* is also used in this sense in 1 Peter 4:13, 2 Thessalonians 1:7, and Luke 17:30. And the word *epiphaneía* is used in this sense in 2 Timothy 4:1 and Titus 2:13.

The contention by the late Professor George E. Ladd, of Fuller Theological Seminary, in his book *The Blessed Hope* (Wm. B. Eerdmans Publishing Co., Grand Rapids, MI), that the word *parousía* is believed by pre-tribulationists to refer only to the rapture of the Church. However, Professor Ladd's claim is unfounded, for it can refer to both the rapture of the Church, which is the coming of Christ for His saints (1 Thess. 4:16, 17) and can refer to the coming of the Lord with His saints (1 Thess. 3:13). The same is true of the words *apokálupsis* and *epiphaneía*. The meaning must be determined by the immediate and general context in which the reference appears.

It would be wrong to assume that the pre-tribulational pre-millennialists attribute only one meaning to each of these words. Some who are not as well-informed may, but not the majority who believe that the Lord is coming at any time and will bring us back with Him. There will be an interval of time between these two stages of His coming, which is equated generally with Daniel's prophecy of the 70th week (Dan. 9:24–27), the time of the great tribulation, which lasted seven years.

Although it is not within the scope of this study to go into the defense and explanation of this position, a careful examination of the entire subject has led me inescapably to this conclusion. If you are seriously interested in pursuing the matter further, I would refer you to *Things to Come,* the voluminous work of my personal friend and fellow scholar, J. Dwight Pentecost, of Dallas Theological Seminary.

I believe that the word *apokálupsin,* "revelation," used by Paul in 1 Corinthians 1:7 refers to the imminent coming of the Lord for His saints, also known as the rapture. I do not believe that "revelation" stands for the great tribulation. Paul emphasizes the imminence of this revelation by using the present tense for their waiting. He tells the Corinthians that they have enriched lives because of what Christ did for them in the past and for what He was yet to do. Their waiting was a continuous looking for the coming of the Lord. Indeed, it seems unlikely that they would be looking forward to this event with such eagerness if they believed that they must first go through the extreme sufferings of the great tribulation.

Nor does this waiting refer to a postponed eager anticipation after the passing of the tribulation, for in that case the participle would have been in the future tense, *apekdeksoménous,* instead of the present tense *apekdechoménous.* Theirs was not a hope that would become true at a certain point in the future after the great tribulation, but it had an immediate effect upon them.

One must not confuse or identify the sufferings of the great tribulation with the general sufferings and persecutions Christians experience today. The tribulation is a distinct intensified period of time in which God judges the world. This judgment has to do particularly with God's plan for Israel, not the Church. The great tribulation is designated as wrath (Rev. 6:16, 17; 11:18; 14:19; 15:1, 7; 16:1, 19; 1 Thess. 1:9, 10; 5:9; Zeph. 1:15, 18); judgment (Rev. 14:7; 15:4; 16:5–7; 19:2); indignation (Is. 26:20, 21; 34:1–3); punishment (Is. 24:20, 21); hour of trial (Rev. 3:10); hour of trouble (Jer. 30:7); destruction (Joel 1:15); and darkness (Joel 2:2; Zeph. 1:14–18; Amos 5:18). The seals, trumpets, and vials found in Revelation 6—21 are descriptive of the specific manifestation of God's wrath during the tribulation. (*Ibid.* J. Dwight Pentecost, pp. 194–5).

> The time is short!
> If thou wouldst work for God it must be now;
> If thou wouldst win the garland for thy brow,
> Redeem the time.
> With His reward
> He comes; He tarries not; His day is near;
> When men least look for Him will He be here;
> Prepare for Him!
>   —Horatius Bonar

Your Personal Stake in Christ's Second Coming

The New Testament clearly indicates that believers of that day were eagerly looking forward to Christ's coming for His Church. No doubt it entered their minds that this revelation was imminent, that is, that it could take place at any time. Otherwise, they would not have been looking forward to it with joy. How could it be called "that blessed hope" (Titus 2:13) if the believers felt they must first expect to go through such tribulation as the world had never known?

As J. Dwight Pentecost points out,

> Many signs were given to the nation Israel, which would precede the second advent, so that the nation might be living in expectancy when the time of His coming should draw nigh. Although Israel could

not know the day nor the hour when the Lord will come, yet they can know that their redemption draws near through the fulfillment of these signs. To the Church no such signs were ever given. The Church was told to live in the light of the imminent coming of the Lord to translate them in His presence (John 14:2, 3; Acts 1:11; 1 Cor. 15:51, 52; Phil. 3:20; Col. 3:4; 1 Thess. 1:10; 1 Tim. 6:14; James 5:8; 2 Pet. 3:3, 4). Such passages as 1 Thessalonians 5:6, Titus 2:13, and Revelation 3:3 all warn the believer to be watching for the Lord Himself, not for signs that would precede His coming. [Things to Come, pp. 202, 203.]

Dr. Pentecost further points out the distinction between the rapture and the second advent, giving a number of contrasts to show that they are not synonymous in Scripture:

(1) The translation entails the removal of all believers, while the second advent entails the appearing or manifestation of the Son. (2) The translation sees the saints caught up into the air, while in the second advent Christ returns with them to the earth. (3) In the translation Christ comes to claim a bride, but in the second advent He returns with a bride. (4) The translation results in the removal of the Church and the beginning of the tribulation, while the second advent results in the establishment of the millennial kingdom. (5) The translation is imminent, while the second advent is to be preceded by a multitude of signs. (6) The translation brings a message of comfort, while the second advent carries with it a message of judgment. (7) The translation is related to the program for the Church, while the second advent is related to the program for Israel and the world. (8) The translation is a mystery, while the second advent is predicted in both Testaments. (9) At the translation believers are judged, but at the second advent the Gentiles and Israel are judged. (10) The translation leaves creation unchanged, while the second advent entails the change in creation. (11) At the translation Gentiles are unaffected, while at the second advent Gentiles are judged. (12) At the translation Israel's covenants are unfulfilled, but at the second advent all her covenants are fulfilled. (13) The translation has no particular relation to the program of God in relation to evil, while at the second advent evil is judged. (14) The translation is said to take place before the day of wrath, but the second advent follows it. (15) The translation is for believers only, but the second advent has its effect on all men. (16) The expectation of the Church in regard to the translation is "The Lord is at hand" (Phil. 4:5), while the expectation of

Israel in regard to the second advent is that the kingdom is at hand
(Matt. 24:14). (17) The expectation of the Church at the translation is
to be taken into the Lord's presence, while the expectation of Israel at
the second advent is to be taken into the kingdom. [Quoted by J.
Dwight Pentecost from W. E. Blackstone's, *Jesus is Coming*, pp. 75–80.]

The word *apokálupsis* actually means "uncovering, revealing."
Although present in our hearts and lives, we believers cannot see
Christ now because we are physical beings with physical eyesight.
Presently we perceive Him with our spiritual being. However
when He comes again, the Lord will reveal Himself differently
to us, even as He did in His incarnation at His First Coming.
When He came the first time, He manifested Himself as a human
being, "And we beheld his glory, the glory as of the only begotten of the Father" (John 1:14). When He returns, He will reveal
Himself in the same physically visible manner. On the Mount of
Olives Jesus, who now had a resurrected body, ascended into
heaven. Angels witnessing the event said, "Ye men of Galilee,
why stand ye gazing up into heaven? this same Jesus, which is
taken up from you into heaven, shall so come in like manner as
ye have seen Him go into heaven" (Acts 1:11).

Such a revelation of the now hidden Christ to our physical
eyes presupposes supernatural power and sovereignty. Paul expresses this sovereignty by using the full name of the Lord:
"Looking forward to the revelation"—not simply of Christ or of
Jesus but "of our Lord Jesus Christ." The Greek word for Lord
is *Kúrios* (2962), which means "having power." No person but
Jesus Christ had the power to appear as a purely spiritual being
for a certain period, take upon himself the form of man, abdicate
that form, and return again into the physical world to be observed
physically. He is *Kúrios*, Lord, powerful; that is why He can do it.

Oh how wonderful for Paul and all believers to be able to
know and claim this powerful One as their very own! Paul does
not say "looking forward to the revelation of the Lord Jesus

Christ," but of "our Lord Jesus Christ." Again this is a declaration of the enrichment of our human lives when we are in Christ. The strongest person, the Creator of life, the transmuter, so to speak, of the spiritual to physical and of the physical to spiritual, is ours when we accept His grace in salvation. Being in Christ our Lord is an advantage no matter what our circumstance. What more could we want in life or in death? On earth we are alive in Christ when we are dying to self and living unto God, and in heaven we are alive in Christ as a new creature void of sin.

Why Submit to Christ's Authority?

Under what conditions are we willing to submit to authority? Our reaction to authority may change with varying circumstances. Fear might even overcome those who are faced with a power that cannot be resisted and must be followed. However, the Lord who is omnipotent does not deal with His children in this way. Instead, there is a miraculous blending of our will with Christ's when He comes to indwell us as we receive Him as Savior and Lord. This is not the obedience of the captive to the conqueror, but a voluntary yielding of ourselves to the One in whom self loses itself to find its divinely and eternally appointed fulfillment.

Recognizing that by submitting to power we can gain safety in the midst of danger may also affect our attitude toward authority. Under the threat of invasion by a dangerous enemy, most men would prefer being under martial law imposed by their own government to being captured by a ruthless foreign power. This is yielding to power, not because they like it, but because they see it as the lesser of two evils. Again, this is not what is involved in the Christian's submission to Christ. True, there is evil in the world, as instigated by Satan and his cohorts, that could mortally engulf us. One reason, therefore, that we should give our obedience to Christ is to come under His protective umbrella. Luke 10:41 assures us that in our relationship and service to Him we are not to be anxious, that is "careful and troubled." As we are purified in our relationship with the Lord, we find our dependence on His power does not exist as a lesser of two evils—fleeing to Him to escape the clutches and enslavement of Satan—but as a gift of life, fully dependent upon the Giver.

"Careful and troubled"—ah, weary one, rest;
Cease thy vain striving and lean on His breast.
He knows the dangers that lurk just ahead,
Knows, too, when heart fails and all hope has fled.

"Careful and troubled"—ah, burdened one, trust.
Why should you fear? God is faithful and just.
He has His covenant honored with you;
Surely the promises given are true.

Nothing is hid from His all-seeing eye,
Never a teardrop, nor even a sigh;
"Careful and troubled" you never need be;
Trust Him completely and doubtings will flee.

What is our real feeling as we call Jesus Christ "our Lord Jesus Christ"? We should feel as though we are under the protection of an all-powerful relative. After all, we know that His power is not meant for our subjugation but for our peace of heart. Knowing this ought to draw us to Him since we know that there are dangers lurking everywhere that can only be met through His protection and help.

One wet, foggy day a little girl was standing on a street corner in London waiting for an opportunity to cross the road. She walked up and down and looked into the faces of those who passed by. Some looked careless, some harsh, some in haste, and she did not find anyone who inspired her with confidence. At length an elderly man, tall and erect, of grave yet kindly aspect, came walking down the street. Looking up into his face she seemed to see the one for whom she had been waiting, and she went up to him and asked timidly, "Please, sir, will you help me cross over?" The old man saw the little girl safely across the street, and when he told the story afterward he said, "That little child's trust was the greatest compliment I ever had in my life!"

Not everyone can be trusted to "help us cross over" in the trials of life. But when we, like Paul, can speak of Jesus Christ as our Lord, indicating dependence and trust in Him, we are really bringing great joy to His heart. Nothing pleases Christ more than our recognition of His Lordship over us, a Lordship of love, safety, and filial relationship.

It is noteworthy that Paul does not say "my" but "our" Lord Jesus Christ. The knowledge and acknowledgment of our common dependence upon a powerful Christ and of His common sovereignty over all is most important. It will keep us from being puffed up when His protection and power seem to be a little more favorable toward us than toward others. When we see our brother or sister in Christ going through great difficulties, we must never conclude that their trust in Christ is necessarily any less than ours. He is "our" Lord, not merely "my" Lord. He is "our" Father in Heaven, not merely "my" Father. Somehow I feel an aversion toward the use of the personal pronoun in this connection. Christ's power seems more real and enjoyable when I feel that it belongs to more than just myself.

This power and Lordship of Jesus Christ will be more apparent to the entire world when He descends from heaven at His revelation, when two men will be working together, and one will be taken up and the other left. Can you imagine a greater event than that of the rapture? Think what it will be like when Christ takes all the believers away from the earth, transforming the living in an instant and raising the dead in their incorruptible bodies! Men may reject Christ now as Lord of the universe because He allows evil a temporary latitude, but the day is coming when He will show that He has always been Lord of Lords

and King of Kings. The promise of His coming again is therefore the most blessed hope of the Christian. It is the hope that
makes suffering tolerable and enriches our lives. Without the
knowledge and assurance of the hope of the Lord's revelation or
coming for His saints, men may be Christians, but their lives are
sadly impoverished.

Dr. Dinsdale T. Young once said, "A wonderful spiritual
enrichment came into my life and ministry because I realized the
great New Testament revelation of the personal return of our
Lord."

> "Till He come!" Oh, let the words
> Linger on the trembling chords;
> Let the little while between
> In their golden light be seen;
> Let us think how heaven and home
> Lie beyond that "Till He come!"

LESSONS:

1. We will never be satisfied by grabbing more than God intends for us.
2. "Not that we are sufficient of ourselves, but our sufficiency is of God"
   (2 Cor. 3:5).
3. God's grace is quite enough for the soul's every need. Seek grace
   (cháris [5485]) rather than gifts (charísmata [5486]).
4. Being rich in and through Christ is not conditioned by what we have
   but by what we are.
5. If we are looking forward to the coming of the Lord, we will tend to
   overlook anything we may be lacking at present. Our riches are not
   counted merely in terms of our present possessions, but in terms of
   what we will possess when the Lord reveals Himself from heaven.
6. To be in Christ our Lord is to be at an advantage no matter what our
   circumstances.
7. Nothing pleases Christ more than our recognition of His Lordship over
   us, a Lordship of love, safety, and filial relationship.
8. Men may reject Christ now as Lord of the universe because He allows
   evil a temporary latitude, but the day is coming when He will show that
   He has always been Lord of Lords and King of Kings.

PRESENT AND FUTURE GIFTS

1 Cor. 1:8

God's Complete Plan for You

Who shall also confirm you unto the end, that ye may be blameless in the day of our Lord Jesus Christ.

If you knew that the Lord would come back tonight, what would your reaction be? The Apostle Paul was not flying on one wing only—that of proclaiming the first coming of the Lord to this earth. He also presented the enriching experience of Christ's future revelation because it has a purifying effect upon our everyday lives. In the light of our Lord's imminent return, how ought you and I to live?

> Is there something you ought to do today?
> Then, do it now!
> Is there some debt you ought to pay today?
> Then, do it now!
> Is there some quarrel you ought to make up?
> Then, do it now!
> Is there a sinner you ought to warn?
> Then, do it now!
> He is coming. Perhaps tonight.

Why will the Lord Jesus Christ come back; why will He reveal Himself? For the sake of the believers. That is what is indicated by 1 Corinthians 1:8, "Who also will confirm you to the end, without condemnation in the day of our Lord Jesus Christ" (a.t.). True, our lives are marred by our present environment and by the very constitution of our bodies. But this will not be forever. We shall experience the personal intervention of the Lord.

Verse 8 begins with the relative pronoun *hós* (3739), "who," referring to this Lord who is ours now. He involves Himself in the scheme of things. The course of the world is not carved by itself. It is not nature evolving, but God executing His own plan, that we see all around us. If we do nothing of importance without first planning our course of action, does it seem reasonable to you that God would have gone about making the world and man without a complete plan?

> I to Christ my life have given
> Ever His alone to be;
> Oh, what peace and blest assurance,
> That He has a plan for me!

What will Christ do for us believers? Paul spoke of what He did for us in verses 4 to 6. He gave us His grace; He enriched us in everything. This enrichment follows the acceptance of His grace, for no one can have the grace of Christ and not be rich. His grace came to us as a result of the witness that has come down to us (v. 6). And then, in verse 7, Paul told us that in this present life we do not lack anything because we have the living hope of Christ's personal return to take us to Himself. We have the past, the present, and—in verse 8—the future: "Who [Christ the Lord] will confirm you to the end, without condemnation in the day of our Lord Jesus Christ."

The verb *bebaiōsei* (950), "will confirm," is in the future indicative, and when referring to persons means "to strengthen, to keep us standing." This is a beautiful picture of the believer's standing in Christ. He gave us His grace; we now have this as a present possession; and we are not going to lose His possession entrusted to us. No matter what the difficulties of the future, they cannot move us. Where would we be if God could not be trusted to keep us?

> How often we trust each other,
>> And only doubt our Lord.
> We take the word of mortals,
>> And yet distrust His word.
>
> But oh, what light and glory
>> Would shine o'er all our days
> If we always would remember
>> God means just what He says.
>> —A. B. Simpson

So many people seem to think that their security depends on their holding fast to God. That is not where Paul found his comfort concerning the future. The verb is in the active voice, and the agent is Christ, "*who* will confirm." He holds us and will never let go of us once we have by faith and submission come to the place of being in Him.

As Moody said, "Trust in yourself, and you are doomed to disappointment; trust in your friends, and they will die and leave you; trust in money, and you may have it taken from you; trust in reputation, and some slanderous tongue may blast it, but trust in God, and you are never to be confounded in time or eternity." Luther gave a similar testimony when he said, "I have held many things in my hands, and I have lost them all, but whatever I have placed in God's hands, that I still possess."

> Let me no more my comfort draw
>> From my frail grasp of Thee;
> In this alone rejoice with awe—
>> Thy mighty grasp of me.

"Who shall also confirm you unto the end." The Greek expression *héōs* (2193) *télous* (5056), "unto the end," does not mean the end of time but the goal reached, the completion or conclusion. God's purpose in our lives does not have a fixed allotment of time. Some die young, some old. Those who live to a ripe old age do not necessarily accomplish more for God than those who die young. After all, our Lord chose to die at the age of thirty-three. And He said as He was dying, "It is finished [*tetélestai* {5055}]" (John 19:30). This word is the same as *héōs télous*. He was not speaking of the termination of His physical life, for that was obvious, but of the fulfillment of His purpose in coming. His death was the goal or "end" that He came to achieve.

The expression, "He shall also confirm you to the end," does not therefore mean to the end of our lives or for a certain fixed period of time, but until the day when He shall appear. His salvation and enrichment of our lives as believers will find its ultimate fulfillment in His Second Coming. That being the most glorious event of the future, we cannot be deprived of our participation in it. Our redemption is based in the past, but its completion is promised in the future. It is not a speculation but a certainty, for the word *bebaiōsei*, "confirm," comes from *bébaios* (949), which means "certain." Christians, Paul was saying, do not look only at the past coming of the Lord but also to His future coming. It is as certain as the past. Prophecy is as firm as history.

The Believer's Position in Christ: Blameless but Not Sinless

The New Testament makes it plain that all who possess a genuine faith in Christ are His "saints." Does this mean that they are perfect and sinless? Hardly, for we find that even the greatest of saints are deeply conscious of their sins. Take Paul, for instance. In writing to Timothy, his "son in the faith," he said, "This is a faithful saying, and worthy of all acceptation, that Christ Jesus came into the world to save sinners; of whom I am chief" (1 Tim. 1:15). Nevertheless, in writing to the believers in Corinth, he assures them that they shall "be blameless in the day of our Lord Jesus Christ" (1 Cor. 1:8). How can sinful creatures be considered "blameless" when they stand before the Lord Jesus Christ at His Second Coming?

The Greek word translated "blameless" is *anénklētos* (410). This term denotes a person against whom there can be no *éngklēma* (1462), "charge or accusation." It is used twice in Paul's epistles concerning elders and deacons in the church who should be blameless (1 Tim. 3:10; Titus 1:6). This refers to their civil ethics: the morality of their lives should be so high that no one could bring an accusation against them with regard to their conduct. In writing to the Philippians, Paul admonished them to "Do all things without murmurings and disputings: that ye may be blameless and harmless, the sons of God, without rebuke, in the midst of a crooked and perverse nation, among whom ye shine as lights in the world" (Phil. 2:14, 15).

As D. L. Moody said, "Christianity isn't worth the snap of your finger if it doesn't change your character." And any belief in Christ that produces no change for the better in a person's life is not true saving faith but mere intellectual assent such as that referred to in James 2:19, where it says that "the devils also believe, and tremble."

The word *anenklētos*, "blameless," is also used in Colossians 1:22, and here, as in 1 Corinthians 1:8, the last judgment is undoubtedly in view. We are told that when the Lord Jesus comes again, He will confirm us believers as blameless. This does not mean that, from the moment we received Christ as Savior and Lord to the day when we see Him face to face at His Second Coming, we have never been guilty of any sin of commission, omission, or intention. James says, "For in many things we offend all" (James 3:2). And John tells us, "If we say that we have no sin, we deceive ourselves, and the truth is not in us" (1 John 1:8). How, then, can all believers be blameless, especially in view of the Lord's statement that a future judgment of sorts awaits them? In Matthew 16.27 we read, "The Son of man shall come in the glory of his Father with his angels; and then he shall reward every man according to his works."

As believers in Christ, we are not sinless but blameless. That is, no charge will be brought against us at Christ's coming because He took our "blame" upon Himself on Calvary's cross, that His righteousness might be imputed to all who came to the Father in repentance and faith through Him. In Romans 8:1 Paul tells us, "There is therefore now no condemnation to them which are in Christ Jesus, who walk not after the flesh, but after the Spirit."

Observe the expression, "to them which are in Christ Jesus." That is the position of the Christian. He is in Christ. Now look at 1 Corinthians 1:4, not as you find it translated in the King James Version but as it is in the Greek: "I thank my God always concerning you for the grace of God which is given to you *in* Christ Jesus," (a.t.) not *"by,"* as the Authorized translation has it. If you are positionally in Christ, you already have the grace of God. And then verse 5 says "that in everything ye were enriched *in* him," not *"by* him," as the translation has it again.

Christ's name occurs nine times in these first nine verses of 1 Corinthians 1. If you go back to the second verse, you will again find mention of our position as saints in Christ. "Unto the church of God which is at Corinth, to them that are sanctified in Christ Jesus, called to be saints." Here the translators correctly rendered the Greek preposition *en* (1722) as "in." Our position and privileges "in Christ" are the subject of the Apostle Paul in the first nine verses of this chapter.

When we believe, our position shifts from the sphere of the unbelieving world to the sphere of Christ. Because of our position, we are without condemnation, without any charge against us. "Who shall lay anything to the charge of God's elect?" asks Paul in Romans 8:33. The word in Greek is the same as in 1 Corinthians 1:8, *engkalései* (1458). "It is God that justifieth. Who is he that condemneth? It is Christ that died, yea rather, that is risen again, who is even at the right hand of God, who also maketh intercession for us" (Rom. 8:33, 34).

Thus our position in Christ is not caused or maintained by our life of faith or our works of righteousness for which we shall be judged (though not unto condemnation), as referred to in the following Scriptures: "Every man shall receive his own reward according to his own labor" (1 Cor. 3:8). "And the dead were judged out of those things which were written in the books, according to their works" (Rev. 20:12). "And, behold," says the Lord, "I come quickly; and my reward is with me, to give every man according as his work shall be" (Rev. 22:12). These Scriptures are all concerned with the reward for our work of faith—everything that we did or did not do, thought or did not think, after we believed on the Lord Jesus Christ and received Him as our Savior. Never labor under the misapprehension that the reward for the selfish and unsacrificing Christian will be the same as for the unselfish and sacrificing Christian. The judgment of unbelievers decides their eternal punishment; the judgment of believers, their eternal reward.

Nevertheless, the basic fact is that all who are in Christ are blameless for the simple reason that they are in Christ. Their saving faith has placed them within the circle of Christ; and all who are in Him, having experienced the new birth, regardless of their degree of spiritual growth, maturity, and fruit-bearing, are going to see the Day of the Lord, are going to be in heaven with Him eternally. It is the same as being heir to a fortune because of your birth into a family. As believers we are all heirs of the kingdom of God, not because of anything that we have done, but because of what Christ did for us.

Watch Out for Mud on Your Shoes!

The New Testament speaks of the believer as inheriting the kingdom by virtue of merely belonging to Christ. The Lord said in Matthew 25:34 that, at the end of the age when He reveals Himself again, He shall "say unto them on His right hand, Come, ye blessed of my Father, inherit the kingdom prepared for you from the foundation of the world." James also speaks of the believers as "heirs of the kingdom" (James 2:5). In the words of the old hymn,

> I once was an outcast stranger on earth,
>   A sinner by choice, and an alien by birth!
> But I've been adopted, my name's written down—
>   An heir to a mansion, a robe, and a crown.
>
> I'm a child of the King, a child of the King!
> With Jesus, my Savior, I'm a child of the King.
>   Harriet Buell

The Apostle Peter speaks with fervent joy of the Christian's "inheritance incorruptible, and undefiled, and that fadeth not away, reserved in heaven for you" (1 Pet. 1:4). Now what is an inheritance? The Greek word translated "inheritance" is *klēronomía* (2817), which in its verbal form occurs 285 times in the Septuagint, the Greek Version of the Old Testament. It plays a great part in the concept of the relationship of Israel to Jehovah (Yahweh).

Inheritance is by birth, by position, and not by gift or acquisition. Paul says in Ephesians 1:11, "In whom [Christ] also we have obtained an inheritance." Observe again the preposition "in," indicative of our position in Christ. This does not refer to the judgment for the rewards of believers mentioned in 2 Corinthians 5:9, 10 and other portions of Scripture, but the judgment affirming that, since these are believers, there is no condemnation, no charge against them, as there is for unbelievers. (See Wilbur M. Smith's book, *The Biblical Doctrine of Heaven*, Chicago: Moody Press, 1968, pp. 177–188, and G.

Kittel's *Theological Dictionary of the New Testament*, Vol. 3, p. 759f.)

All believers are "heirs of the kingdom" because they are members of the family of God by virtue of their position "in Christ." Even so, not all the children in one and the same family enjoy their relationship to the family, or work for the family in equal measure. Our position in Christ is by grace, through faith, plus nothing. Because of this position, we shall see the Lord, and nobody can accuse us of not belonging with Him in the life to come. But our growth in that relationship and our enjoyment of it depend on how by faith we use our privileged position. Our reconciliation to God is effected the moment we believe in the Christ of history and is fulfilled in the day when we shall see the Christ of prophecy. Only, therefore, "on the basis of the justification effected by the death and resurrection of Christ, Christians are spotless and irreproachable before God" (G. Kittel, *Theological Dictionary of the New Testament*, Vol. 1, p. 357).

When will this judgment affirming our eternal salvation in Christ take place? "In the day of our Lord Jesus Christ," Paul tells us. From the moment we believe on the Lord Jesus Christ, Satan tries to cast doubt on our salvation, safety, and security in Him. But Paul comforts us with the assurance that the day is coming when final affirmation will be given by the Judge, the Lord Himself. Why wait till then, however, to enjoy your redemption? It is as sure as the Word of the Redeemer Himself. Listen to what He says: "And I give unto them eternal life; and they shall never perish, neither shall any man pluck them out of my hand" (John 10:28).

There is no doubt that "the day of our Lord Jesus Christ" is His revelation referred to in 1 Corinthians 1:7. When He shall appear again for His saints, it will be His day. Presently, man has his day, the day of God's tolerance. In this day the consequences of his disobedience to God's law and the rejection of His offer of mercy are suffered by unbelievers and in some measure by believers. Although the latter do not deserve to suffer the consequences of evil since they are in Christ, by the nature of things in the overall plan of God they do. We live in a day in which both good and evil exist, though not on the same plane or in the same degree, and we cannot escape rubbing up against our sinful environment. We are in the world though not of the world. Today is the day of God's offer of grace through Christ, but it is not yet His day of the complete subjugation of evil and the elimination of its consequences.

As we walk through this earthly field, our garments are not likely to gather fragrant spices, but defiling dust, thorns, and burrs. I never remember coming home from a walk with my shoes highly polished as a result of my excursion, but I have often come home with mud on them. Since we can easily be soiled by all that is around us, we must be very careful to keep ourselves "unspotted from the world" (James 1:27).

A group of young people were about to explore a coal mine. One of the girls was wearing a white dress. A friend urged her to go home and change. Not liking the interference, she turned to the guide who was to conduct them and asked, "Can't I wear a white dress to go into the mine?" "Yes, ma'am," was his reply. "There's nothing to keep you from wearing a white dress down there, but there'll be plenty to keep you from wearing one back!"

There is nothing to hinder a Christian from conforming to the world's standard of living, but there is a good deal to keep him from being unspotted if he does. Christians were put into the atmosphere of this world to purify it, not to be poisoned by it. Let us be like those few even in Sardis, "who have not defiled their garments"; for the Lord Jesus says of them, "They shall walk with Me in white, for they are worthy" (Rev. 3:4).

God's Complete Plan for You

Will You Be In the Storm or Above It?

Will there really be a day of judgment that will overtake the world? Some may scoff at the idea, but any thinking individual must realize that true justice demands it. The undeserved suffering of the righteous at the hands of evil men in this life must be compensated for in the next; and all who commit evil in this life, many of whom escape the consequences of their evil deeds now, must one day give account for them before a righteous Judge. God Himself has said there will be a judgment day, and no amount of hiding one's head in the sand can alter its occurance. In Old Testament times, when Israel was beset by enemies, God told His people to set a watchman to warn the people of their approach by blowing a trumpet. "Then whosoever heareth the sound of the trumpet," God told them through the prophet Ezekiel, "and taketh not warning; if the sword come, and take him away, his blood shall be upon his own head. . . . But he that taketh warning shall deliver his soul" (Ezek. 33:4, 5).

W. A. Dessain tells the story of a young farmer in North Dakota who one day brought home a fancy barometer:

> In the following days he watched it avidly as it predicted the weather. On one of the walls of his home it hung in an honored place. But the day came when for three days it predicted "storm" while the sky was turquoise and clear. So he took it off the wall and back to town where he demanded his money back.
>
> Returning home, he and his wife became alarmed when they saw evidence of a storm ten miles out. When they turned in their yard, their home had blown away. The furniture was up in the apple trees, and the bathtub three blocks away in a pasture. Where were the kids? The grandmother had believed the barometer, and when a dark cloud appeared she took the two small children and went to the shelter in the old storm cellar, long unused, and they were all saved.

God's Word warns us that a day of judgment is surely coming. Those who heed His warning and flee to Christ will be safe with Him on that dreadful day.

> We shall see earth's last red, bloody sunset,
>   We shall behold the Avenger's form,
> We shall see the Armageddon onslaught,
>   But we shall be above the storm.

Two distinct expressions in Scripture which refer to this judgment period are the Day of the Lord and the Day of Christ. When we read of the Day of the Lord or the Day of Christ, we are not to think of a twenty-four hour day but of a period of time during which the judgments of the Lord Jesus Christ will take place. It is a time of judgment.

The Day of the Lord is mentioned in Isaiah 2:12; 13:6, 9; Ezekiel 13:5; 30:3; Joel 1:15; 2:1, 11, 31; 3:14; Amos 5:18 (2), 20; Obadiah 15; Zephaniah 1:7, 14 (2); Zechariah 14:1; Malachi 4:5; Acts 2:20; 1 Thessalonians 5:2; and 2 Peter 3:10. Although some versions of the Bible translate 2 Thessalonians 2:2 as "Day of the Lord," the correct rendering is "Day of Christ," as in the King James Version. In addition, the phrase "that day" or "the day," or "the great day" occurs more than seventy-five times in the Old Testament.

All of these passages speak of judgment. I agree with J. Dwight Pentecost who states,

> This judgment includes not only the specific judgments upon Israel and the nations at the end of the tribulations that are associated with the second advent, but includes judgments that extend over a period of time prior to the second advent (the time when the Lord returns with His saints). Thus it is concluded that the Day of the Lord will include the time of the tribulation. Zechariah 14:14 makes it clear that the events of the second advent are included in the program of the Day of the Lord. 2 Peter 3:10 gives authority for including the entire millennial age within this period. If the Day of the Lord did not begin until the second advent, since that event is preceded by signs, the Day of the

Lord could not come as a "thief in the night," unexpected and unheralded, as it is said it will come in 1 Thessalonians 5:2. The only way this day could break unexpectedly upon the world is to have it begin immediately after the rapture of the Church. It is thus concluded that the Day of the Lord is that extended period of time beginning with God's dealing with Israel after the rapture at the beginning of the tribulation period and extending through the second advent and the millennial age unto the creation of the new heavens and new earth after the millennium [J. Dwight Pentecost, *Things to Come*, Dunham Publishing Co., Findlay, Ohio, 1958, pp. 230, 231].

The expression "the Day of the Lord Jesus" or "the Day of Christ" occurs in 1 Corinthians 5:5, 2 Corinthians 1:14, Philippians 1:10; 2:16, and 2 Thessalonians 2:2. Naturally this is a New Testament expression and relates to the Lord's plan, particularly for His Church.

Two different plans are in view in these two expressions, "Day of the Lord" and "Day of Christ," but they fall within the same time period. "Thus the two days may have the same beginning, even though two different programs are in view" (*sorcery*, p. 232).

Interestingly, in 1 Corinthians 1:8 Paul combines the two expressions into one when he speaks of "the day of our Lord Jesus Christ." Apparently, this follows the pattern that the Lord's primary interest is in believers. His redemption, His election, His predestination, His whole plan, are for those "in Christ," and by necessity there has to be an eternal destiny for those who have chosen to remain outside of Christ. These have rejected God who has given them whatever opportunity, veiled or unveiled, to receive Him or reject Him, either as the Messiah who was to come or as the Redeemer of Calvary. God does not determine that anyone should be eternally lost, but He does set the consequences for those who refuse to believe in Him. Setting such consequences, however, does not occupy the primary place in God's planning but is simply a necessary corollary of His program for believers.

In the first chapter of 1 Corinthians Paul speaks not of the poverty and misery of the unbelievers but of the riches of the believers. They are looking forward with eager anticipation to the Day of Christ Jesus. It is Christ's activity, Christ's program, particularly for them. It is their coronation day, the day of their ultimate enrichment in Christ. What a glorious expectation, what a blessed hope!

The Christian's Responsibility to the Lost

Throughout the 15th chapter of 1 Corinthians, the Apostle Paul speaks in great detail about the resurrection of believers emphasizing the enrichment of the believer in Christ. Paul makes reference to the resurrection of unbelievers but does not dwelt on it. Christ who "is . . . not willing that any should perish" (2 Pet. 3:9) finds it unpleasant every time He must reveal the end of the impenitent. He dwells upon it as little as possible, but never doubt that it is so.

Observe how 2 Peter 3:10 follows this expression of God's unwillingness that any should perish. It says, "But the Day of the Lord will come as a thief in the night; in the which the heavens shall pass away with a great noise, and the elements shall melt with fervent heat, the earth also and the works that are therein shall be burned up." The judgment of unbelievers is sure, but it will come only as the corollary of what God intends to do for those who are in Christ. Therefore, in 1 Corinthians 1:8, Paul includes it in speaking of "the Day of our Lord Jesus Christ." It is both "the Day of Christ"—and, primarily so, the day when believers will be cleared of any condemnation—and "the Day of the Lord," when the unbelievers, those outside of Christ, will be condemned finally and forever. Judgment has to be passed on both classes of people, and there are only two, those "in Christ" and those "outside Christ."

It may be that the reason Paul combines "the Day of the Lord" with "the Day of Christ" in the phrase "in the Day of our Lord Jesus Christ" is to arouse the compassion of the Corinthian Christians on behalf of those who are without Christ. True, he tells them, you can look forward with great and satisfying anticipation to that day, for you will be found blameless because of your position in Christ, but how about those who will be eternally condemned? You ought to witness to them; you ought to sacrifice all that you have so that they might also have the opportunity of being found in Christ in that day. While you think of your eternal joy, Christian, think also of the eternal condemnation of those who must be given an opportunity to know Him. How can we as Christians rejoice wholeheartedly in the assurance of our own salvation without having done all in our power to bring others to the saving knowledge of Christ?

> When the voice of the Master is calling
>   And the gates of Heaven unfold,
> And the saints of all ages are gathering
>   And are thronging the city of gold;
> How my heart shall o'erflow with the rapture
>   If a brother shall greet me and say,
> "You pointed my footsteps to Heaven;
>   You told me of Jesus, the Way."

The question that immediately arises for the Christian is, when are we to expect this Day of our Lord Jesus Christ? I believe, as I have said before, that one of the reasons the two otherwise separate expressions, "the Day of the Lord" and "the Day of Christ," are combined in 1 Corinthians 1:8 is to show that they have the same beginning, even though two different programs are in view. The Christian begins to rejoice at his salvation day. This is what is described in 1 Thessalonians 4:16–18.

as the rapture of the church. This event can take place at any time. It is imminent; it has always constituted the blessed hope of all Christians from apostolic times on.

The Corinthian Christians and Paul were eagerly looking forward to the rapture (*apekdechoménous* [553]), as verse 7 so unmistakably declares. The revelation of our Lord Jesus Christ, the *apokálupsis* (602) of verse 7, must be interpreted as the rapture that will take place at the time of the *parousía* (3952) or "personal presence or appearing" of the Lord Jesus. Certainly this will precede the Great Tribulation period, which will last for seven years (Dan. 9:24–27; Matt. 24:15–22; Mark 13:14–20; Rev. 11:2, 3; 12:6, 14; 13:5). Let me once again state that if the Christians to whom Paul was writing were eagerly anticipating this day of the revelation of their Lord, it was considered a period of great rejoicing, not a time of suffering and great tribulation such as the world had never seen. Indeed, it is inconceivable that this jubilant expectation is to be delayed until the end of the seven-year Great Tribulation. The term *anénklētos*, "faultless, without cause for legal condemnation," also refers to the exemption from this time of tribulation, which begins after the taking up of all believers.

The Day of Christ will not take the believers by surprise, but the Day of the Lord will certainly surprise and shock the unbelievers. The believers are eagerly expecting their Lord's coming. It will be the day of their liberation from their present sufferings and from the Great Tribulation that is about to come upon the world. That is why Paul says in 1 Thessalonians 5:2, "The Day of the Lord so cometh as a thief in the night." Peter connects the Day of the Lord with the destruction of our earth by fire through what may well be some sort of nuclear explosion. "But the Day of the Lord will come as a thief in the night; in the which the heavens shall pass away with a great noise, and the elements shall melt with fervent heat, the earth also and the works that are therein shall be burned up" (2 Pet. 3:10).

The term "thief" used in this passage is not descriptive of the Lord's character but of the manner in which He works. Certainly we are not able to attribute the character of a thief to the Lord.

Believers are urged to be in an attitude of expectation: "Watch therefore: for ye know not what hour your Lord doth come" (Matt. 24:42). One reason we are not told the exact time of His return may be so that we do not lose the joy of expectancy. We are to occupy until He comes. If we knew exactly when that would be, because of our human frailty we might become slothful. The Lord wants this expectation to be the blessed hope and privilege of all generations of Christians, and not only of one, as would be the case if the exact time had been revealed. Therefore, He admonishes us, "Be ye also ready: for in such an hour as ye think not the Son of man cometh" (Matt. 24:44). Since we do not know the exact time, but know that He will come as a thief in the night, we live on guard, constantly on the watch. Living in this way we have great blessing.

Overtaken by Surprise

Not only is there great blessing in expecting the Lord to return at any time, but the expectation also has a purifying effect on our lives. In 1 John 3:2, 3 we read: "Beloved, now are we the sons of God, and it doth not yet appear what we shall be: but we know that, when he shall appear, we shall be like him; for we shall see him as he is. And every man that hath this hope in him purifieth himself, even as he is pure." By looking to Christ, we will get a clear notion of what purity really is. By communing with Him daily we have a tender conscience that makes us more aware of our faults. And by determinedly and vigorously resisting the devil and the suggestions of our lower nature, we will overcome them through the power of the indwelling Christ who was

"manifested that he might destroy the works of the devil"
(1 John 3:8).

> Still, still we wait,
>   And for His footsteps hearken;
> Still, still we watch
>   And cry, "Lord Jesus, come!"
> Earth's gathering clouds
>   Of woe more deeply darken,
> And God's redeemed ones
>   Surely long for home.
>
> A little while—
>   Perchance a moment fleeting—
> And then the shout,
>   The trump, the call away;
> Then, oh, the joy,
>   The wondrous, rapturous meeting
> —Our blessed hope—
> It might take place TODAY.
>   —J. Danson Smith

The suddenness of something that is expected is never as shocking as something that is not expected, especially when the expected event is desirable. When Christ comes again, believers will be expecting Him; and though the event will be sudden, it will bring great joy. As believers we qualify for the Day of Christ because we are in Christ, but we are exempt from the Day of the Lord. That is what the term *anénklētos,* "faultless or blameless," means in this context. We are exempt from the day of judgment.

This is the day of final distinction between believers and unbelievers. The Greek word *krísis* (2920), "judgment," comes from the verb *krínō* (2919), which basically means "to separate, to distinguish, to select." This judgment does not involve the degree of faithfulness and devotion of those who are in Christ and the degree of unfaithfulness and evil of those who are outside of

Christ. It concerns the mere distinction between the two groups, the saved and the unsaved, the redeemed and the unredeemed.

The simile of the Lord coming as a thief in the night introduces the element of suddenness. For the unbelievers it is going to be both unexpected and sudden. The suddenness of the undesirable will be far more shocking. Those who are true Christians are constantly referred to as not overtaken by that day as by a thief in the night. "For you know perfectly that the Day of the Lord so cometh as a thief in the night. For when they shall say [not when you, the disciples, shall say], Peace and safety; then sudden destruction cometh upon them, as travail upon a woman with child; and they shall not escape" (1 Thess. 5:2, 3). Then Paul adds in verses 4 and 5, "But ye, brethren, are not in darkness, that that day should overtake you as a thief. Ye are all the children of light, and the children of the day: we are not of the night, nor of darkness." The coming of the Lord for the believer presages liberation from the environment of worsening evil, but for the unbeliever it presages accounting and punishment for the evil perpetrated. It is sudden reward for the believer and sudden punishment for the unbeliever.

As Canon Liddon says, "To keep watch for that which is certain, which will come unexpectedly, which will affect us most intimately, is only common sense" (Liddon's *Advent Sermons*, p. 377). All the admonitions of Scripture for believers, therefore, are that we may be expectant, although "of that day and that hour knoweth no man . . . but the Father" (Mark 13:32). Canon continues:

> Christ's coming is as certain as His Word is sure. But are we looking out for it? It may not come to us on this side of the grave, but it will practically have come to us at death. At once certain and uncertain—it bids us at least keep watch for it. A Christian's first practical anxiety should be expressed in his Master's words, "Lest coming suddenly he find [me] sleeping (Mark 13:36)" [sorcery, p. 378].

GOD'S COMPLETE PLAN FOR YOU

The Day of the Lord is an event which, no matter how hard men try, they cannot avoid or prevent. Believers pray for the Day of the Lord to come, as did John in exile on the island of Patmos when he said, "Even so, come, Lord Jesus" (Rev. 22:20), but the Day of the Lord will come upon unbelievers so unexpectedly, so suddenly that they will not have time to do anything about it even if they could. The great tribulation that begins for the unbelieving world after the believers' translation into heaven will find man helpless. It will spell the end of man's day and the beginning of the Lord's day. "Behold, he cometh with clouds; and every eye shall see him, and they also which pierced him: and all kindreds of the earth shall wail because of him" (Rev. 1:7).

> Jesus is coming to earth again; what if it were today?
> Coming in power and love to reign. What if it were today?
> Coming to claim His chosen Bride, all the redeemed and purified,
>> Over the whole earth scattered wide. What if it were today?
> Faithful and true would He find us here, if He should come today?
> Watching in gladness and not in fear, if He should come today?
> Signs of His coming multiply. Morning light breaks in eastern sky;
> Watch, for the time is drawing nigh. What if it were today?
>> —Lelia Morris

Life's Greatest Question

What will be the procedure when Christ comes to earth again, and all nations are gathered before Him? The judgment on the Day of the Lord will not be similar to the legal trials man faces today. When an accused person is arrested, he is considered innocent until proven guilty, and he has the right to a trial by a jury of his peers. But in that day the Judge will not need to hear evidence or review the life of the person whom He is about to judge.

As Liddon says,

> It is not to be supposed for an instant that a day is yet to come on which, like some human judge on the circuit, He will discover for the first

time, by some laborious legal process, by arguments pleaded before Him, or from witnesses examined, what manner of men we severally are. "Thou art about my path, and about my bed, and spiest out all my ways. For lo, there is not a word in my tongue but thou, O Lord, knowest it altogether" (Ps. 139:3, 4). But on that day, the Day of the Lord, the Day of Judgment, what is always true will become, so to speak, visible, palpable, acknowledged; will inflict itself with terrific and resistless force upon the reluctant senses and imaginations of men. "When the Son of man shall come in his glory, and all the holy angels with him, then shall he sit upon the throne of his glory: and before him shall be gathered all nations: and he shall separate them one from the other, as a shepherd divideth his sheep from the goats (Matt. 25:31, 32)" [*Ibid.* p. 371].

If you are an unbeliever, there is a difference between the loss that you will suffer in that Day of the Lord and all the other losses that you may have experienced. "The loss of wealth is nothing; the loss of health is a sad thing, but it is not a finally fatal thing; the loss of your good name may be retrieved, but the loss of that day will be far greater. The discovery will then be made that the soul is lost, and its salvation forever impossible" (author unknown). If you lose your wealth, you can regain it with hard work. If you lose your health, you may regain it through the intervention of medical science, but the loss of your soul in the Day of the Lord will be final; it is a loss you can never recover.

Ask yourself seriously, solemnly, "What is to become of me?" Even science assures you that, since nothing is annihilated, your personality cannot be annihilated either. Are you going to be found faultless and blameless in that day simply because through faith in the finished work of Christ for you, you placed yourself "in Christ"? Or are you going to suffer the irretrievable loss of your soul? There can be no greater tragedy for you than to be lost at the feet of the One who gave His life that you might be saved.

Not only is the loss in the Day of the Lord irretrievable, but there is no possible compensatory element that comes into play to mitigate the intensity or lighten the darkness of that terrible loss. If you lose your eyesight, your hearing becomes more exquisitely acute, and hence blind people are often the best musicians. If you lose your hearing and sight together, by a beautiful compensatory law your touch becomes more exquisite; so that the touch of a deaf and blind man is almost as acute and sensitive as the eye and the ear; it becomes a sort of extended sight and hearing.

If you lose your riches, friends will be raised up who sympathize with you and for you. If you lose your nearest and dearest ones, hopes that stretch beyond the grave lighten its gloom and shine in upon your heart. There is not a loss in this world for which there is not some compensatory element instantly or remotely attending it. However, if you lose your soul, there is no compensatory element in reserve!

Regarding the time in which the Day of our Lord Jesus Christ will return, there is one thing of which we can be sure. It is nearer today than in the day when Paul wrote 1 Corinthians 1:8. It is nearer today than it was yesterday, and it will be nearer tomorrow than it is today. What a solemn thought to know that only two great and opposite divisions of mankind will be found then and there, and you and I must be found in one or the other. For what does Paul say will be the lot of believers; what will they receive on that day? "To you who are troubled rest with us, when the Lord Jesus shall be revealed from heaven with his mighty angels" (2 Thess. 1:7).

But what will He do to the unbelievers at His coming? "In flaming fire taking vengeance on them that know not God, and that obey not the gospel of our Lord Jesus Christ: who shall be punished with everlasting destruction from the presence of the Lord, and from the glory of his power" (2 Thess. 1:8, 9).

When He comes, it will be "to be glorified in His saints, and to be admired in all them that believe . . . in that day" (2 Thess.

1:10). In which of these classes will you be? That is the most momentous question and involves the prior question, Is your soul saved or not saved? (See John Cumming, *The Great Preparation*, 1860, pp. 140–156.)

D. L. Moody once said that he believed there was

> a day of decision in our lives—a day upon which the crisis of our lives occurs. There is a day when the Son of Man comes and stands at our heart and knocks for the last time and leaves us forever. I can imagine when Pilate was banished, how this recollection troubled him day and night. He remembered how the people had clamored for His life, and how he did not have the moral courage to stand up for the despised Nazarene, and that preyed upon his mind, and he put an end to his miserable existence.

In his hymn, "What Will You Do With Jesus?" A. B. Simpson asks,

> Will you evade Him as Pilate tried?
> Or will you choose Him, whate'er betide?
>
> What will you do with Jesus?
> Neutral you cannot be;
> Some day your heart will be asking,
> "What will He do with me?"

<u>LESSONS</u>:

1. The course of the world is not carved by itself; it is not nature evolving, but God executing His own plan.
2. Our security as Christians does not depend on our holding fast to God. Rather, Christ holds us and will never let go of us once we have by faith and submission come to the place of being in Him.
3. As believers in Christ, we are not sinless, but we are blameless. Christ has taken our blame upon Himself.
4. Today is the day of God's offer of grace through Christ, but it is not yet His day of the complete subjugation of evil and the elimination of its consequences.
5. True justice demands a day of judgment that will overtake the world.
6. The Day of the Lord is the Day of Judgment that will take unbelievers by surprise. The Day of Christ will fall within the same time period but

is a day for the believers' ultimate enrichment in Christ, a day for which believers wait with eager anticipation.

7. As believers we qualify for the Day of Christ because we are in Christ, but we are exempt from the Day of the Lord. The coming of the Lord for the believer presages liberation from the environment of worsening evil, but for the unbeliever it presages accounting and punishment for the evil perpetrated.

8. The loss of your soul in the Day of the Lord will be final; it is a loss you can never recover.

9. Not only is the loss in the Day of the Lord irretrievable, but there is no possible compensatory element that comes into play to mitigate the intensity or lighten the darkness of that terrible loss.

1 Cor. 1:9

Fellowship with Our Lord

God is faithful, by whom ye were called unto the fellowship of his Son Jesus Christ our Lord.

When some unexpected honor is conferred on you or some wonderful bit of good fortune or good news comes your way, your first reaction is likely to be, "I can hardly believe it! It's almost too good to be true!"

When the Apostle Paul wrote of the Day of the Lord to the Corinthians in verse 8, their first thought most likely was that this would be the day of God's wrath upon disobedient humanity. But Paul's first thought was to present it as the Day of Christ for the believers, the day of liberation from the awful judgment of God in the coming great tribulation.

It was natural that some should doubt their privileged position. It seemed too good to believe that they should escape God's wrath. That is what some people think even today. To answer such doubts Paul made an emphatic statement about the character of God in verse 9: "Faithful [is] the God by whom ye were called unto fellowship of His Son Jesus Christ our Lord" (a.t.).

The One Unchanging Certainty in a Changing World

Verse 9 begins with the word *pistós* (4103), meaning "faithful." Paul uses this word for emphasis. The adjective *pistós* can be used in an active or passive sense. When man is said to be *pistós*, "faithful," it is used in an active sense to indicate he is putting trust in someone else. But when *pistós* is used in a passive sense, as here, it means "worthy of trust, reliable." The word is not used of things; it is used only of persons and of matters constituted or pursued by them. It has reference to character, to personal conduct.

There are two directions in which we must look when we speak of the faithfulness of God—the past and the future. Both are involved in this passage. God was faithful, Paul told the Corinthian believers in verse 4, in that He enriched your lives through the Lord Jesus Christ. He confirmed His testimony in you and among you (v. 6). And His faithfulness extends to the future as you wait for His revelation when He will come to take you from this sinful world.

Very interestingly, this same adjective, *pistós*, is used to describe God in 1 Peter 4:19, where the apostle is endeavoring to comfort those who suffer according to the will of God. When we suffer undeservedly, in spite of our righteousness, we sometimes find it difficult to maintain our righteous and charitable behavior. Even though we are saints, it is hard to take when our helpful acts are rewarded with suffering. That is when we may be tempted to give up well-doing. In such circumstances, Peter asks us to remember that God is "a faithful Creator." "Wherefore let them that suffer according to the will of God commit the keeping of their souls to him in well doing, as unto a faithful Creator" (1 Pet. 4:19). We must not let suffering cause us to give up hope. God is faithful, a trustworthy Creator.

In other words, God has moral character. His omnipotence can be trusted, both in His creation and sustaining of all things. There is nothing more frustrating and miserable in human relationships than to have to depend on someone who is unreliable. Just imagine how much anxiety we would have if we were not sure that the sun would rise at the expected time each day.

If we can depend on the laws of nature, then we can all the more depend on the God who ordained these laws. He is the God in whom there "is no variableness, neither shadow of turning" (James 1:17).

In Psalm 36:5 we find an interesting example of this concept of God's faithfulness: "Thy mercy, O Lord, is in the heavens; and thy faithfulness reacheth unto the clouds." There is nothing more changeable than the movements of the clouds. They appear only to disappear. They are never the same two moments together. And because we live in a world in which so many things are changeable, it is easy for us to slip into the unconscious suspicion that God is also changeable. We need to remember that, amid all that changes, His faithfulness abides. Behind all that is subject to change, there is One who is absolutely constant.

In reality there is an unchangeableness at the heart of all things. The eternal laws of God are the same. Gravity does not change with the passage of time. There is an essential constancy in the very heart of all that is shifting. Even though the air we breathe today is polluted, it is basically oxygen. I doubt if Adam breathed anything else to live. Even the apparently drifting clouds are not vagrants of the wind, driven by purposeless caprice. God's hand is upon them. His faithfulness controls their changeableness. They appear at His command and they vanish at His command. "Thy faithfulness reacheth unto the clouds" (Ps. 36:5). The greatest uncertainties are chartered and move on purposed missions.

These clouds that are controlled by a faithful and unchangeable God in spite of their uncertain movements are symbols of the shifting uncertainties of human life. Our cloudy experiences can never be reduced to system and calculation. We cannot escape them but, by putting our trust in the God who controls them, we rob them of their terror. Whatever our present circumstances and whatever awaits us, we should accept this basic fact about God's character as Creator—His providential decrees have authority and dominion even in the realms of uncertainty.

Our clouds are not unchartered. Our shadowy experiences are not bereft of God. "Lo, I come unto thee in a thick cloud," said the Lord to Moses (Ex. 19:9). He "maketh the clouds his chariot" (Ps. 104:3). The one supreme certainty in all our uncertainties is God's luminous and loving sovereignty. The shifting clouds are not out of hand. "Even the winds and the sea obey him" (Matt. 8:27). While the world may reject the sovereignty of God, it ought to be the comfort of believers.

Be assured of this one thing, that our cloudy experiences are weighted with benefits. "Thou visitest the earth, and waterest it. . . . thy paths drop fatness" (Ps. 65:9, 11). We would perish of starvation and thirst if it were not for the clouds.

God has a purpose in permitting the clouds to form, the thunder to roar, and the lightning to dazzle us. Concerning the disciples on the Mount of Transfiguration we read, "And they feared as they entered into the cloud" (Luke 9:34). The faithful God permits change and uncertainty to inspire fear. Do not revolt against the idea of fear. Far better to fear than to remain insensitive. Better to have dread than irreverence. Better to end up in heaven through fear than to laugh your way frivolously and insensitively into hell. Dr. William Pettingill used to say, "I would rather scare a person into heaven than lull him into hell."

Our deadly peril is insensitiveness. Unrelieved carelessness is the only terrible hopelessness. Better to be afraid of God than to care nothing about Him. God permits you to enter the cloud to stir up wholesome fear in you. The only remedy is knowing the faithfulness of God that reacheth even unto the clouds. Our fear caused by God's clouds will be steadied and subdued into reverence, and we shall find the cloud to be a fountain of life.

And indeed, if we remember that the cloud is the home of our God, our fear will most surely be chastened into reverence,

and in the very midst of the cloud we shall have rapt communion with the transfigured Lord.

> Ye fearful saints, fresh courage take,
> The clouds ye so much dread
> Are big with mercy, and shall break
> In blessing on your head.

(See "Even Unto the Clouds," by J. H. Jowett, in *The Christian
World Pulpit,* Vol. 81, London: James Clarke & Co., 1912, p.
291.)

You Can Depend on God

God never asks His children to be something that He is not.
"The servant is not greater than his lord," said Christ (John
13:16). Does God ask you to be pure, loving, generous, forgiving, and faithful? Then you may be sure that He is far more holy,
loving, generous, forgiving and faithful than you could ever
be. These are His inherent characteristics, perfect and undevi-
ating. Thus, when the Apostle Paul tells us that "God is faithful," he is telling us that we can absolutely rely on Him.

"God is faithful" also means that God has method in what
He does. Regular habit or methodical action is a quality of
faithfulness. God followed method and order in creation, as we
see in the first two chapters of Genesis. He has regular habits of
procedure. He does not deal with His creation now on one plan
and then on another. He has not left His myriad worlds lying
haphazardly all over space wherever they happened to fall. He
does not let His divine affairs run on by themselves without
thought, system, or order. The faithful Creator is the God of regular habit, the God of system, the God who has His own time
and place for everything. Just think how much it means for us to
know that God has regular habit, that He is methodical, whether
in the realm of nature or of redemption.

Because all through nature and history God has been following His one chosen method, we can study what He has
been doing and find out to some extent what His method is.
Likewise as we gain more and more knowledge of it, we can trust
it and adjust our plans of life, efforts, and hopes to it.

Because God is faithful we can be scientists. If everything
depended on chance, science could not exist. We can live con-
fidently, as we live in accordance with God's method. As we sci-
entifically discover His method in nature, we may learn to use
it in our own activities. Our universities are actually founded on
God's faithfulness, whether they recognize it or not. This is
true in all our experiences. We drive our cars, we fly in planes,
we light our homes, we run our machinery, we multiply our
conveniences because we have found out something about God's
regular habit or method with regard to gas, gravity, light, and
electricity—the admirable mechanics of the creation to which
He has been faithful from the beginning.

There is a fundamental difference between the basis of God's
methods and ours. His have been formed in wisdom. He knew
they were good before trying them out, while ours are the result
of trial and error, by experience. His methods cannot be improved
upon; ours can. His methods are fixed and immutable, not to be
frustrated so that we can commit our hope to them as to a
faithful Creator.

God is faithful: that means not only that God has character,
that He has method, but also that He has aim or goal. Faithfulness is fidelity to one's life purpose. It requires that the goal
be kept in sight. The faithful man lives and toils for certain
ends, and he will not be diverted from them.

What was God's goal when He created man? To impress His
image upon man and to have fellowship with him. This original image and fellowship were lost because of sin. But God
could not be unfaithful to His goal. He had to regain man to

himself. To do this, He sent His Son, the Lord Jesus Christ, into the world to redeem man. "He abideth faithful: he cannot deny himself" (2 Tim. 2:13). "If we confess our sins, he is faithful and just to forgive us our sins, and to cleanse us from all unrighteousness" (1 John 1:9).

With regard to believers, God's object is to liberate them from the suffering caused by the weak and corruptible body and the sinful environment in which they now live. How and when will this be accomplished? Through the revelation of our Lord Jesus Christ when He shall appear to take us unto Himself. He said He would come again. He is faithful. He will keep His word.

One final thing is implicit in Paul's declaration that God is faithful. He is responsible. His responsibility extends to the world at large and to each individual, whether believer or unbeliever. He has declared what the end of the world will be and what our end will be, depending on our attitude toward Him. If we regard the history of the world and our own life as simply a series of unrelated events, we are missing the whole point. Behind everything that takes place is the hand of God that is responsible either in directing or permitting these events. If we do not believe that God is responsible, we can lose our way trying to figure out what life is all about, or by trying to make sense of it. How can we, since we are not the ones who determine the goal to be reached? He who is faithful is also sovereign and also responsible.

When Martin Luther was hard pressed and inclined to be over-anxious concerning the prospects of the Reformation, quiet Philip Melancthon would say to him, "Martin, let God be governor of the world." The faithful Creator is the responsible One. He alone is capable of being governor. There is not a verse written by prophet or apostle, there is not a word spoken by the Lord Jesus, that would lead us to suppose for an instant that God on high would avoid His responsibility for His world; or that He would put upon any man the least of His divine responsibility for its affairs. The faithful Creator and Sustainer is responsible for all things. God is the missionary to this world; and all our responsibility rests on His work. All our missionary work can be of service only when it has first been God's work. Were it not for God's prior and final responsibility as the faithful One from eternity, we would have no hope for better things. Let us therefore do with all our might whatever our hands find to do because we are but servants, and the responsibility is God's.

"God is faithful" may finally be summed up in this: God never made anything simply to break it, like a child, still less such a wonderful thing as a human heart. We are responsible for ourselves as we use aright what He has given, but we, all of us, live our lives under a grander responsibility over us, even God's, our Creator and our Redeemer. Trust Him to fulfill it. (See "God's Faithfulness," by Newman Smyth, in the *Christian World Pulpit*, Vol. 50, pp. 43–45.)

> Great is Thy faithfulness, O God my Father,
> There is no shadow of turning with Thee;
> Thou changest not, Thy compassions they fail not;
> As Thou hast been Thou forever wilt be.
> —Thomas Chisholm

A Bridge That Only God Could Build

Does it seem a long time to you since Christ first promised that He would one day return to earth? Do you sometimes wonder just how long it is going to be before this promise is fulfilled? With the passing of time, and all things continuing as they have been, two attitudes may develop in the minds of men—one in the believer and the other in the unbeliever.

The believer, seeing evil rampant and unabated and suffering not eliminated from this world, gets discouraged. He may be tempted to cry out, "Where is the fulfillment of Christ's promise to come back and right what is wrong?" Perhaps there has never been a time in history when Christian believers looked more to the coming of the Lord as the only apparent hope out of an impossible situation. It was while in exile on the island of Patmos that the Apostle John prayed, "Even so, come, Lord Jesus" (Rev. 22:20). As if Paul anticipated this feeling of anxiety and possible discouragement, he spoke in 1 Corinthians 1:8 of "the Day of our Lord Jesus Christ," the day of His return, and immediately added in verse 9, "Faithful is God."

Do not take Christ's delay as a failure or denial of His promise. His "Surely I come quickly" still stands (Rev. 22:20). The word "quickly" is in the context of eternity, for it is the eternal and infinite Christ who speaks. We are likely to attribute the wrong timing to it because we think of time only within the context of the present.

The Lord's coming will be a day of great deliverance for believers. "And ye now therefore have sorrow," said Christ to His disciples, "but I will see you again, and your heart shall rejoice, and your joy no man taketh from you" (John 16:22). Paul seems to ask, "Has it seemed too long to wait? 'Faithful is God.'" While our Lord Himself admonishes us, "Watch ye therefore: for ye know not when the master of the house cometh, at even, or at midnight, or at the cockcrowing, or in the morning: lest coming suddenly he find you sleeping. And what I say unto you I say unto all, Watch" (Mark 13:35–37). If you believe in God's faithfulness, in His trustworthiness, you will not grumble under any circumstances, but will be constantly watching for Him.

A little girl had been listening while her mother's friends were speaking about the imminent return of the Lord. After some time she was missed, and her mother went in search of her. She found her looking out a window at the top of the house. Asked what she was doing she said, "Oh, Mother, I heard you say Jesus might come today, and I wanted to be the first to see Him. Look, I washed myself and put on a clean dress."

That is how Christians should wait for their Lord. God is faithful. He will return. This should have a purifying effect on our lives, producing "holy behavior and godliness," not discouragement and loss of faith in God's promises (2 Pet. 3:11).

On the other hand, the unbeliever is emboldened in his belief that it will be his day forever because of the seeming delay of Christ's return. Nothing seems to be stopping Satan in his tracks. Though the unbeliever is not likely to bend his ear toward God's voice, Paul has a word for him also. "Just a minute," he seems to be warning, "God is faithful." Hear the words of Christ in John 12:48: "He that rejecteth me, and receiveth not my words, hath one that judgeth him: the word that I have spoken, the same shall judge him in the last day."

Unbelievers, take God's warning to heart while you have an opportunity to repent and be reconciled to Him. Otherwise, what you refuse to heed as a warning of the future will one day confront you as a fact of history. John tells us of this historical fact to come in Revelation 6:15–17 when he records a vision in the past tense as though it had already occured. "And the kings of the earth, and the great men, and the rich men, and the chief captains, and the mighty men, and every bondman, and every free man, hid themselves in the dens and in the rocks of the mountains; and said to the mountains and rocks, Fall on us, and hide us from the face of him that sitteth on the throne, and from the wrath of the Lamb: for the great day of his wrath is come; and who shall be able to stand?"

Do not shrug these off as empty words. "God is Faithful." Better to be safe than sorry. Repent and accept Christ as your Savior from sin. Then you will live in the daily expectation of His glorious appearing—glorious for Him and glorious for you, but terrible for those who are not ready to welcome Him.

After telling us that "God is faithful," Paul goes on to say that He is the One "through whom ye were called unto the fellowship of His Son Jesus Christ our Lord." He is not only the Rock of safety for any human being, but He is also the provision of the way by which a man can climb upon that Rock. He is the loving Father who prepares a wonderful home for us to live in and also opens the way and leads us into that home. He provides salvation and the faith to appropriate it. This is intimated by the preposition *diá* (1223), "through," translated as "by" in the King James Version. The Greek word for "by" is *hupó* (5259), not *diá*. The preposition *diá* is found in the prefix of English words such as "diaphragm, diathermy," etc.

On one hand we have God who is declared faithful, and on the other we have man who is dependent on God's faithfulness toward him. Whatever man does or is presupposes God's faithfulness. We could not work if we could not breathe, and we could not breathe if God did not provide an atmosphere filled with oxygen. There is no such thing as human independence, whether it be in the physical or spiritual realm. Through God we have our being, as Paul said to the Athenian philosophers: "Seeing he giveth to all life, and breath, and all things" (Acts 17:25). Even the means of appropriating what is God's comes from Him. Through Him we have fellowship with the Lord Jesus Christ.

"Through whom ye were called." Observe that Paul speaks about the person of God. It is not through a set of doctrines or practices, but through God Himself that we come to know Him. God jealously guards His personal prerogatives in the lives of men. There are no means of grace as such—not baptism or communion or good works or prayers. These are but evidences of the prior appropriation of the grace of God. God is the sole means of grace; He calls us and provides the bridge between heaven and earth. We on our own, or through anything we could do, could never build a bridge to heaven. Only a bridge descending from heaven to earth could effect our salvation.

The Greatest Joy Life Can Hold

How can we imperfect and sinful human beings ever hope to be in fellowship with God—so high, so omnipotent, so superior, so holy? We are not allowed to walk into the White House or Buckingham Palace and make ourselves at home. We are brought there only by the consent and invitation of the President or of the Queen. Similarly, we are brought, or called, into the presence of God through Him. The verb *eklḗthēte* (2564), "were called," is in the passive voice, which perfectly agrees with the meaning of the preposition *diá* with which 1 Corinthians 1:9 begins. It stresses the agent of our calling into this fellowship. This reminds us of Ephesians 2:8, "For by grace are ye saved through faith; and that not of yourselves: it is the gift of God."

The verb *eklḗthēte* is the same basic verb from which the adjectival nouns *klētós* (2822) *apóstolos* (652), "called apostle," of verse 1, and *klētoís* (from *klētós*) *hagíois* (40), "called saints," of verse 2, are derived. It refers to the effective call of God. It is equivalent to "ye were called unto salvation." It is the same word used in Romans 8:30: "Moreover whom he did predestinate, them he also called [*ekálesen* {2564}]: and whom he called [*ekálesen*], them he also justified: and whom he justified, them he also glorified." This is an effective calling implying response by the persons called and their consequent justification by God.

One must be saved to be accepted into the fellowship of the Lord Jesus Christ. Furthermore, this verb *eklḗthēte*, "were called" is in the second aorist tense, indicating that this effective call of God occurs at some particular time in the past. It refers to the entrance of man into the family of God. One must be born or adopted into a family to be eligible for the privileges of sonship. No wonder the Lord said to Nicodemus, "Ye must be born again" (John 3:7). There is no other way. Do you know the time when you were drawn into the family of God and became His child? "But as many as received him, to them gave he power to become the sons of God" (John 1:12). We become "sons" at a certain distinct time. It is the prerequisite to fellowship with the Lord Jesus Christ. "And if [we are] children, then heirs; heirs of God, and joint-heirs with Christ" (Rom. 8:17). We can only be heirs of God if we are children of God, and this only because of Christ.

We have said that the verb *eklēthēte*, "were called," is in the passive voice, indicating that the agent is God. Our call to salvation and fellowship with Christ is not prompted and effected by us but by God Himself, and it is part and parcel of the demonstration of His faithfulness. We owe everything to God's mercy, all that we experience now, all that we hope for in the enjoyment of Himself. We know that but for His grace we could at this moment be running in the paths of sin and sliding downward into death.

We look back upon our past lives with amazement and thankfulness. Were it not for Christ, we may have already slipped or gotten lost. By the grace of God, we are what we are and where we are. Every Christian should be able to confess a contrast between his sinful, worldly past and his spiritually living, joyous, and hopeful present, for the verb *eklēthēte*, refers not only to an act of God in the past, but also speaks of our state at the present time. We are in Christ, and as we look back we make God the author of our whole salvation. Romans 9:11 says that it is "not of works, but of him that calleth [*kaloúntos*, 2564]." Here is an influence that goes along with the invitation to make it effectual. This is the power of the Holy Spirit.

Whenever any of us have fellowship with an important personage, such as a president or king, it is always by invitation. Likewise, we did not choose God for our company. We are too depraved to do that. Remember Adam tried to hide from God after his fall (Gen. 3:8). He could no longer find pleasure in God's presence. Similarly, in the parable of the Prodigal Son, the younger son wanted to leave the father's house. If no agreement on basic attitudes exists, what joy is there in being together? People enjoy each other's company when they are of one purpose, one desire, when they love each other.

Man, having been estranged from God, does not seek His company anymore. "Behold, I was shapen in iniquity; and in sin did my mother conceive me" (Ps. 51:5). "The wicked are estranged from the womb: they go astray as soon as they are born, speaking lies" (Ps. 58:3). "There is none righteous, no, not one: there is none that understandeth, there is none that seeketh after God. They are all gone out of the way" (Rom. 3:10–12). Therefore, any fellowship with God must be initiated by Him and be preceded by a call that leads to salvation.

The preposition *eis* (1519), "unto," in the expression "Ye were called unto the fellowship of his Son," is indicative of movement. When God called us unto salvation, He called us to a different sphere of existence altogether. There are only two spheres in which men exist in this world—the sphere of those who are outside of Christ and the sphere of those who are in Christ. The greatest joy of those who live in Christ is their fellowship with Him, and the greatest punishment of those outside of Christ is being shut out from His presence. When we are born again, we are removed from the one sphere to the other.

The tense of the verb *eklēthēte*, "were called," indicates that this movement is a once-and-for-all transfer. Our greatest treasure then becomes our fellowship with Christ. We are like that little fellow who nestled very close to his father and, in answer to the question, "What do you want now?" replied, "Just to be near you, Daddy." We can gain nothing greater when we are

FELLOWSHIP WITH OUR LORD

saved than the joy of being close to Christ. When we have Him, we have everything.

A happy Christian met an Irish peddler one day and said to him, "It's a grand thing to be saved." "Aye," said the peddler, "It is. But I know something better than that." "Better than being saved? What can you possibly know better than that?" "The companionship of the Man who has saved me," was the reply. When we know that, we can rejoice with John and say, "Truly our fellowship is with the Father, and with his Son Jesus Christ" (1 John 1:3).

Your Personal Relationship With Christ

God calls sinners to repentance because He longs to save them from the present and future consequence of their sins. He knows more than any one of us, both the temporary misery of our sinful state and the ultimate and eternal suffering to which it leads. He knows what that awful pronouncement in Revelation 21:8 entails: "But the fearful, and unbelieving . . . shall have their part in the lake which burneth with fire and brimstone: which is the second death."

Some may laugh at this fearful prospect. But what if it were true? The Lord Jesus Christ knew it to be true, and that is why He left His heavenly glory to become man, to die for us, to call us unto salvation and fellowship with Himself forever. God calls us even here and now because He knows what our lives on earth would be like without Him. John Bradford, when he saw a cartful of men going off to Tyburn to be hanged, said, "There goes John Bradford, but for the grace of God."

A good Scotsman called to see Rowland Hill, an eminent English clergyman who did so much for the betterment of his countrymen, and without saying a word sat still for some five minutes looking into his face. At last Mr. Hill asked him what engaged his attention. Said he, "I was looking at the lines of your face." "Well, what do you make out of them?" "Why," said he, "that if the grace of God hadn't been in you, you would have been the biggest rascal living!"

We shall better understand what is involved when God calls us to become His partners, to enter His sphere of influence and fellowship, if we understand the terminology that Scripture uses. Consider the word "fellowship." People are attracted to each other by something that they hold in common. We have art fellowships, business fellowships, religious fellowships, and many others. The word "fellowship" in Greek is *koinōnía* (2842), the abstract noun from the adjective *koinós* (2839), "common." In fact, it is the very word that corresponds to our English noun "society." Society means the fellowship of people. Social interests are the interests directed toward people. When we are effectively called by God unto salvation, we move into a new society of saved people. The common bond in this society is the Lord Jesus Christ.

When we are saved by Christ, we become partakers of His divine nature. "According as his divine power hath given unto us all things that pertain unto life and godliness, through the knowledge of him that hath called us to glory and virtue: whereby are given unto us exceeding great and precious promises: that by these ye might be partakers of the divine nature, having escaped the corruption that is in the world through lust" (2 Pet. 1:3, 4).

Such a unique relationship as that between the believer and Christ is not found in any of the religions of the world. In the society of Christians, the living Christ holds them together and communicates with them and they with Him. That Christ was crucified is only part of the gospel. He is alive, and because He is, we can have fellowship with Him. We do not merely have fellowship with Christ because of our love relationship with

FELLOWSHIP WITH OUR LORD

Him. Christianity is not merely gaining what God gives but having fellowship with God Himself.

This fellowship is primarily a fellowship of two persons, Christ and the believer. When we accept Him as our Savior, He causes us to become like Him, and because we are like Him we desire His company—in fact we can do nothing without Him, and conversely we can do all that He requires of us through Him. Our entire commitment and surrender to Christ are the terms of our fellowship or partnership together. We are the zero, and He is the unit in front of us. We are nothing without Him and are something only because of Him. In our relationship to Christ as Savior, trust is reliance; in our relationship to Christ as ruler, trust is obedience; to Christ as a leader, trust is homage; to Christ as a man, trust is sympathy; to Christ as a brother, trust is affection; to Christ as God, trust is worship. In one word, fellowship with Christ is complete surrender of the whole soul to Him, however He may present Himself to us.

There is a danger, however, that we may pick up one aspect of Christ and choose to enjoy only that instead of Christ in all His aspects. We may take Him as teacher but not as Savior; as Savior but not as King; as man but not as God. Beware! Observe how Paul designates Christ in 1 Corinthians 1:9, when he speaks of our entrance into His fellowship. He calls Him "His [God's] Son Jesus Christ our Lord." Here we have His comprehensive name and title. We must hold fellowship with Him as God's Son, taking into full account His relationship with His Father. Let our fellowship with God be on the same level as Christ's fellowship as a Son with the Father.

Is that not the burden of His heart in His high-priestly prayer in John 17? Read it carefully in the light of this relationship. Listen to His words: "That they all may be one; as thou, Father, art in me, and I in thee, that they also may be one in us . . . that they may be one, even as we are one: I in them, and thou in me, that they may be made perfect in one" (vv. 21–23). The only way in which we as believers can be one as Christ desires us to be, is for our relationship with God to be what His is with the Father. The Lord never desired our fellowship merely as a society of Christians, or that our union be based on the sacrifice of the personal relationship with Him as God's Son, the Redeemer, but only on our conformity with Him, even as He and the Father are one in nature, interests, and purposes.

> My Jesus, as Thou wilt! Oh, may Thy will be mine!
> Into Thy hand of love I would my all resign;
> Through sorrow, or through joy, conduct me as Thine own,
> And help me still to say, My Lord, Thy will be done!

A Most Profitable Partnership for You

When two people enter into a business venture together, often they do not put themselves into the partnership, but rather invest their money or talents—what they have rather than what they are. And, if they want to absolve themselves from personal responsibility, they form what is known as a corporation. In a corporation they risk only what they put into it. If the corporation as such incurs debts, the creditors cannot come to them and take away their uncommitted assets.

But the partnership or fellowship with Christ of which Paul speaks in 1 Corinthians 1:9 is not so much a partnership of possessions as of beings. It is not a corporation of restricted responsibilities for the partners—Christ and you—but an unreserved blending of selves. It involves the loss of your will in His, in that, through the miraculous change He has worked in you, you have willed your will to become His will.

We have previously considered the term "fellowship" in relation to the effective calling of God. The second term for us to consider in 1 Corinthians 1:9 is the name "Jesus." "Faithful is God, through whom you were called unto the fellowship of his Son Jesus Christ our Lord." In order for us to acquire God's nature and thus enter into partnership with His Son, it is necessary that we accept Him as God made manifest in the flesh. "Jesus" was His earthly, human name. It means "Savior." That was the name announced to Joseph by the angel in Matthew 1:21: "And she [Mary] shall bring forth a son, and thou shalt call his name JESUS: for he shall save his people from their sins." You must believe that in the Babe of Bethlehem, in that man called Jesus who walked the streets of Palestine, dwelt "all the fullness of the Godhead bodily" (Col. 2:9). He was Jesus the man, yes, but He was also the Christ, the anointed of God. He is the God-Man, and only as such could He effect this fellowship between us and God. "And ye are complete in him," Paul adds in verse 10. In whom? In the man Jesus in whose body dwelt all the fullness of God.

In our individual fellowship with God through His Son Jesus Christ, He must be Lord; otherwise the fellowship will not be a source of joy but of heartache. That is why Paul stresses His whole name and title here, "His Son Jesus Christ our Lord." The word for "Lord" here is *Kuríou* (2962), meaning "the strong one." In this partnership He must be the dominant one. When we consider who it is that takes us into this partnership, in comparison with who and what we are, we can only marvel that He ever saw fit to call us to Himself at all.

God calls us into His fellowship through Christ as we are. He wants us. Let us not make the mistake of trying to please Him by giving Him what is ours and withholding ourselves. He is no beggar. He is not trying to take advantage of our possessions in this partnership. He is not going to benefit as much as we are. The partnership is primarily for our benefit. How can we dare accept Him, with all the resources of His being, and only put into the partnership a tiny pittance of our possessions or talents? It is each one of us He wants—all that we are—in order that He may make us all that He desires us to be.

In 2 Corinthians 8:1–5, Paul compares the giving of the Macedonians with that of the Corinthians. Though the Macedonians gave far less than the Corinthians, Paul commended them because they "first gave their own selves to the Lord" (v. 5). It makes no difference, Paul intimates, how much we actually give, as long as we give ourselves. Because the Macedonians first gave themselves to the Lord, they gave more of their worldly goods than they could afford; while the more affluent Corinthians because they held themselves back, gave less than they could afford.

Partnerships confer privileges commensurate with the contributions the partners make. Just stop to think what Christ put into this partnership and what we put in. The terms are not equal. We take nothing into it but weakness and poverty. Without Him we can do nothing, but with Him we will jointly realize God's ideal for humanity. In this partnership, we must never boast of doing anything ourselves. Since Christ brought in so much and we so little, let us give Him all the glory for the achievements. (See "Fellowship with Christ," by J. M. Charlton, in the *Christian World Pulpit*, Vol. 14, pp. 337–39.)

In its simplest form, our fellowship in and with Christ is a matter of holding everything in common with Him and those that are His. An illustration of this is to be found in the Apostolic Church. In Acts 2:44 we read, "And all that believed were together, and had all things common." That word "common," *koiná* (2839) in Greek, is the word from which *koinōnía* (2842), "fellowship" or "society," and *koinōnós* (2844), "partaker," are derived. Now that is not communism, as some have thought. Communism advocates forcibly taking from those who have and giving to those who have not. Fellowship in the Apostolic Church consisted of the voluntary sharing of what every believer had. That is the fundamental difference. Our fellowship with Christ and with other believers is never based on coercion but on voluntarily placing ourselves by faith in the sphere or society of Christ by being born again of the Holy Spirit, after which Christ voluntarily shares with us all that is His, and we share with Him all that is ours. In this partnership we are always the ones who profit.

The story is told of a missionary who came into contact with a proud and powerful Indian chief. The chief, trembling under conviction of sin, approached the missionary and proffered his belt of wampum as atonement. "No!" said the missionary, "Christ cannot accept a sacrifice like that." The Indian departed, but soon returned offering his valuable rifle and the most beautiful skins that he had taken while hunting. "No!" was the reply, "Christ cannot accept those either." Again the Indian went away, only to return with a conscience more troubled than ever; and this time he offered his wigwam, together with his wife and child—everything for peace and pardon. "No," was the reply even to this, "Christ cannot accept such a sacrifice." At this the chief seemed utterly oppressed with surprise, but suddenly he somehow sensed the deficiency, for, lifting up tearful eyes, he feelingly cried out, "Here, Lord, take this poor Indian too!" That is the condition for fellowship with Christ, and only on those terms will He consent to go into partnership with us.

What Partnership With Christ Involves

The great Bible expositor, G. Campbell Morgan, has said that partnership with Christ means at least three things: mutual interests, mutual devotion, and mutual activity. The Lord is interested in each one of us—in our development and our spiritual and temporal welfare. He has a goal that He would like us to reach. Thus the question is, "Are we interested in Him?" Of course, our partnership with Him will not accomplish anything for the One who is already perfect, but we can help Him to achieve His plan and further His interests in this sinful world and in the society of believers. In this partnership of mutual interests, however, we must be careful not to try to impose our interests on Christ. We cannot drag His interests down to the level of helping us achieve our purely selfish aims.

A man who was fond of having his own way at home made sure that he got it by the simple expedient of constantly reminding his wife that the Bible said she was to obey her husband. He used this excuse for foisting off on her any tasks he found too distasteful for himself so that she became a virtual slave to his comfort and to that of his relatives. He conveniently overlooked the biblical admonition to husbands to give "honor unto the wife, as unto the weaker vessel" (1 Pet. 3:7). His feeling was that God had made him lord and master in his own home, and he was fully exploiting this prerogative. This is not what partnership with Christ involves. We do not invoke Him and His Word to serve our own ends.

Fellowship or partnership with Christ also involves mutual devotion. The resources of Christ are ours in whatever we undertake to do, as long as a common interest exists. Once we have been admitted into His fellowship, all things are ours. In earthly partnerships, it seldom happens that every partner is given unlimited power to draw upon the common resources. The bank account is strictly guarded, and the available funds are meted out, not according to need or desire, but according to the legal claim each has on them.

For sinful men who have been regenerated and adopted into partnership with God, all this is blessedly otherwise. The treasury of grace is the fullness of God. There is "enough for all, enough for each, enough for everyone!" "But all He hath for mine I claim." If you really want to know of the wealth you can share with and in Christ Jesus, read His own words in John 17:22: "And the glory which thou gavest me I have given them." His glory mine! His glory yours! The glory of Christ is given to His people. That glory consists in what He is and what He has; the riches of life and the gifts of love. Realizing this, would you hesitate to place what you are and have at His disposal? (See G. W. Olver, in *The Biblical Illustrator*, 1 Corinthians Vol. 1, p. 20.)

But this partnership is not one that involves work only by the stronger and more capable partner. It is a partnership of mutual activity. True, Christ sometimes accommodates Himself to our weakness. This does not mean that He becomes weak. He is like the father who slows down his pace while walking with a child. When Christ slows His pace to ours, it does not mean that He is slow but that He humbles Himself to our level so that we may be able to walk with Him. Even so, let us at least try to quicken our pace.

In Hebrews 4:15, 16, the apostle makes clear the truth that the Lord accommodates Himself to our weakness without Himself becoming weak. "For we have not an high priest which cannot be touched with the feeling of our infirmities, but was in all points tempted like as we are, yet without sin. Let us therefore come boldly unto the throne of grace, that we may obtain mercy, and find grace to help in time of need." "The Lord fainteth not, neither is weary" (Is. 40:28). He accommodates Himself to our weakness. He waits for us, and when our footsteps falter, He pauses by our side. To quote G. Campbell Morgan again:

> I remember hearing a very dear friend of mine in a conference say that, if the Lord leads us into difficulties, He leads us out, but that, if we get into difficulties of our own making, we have to get out ourselves. I thank God that is not true of my life. That is not what I have found out. Yes, it is true, if He leads me into difficulty, He will lead me out, but if I wander in my own foolishness, He will still follow me, and lead me out.
>
> Fellowship, mutual activity; He accommodating all His power to my weakness and my faltering; and I—oh, yes—rising in cooperation with His power through that fellowship. Not only does He accommodate Himself to my weakness, He gives me power that enables me

to do things impossible to me outside the fellowship. [See G. Campbell Morgan, in *The Corinthian Letters of Paul*, p. 16.]

James Hastings also addresses this:

> Christ's strength loves to work in weakness, only the weakness must be conscious, and the conscious weakness must have passed into conscious dependence. There, then you get the law for the Church, for the works of Christianity on the widest scale and in individual lives. Strength that counts itself strength is weakness: weakness that knows itself to be weakness is strength. The only true source of power, both for Christian work and in all other respects, is God Himself; and our strength is ours but by derivation from Him. And the only way to secure that derivation is through humble dependence—which we call faith—on Jesus Christ. [See James Hastings' *Great Texts of the Bible, 2 Corinthians and Galatians*, pp. 305, 306.]

> Thou knowest, Lord, that we alone
> Should surely fail;
> We have no wisdom of our own
> That could prevail;
> Yet Thou, through human helplessness,
> Canst work Thy will—canst help and bless.
>
> Take these weak hands, and hold them, Lord;
> Our Helper be; In Thee is all our fullness stored;
> We come to Thee,
> And know that, by Thy Spirit's might,
> We must be victors in the fight.
> —Edith H. Divall

Your Responsibility in Your Partnership With Christ

Sometimes I hear people say, "A man's religion is his own business." But if you look at the root meaning of the word "religion" you will find that it comes from the Latin *re*, meaning "again," and *ligo*, "to bind," so that to be religious is to be bound back to partnership with God. Religion is God's business as well.

To make this partnership possible, God committed Himself to us fully, with all the resources at His command. In His incarnation He shared His nature with us through Jesus Christ. His Word tells us that through this incarnation we can become "partakers of the divine nature" (2 Pet. 1:4). Christ shared our lot in order that we might share His. That was how our redemption was accomplished. And thus, being found in Christ, Paul tells us in 1 Corinthians 1:5, we are enriched in all things.

Christ truly became a man. He was born; He grew; He acquired knowledge; He labored; He was tempted; He suffered; He died. His partnership in our nature was real. "Forasmuch then as the children are partakers of flesh and blood, he also himself likewise took part of the same" (Heb. 2:14). In order for us to share in the divine nature, it was necessary for God to come down and live as a man among men. Redemption for man occurs when he is regenerated, when he receives God's nature.

Partnership with Christ does not mean an external imitation of Christ, taking Him as a kind of copybook pattern, but having Christ Himself living in us. It means, not Christ outside of us as a model, but Christ within us as a power. "Abide in Me, and I in you," He told His disciples, "for without me you can do nothing" (John 15:4, 5). Paul recognized his partnership with Christ when he said, "I live; yet not I, but Christ liveth in me" (Gal. 2:20). What, then, is a Christian? He is one who has a nature in common with Christ. That is how the divine-human partnership starts—with a change of nature.

After we become a Christian by partaking of Christ's nature, we become a partaker of His life. The Bible expresses this by saying that we are "partakers of Christ's sufferings" (1 Pet. 4:13). God is love; and love by its very nature is sacrificial. Christ's love showed itself in sacrifice and suffering. "The Son of God, who loved me, and gave himself for me" (Gal. 2:20). All the suffering and sacrifice of the incarnation and the cross were implicit in this love. As soon as we become partakers of Christ's love, which is His divine nature, we are bound to become partakers of sufferings that love always involves.

Of course, from one point of view, the sufferings of Christ are unshared and unshareable. No one could possibly have been a substitute for Christ or assisted Him in His work on the cross. Nothing is more solitary than Christ's cross. He offered the one full and perfect oblation and sacrifice for sin. Not one of us can share in this atoning work.

However, in the condition of discipleship we not only may but also must share Christ's sufferings. We cannot take up His cross, but we must take up our own cross. "Whosoever doth not bear his cross, and come after Me, cannot be My disciple" (Luke 14:27). Every partnership with Christ involves a cross, involves suffering for His sake, even as He bore His cross for our sakes. It is impossible for a man who is a partaker of the divine nature to be unconcerned in the presence of sin. Just as the Lord Jesus, in sheer agony of soul, wept over Jerusalem, so the Christian will weep for the sins that abound around him. He knows that Christ is the first step and the source of spiritual life. And then comes "the fellowship of his sufferings" (Phil. 3:10). That is how Paul looked at his partnership with Christ, and that is the spirit in which he took his sufferings. Paul was stoned at Lystra, scourged at Philippi, fought with wild beasts at Ephesus, was ship-wrecked at Malta, and was finally put to death in Rome.

To be more specific, in the course of our partnership with Christ we have certain obligations. First, we must surrender our personal independence. Once we possess Christ's nature, we cannot act purely as an individual. We are compelled to think of the well-being of the joint enterprise. We know how true that is in the marriage partnership as well as in a business partnership. In a partnership we have to surrender the liberty of acting as individuals. For instance, we cannot guarantee debts for friends because that might involve the partnership. Similarly, if we are going to be a partner with God, we must act, speak, and think in the realization that His interests are at stake with our own. At all times we must consult Jesus Christ, our Partner in life, for everything. We are involving Him with all that we do and say. Let us be careful lest His kingdom, His cause, suffer as a result of His condescension in becoming our partner. If we think back over our lives, we will see how much richer it could have been had we consulted Christ our Partner in all that we ever attempted.

A famous journalist abandoned a lucrative position for reasons of conscience. A friend asked, "Can you afford to do this?" "Well," said the journalist, "you see, I have a very wealthy partner." "Who is he?" asked the friend in surprise. "God Almighty," was his reply. A man who is in partnership with God can afford to lose his own independence, to surrender it to the interests of the kingdom of God, to accept the Divine dictates because the wisdom and spiritual resources of the heavenly Father are at his disposal.

Secondly, our partnership with God demands the sharing of our time with Him. Nothing is achieved in this world without the investment of time. Our marriage cannot be a satisfactory partnership unless husband and wife spend time at home together. The same holds true for success in business. We would not want a partner in our business who did not care to devote his time to it. Success in partnership requires that the partners give it priority with regard to their time. Divided loyalties spell failure.

Honestly, how much time do we spend with God? Perhaps the reason our partnership with Him is not as happy or successful as it might be is that we devote so little time to it. His love, fellowship, and counsel, if only we made time for them, would dispel our fears, our restlessness, and our overwrought life. Patiently He waits for us, ready and willing to enrich us with every good thing. Shall we refuse the partnership He offers because we have no time for Him?

Thirdly, a partnership necessitates the investment of money. Partnership in the home, in industry, and in the community is utterly impossible without money. We cannot expect a wife to keep a home going unless she is given money. Businesses prosper according to the amount of capital they have. If they wish to expand, they seek for partners to put further money into the concern.

"How can one get rid of so many appeals for money?" asked a lawyer. "That's easy enough," was the reply. "Just stop giving altogether, and in a little while the public will find it out and will let you alone, as they do many others." "Yes," said the lawyer, "I suppose that is so, but what would be the effect upon me if I should stop giving?" "Why, your soul would grow small just in proportion as your bank account grew large," was the response.

The source of our partnership with Christ is His divine nature which we acquire as we begin our partnership with Him through a new spiritual birth. Our course of partnership occurs as we live in partnership with Christ all our lives, tasting the indispensable results of sharing in His love and sufferings. Finally there comes the end or goal of our partnership, as expressed by Peter, "a partaker of the glory that shall be revealed" (1 Pet. 5:1). We may suffer on the way, but glory is at the end of the road. "Our light affliction, which worketh for us a far more exceeding and eternal weight of glory" (2 Cor. 4:17). As for Christ, so for the disciple, the cross is the way to the crown. If we want to be partners in His glory, let us willingly be partners in His sufferings. (See J. D. Jones, *The Hope of the Gospel*, pp. 271–284, and "Partnership," by Norman Castles, in the *Christian World Pulpit*, Vol. 148, pp. 52, 53.)

LESSONS:

1. God's providential decrees have authority and dominion even in the realms of uncertainty.
2. When the Apostle Paul tells us that "God is faithful," he is telling us that we can absolutely rely on Him, that He has method in what He does, that this method includes an aim or goal, and that God is reasonable.
3. God is faithful. He will return. Christians can wait for the Lord fully expecting His return at any time.
4. God not only provides salvation to believers but also the faith to appropriate that salvation.
5. We can only be heirs of God if we are children of God, and this only because of Christ.
6. When we are effectively called by God unto salvation, we move into a new society of saved people. The common bond in this society is the Lord Jesus Christ.
7. The greatest joy of those who live in Christ is their fellowship with Him, and the greatest punishment of those outside of Christ is being shut out from His presence.
8. Our fellowship with Christ is an unreserved blending of ourselves with Christ. It involves the loss of our will in His, in that, through the miraculous change He has worked in us, we have willed our will to become His will. Christ Himself lives in us.
9. The only true source of power, both for Christian work and in all other respects, is God Himself. Our strength is ours only by derivation from Him.
10. A Christian is one who has a nature in common with Christ. One way we partake of Christ's nature is when we become "partakers of Christ's sufferings" (1 Pet. 4:13).
11. In our partnership with Christ we have certain obligations: 1) we must surrender our personal independence, 2) we must share our time with Him, and 3) we must share our money with Him.

1 Cor. 1:10

No Divisions Among Brothers

Now I beseech you, brethren, by the name of our Lord Jesus Christ, that ye all speak the same thing, and that there be no divisions among you, but that ye be perfectly joined together in the same mind and in the same judgment.

When Paul wrote to the Christians at Corinth—those who had been called into the fellowship of God's Son, their Lord Jesus Christ—he called them "saints." You might think from this designation that they were perfect angels, but this is not so. They were in Christ and thus were saved. Paul had told them so, and of their riches in Christ, and he had spoken of the expectation of the revelation of the Lord from heaven in 1 Corinthians 1:1–9. But their daily conduct left much to be desired.

It is always a struggle to conform to the perfect image of Christ. Disagreements arise within the Christian society or fellowship that grieve Christ and that must be corrected. Paul proceeds to do this in verses 10 through 17.

He begins this section with an expression of gentleness and a conjunction of contrast: "But I beseech you" (not "Now I beseech you," as the King James Version has it). There is always a "but" while we are in the flesh and surrounded by so many evil influences. We are a society of believers in Christ, but our society exists within a larger society of unbelievers, and we cannot help but be influenced. Often we are not even aware of what brushing up against the world does to us. When spiders spin their webs in bushes, they leave nothing we can see in the dark. But the next morning the dew that has clung to the webs reveals them, and then we can see that the bushes were covered with them. Similarly the influences that men exert upon us are not always apparent at the time. It is only when they are subsequently revealed in our lives that we become aware of them. Thus, when we find ourselves being critical of our congregation and the preacher, and at variance with the brethren, the fault may not lie so much in them as in our attitude that has been influenced by our worldly environment and friends.

Three surprising things stand out concerning the divisions that arose in the Corinthian church: (1) It had been only about five years since Paul established the congregation in this city. (2) Its greatest danger had arisen, not from its sinful environment, but from within; the church was bleeding from wounds inflicted not by her enemies but by her own children. (3) The divisions were not occasioned by fundamental differences in doctrine but by attachments to human personalities.

Who Is Your Brother?

In spite of divisions within the church of Corinth, Paul continued to consider these feuding Christians his brethren. These are the people he calls "the church of God which is at Corinth—the sanctified ones in Christ Jesus" (1 Cor. 1:2). Church saints feuding! Paul admits they are blameworthy with traits that need correction, but he does not consider this a reason to call them heretics. He addresses them by the loveliest of all appellations, "brethren." Gentleness in rebuke can often win over erring ones, where blunt severity cannot.

John Wesley and a preacher of his acquaintance were once invited to lunch with a gentleman after the worship service. Wesley's preacher friend was a man of very plain speech. While talking with their host's daughter, who was remarkable for her beauty and who had been profoundly impressed by Wesley's preaching, this well-meaning man noticed that she wore a number of rings. During a pause in the meal he took hold of the young lady's hand, and raising it called Wesley's attention to the sparkling gems. "What do you think of this, sir," he asked, "for a Methodist hand?" The blushing girl turned crimson. The question was extremely awkward for Wesley, whose aversion to all display of jewelry was well known. With a quiet, benevolent smile he looked up and simply said, "The hand is very beautiful." He had not denied the implied rebuke, but had taken the sting out of it. The young lady appeared at evening worship without her jewels and became a firm and dedicated Christian.

Paul knew his duty to correct the Corinthians. He could not allow wrongs to go unmentioned and uncorrected. But he wanted to attract those he corrected, not repel them. Paul had neither patience nor the time for those who rejected the basic truth of Christianity, whom he called heretics. These heretics were to be distinctly marked and not tolerated in the fellowship of Christ, for they were none of His. "For there must be also heresies among you, that they which are approved may be made manifest among you" (1 Cor. 11:19). "There must be" does not mean that Paul wanted them to be, but that there inevitably would come heresies, brought in by people who denied the truth. Such people had to be clearly known among believers. After all, an undetected rotten apple can do a great deal of harm to a basketful of good apples.

In this same vein, Paul wrote in Titus 3:10, "A man that is an heretic after the first and second admonition reject." And in Colossians 2:8 he said, "Beware lest any man spoil you through philosophy and vain deceit, after the tradition of men, after the rudiments of the world, and not after Christ." In Hebrews 13:9 we find the admonition, "Be not carried about with diverse and strange doctrines." In 1 Timothy 4:1, 2, Paul does not mince words, nor does he call false teachers "brethren." Listen to these stinging words: "Now the Spirit speaketh expressly, that in the latter times some shall depart from the faith, giving heed to seducing spirits, and doctrines of devils; speaking lies in hypocrisy; having their conscience seared with a hot iron." Harsher words than these are given for false teachers in Titus 1:10, 11: "For there are many unruly and vain talkers and deceivers, specially they of the circumcision: whose mouths must be stopped, who subvert whole houses, teaching things which they ought not, for filthy lucre's sake."

We must clearly differentiate between brethren in Christ and unbelievers. Each has the right to his own beliefs and doctrines, but unbelievers cannot claim acceptance in the community of saints. They must bear their proper name; they must be known for what they are. At the same time, we must recognize that in the fellowship of Christian believers there will be those who allow their human weaknesses to get the best of them. They may allow certain people to come first in their lives. These may be good, sound teachers of the gospel, whose views occasion minor differences and special attachments to arise among believers. This should not make us exclude their adherents from our fellowship in Christ. As long as they are born-again believers, they are children of God—according to John 1:12—and we have no right to refuse to call them our brethren.

A saintly bishop once said, "For the last forty years I have been trying to see the features of Jesus Christ in every man that differs from me." The truth is that many of our brethren differ from us, but this is no reason for not calling them "brethren." All too often, I am afraid, we are like that man who said,

> Believe as I believe, no more, no less;
> That I am right, and no one else, confess;
> Feel as I feel, think only as I think;
> Eat what I eat, and drink but what I drink;
> Look as I look, do always as I do;
> And then, and only then, will I fellowship with you.

Do not misunderstand me. I do not advocate having spiritual fellowship with those who deny the Lord Jesus Christ, but, when a man is born again of the Spirit of God, I do not believe we should turn our backs on him because he may be in error, or may differ from us on some points which do not affect our salvation.

How to Keep Harmony in the Church

When the Apostle Paul found it necessary to correct the erring brethren in Corinth, he did not point out their faults with a stick in his hand but with a heart of love. 1 Corinthians 1:10 begins with the gentle word *parakaléō* (3870), "I beseech, I beg, I ask, I exhort." It is the verb from which we derive one of the names of the Holy Spirit (the Paraclete or Comforter). This verb comes from the preposition *pará* (3844), meaning "near," and the verb *kaléō* (2564), meaning "call." It is as if Paul were saying to the Corinthians, "Come near to my side. I want you to feel the warmth of my love as I speak to you of what is on my heart."

> It is not so much what you say
>   As the manner in which you say it;
> It is not so much the language you use
>   As the tones you use to convey it.
>
> For words come from the mind,
>   And grow by study and art;
> But tones leap forth from the inner self
>   And reveal the state of the heart.

No Divisions Among Brothers

The word *parakaleō*, "I beseech you," sets the tone for all Paul is about to say to the Corinthians for their correction. As he admonishes them, Paul involves the Lord Jesus Christ because he wants to make sure that what he says does not come from or concern only himself.

"But I beseech you, brethren, through the name of the Lord Jesus Christ. . . ." The prepositional phrase in this verse is in the genitive case, which makes the name the instrument of Paul's appeal. It is not "for the sake of" the Lord Jesus Christ, which would have been indicated by the accusative case, but "through" Him. The full name of the Lord is used repeatedly in these verses.

What does Paul intend to invoke by using the name of the Lord? He wants to impress on the Corinthians that only through Christ is he able to get through to them to accomplish the desired goal. None of us who teach or preach God's revelation can accomplish anything or effectively correct anyone but through Christ. It is He who does it all. The name of the Lord stands for His character, for His revelation. Paul tells them right at the outset what is in full agreement with the character and revelation of the Lord Jesus Christ.

Observe that Paul does not speak here of "the" Lord Jesus Christ. He is the common possession of Paul and the ones to whom he is writing. They are his brothers, and Jesus Christ is Paul's Lord and theirs. This tells us at once that Paul is not about to rebuke them for heresy, which would deprive them of the right to own Jesus Christ as their Lord. We must be careful not to disqualify a brother from Christ's fellowship because of some peculiarity of behavior or an over-attachment to a servant of Christ instead of to Christ, as was the case in Corinth.

What was the burden of Paul's heart? It is expressed in the telic word *hína* (2443), "that," or "so that," which is indicative of the end desired. "I beseech you . . . that [or so that] all of you speak the same thing." The exact order of the Greek text is, "so that the same thing ye speak all." The word for "all," *pántes* (3956), comes at the end. Now how could all the Christians in Corinth possibly speak the same thing? This expression is taken from Greek political life, and means "be at peace," or, as here, "make up differences." (*International Critical Commentary*, 1 Corinthians, p. 10.) Paul is not exhorting the Corinthians to actually repeat the same phrases in unison in their worship services, as many liturgical Christian churches are accustomed to do. Furthermore, Paul wants no parrots either in Christian worship or conversation. The verb he uses is not *laléite* (2980), which would fit in more with the automatic repetition of sounds, but *légeite* (3004), which involves not only speech but consent of the mind, of the intellect. It means agreement of thought. Paul does not wish the Corinthian Christians to stop thinking and blindly follow a leader, be he Paul or any other dignitary of the church.

"And let there be no divisions among you," actually explains the previous expression, "so that you all say the same thing," that is, "so that there be thoughtful harmony among you." The opposite of harmony is divisiveness because of discord. Paul first states what he means positively and then proceeds to state it negatively. It is just like saying "Do good," and then "Here is the evil that you should avoid." A negative often makes the positive clearer, just as black brings out the contrast of white. The negative sometimes makes the command more specific, as it surely does in this instance.

Instead of using a direct second person plural in this negative command as "You'd better not create any divisions among yourselves," Paul puts it in the third person singular, "Let there not be." He does this to show that these divisions came about, not because the Corinthians had sought them, but because they were not on their guard. Divisions can easily creep in if we are not careful. Again this is part of Paul's gentle way. He is a psychologist par excellence. It is as if he were saying "I'm not blaming you for creating this situation, but it is here; it is a reality, whoever is to blame, and it must be corrected." We can take his admonition to heart even today. The state of your congregation or mine may not be the result of anything we have done, but we are definitely responsible for doing something about anything that may be wrong in it, recognizing the situation for what it is.

The word used for "divisions" here is *schísmata* (4978), transliterated into English as "schisms." This noun comes from the verb *schízō* (4977), which means "to rip or rend" as a piece of cloth is ripped. It has the meaning of separation from the whole, and could be paraphrased as "dissensions." In an orchestra or choir, each person contributes his part to the whole. Each part is not identical with the others; it is distinctive, but it complements the others to produce harmony. Paul is speaking of dissension versus harmony in the Christian Church. Our individualistic attachments can mar the harmony of the chorus. If one sings without regard to the other voices, only for the display of his own, his part is out of proportion and the effect is inharmonious. The part that each one of us sings or plays cannot be the same, but it must contribute to the harmony.

God Gave You a Mind to Think With

Do we as individuals have the right of private judgment within the Christian Church? Of course, every Christian has the right to search the Scriptures for himself and to communicate directly with the Lord. But he has no right to examine and judge under the influence of prejudice, or form opinions contrary to the clear and basic teachings of Scripture. Read Romans 14 carefully to see how Paul tackles the problem of private judgment with regard to certain customs of our daily life.

The first consideration in this matter of private judgment should be to acknowledge the primacy and Lordship of Christ. There is no doubt that He is the Alpha and the Omega in the revealed Word of God. "For whether we live, we live unto the Lord; and whether we die, we die unto the Lord: whether we live therefore, or die, we are the Lord's" (Rom. 14:8).

The second consideration by which to judge our divergent action or mode of life is the impact it has on our brothers or on the world. Paul gives us the rule in Romans 14:13: "That no man put a stumblingblock or an occasion to fall in his brother's way." Each time we are about to make a judgment or decide upon a course of action, we must ask ourselves if we are putting Christ first in the matter how it affects those around us.

A problem must be understood before it can be solved. Just as there were dissensions and divisions in the Corinthian church, we find them in our congregations today. What are the causes?

The fundamental cause, I believe, is a radical misunderstanding of the nature of truth. God's truth is infinite. Man's mind is finite. In the nature of things, then, it is impossible that we with our limited capacities should be able to comprehend the whole of truth. All we can grasp are some fragments—here a little, there a little—enough indeed for our personal necessities, if we seek aright in faith and patience, but immeasurably falling short of reality. Indeed we fall short of the reality of truth even in our comprehension of finite objects. Who can truly say that he understands all that there is to know about a drop of water? When I say I see you, do I really see the millions of nerves and other components that make up your body? I can see only part of you.

If, therefore, our knowledge even of the finite is at best partial, though sufficient for practical uses, how much more partial is our knowledge of the infinite, be it truth or the person of God or the Lord Jesus Christ? At best, as Paul expressed it in 1 Corinthians 13:9, "we know in part." We cannot know all that is in a drop of water, but we know enough to drink it to sustain life. So it is with God, with truth, with the revealed will of God in His Word.

Therefore, since our views of truth are partial and disjointed, it is inevitable that men with minds differently trained should understand different parts and aspects of the truth. Variety is not of itself an evil. In fact, it is God-given; and what God gives is never evil. He made each of us with a basic identity and yet with a diverse makeup. There are no two people who look or think absolutely alike. Even identical twins differ in some respects. These differences are not of our making. The hand of the Creator is behind them all.

Because God has made us different, we form different views of God as we read His Word and view His world. This is not wrong. Views only become wrong when they exclude others, or when they are antagonistic instead of complementary. For instance, both views cannot be right when one man views God as righteous and another regards Him as unrighteous. When my view is opposite to yours instead of complementary, then there must be a standard of self-evident truth that can serve as a criterion.

Differences should not be ignored or dissembled but frankly acknowledged. In fact, "combination in diversity" is a characteristic feature of Holy Scripture. It uses the records of the four Evangelists, written in different styles and from different viewpoints by different personalities, to give a true picture of the Son of Man in His earthly ministry. We are not to regard one as more faithful to the truth than another, not to take any one as complete in itself, but to find, in the harmony of all, the true delineation of that perfection that we can only realize by contemplating it in its several parts. Paul, James, Peter, John, each offer us different aspects of the truth. One is the apostle of faith, another of works proving the existence of faith, one of hope, another of love. But though they each have some special grace or duty upon which they lay emphasis, it is not to the neglect or exclusion of other graces and duties, nor are we to pit them one against the other.

Although I have used the illustration before about the six blind men who went to view the elephant, it bears repeating. Each man put out his hand to touch some part of the elephant's anatomy and thought he had grasped the whole. To one the elephant was like a tree, to another like a wall, to a third like a fan, to a fourth like a snake, to a fifth like a spear, and to a sixth like a rope—depending on whether they had touched his leg, his side, his ear, his trunk, his tusk, or his tail. The poem in which this fable is contained concludes that all of them were right, though each of them was wrong. It takes a synthesis of all aspects of God and His creation to get a complete picture of Him—and none of us is so gifted as to be able to comprehend this, though we make some progress as we open our hearts and minds to the various facets of truth we encounter on our heavenward journey.

Various schools of thought are necessary for the full representation of truth, instead of thoughtless blind obedience to a particular representation of the truth, as some churches have demanded. If God does not ask you to set thought aside in your decision to follow Him, no ecclesiastic in the name of God should do so either. In fact, the first and foremost command of Christ to man is to repent, which in Greek is *metanoéite* (3340), meaning "to change your mind." Obviously you cannot change it without exercising it. When by the grace of God the bondage of sin is broken, one of the best evidences is the sense of intellectual freedom, accompanied by a new spirit of humility and obedience, a fresh love of truth, and a re-adjusted perspective.

Can Any Man Know the Whole Truth?

Someone has said that various schools of thought supply "that antagonism of influences which is the only real security for continued progress." Is this not true in economics, in business, in manufacturing? In an organization of "yes-men" you may have peace and harmony, but there will be no healthy interchange of ideas to spark progress. Which countries are most advanced—those that allow individual initiative for the good of all, or those whose governments determine what each person can and cannot do? This may also be applied in the Christian church, where the matter of disagreement arises with far more frequency than many have thought desirable.

I think the whole matter of private judgment is progress if it is safeguarded by that beautiful Greek word *sōphrosúnē* (4997), usually translated "sobriety." An illuminating verse in which this word occurs is Romans 12:3. I wish you could read it in the Greek text, but here is a literal rendering: "For I say, by the grace given unto me, to every one who is among you, not to think more highly [*huperphronéin* {5252}, made up of *hupér* {5228}, "higher," and *phronéin* {5426}, "to think"] than he must think, but to think [*phronéin*] so that he may think soberly [*sōphronéin* {4993}], each one according as God hath given a measure of faith (a.t.).

Think, Christian, but place limitations on your thoughts, realizing that someone else's thoughts may be as great as, or greater than, yours. His interpretation of truth may indeed supplement and complement yours. A person who is free places voluntary limitations on his freedom, and a Christian who thinks sets up a wall on one side called "God" to keep him within the bounds of truth, and a wall on the other side called "others" that keeps him in touch with other people's thinking about truth.

The danger, however, is that schools of thought, or denominations, or congregations, are painfully liable to degenerate into parties. We naturally and rightly concentrate our attention upon that fragment of truth that we have realized for ourselves to be real and precious. But gradually we may grow to think that this is the whole of truth. We tend to divide the swelling river of truth into a thousand paltry streams, and each of us cries, "Come, drink at my stream; for it, and it alone, is pure and uncontaminated."

We must watch ourselves lest we reach that place where we declare our little stream to be the only stream of living water. If it were, would it be sufficient for the whole wide world to drink from it? Such an attitude leads us to look at other streams with contempt and to reject them as impure. We begin to resist others who are in the same family of the redeemed as ourselves. This leads to hot-headed controversy in which love is easily forgotten. Thus the party strife in the Christian church becomes a spectacle that provokes the scornful laugh of the world and devils. This moves our angelic watchers to tears.

The absence of humility, the stubbornness of self-will, the spirit that desires victory rather than truth, all contribute a dire result; and the imperfection of our knowledge is perverted by our sinful folly into a source of incalculable harm to ourselves and those around us. Be careful lest you unduly cherish your own individual discovery of an aspect of truth and proclaim it as the one vital element of truth to the exclusion of others that in reality are no less important.

As you read Paul's letters to the Corinthians, notice how true this attitude was of them. Apparently they were using names and phraseology indicative of partisanship. "I am of Paul," said one faction. "I am of Apollos" (or "Cephas" or "Christ"), said still others. These clichés accentuate the differences between various schools of thought. As Christian brethren, we must recognize that extremes beget extremes. If one set of men form themselves into an exclusive party, with narrow views and aims, the almost-certain consequence is that those who have opposite views and aims will form a party to resist them.

We shall do well to look at the evils arising from such divisions. Party spirit causes the decay of spiritual life, for love is the breath of life, and where love is not, life must wither and die. Love and controversy cannot co-exist for long. As each party circle ceases to hold communion with its neighbors, and feeds more exclusively upon its own limited truths, there is peril that even these will grow lifeless and become petrified into hard, unmeaningful, theological formulas. The consequences of such isolation may include loss of knowledge, narrowness of sympathy, and even death.

Party spirit is a grievous hindrance to the growth of the Church of Jesus Christ. It is a stumbling block to weak believers. It is a laughing-stock to unbelievers. "See how these Christians fight with each other!"

What remedy is there for this spirit of divisiveness and partisanship within a congregation? We must remember that we are Christ's—not primarily in outward organization, however valuable; not in creeds, however necessary, but in living union with our Head. And then we must recognize that variety in the Church of Christ is not only not wrong but is natural and necessary because the views of any one individual or group of individuals can be at best only partial embodiments of the whole truth.

Let us candidly and patiently examine the views of those who differ from us. This will do much to moderate party spirit. Born-again men of undeniable honesty, conscientiousness, zeal, and holiness, differ from us. Why is this? They cannot be entirely in the wrong. No holy life is based entirely on false premises. Let us cooperate on a practical basis with those with whom we differ. If controversy should become unavoidable, as it may be on some occasions and with some individuals, we must take heed that it is conducted with calm sobriety, temperate reason, and with a desire for truth, not success.

An eminent preacher has said, "I was walking in a beautiful grove where the trees were wide apart and the trunks were straight and rugged. But, as they ascended higher, the branches came closer together, and still higher the twigs and branches interlaced. I said to myself: Our congregations resemble these trees. The trunks near the earth stand stiffly and rudely apart; the more nearly toward heaven they ascend the closer they come together, until they form one beautiful canopy, under which men enjoy both shelter and happiness. Those who have the Spirit of Christ will be like-minded."

Where Do You Fit in the Picture of the Church?

After the Apostle Paul's negative admonition to the Corinthian Christians not to have divisions among themselves, he proceeds to give them constructive positive advice on how to accomplish this. "But become fitted together in the same mind and in the same opinion" (1 Cor. 1:10 [a.t.]).

Paul is not correcting the existence of denominationalism as we know it today, but the party divisions within one local church. As long as we are human with individual minds and dispositions, there will be differences of opinion that lead to party formation. Satan is to a great extent responsible for these. He is the instigator of divisions within the Church and among Christian brethren. His favorite place is in a good assembly of believers.

But Paul does not altogether throw the burden upon the devil. After saying, "Let there be no divisions," he immediately adds, "but become fitted together." This brings to mind the apt warning of our Lord in Matthew 18:7, "Woe unto the world because of offenses! for it must needs be that offenses come [that is, they are unavoidable as long as Satan is around], but woe to that man by whom the offense cometh!"

We see here a case of double responsibility. A missionary in India was trying to explain this matter to a group of natives near a river. A Brahmin countered by saying, "Sir, don't you say that the devil tempts men to sin?" "Yes," answered the missionary. "Then," said the Brahmin, "certainly the fault is the devil's; the devil, therefore, and not man, ought to suffer punishment." Just then the missionary caught sight of a boat on the river with several men on board. "Do you see that boat?" he asked the Brahmin. "Yes." "Suppose I were to send some of my friends to destroy every person on board, and bring me all that is valuable in the boat—who ought to suffer punishment—I for instructing them, or they for doing the wicked act?" "Why," answered the Brahmin with emotion, "you ought all to be put to death together." "So, Brahmin," replied the missionary, "if you and the devil sin together, the devil and you will be punished together."

Paul recognizes that the devil cannot be restrained. God permits his activity in this world until the day that he is bound, as prophesied in Revelation 20. But there is something definite that we as children of God can do to resist him and foil his plans—not so much in the world in general, but within the fellowship of Christ. As Martin Luther said, "We cannot prevent the birds from flying over our heads, but we can certainly prevent them from building nests in our hair."

What, then, can we do about evil or divisions within the Christian community? Paul answers this by using the word *katērtisménoi* (2675), "perfectly joined together" (as the King James Version has it) which shows his recognition of the diversity of the individuals making up the body of Christ or the fellowship of believers in a local church. He elaborates on this in the 12th chapter of 1 Corinthians. This word comes from *ártios* (739), which means "complete, capable, proficient," and occurs only in 2 Timothy 3:17, where it is translated "perfect." "That the man of God may be perfect, thoroughly furnished unto all good works." Actually, "perfect" here means neither faultless nor sinless. It means "fitting, useful." *Ártion* for the Pythagorean philosophers was the opposite of *péritton* (cf. *périssos* [4053]), "unnecessary." It is that which is necessary for the whole.

NO DIVISIONS AMONG BROTHERS

As Christians we are like the parts of a jigsaw puzzle that have to be ártia, "perfect, fitting," so they can be placed where they belong. They are of various shapes, but each one has its particular place and is necessary to make up a whole that can be admired. That is what the Church of Jesus Christ should be, a fellowship of different individuals, each of whom must find his place of usefulness and allow Christ to fit him for it. You may seem a very small and insignificant part of the whole, but without you the picture would be incomplete.

Katartízō, then, means "to order, to put together." In Hebrews 11:3 we read, "Through faith we understand that the worlds [*aeons*, 'ages'] were framed [*katērtísthai*] by the word of God." The ages were put together, fitted into each other, by the Word of God; and this Word is also responsible for taking sinful individuals like those in Corinth and fitting them together into a unified whole. It takes faith to understand this and yield ourselves to this "fitting" process. Thus, when Paul tells the Corinthians to be *katērtisménoi*, "fitted together," he calls upon them to understand that they are not all alike. Just as no two puzzle pieces and no two snowflakes are exactly alike, so no two Christians are exactly alike. When we become members of the fellowship of Christ, we do not lose our identity or our idiosyncrasies, but we are cut to fit into the whole body, in the place where we are needed to complete the picture.

The second thing Paul wants us to recognize is that there is nobody just like us, and therefore, if we do fill our place, there will be a certain imperfection or incompleteness in the body of Christ. And thirdly, no individual, as a part of the whole, can be the whole body. Paul or Apollos or Peter are not the body. They are only part of it, and so are you and I. The moment the part assumes so much importance that it wants to appear as the whole, the Church is in trouble.

No Divisions Among Brothers

The story is told of a heavy bronze bell that had sunk into a river in China. The efforts of various engineers to raise it had been to no avail. At last a clever native priest asked permission to make the attempt, on condition that the bell should be given to his temple. He then had his assistants gather an immense number of bamboo rods. These are hollow, light, and practically unsinkable. They were taken down by diverse, one by one, and fastened to the bell. After many thousands of them had been thus fastened, the bell began to move. When the last one had been added, the buoyancy of the accumulated rods was so great that they actually lifted that enormous mass of bronze to the surface. You may think that your bamboo rod is too small and light to make any difference, but it is necessary in God's sight to lend strength to the whole.

Should All Christians Agree on Everything?

Sometimes we think if we could go back to the days of the early Church, we would find perfection. But that is not the way it was, for we find many admonitions in the letters of the Apostle Paul against the errors that were creeping into the local assemblies of believers. He not only warned the Corinthians about their spirit of divisiveness, but also told the Thessalonians there was something lacking in their faith that he wanted to make up for by his presence among them, to strengthen, establish, and confirm them. That is a meaning of the word *katartízō*, "to establish, to confirm," as we find it used in 1 Thessalonians 3:10. "Night and day praying exceedingly that we might see your face, and might perfect [*katartísai*] that which is lacking in your faith."

As Christians, we need each other if we are going to present a picture of a unified whole to the world, of parts aptly fitted together. If we prove a misfit, we may prevent many others from finding their positions. The participle *katērtisménoi* here is the perfect tense and passive voice of *katartízō*, which denotes a stable condition brought about by someone other than oneself, in this instance by God. We must allow God to cut and fit us into our proper place. When He does the fitting, it is stable, it is fixed.

Christians need to fit into the community of believers "In the same mind and in the same opinion." First of all, let us find out what these two Greek words, *noí* (dative singular of *noús* [3563], "mind") and *gnómē* ([1106], "opinion"), mean here. *Noús* is used twenty-one times by Paul, and outside of his epistles it occurs only in Luke 24:45 and Revelation 13:18; 17:9. *Noús* is more of a general term indicating the whole intellect, that part of that enables us to think. *Gnómē* means "opinion," and is a little more restrictive in its use. We use these two words in both Ancient and Modern Greek. *Noús* is the general inner thought and attitude, while *gnómē* is the formulation of an opinion concerning a particular matter.

Thus Paul tells the Corinthians that in their general mental attitude and in their opinions on individual matters they should be one. Does that mean conformity of thinking and opinions? Should all Christians agree on everything and, unless they do, be excluded from fellowship with each other? No, this is not Paul's meaning here. The same mind and the same opinion to which he refers are the mind and opinion of Christ. In 1 Corinthians 2:16 he makes this clear: "But we have the mind of Christ." You must be fitted into the same mind, he tells them, and that mind is Christ's—not Paul's, not Apollos,' not any man's. Is your conscious aim to make your general attitude and your every opinion fit into that one mind of Christ? Whom are you more eager to please, Christ or some particular preacher or teacher?

A famous evangelist of our day who preaches the gospel has become a bone of contention in some circles. There seems to be almost a war between two camps, those who are for him and those who are against him. Fellowship no longer hinges on "What do you think of Christ?" but on "What do you think of

Preacher so-and-so?" The preacher should not be the criterion of our faith and fellowship, but Christ alone. That was the trouble in Corinth. Each of three preachers—Paul, Apollos, and Peter—was loved so much by a certain group that they said, "I am of Paul," or "I am of Apollos," or "I am of Peter."

Let us examine our hearts. In our general attitude and in our particular decisions, do we seek to please a preacher, whether one of national fame or one of local repute? If we do, disregarding "the mind of Christ" in the matter, we are grieving the heart of the Lord and bringing confusion to the cause of Christ. No person or thing should dethrone Christ in our minds and hearts at any time. We should ask ourselves at all times: Is my attitude and are my decisions able to fit together in the mind of Christ in general and in particular? When we are faced with a decision, we should question ourselves in all honesty, What would the Lord Jesus do if He were in our place?

Remember that incident when the Lord asked the disciples what they had been fighting about amongst themselves on the way to Capernaum? They kept quiet because the quarrel was about who would be the greatest among them. The Lord took a child and set him in their midst to teach them a lesson in humility. Then John said, "Master, we saw one casting out devils in thy name, and he followeth not us: and we forbad him because he followeth not us" (Mark 9:38). Unfortunately, that spirit prevails even in our day. The disciples were wrong in this matter, and so are those who follow their example. "But Jesus said, Forbid him not: for there is no man which shall do a miracle in my name, that can lightly speak evil of me. For he that is not against us is on our part" (Mark 9:39, 40).

On a blank leaf of his Bible a man had drawn a circle with several radii converging on the center, which he called "Christ," while on the radii were written the names of different denominations of Christians. Underneath were written the words, "The nearer to the center the nearer to one another."

<u>LESSONS</u>:

1. Gentleness in rebuke can often win over the erring ones, whereas blunt severity cannot.
2. We must not maintain spiritual fellowship with those who deny the Lord Jesus Christ, and when a man is born again of the Spirit of God, we should not turn our backs on him if he may be in error or holds to slightly different doctrines.
3. No one can accomplish anything or effectively correct anyone except through Christ.
4. Before we privately judge issues within the Christian Church we must acknowledge the primacy and Lordship of Christ and consider how others will be affected by it.
5. "Combination in diversity" is a characteristic feature of Holy Scripture. It also should be a characteristic feature of our relationship with Christian brothers.
6. Variety in the Church of Christ is not wrong but is natural and necessary because the views of any one individual or group of individuals can be at best only partial embodiments of the whole truth.
7. When we become members of the fellowship of Christ, we do not lose our identity or our idiosyncrasies, but we are cut to fit into the whole body in the place where we are needed to complete the picture.
8. Nobody in the Church is just like us; and therefore, if we do not fill our place, there will be a certain imperfection or incompleteness in the body of Christ.
9. Each individual is a part of the whole body of Christ. No individual should presume to make up the whole body, himself.

1 Cor. 1:11,12 | *What Kind of Christian Are You?*

For it hath been declared unto me of you, my brethren, by them which are of the house of Chloe, that there are contentions among you. Now this I say, that every one of you saith, I am of Paul; and I of Apollos; and I of Cephas; and I of Christ.

What is the basis of our agreement as members of the fellowship of Christ? What is the mind of Christ into which we must fit our own thinking? Notice that Paul mentions two main things in 1 Corinthians 1:10–17. He refers to the crucifixion of Christ and to the ordinance of baptism, and does so in a manner to draw attention to the difference in importance between them. He asks, "Was Paul crucified for you? or were ye baptized in the name of Paul?" (v. 13).

Is it clear that baptism is not of equal importance with the crucifixion by what Paul says in verse 17: "For Christ sent me not to baptize, but to preach the gospel: not with wisdom of words, lest the cross of Christ should be made of none effect." The cross is the focal point, the means of redemption of the human soul. It is through the blood of the cross that we have the forgiveness of sins. The basis of our oneness is the redemption secured for us by Christ. We are brothers, even if we differ in the matter of baptism, but we cannot be brothers in Christ unless and until we have gone to the cross of Christ to obtain our redemption from sin. This is the very heart of the gospel.

"Oh," said a woman to a minister, "do you belong to us?" "Well," said the minister, "who are 'us'? I belong to Christ." Then, seeing that this explanation still did not satisfy her, he continued, "I like the Augustinian creed: 'A whole Christ for my salvation, the whole Bible for my study, the whole Church for my fellowship, and the whole world for my parish, that I may be a true catholic and not a sectarian.'"

In verse 11, Paul explains where he received information about divisions that existed among the Corinthians. He does not try to hide the identity of his informants. In fact, the verb that he uses is *edelōthē* (1213), which means "it was made evident or clear to me." Even in Modern Greek the deposition one makes under oath before a judge is called *dēlōsis*—the declaration of what one knows to be true. In other words, this is not hear-say. Paul would not write about it if he did not know it to be true.

It is our duty, especially if we hold any responsibility for the flock of Jesus Christ, to be straightforward in facing a factual situation. If something needs to be corrected, we must speak up. Paul could have kept quiet about the problem in the Corinthian church, but he did not. He wrote the Corinthians—in the kindest way possible—to tell them that the cause of Christ was being hurt by the divisiveness that existed in Corinth. His purpose was not simply to criticize them but to correct them. When you feel impelled to utter or write a criticism of or to anyone, reflect a moment on why you are doing it. If it is to redress a personal affront or to get even, it is wrong. It is better not to do it. But speak up when the cause of Christ is at stake.

Observe that Paul was informed personally: "For it hath been declared unto me." It was not some rumor that he happened to pick up, but something that specific individuals who had personal knowledge of the situation had come to pour out their hearts to him about. "They told me," not "They told somebody to tell me." First-hand information is the best information. It is always best to talk to the people about whom you have received a complaint.

Paul writes them a letter of love and understanding, not of anger. He calls them brethren for the second time but makes the appellation a little more intimate by prefacing it with the word "my." He includes all of them as "my brethren," even those who were schismatics.

Paul then goes on to identify the source of his information: "those of the house of Chloe." We are told absolutely nothing about this woman. We may suppose that she was living in Ephesus, from which city Paul wrote this epistle. Some of her relatives or servants may have visited Corinth and brought back the news about the state of the congregation there. Undoubtedly, Chloe must have been known to the Corinthians, since Paul does not find it necessary to explain who she was. It seems likely that there was more than one informant, and that Paul was practicing what he preached when he wrote to Timothy, "Against an elder receive not an accusation, but before two or three witnesses" (1 Tim. 5:19).

What was the news from Corinth? "That there are contentions among you." We have noted before that Paul does not put the blame on specific individuals. It is the general situation that concerns him. The word for "contentions" here is *érides* (2054), "quarrels," which is a little harsher than the word *schísmata* (4978), "divisions." One may form a party or a schism or leave a group without hard feelings. But *éris* (the singular form of *érides*) involves a feeling of enmity that is expressed outwardly. Apparently there was quarreling among the various groups and between individuals.

This quarreling or strife is an evil which Paul includes in a list in Galatians 5:19–21. In this passage we also find what company strife keeps: "Adultery, fornication, uncleanness, lasciviousness, idolatry, witchcraft, hatred, variance, emulations, wrath, strife, seditions, heresies, envyings, murders, drunkenness, revellings, and such like." Pretty bad companions, wouldn't you say? Strife ought not to be known among Christians.

The trouble with the Corinthians is diagnosed by Paul in 1 Corinthians 3:1, "And I, brethren, could not speak unto you as unto spiritual, but as unto carnal, even as unto babes in Christ." The word for "carnal" is identical in its root (*sárkinos* [4560], "fleshly") with the word "flesh" in Galatians 5:16, 17, 19. A carnal Christian is one who allows the flesh to win over the spirit. This battle goes on within the Christian as long as he is in the flesh. Paul himself had a terrific battle, as he confesses in the sixth chapter of Romans. It is all too easy to fall prey to the weaknesses of the flesh.

The most unfortunate aspect of this is that the world around us cannot make the distinction between spiritual and carnal Christians. They are scandalized and offended when they observe the carnality of some Christians, and are amazed and blessed when they see the spirituality of others. Praise the Lord, there are Christians who bring glory instead of shame upon the Lord.

A non-Christian who read the New Testament for the first time said to a friend, "Parts of it are most beautiful, but I do not see what these people around here who are called Christians have in common with this book!" Can that be said of us?

Are You a Divisive Christian?

A missionary speaking to a group of Hindu women was surprised to see one of them get up and walk away. Soon she returned and listened more intently than before. "Why did you leave in the middle of my message?" asked the missionary. "I was so interested in the wonderful things you were saying that I went to ask your servant if you live like you teach. He said you do. So I came back to hear more about Jesus," said the woman.

This missionary must have been a truly spiritual Christian. If only the world could make the distinction between the spiritual and carnal members of Christ's Church. This is one more reason Christians should move from carnality to spirituality, as they submit to Christ through the crucifixion of self.

A quarrelsome spirit is a carnal spirit. No group of Christians should quarrel with another group. No Christian should entertain hatred toward or speak evil of another Christian, one who is under the shadow of the same cross of Christ. Just think of how the crucified Christ feels as He listens to our strife. Face it; if we seek a quarrel with a fellow Christian, we are carnal. If we avoid one, even when challenged to fight a fellow Christian, that is proof that we are spiritual.

I do not know if you are old enough to remember the organ grinder who used to go around with a little monkey to collect pennies in the streets. One such entertainer had an especially clever monkey. When a big dog broke away from some children with whom he had been playing and made a dash for the monkey, the bystanders were surprised to see that the monkey did not seem in the least afraid. He stood perfectly still in evident curiosity, waiting for the dog to come up to him. This disconcerted the dog, for he would have much preferred to chase something that would run and not stand its ground.

As soon as the dog reached the monkey, the funny little scarlet-coated creature courteously doffed his cap. Instantly there was a laugh from the audience. The dog was nonplused. His head drooped and his tail dropped between his legs. He looked like a whipped cur and not at all like the fine dog he really was. He turned and ran back home, and the laughing children could not persuade him to return. As for the monkey, he climbed up on his master's organ and went peacefully on his way.

WHAT KIND OF CHRISTIAN ARE YOU?

Evidently, although only a monkey, he wanted no disagreement, and he knew instinctively that it took two to make a quarrel. You can often avoid strife by being the one who refuses to fight with a brother in Christ, even if he is somewhat different from you or belongs to another group.

The strifes in the Corinthian church took root when the believers there attached themselves to various individual preachers, each one thinking that his preacher could not be excelled. The moment we believe we have an exclusive corner on truth, we are on dangerous ground. As we consider ourselves members of the body of Christ and others members of the same body, how can we strive with another member of the body to which we belong?

Someone once remarked, "There are two sides to every question—my side and the wrong side." An illustration of this concerns the argument that arose between two young chaplains of different denominations. The senior chaplain said, "Let us bury the hatchet, my brother. After all, we are both doing the Lord's work, aren't we?" "We certainly are," said the junior chaplain, quite disarmed. "Let us do it, then, to the best of our ability, you in your way, and I in His!" I'm afraid too many of us are inclined to think our ways are the Lord's ways, and the ways of other fellow Christians fall short of that standard.

Paul does not stop with generalities when he tells the Corinthian Christians that they are carnal for quarreling with each other. When he speaks of the contentions or strifes among them, he proceeds to explain what he means. He begins verse 12 with the words, "And I say this"—in other words, "this is what I mean." He uses the Greek verb *légo* (3004) for "say," which refers not to mere talk but to a declaration that has thought behind it. It comes from the word *lógos* (3056), meaning logic or intelligence. This is an intelligent accusation Paul is making against unseemly conduct among Christians.

Just what is this accusation? "That each of you says, I am of Paul; and I am of Apollos; and I am of Cephas; and I of Christ." Observe that Paul is not concerned with the claims of the groups as parties but with the individuals within the groups. Having different parties is not wrong in itself; it is rejecting fellow Christians who belong to another group that is wrong.

Although it seemed natural that Paul ought to be honored in Corinth because he was its pioneer missionary, he condemns those who place him higher than he should be in the esteem of the people. Placing any human on an equal basis with Christ is wrong no matter how worthwhile his labor. Preeminence must belong to the Lord in all things. Thus fault lay in thinking too highly of men and not highly enough of Christ. If we allow anybody or anything to stand on an equal footing with Christ, our vision is blurred and our mind is dulled.

A white-haired old man standing in a museum gazed with fascination upon a picture of Christ. Having looked upon it for a few moments, he murmured to himself, with a glowing face, "Bless Him, I love Him!" A stranger standing near overheard him and said, "Brother, I love Him, too," and clasped his hand. A third caught the sentence and said, "I love Him, too"; and soon there stood in front of that picture a little company of people with hand clasped to hand, utter strangers to one another, but made one by their common love of Christ. As they talked with one another they found they belonged to different Christian denominations. But this did not disturb their fellowship in Christ.

Many people turn denominational adjectives into nouns. Instead of saying "I am a Baptist Christian, a Presbyterian Christian, a Catholic Christian, or an Orthodox Christian," they say, "I am Baptist; I am Presbyterian; I am Catholic; I am Orthodox," and so on. In doing so, they distort proper values for being a Christian is the important thing, and what kind of Christian you call yourself is purely secondary.

What Kind of Christian Are You?

Are You an Exclusive Christian?

In my library the other day I came across an article that asked, "Are You Exclusive?" in which the writer went on to say:

> What a lot we all lose by exclusiveness. We get ourselves together into sets and groups and cliques, and let the rest of the world go. Those sets and groups may be in themselves quite natural. They are formed on the basis of some common interest or neighborliness and they lead quite often to friendship. But the word "clique" by itself explains the attitude that I mean. In my mind it paints a picture of a man or a handful of people putting up a fence because they want nobody but themselves inside that fence and are very anxious to keep others out.
>
> What they do not see is the obvious fact that anybody who puts up a fence fences out far more than he can fence in. Moreover, the fence is a mild display of superiority which in a world like this we can very well do without. There is something unhealthy always about exclusiveness. It reminds me of a room where all the windows are kept shut. The atmosphere is heavy and stuffy and a little poisonous. There are minds like that, too, shut in by all sorts of prejudices, barring up the windows lest some new idea should get in. We are suffering a lot from that in these days [W. H. Elliott, *Day by Day*, p. 195].

Indeed Paul strenuously objected to such exclusive actions of the Christian Corinthians of his day. He did not object to the preachers to whom the various parties in Corinth were attaching themselves, but rebuked them for the party-strife among them, causing divisions in the Church and bringing reproach to the name of Christ.

What is known about these preachers around whom cliques were forming? We know Apollos came to Corinth following Paul's sojourn there. He preached there and many became attached to him. He was a brilliant man, an actor and a philosopher. He was also a faithful servant of God. Because of this faithfulness I do not think we can attribute to him, or to any of the others mentioned, the responsibility for the excessive devotion their hearers gave them.

Cephas probably never visited Corinth, though apparently he had a strong following there. With the exception of a passage in Galatians, Paul always spoke of Peter as Cephas. Ever since the conflict that he had with him concerning circumcision (Gal. 2:7–9, 11–14), He called him by his Jewish name. Probably those who became attached to Peter were Jews converted to Christ, who found it easier to give their allegiance to him.

The real puzzle is why Paul should censure those who were of the "Christ party." What is wrong with anyone claiming he belongs to Christ's group? It is certainly a delight to your heart to sing, "I am His and He is mine." Fellow Christians ought to rejoice when they hear someone declare that he belongs to Christ. Why, then, should Paul object to that group in the Corinthian church who were claiming, "We belong to Christ"? It was because by this they meant that others who were not with them in the group did not belong to Christ. These were the exclusivists.

Second Corinthians 10:7; 11:4–23 throw light on a situation that must have arisen. Apparently some preachers had come along who declared themselves against Paul and wanted to devalue him in the esteem of the Christians there. Perhaps this particular party of exclusivists was the most harmful and thus occasioned the writing of Paul's Second Epistle. He says, "If any man trust to himself that he is Christ's, let him of himself think this again, that, as he is Christ's, even so are we Christ's." How different, how tolerant, was Paul's spirit toward this group. He did not discount their belonging to Christ simply because they had wronged him. Instead of answering them in kind he answered them with kindness. Of course, he did not appreciate their efforts to lower him in the esteem of others. "For I suppose," said he, "I was not a whit behind the very chiefest apostles."

Probably this group adhered even more closely to the Mosaic Law than the followers of Peter. Paul took a stand against the necessity of Christians keeping the Mosaic Law, as can be seen from all his epistles, especially the one to the Galatians. In Acts 21:20, 21 we find that there were thousands of Jews who believed in Christ but were still zealous of the Law. "And they are informed of thee, that thou [Paul] teachest all the Jews which are among the Gentiles to forsake Moses, saying that they ought not to circumcise their children, neither to walk after the customs."

This matter of holding tightly to Mosaic Law took a long time to be resolved in the early Church, and in fact it is still unresolved in certain sectors of the Church today. To these sectors Paul would say, as he did to the Galatians, "This only would I learn of you, Received ye the Spirit by the works of the law, or by the hearing of faith? Are ye so foolish? having begun in the Spirit, are ye now made perfect by the flesh? But that no man is justified by the law in the sight of God, it is evident: for, The just shall live by faith" (Gal. 3:2, 3, 11).

> Free from the law, oh, happy condition!
>   Jesus has bled, and there is remission.
> Cursed by the law, and bruised by the fall,
>   Grace hath redeemed us once for all.
>
> "Children of God!" oh, glorious calling!
>   Surely His grace will keep us from falling;
> Passing from death to life at His call,
>   Blessed salvation once for all.

LESSONS:

1. A carnal Christian is one who allows the flesh to win over the spirit. This battle goes on within the Christian as long as he is in the flesh.
2. A quarrelsome spirit is a carnal spirit. No group of Christians should quarrel with another group. No Christian should entertain hatred toward or speak evil of another Christian, one who is under the same shadow of the cross of Christ.
3. Strifes in the Corinthian church took root when the believers there attached themselves to various individual preachers, and each one think-

WHAT KIND OF CHRISTIAN ARE YOU?

ing his preacher could not be excelled.

4. Having different parties within a church is not wrong in itself; it is rejecting fellow Christians who belong to another group that is wrong.

5. Paul did not object to the preachers to whom the various parties in Corinth were attaching themselves. It was the party-strife among the Corinthians, causing divisions in the Church and bringing reproach to the name of Christ, for which he rebuked them.

WHAT KIND OF CHRISTIAN ARE YOU?

1 Cor. 1:13 — *Is Christ Divided?*

Is Christ divided? Was Paul crucified for you? or were ye baptized in the name of Paul?

The Apostle Paul was an expert with the *reductio ad absurdum* method of reasoning. This type of reasoning involves the ability to disprove a proposition by showing the absurdity to which it would lead if carried to its logical conclusion. He often used this suppositional form of argument by stating a wrong premise and then drawing from it a conclusion that was patently absurd. For instance, he argues in 1 Corinthians 15:13–19 that if it is impossible for the dead to rise, then Christ did not rise. Nevertheless since there is historical evidence that He did rise, this supposition must be wrong. He therefore concludes that it is possible for the dead to rise.

Once again, he uses this kind of reasoning to deal with the Corinthians concerning their issue of allegiance. As we have seen, the Corinthian Christians had separated into groups claiming allegiance to Paul, Apollos, Cephas, and even Christ. Although the ones claiming to be of Christ had the correct person, they also had the wrong motive. Their motive was one of exclusion, one which threw out the possibility for others to belong to Christ. Paul therefore reasoned with these groups of Corinthians, saying to them that if their allegiance belonged to a person other than Christ, that person had to have done what was necessary for their salvation. Thus, since they knew the person they were showing allegiance had not done so, they had to conclude their supposition was wrong.

Are You Exalting Men or Christ?

Paul asks a number questions to counter the absurdities of the Corinthians' arguments. The first question he asks is, "Is Christ divided?" The Greek verb here is *meméristai* (3307), derived from *méros* (3313), meaning "part." Has Christ been cut up into parts so that one group has one part, the next group another part, and so on? Ridiculous. Among the various believers in Christ, no group can have only part of Christ or the whole of Christ exclusively. The whole of Christ is for every group of believers and for each believer individually. Christ cannot be cut up into bits and pieces. Yet, when we have Christ, we do not possess Him to the exclusion of others, for He is infinite and as such He can fill every finite group or believer He chooses to indwell. The understood answer to the question, "Is Christ divided?" is, of course, an emphatic No. Thus we could say that this first question is an answer to the last statement of verse 12, "I am of Christ [and others are excluded]."

Another question Paul asks answers the statements of verse 12, "I am of Paul . . . of Apollos . . . of Cephas." Paul wisely puts himself on the spot by asking, "Was Paul crucified for you?" He indicates his disapproval of being unduly elevated by some of his followers. Had he said, "Was Cephas crucified for you?" some might have concluded that Paul was simply jealous that Peter was more highly regarded than himself.

Paul had courage to ask this question. A leader would rather boost the confidence and loyalty of his friends than be honest and tell them that he is not the model of perfection that they have made him to be. It is not difficult to find fault with those who oppose us. Our self-love whispers that if they were not wrong, they could not be our opponents. It is a rare thing for a leader to tell the whole truth about himself to his friends. He will do anything to keep from losing or dividing them.

Eli, though a priest and judge in Israel, could not bear to be honest with his family. Thus, while his sons discredited the priesthood, he kept silent (1 Sam. 3:13). Who of us is not tempted to hide the weaknesses of our loved ones? However, Paul was enabled by the grace of God to tell the unwelcome truth to his devoted friends. He asked the men who showed such mistaken adulation for him, "Was Paul crucified for you?"

Of course the answer to this question was also No. This question was asked rhetorically to make the Corinthians think. After all, the Apostle Paul knew that they were not ignorant of the One who was crucified for them. Canon Liddon suggests that Paul also asks this question to appeal to the sense of historic absurdity. For certainly Paul could not have been the one crucified as he was alive to write them this letter.

"Was Paul crucified for you?" further suggested the question, "Who then was crucified?" Paul asks this rhetorical question to emphasize that it was Christ, not him, who was crucified. This second question highlights the impassable chasm between the personalities of Paul and Christ. Certainly only Christ could have been crucified and have accomplished what He did. Thus Paul points out the uniqueness of the death of Christ. Other people had died, even by crucifixion. In fact, two thieves were crucified the same day as Christ. Unlike Christ, their crucifixion had no efficacy for others. Observe the wording of the question, "Was Paul crucified for you?" The expression "for you" is *hupér* (5228) *humōn* (5216) in Greek, meaning "on your behalf." Paul too was martyred, probably beheaded, but his death had no redemptive efficacy for others.

Is Christ Divided?

Paul did not ask questions such as, "Was Paul transfigured on the mount? Did Paul raise Lazarus from the dead the fourth day?" People in our day who esteem Christ more for what He taught than for what He did would have asked, "Did Paul preach the Sermon on the Mount?" The central fact about Christ in Paul's estimation was His crucifixion for us. He used his writings to disclose the centrality of his feelings on the crucifixion of Christ. In Galatians 3:1 he said, "O foolish Galatians, who hath bewitched you, that ye should not obey the truth, before whose eyes Jesus Christ hath been evidently set forth, crucified among you?" Later Paul wrote to the Corinthians, "I determined not to know anything among you, save Jesus Christ, and him crucified" (1 Cor. 2:2). "God forbid that I should glory," he wrote again to the Galatians, "save in the cross of our Lord Jesus Christ" (Gal. 6:14). Paul very clearly placed the death of Christ above His teaching. None of us can be saved by His teaching because none of us can live up to it; we must be redeemed by the blood He shed on the cross.

Peter says we were redeemed "with the precious blood of Christ, as of a lamb without blemish and without spot" (1 Pet. 1:19). John tells us, "The blood of Jesus Christ his Son cleanseth us from all sin" (1 John 1:7). His death was in payment for our sins. Scripture calls this a propitiation for sin (Rom. 3:25). It was a redemption or deliverance from the guilt and penalty of sin (1 John 2:2; 4:10). "We have redemption through his blood, even the forgiveness of sins" (Col. 1:14; see also Eph. 1:7). We sinners were reconciled to God through the cross of Christ (Rom. 5:10; 2 Cor. 5:18–21). The New Testament credits Christ's death with effects attributed to no other death in human history. It is to this solitary and salutary efficacy of Christ's death that Paul tacitly referred in the question, "Was Paul crucified for you?"

True, Paul's death was a noble martyrdom for the sake of Christ, but it did not act as a propitiation for anyone's sins before

God. It did not buy anyone back from the guilt and penalties of sin. It did not reconcile God and man. The consequences following the death of our Lord differed in both degree and kind from the consequences that have followed the death of any of His servants.

> There was no other good enough
>   To pay the price of sin;
> He only could unlock the gate
>   Of heaven, and let us in.
>
> Oh, dearly, dearly has He loved!
>   And we must love Him, too;
> And trust in His redeeming blood,
>   And try His works to do.
>   —C. F. Alexander

Whose Word Weighs More With You, God's or Man's?

A group of young tourists arose early one Sunday in Yosemite Park. The only Christian in the group suggested they attend chapel service there. To be congenial, the others agreed to her wish and sat through a sermon that stressed the efficacy of the death of Christ. Afterward, one young man asked, "What was so unusual about the death of Christ? Have not many people died in even greater agony for a cause they believed in, or to save the lives of others? Why was His death any different from theirs?"

What makes Christ's death so unique? Christ is the God-Man whose redemptive death has an efficacy all its own. Even as man He was unique in two respects—He was sinless, and He was representative of the whole human race. No mere man can make these claims. Christ was sinless in His birth and in His life. He could silence His enemies with the question, "Which of you convicts me of sin?" (John 8:46). This sinless One was made "to be sin for us, who knew no sin; that we might be made the righteousness of God in him" (2 Cor. 5:21). This sinless nature, representing a world of sinners, hung in death upon the cross.

When He died, our Lord's human nature, being sinless, was also representative of the race. When the Eternal Word or Son of God was made flesh, He united Himself, not to a human person but to human nature. His humanity had nothing about it that was local or particular, appropriate only to a single historical epoch, a century, or a race. He was born of a Jewish mother in Palestine, yet He was without the narrowing characteristics of His ethnic origin. All races, all countries, all ages had a share in Him, yet none could claim Him exclusively.

Therefore Paul called Him the Last Adam (1 Cor. 15:45). The first Adam represented all that was sinful in humanity. The Second Adam represented the human family, not as the common source of bodily life, but as a moral and spiritual existence. The children of the first Adam might receive this existence from Him if they would.

Notice that Paul refers to the Lord not as Jesus, which was His human name, but as Christ. "Is Christ divided?" Although the Lord in His manhood was both sinless and representative of humanity, He was much more than man. In truth, His manhood was only a robe that He had folded around His person when He condescended to come among us. In the true seat of His being He was much more than man. He was, as Paul says, the One who is "over all, God blessed forever" (Rom. 9:5). "Before Abraham was, I am," Christ said (John 8:58).

When Christ died, nature around was visibly troubled; the earth quaked and the rocks were torn asunder. The bodies of many dead arose. No wonder the pagan centurion cried out, "Truly this was the Son of God" (Matt. 27:54). Never lose sight of the fact that the death of Christ was different, for He was different from any other who walked upon the face of this earth. He was God walking, working, suffering, dying as man.

Had He not become man, He could not have died. The incarnation was prerequisite to the crucifixion. The scourged flesh was the flesh of the incarnate Son of God; the pierced hands were His hands; the thorn-crowned brow and the buffeted and spat upon face were His brow and face. The blood that flowed from His wounds was rightly credited with cleansing power. This was the crucifixion as Paul saw it. He thought of it as the decisive moment of the world's redemption because the Redeemer was indisputably God made manifest in the flesh.

One can only imagine how Paul felt when he realized what his friends were doing by giving him a place that can be occupied only by the Lord Jesus Christ. What disgust and pathos must have prompted his indignant question, "Was Paul crucified for you?" He realized he could never do the work of God on the cross, for he was not God. Nor should he allow any human to bestow on him the confidence, trust, and adulation that belong exclusively to God. Our crucified Savior must have first place in the thought and heart of every believer. No other man or angel has remotely comparable claims. Make your heart, therefore, a throne for the crucified One. Expel all rival affections that would usurp what should belong only to Him.

> O let my heart no further roam,
>   'Tis Thine by vows, and hopes, and fears
> Long since. O call Thy wanderer home
>   To that dear home, safe in Thy wounded side,
> Where only broken hearts their sin and shame may hide.
> —Hymn for Good Friday
> [See H. P. Liddon's *Passiontide Sermons*, pp. 34–49.]

How careful we as Christians must be to distinguish between the honor we owe to Christ and the honor we render to those who preach the message of Christ. We who preach the gospel must be careful lest, wittingly or unwittingly, we steal from the luster that belongs to Christ alone. Is there any man, dead or

alive, whom you honor as much as Christ? I am afraid that
sometimes the statement, "Pastor So-and-So says," is allowed to
weigh more heavily with us than "the Lord Jesus says." This is
certainly true of those who follow false teachers. Ask yourself
about the spiritual leader whom you allow to have such great influence over you, "Was he crucified for me? Is he God?"

A friend of mine relates that once when he was attending a
meeting held by Dr. Donald Barnhouse in New York City, this
highly esteemed Bible teacher told his hearers that the thing that
would make him stop his Monday night meetings at once would
be for them to go out and say, "Dr. Barnhouse said it." Instead,
he told them, they ought to go home and check his teachings in
the Bible for themselves.

An amusing radio comedian of many years ago, known as the
Baron Munchausen, used to spin wild and improbable tales;
and when anyone challenged him he would ask, "Vas you dere,
Sharlie?" God was there before there was any beginning; He was
there in the person of his only begotten Son, who came into the
world. And in the person of the Son, He was there on the cross,
suffering, bleeding and dying for you and me. To anyone who
questions this, you can retort, "Were you there? God was, and I
prefer to take His Word for it."

The Connection Between Baptism and the Crucifixion

The Apostle Paul was aware of the debt the members of the
Corinthian church owed him, and of what he himself went
through to make Christ known to them. The Jewish Christians owed him the debt of liberation from the Law. Liberated
from centuries of spiritual darkness, it was only natural that
the Christians were redeemed from paganism should become attached to the one who led them to the truth that set them free.

Paul suffered a great deal in his work of preaching the
gospel to the Jews and pagans of Corinth. He came to Corinth

without any outside pledge of support. He worked at his trade of tentmaking as he preached. When he was cursed in the synagogue and excommunicated, he began to preach in the home of Justus. He was brought to trial before Gallio. Despite all this, he stayed in Corinth for a year and a half. However his sufferings for them did not entitle him to their worship, a position belonging exclusively to Christ. He suffered and sacrificed, but he dared not let the Corinthian Christians equate his sufferings with those of Christ.

The difference between the sufferings of Paul and those of Christ was not only a difference in degree but also in kind. The relation of the Apostle to Christ was altogether unlike that which ever existed or could exist between the pupils of a great human teacher and their master. Take Socrates, the father of philosophy, for example. He founded a school. His pupils took up his work, adding to the school of thought. From first to last, the master and his successors were on a virtual level. All alike were teachers. If they taught any truth, they taught something that was independent of them all. One might have taught a subject just as well as another. If a master ended his life drinking a cup of hemlock, people may have discovered how he valued some of his speculations. They may even discover his findings of the fickleness or injustice of his fellow citizens. Nevertheless, he became of no true importance either to his pupils or to mankind in his death.

When Paul asked, "Was Paul crucified for you?" he implied an utterly different relation to Jesus Christ from that of his pupils to Socrates. For Paul did not think of Christ only or chiefly as a great teacher whose work he had continued, after the fashion of a second Plato, in a way peculiarly his own. To Paul Christ was not merely the Author of Christianity but its Subject and its Substance. Christianity is not only what Christ taught, important as that may be, but it is also the Apostle's teaching about Christ. It is the true account of the work and person of Christ. It is not merely what He said while He was on earth, but also what He did and suffered and who He is, that invest His sufferings and acts with a transcendent interest.

Paul was not crucified on a cross; he was beheaded some years later as a martyr for Christ in Rome. Except for the testimony that he bore to the truth that he preached, his death had no redemptive results for Roman Christians and the world. He was beheaded on behalf of no one. Surely, had he been crucified at Corinth, the sin of no single Corinthian would have been washed away by his blood; not one soul would have been placed in a new relation to God by his sufferings. No matter how well he taught, no matter how much he did or how greatly he suffered, Paul was not a Savior; he was only a disciple. (See Liddon's *Easter Sermons*, Vol. 2, pp. 224–39.)

After asking "Was Paul crucified for you?" he went on to ask, "or were ye baptized in the name of Paul?" and he immediately exclaimed, "I thank God that I baptized none of you, but Crispus and Gaius; lest any should say that I had baptized in mine own name. And I baptized also the household of Stephanas: besides, I know not whether I baptized any other. For Christ sent me not to baptize, but to preach the gospel" (1 Cor. 1:13–17).

In the early church baptism was a believer's public confession of belonging to Christ. One could be a believer without being baptized, as in the case of the thief on the cross. To declare publicly through baptism one's inner belief often resulted in severe persecution.

Paul connected the baptism of believers with the death of Christ. Romans 6:3, 4 states it clearly: "Know ye not, that so many of us as were baptized into Jesus Christ were baptized into his death? Therefore we are buried with him by baptism into death; that like as Christ was raised up from the dead by the glory of the Father, even so we also should walk in newness of life." In 1 Corinthians 1:13, having asked the question, "Was Paul crucified for you?" he then added, "or were ye baptized in the name of Paul?" Again baptism was connected with the crucifixion of Christ.

This question clearly shows that those who believed among the Corinthians were baptized. Otherwise why ask the question? Jesus Himself submitted to baptism by John (Mark 1:9), though He did not baptize anyone. "After these things came Jesus and his disciples into the land of Judea; and there he tarried with them, and baptized—(Though Jesus himself baptized not, but His disciples.)" (John 3:22; 4:2). Of course, for Jesus, baptism did not involve prior repentance and forgiveness, for He was sinless, but it was His dedication as the Messiah. As He identified Himself with the sinner on the cross, so also did He in baptism.

According to Mark 10:38 and Luke 12:50, the Lord Jesus described His own death as a kind of baptism. The word *baptízō* (907), akin to *báptō* (911), means "to dip or to immerse" and in a wider sense "to envelope" as in 1 Corinthians 10:2. In the Christian community, baptism in water was undoubtedly practiced from the very first (Acts 2:38, 41; 8:12; Rom. 6:3; 1 Cor. 12:13). The disciples were commissioned by the risen Christ, in Matthew 28:19, "Go ye therefore, and teach all nations, baptizing them in the name of the Father, and of the Son, and of the Holy Ghost." (See also Mark 16:15, 16.)

The physical element of baptism was water. John the Baptist said, "I indeed have baptized you with water: but He [the Lord Jesus Christ] shall baptize you with the Holy Ghost" (Matt. 3:6, 11; Mark 1:5, 8; Luke 3:16; John 1:26, 31, 33; Acts 1:5; 11:16). Undoubtedly, Paul is referring to water baptism in 1 Corinthians 1:13–17. This baptism is consequent to acceptance of Christ's redemption through His blood shed on Calvary's cross. Because the death of Christ has no significance without baptism there is a close connection between these events.

Is Your Worship More Material Than Spiritual?

Three days after Paul met Christ on the road to Damascus, he followed His example and command and was baptized (Acts 9:18). However, as much as his baptism must have meant to Paul, like His Master, he did not consider baptizing his main task (1 Cor. 1:14, 17). When he asked the Corinthian believers, "Were ye baptized in the name of Paul?" he was not implying that baptism in water was unnecessary. These believers were baptized, not indiscriminately as has been done in so many instances, but as an external individual confession of their inner redemption through the blood of Christ. To baptize means technically "to dip or immerse in water." Hence, here and elsewhere it will be unnecessary to specify the medium.

Who were thus baptized? Undoubtedly those who had believed as a result of Paul's preaching in Corinth. In Acts 18: 8 we read, "And many of the Corinthians believed, and were baptized." Belief had to precede baptism. Baptism could not have substituted for faith in Christ. Paul did not start baptizing the masses into the Christian Church, as was later by others in many parts of the world. Baptism without saving faith in Christ means nothing.

What did Paul intend by asking them if they had been "baptized in the name of Paul"? The command of the Lord Jesus Christ in Matthew 28:19 was that the disciples should go "and teach all nations, baptizing them [the individuals who would believe] in the name of the Father, and of the Son, and of the Holy Ghost." Notice that He says "name" and not "names." There are three persons mentioned here, but the form of the word "name" is singular, not plural. This expresses the unity that exists in the Trinity.

Generally speaking, the expression *eis tó* (3588) *ónoma* (3686), "in the name of," means "with respect or regard to because of."

In Matthew 10:41 we read, "He that receiveth a prophet in the name of a prophet shall receive a prophet's reward." This means that he that receiveth a prophet with respect to the fact that he is a prophet, or because he is a prophet, shall receive a prophet's reward. And Matthew 18:20 says, "For where two or three are gathered together in my name [that is, in relation to Me, *eis tó emón* {1699} *ónoma*], there am I in the midst of them."

Paul did not use the phrase "baptizing in the name of Jesus Christ," but judging from his expression, "Were you baptized in the name of Paul?" he was probably familiar with it. Elsewhere he simply refers to baptism *eis Christón* (5547) *Iēsoún* (2424), "In Christ Jesus" (Rom. 6:3) or "in Christ" (*eis Christón*) (Gal. 3:27). The name means the person. Therefore, baptized into, in, or unto the name of Paul means baptized unto Paul himself. It has a final sense. It means to declare one's attachment to a person. (See the *Theological Dictionary of the New Testament*, ed. by Gerhard Kittel. Grand Rapids, Michigan: Wm. B. Eerdmans Publishing Co., 1964, Vol. 1, p. 539; Vol. 5, pp. 271, 274–76).

When, therefore, Paul asked, "were you baptized in the name of Paul?" it was as if he asked, "When you were baptized, was it to become attached to Paul?" It implies, of course, that these Corinthian believers were baptized, not in his name, but in the name of Christ. Therefore, it was to His name, to His person, that they were to be attached, not to the name and person of Paul.

As Paul looked back on his ministry in Corinth, he evidently thought, "Had I baptized many of these believers, they would have had at least some reason for their undue attachment to me. But I didn't even do that." In verse 14 he states, "I thank God that I immersed none of you, but Crispus and Gaius."

From this we learn that Christians attached themselves in some special way to those who baptized them, to the ones who humanly accepted their public confession of Christ. We are always tempted to become attached to those we apprehend with our physical senses, giving more importance to material performances than to our spiritual relationship with Christ, the unseen Lord. Faith in Christ, which is a spiritual exercise, is more important, more essential, than the physical act of baptism. When we are baptized, the important person is not the one who baptizes us but the One in whose name we are baptized, the Lord Jesus Christ, to whom we are joined. It is far too easy to follow the adage, "When you can't be with the one you love, love the one you're with." We should never let material forms at hand blur from our spiritual sight what is removed from our physical vision. We must never let our worship consist mainly of certain external practices, such as bodily movements, lighting candles, and kissing objects, instead of that inner spiritual fellowship with Christ, the unseen Lord who is Spirit (John 4:24).

It may be that, in this human weakness of attachment to individuals, lay the reason for Paul's refusal to immerse most of his converts in Corinth. They must have been numerous, for we read that "many of the Corinthians hearing believed" under Paul's ministry (Acts 18:8). Their faith was unto salvation. This salvation was a spiritual transaction between their spirits and God who is Spirit. Following their belief, it says they were baptized. This baptism was a physical transaction; they were immersed in water as a testimony to their burial and resurrection with Christ (Rom. 6:4). Now an interesting question arises. Were these Corinthians saved before their baptism? We shall consider this in our next study.

LESSONS:

1. Christ is not divided. Among the various believers in Christ, no group can have only part of Christ or the whole of Christ exclusively.
2. The New Testament credits Christ's death with effects attributed to no other death in human history. His death was unique because He was

different from any other who walked upon the face of this earth. He was God made manifest in the flesh.

3. To Paul Christ was not merely the Author of Christianity but its Subject and its Substance. Christianity is not only what Christ taught, important as that may be, but it is also what He did.

4. In the early church baptism was a believer's public confession of Christ. Paul connected the baptism of believers to the death of Christ by comparing the believers' immersion into water and rising from it with their dying and rising with Christ.

1 Cor. 1:14–16 | *Paul's Record of Baptism Among the Corinthians*

I thank God that I baptized none of you, but Crispus and Gaius; lest any should say that I had baptized in mine own name. And I baptized also the household of Stephanas; besides, I know not whether I baptized any other.

How odd that Paul would thank God that he baptized only a few Corinthians. Most Christian missionaries would rejoice at being able to baptize large numbers of new believers. However, considering the controversy within the Corinthian church, Paul was glad that he had not added to it by baptizing more than a few of the Christians there. If baptism had been necessary for salvation, Paul would certainly have thought differently.

Some Christian denominations today believe that a person cannot be saved simply through faith in Christ, but must also be baptized. If this were so, then it is very strange that the Apostle Paul—who yearned to see people converted—should have thanked God that he had not baptized any of the Corinthians but Crispus and Gaius and the household of Stephanas. By this line of reasoning this would be the same as saying that he thanked God he had led no one else to salvation but these few.

Is Baptism Necessary for Salvation?

If you study all the passages of the New Testament on baptism and consider their total teaching, no one will be able to convince you that you are not saved until you are baptized, or that you are saved simply because you have been baptized. Both of these views are wrong in the light of all that Scripture has to say on the matter.

Those who believe in baptismal regeneration often quote Matthew 28:19, "Go ye therefore, and teach all nations, baptizing them in the name of the Father, and of the Son, and of the Holy Ghost." What the disciples were to teach, however, undoubtedly included the fact that redemption is through the blood of Jesus Christ and not through an external act of being dipped into water.

That baptism is a step consequent to salvation, and not a prerequisite, is the only conclusion to which we can come if we are to avoid contradictions in our interpretation of the teaching of the New Testament. In Acts 2:38 we read, "Repent, and be baptized every one of you in the name of Jesus Christ for the remission of sins," and in 1 Peter 3:21, "The like figure whereunto even baptism doth also now save us (not putting away of the filth of the flesh, but the answer of a good conscience toward God,) by the resurrection of Jesus Christ." Here we have two statements: (1) that he who repents and is baptized has the remission of sins, and (2) that baptism saves.

For every such statement in the New Testament, you will find literally hundreds that contradict them, if they are taken as meaning that faith is insufficient for a person to obtain eternal life and become a member of the body of Christ. If baptism is necessary for salvation, then any statement about salvation that does not include baptism is insufficient. Such a view would necessarily make the following cardinal statements of the New

Testament only partially true, if not altogether false, and those who made them ignorant persons or deceivers.

Take the words spoken by the Lord Jesus Himself. In Mark 1:15 He said, "Repent ye, and believe the gospel." He did not add "and be baptized." In Mark 2:5 He said to a paralyzed man, "Son, thy sins be forgiven thee." But this man was not yet baptized. Was Jesus not telling the truth, then, when He said this man's sins were forgiven? You will find many such instances in the four Gospels.

In John 3, the classic chapter concerning the new birth, Christ said to Nicodemus, "Except a man be born again, he cannot see the kingdom of God" (v. 3). Those who believe that this new birth occurs when people are baptized base this on the words of Christ in John 3:5, "Except a man be born of water and of the Spirit, he cannot enter into the kingdom of God." They believe that water here refers to baptism. But if you examine this whole passage carefully, you will find that it has nothing to do with baptism at all. Consider also that the Lord refers to a spiritual experience when he tells Nicodemus of the new birth, but Nicodemus reacts with surprise because he attributes a physical significance to it, saying, "How can a man be born when he is old? can he enter a second time into his mother's womb, and be born?"

The Lord then carefully makes it clear to Nicodemus that we are to keep the physical and spiritual realms separate in our understanding. Man is both flesh and spirit, and in John 3:5, 6 Jesus uses the simile of natural birth to illustrate spiritual birth. That which is "born of water" in verse 5 corresponds to that which is "born of flesh" in verse 6. All men born into the world have been born of water since a child develops in the amniotic fluid of its mother's womb. These verses also tell us that similarly unless a person is born "of the Spirit" (v. 5) "he cannot see the kingdom of God" (v. 6). It is the Spirit of God that ushers us

Paul's Record of Baptism Among the Corinthians

into His kingdom, not anything physical that we have done of ourselves. Verse 6 reiterates that a physical act is fleshly, whereas the spiritual act does not involve the flesh. It is purely spiritual.

If this reference to "water" meant baptism, then at least it would have been alluded to in the following statements of the Lord: "Whosoever believeth in him [Christ] should not perish, but have eternal life" (John 3:15). This clearly states that eternal life comes through believing on the crucified Christ, without any reference at all to the necessity of first being baptized.

If baptism is essential to salvation, then the Lord omitted an important truth when He said, "For God so loved the world, that he gave his only begotten Son, that whosoever believeth in him should not perish, but have everlasting life" (John 3:16).

Here is something else to ponder. If baptism were essential to salvation, there would have been at least one Scripture verse stating the truth negatively, that he who is not baptized is condemned. However, there is no such declaration, although there are many regarding lack of belief, such as "He that believeth on him is not condemned: but he that believeth not is condemned already"—and this, not because he is not baptized, but "because he hath not believed in the name of the only begotten Son of God" (John 3:18).

Only the central passages to apostolic declarations of this nature need be mentioned here. One such passage is Ephesians 2:8, "For by grace are ye saved through faith; and that not of yourselves: it is the gift of God." Another such passage is Romans 10:9, "If thou shalt confess with thy mouth the Lord Jesus, and shalt believe in thine heart that God hath raised him from the dead, thou shalt be saved." How strange that baptism is not also listed as a requirement. Again in Romans 3:23, 24, we read, "For all have sinned, and come short of the glory of God; being justified freely by His grace through the redemption that is in Christ Jesus." Again no baptism required.

PAUL'S RECORD OF BAPTISM AMONG THE CORINTHIANS

It is therefore safe to conclude that, though baptism is a commandment of Christ, its fulfillment is not connected with our redemption but with our discipleship.

Putting First Things First

If there is one principle of Scriptural interpretation more than any other that will help you to understand what the Bible teaches, it is this: Do not attempt to found a doctrine on a single verse of Scripture, or on one taken out of context. Study every passage on a given subject, to get a consensus of biblical teaching on the matter.

This is what I have attempted to do in my studies on baptism. For instance, when we read, "Repent, and be baptized every one of you in the name of Jesus Christ for the remission of sins" (Acts 2:38), we must not jump to the conclusion that forgiveness of sins is effected through both repentance and baptism, since in other passages of Scripture we find remission of sins and forgiveness attributed to repentance only.

If it is in harmony with the rest of Scripture, the interpretation of 1 Peter 3:21, "baptism doth also now save us," must include the essential element of saving faith. It is the same as if we were to say, "All properly baptized people are saved." This is true, not because there is salvation in baptism, but because the word "properly" here refers, not to the mode of baptism, but to the fact that immersion should only be administered to those who are already saved. Today, however, baptism has so degenerated in some quarters that individuals are being baptized without first having believed on the Lord Jesus Christ as their personal Savior. In such instances, it seems, the actual physical rite of sprinkling or dipping in water is thought to have saving power contrary to the entire teaching of Scripture on the way of salvation.

PAUL'S RECORD OF BAPTISM AMONG THE CORINTHIANS

In 1 Corinthians 10:1, 2, Paul expresses that baptism symbolizes discipleship. When the Israelites passed through the Red Sea, they cut themselves off from Egypt forever. Figuratively speaking, in that immersion they were baptized unto Moses, for thereby they declared themselves his followers and left everything to go with him. Thus Paul argues: To whom were ye then baptized? To whom did you pledge yourselves in discipleship? If to Christ, why do you name yourselves by the name of Paul? (See F. W. Robertson, in the *Biblical Illustrator*, 1 Cor. 1.)

Why did Paul not baptize anyone except Crispus, Gaius, and the household of Stephanas? The answer is found in verse 17, "For Christ sent me not to baptize, but to preach the gospel." It was a matter of priority with Paul. Preaching the gospel was more important because that saves a person from sin, not the physical act of baptism. If baptism were as important, then Paul would have instantly followed through with it.

Another question arises as we discuss the importance of baptism—how long after a person expresses belief in Christ, and accepts Him as personal Savior, should he be baptized? The Word of God gives instruction on this matter. In areas of the world where Christians are in the minority, the convert is placed on probation for a period of time to prove his profession of faith by his daily conduct. The one who declares his faith through baptism but fails to live a Christ-like life before the eyes of the world brings great shame to the name of Christ. On one hand, believers in some foreign lands have to wait several months and prove themselves worthy of the name of Christ before they are given the privilege of publicly confessing their faith in baptism. On the other hand, in the United States, some preachers will baptize a person within a few minutes after his profession of faith.

Which method is right and which is wrong? We cannot say with any degree of assurance. In Corinth, where paganism was rampant and worldly influences were great, there was probably a period of waiting. On the other hand, in Acts 2:41 we read, "Then they that gladly received His word were baptized: and the same day there were added unto them about three thousand souls." It is apparent that three things happened in one day: 3,000 people accepted Christ, were immersed, and were received into the visible body of Christ.

Clearly, according to 1 Corinthians 1:13–17, there is no need for a believer to be baptized by the same person who preached the gospel to him. Certainly this was the case in Corinth. If Paul baptized so few in the year and a half that he labored there, who baptized most of the Corinthian believers— since we read that "many of the Corinthians hearing believed, and were baptized" (Acts 18:8)? We do not know. Perhaps it was Paul's co-workers, Silas and Timothy, who came down from Macedonia to join him, or even Aquila, who extended hospitality to him when he first arrived in Corinth.

One can make speculations why Paul even chose to baptize a certain few individuals. It is quite possible he felt a special attachment to them. For instance, he mentions baptizing Crispus. Crispus, the chief rabbi in the Corinthian synagogue, had apparently excommunicated Paul when he declared Jesus as Christ. Some time later, Paul preached next door to the synagogue in Justus' home and Crispus believed. Not only would his conversion give Paul a special attachment to him, but it might also have compelled Paul to glorify God in the advancement of the gospel in the surrounding community. After all, imagine the uproar when people learned their chief rabbi accepted Christ for which he had ejected Paul from the synagogue for proclaiming the same belief (Acts 18:17). Oh that we too would not hesitate to do our best to glorify Christ and advance the gospel!

Who was Gaius, the second person Paul mentioned that he baptized? Apparently he was a resident of Corinth and allowed

Paul to write his epistle to the Romans in his house. In Romans 16:23 we read, "Gaius mine host, and of the whole church, saluteth you." Most likely John wrote his third epistle to this same Gauis, for in the first verse of his epistle, John calls him "the well-beloved Gaius, whom I [myself] love in the truth [or truly love]." It is also probable that Gaius opposed Diotrephes (3 John 9), a man said to have loved preeminence and to have caused some difficulties in Corinth.

Gaius was a hospitable man who opened his home not only to Paul but also to the entire church to conduct their worship there. Host to an apostle and host to the whole church! What blessings extend from Christian hospitality. Is your home open to God's servants and to those who love the Lord? If so, you are fulfilling scriptural admonition. It was Paul who wrote in Romans 12:13 that we are to be "given to hospitality." He was enjoying Gaius' hospitality even as he penned this advice. It is no wonder that Paul consented to baptize him personally. Each man must have expressed affection for the other.

Christian hospitality opens the heart and home to many an "angel unawares." Had Abraham coldly turned away the three strangers who approached his tent on the plain of Mamre, he would have missed one of the greatest blessings of his life—the opportunity to entertain three heavenly visitors. These visitors announced that God would shortly fulfill His promise that Abraham would have a son in whom all nations of the earth would be blessed. Had the Shunammite woman and her husband not furnished Elisha with a little "prophet's chamber" in their home, he would not have been there on the day their son suffered sunstroke to restore him through his prayers. Of course, we are not to extend hospitality to receive a reward. Instead Christians find God's blessing when they are open-hearted in hospitality.

PAUL'S RECORD OF BAPTISM AMONG THE CORINTHIANS

Deciding What God Has Called You to Do

An ancient maxim says, "Men must be decided on what they will not do, and then they are able to act with vigor in what they ought to do." The Apostle Paul felt fully justified as he looked back on his decision to avoid baptizing those converted under his preaching. As it was, too many Corinthian believers had become unduly attached to him, and had he baptized more, who knows how many would have joined their ranks. He adopted this policy "So that no one may say that in my own name you were baptized" (1 Cor. 1:15). Having a great following would certainly have caused division in the body of Christ.

Although it seems likely that Paul's main objective in not baptizing many was to avoid church conflict, the Christian Church today would do well to follow his example. Certainly we should not do anything that, while it is not wrong in itself or may even be as commendable as baptizing believers, could cause divisions in the body of Christ.

In verse 16, Paul mentions that he baptized the household of Stephanas also. Is this an afterthought on his part, a sudden recollection of something he had almost forgotten? No, I believe it is simply an indication that he classified Stephanas and his family differently. The Corinthians knew Stephanas. He was a traveling evangelist who was with Paul in Ephesus at the time he was writing this epistle. Most likely he was saved as a result of Paul's ministry in Athens. He may have been among the "certain men" who believed, mentioned in Acts 17:34. This would agree with 1 Corinthians 16:15, which tells us that Stephanas was among the first believers in Achaia. Athens was and is the principle city of that region. It is probable that Paul baptized Stephanas in Athens, not Corinth. Stephanas was saved before Crispus and Gaius. He belonged to a different category because he was not saved in Corinth as they were and probably not baptized there as they were, either. This must also have been true of his household.

Therefore those who say that Paul writes as if he had forgotten Stephanas and his family are not justified. He simply recognizes them as belonging to a different category—strangers who came to Corinth as baptized believers. And how wonderfully they served the saints there! They probably traveled from Athens, only fifty miles away, to assist Paul in his ministry in Corinth. Of this household Paul writes, "Ye know the house of Stephanas, that it is the firstfruits of Achaia, and that they have addicted themselves to the ministry of the saints."

The word *oíkon*, from *oíkos* (3624), translated "household," does not mean only "family," but also includes the domestics living with the family. (See Acts 7:10; 10:2; 11:14; 16:15, 31, 1 Tim. 3:4, 5, 12; Luke 10:5; 16:27.) Some argue that Stephanas' "household" must have included children, and therefore baptism was administered to babies. However this cannot be proven. First, the Bible does not state that every member of the household was baptized. No doubt most of them were believers, and Paul did baptize them, since they were the "firstfruits of Achaia," that is, among the first who believed there. Second, they were probably adults, for children can hardly be said to have "addicted themselves to the ministry of the saints." Children are not ordinarily characterized by such altruistic benevolence.

Now we come to a phrase that is both misunderstood and misapplied by those who do not believe in the inspiration of the Bible. In 1 Corinthians 1:16, Paul says, "Besides, or beyond that, I know not if I baptized anyone else." In this passage the verb *oída* (1492), "know," connotes "belief." Therefore we know that Paul is not expressing that he is ignorant, having memory failure, of his past actions. He is not expressing opposition to baptism either. He simply uses a common expression to politely state that he has baptized only a few.

PAUL'S RECORD OF BAPTISM AMONG THE CORINTHIANS

Indeed, it is much safer for us to attribute politeness rather than a weak memory to Paul because he had a brilliant mind. In fact, the Greeks today still have a polite expression of the archaic verb *oída,* know.

In verse 17 Paul explains why he had immersed so few: "For [or because] Christ sent me not to baptize, but to preach the gospel." The first statement is negative, "Christ sent me not to baptize." To have time for what we are called to do, we must first recognize what we are not to do. Had Paul taken time to baptize all whom he led to a saving knowledge of Christ, he would not have had time to reach so many others, either in Corinth or elsewhere. First things first. Our time is so short, and there is so much to be done, that we must place priorities on our activities. Especially those in the Lord's work must decide what God has primarily called them to do and what He has not called them to do. Although Paul is not so rigid that he refused to recognize that there should be exceptions, he did baptize a few, but he would not allow baptizing to become his primary task.

LESSONS:

1. Baptism is a step consequent to salvation and not a prerequisite. Its fulfillment is not connected with our redemption but with our discipleship. It is a physical act confirming the spiritual transformation of an individual.
2. Paul did not consider baptizing converts to be his ultimate task. Except for a few, he did not baptize people at Corinth, but instead busied himself with the preaching of the gospel. Especially those in the Lord's work, must decide what God has called them to do primarily and what He has not called them to do.

1 Cor. 1:17

The Proper Aim of Christian Service

For Christ sent me not to baptize, but to preach the gospel: not with wisdom of words, lest the cross of Christ should be made of none effect.

The Apostle Paul recognized a divine call on his life that he obeyed. "For Christ did not call me to baptize," he said, "but to evangelize or preach." No doubt he had a natural gift of speaking. But he did not consider that enough. Natural gifts, even when used in the work of the Lord, without the definite call of God, are not good enough. Paul wanted to make it clear that he preached because God had called him to that work, not because he had a natural inclination for oratory. Take a few moments to read Acts 14:8–12, and you will get a glimpse of Paul's fascinating and spellbinding speaking ability. His preaching was far more effective than his other abilities. Even the pagans of Lystra recognized his gift of eloquence when they called him "Mercurius," after the mythological Greek god, "because he was the chief speaker" (Acts 14:12).

Interestingly God did not call Paul to do something he was not naturally gifted to do. It is painfully obvious that some preachers should not have entered that ministry at all. They are trying to do something for which God has given them no ability, and their desire to enter the ministry has mistakenly led

219

them to assume that they had a divine call. After all, are not our innate abilities God-given? If someone is a gifted speaker and only a poor singer, why should God call him to be a vocalist instead of exercising the natural gift He has bestowed on him? God recognizes that when He made us, He gave us certain talents and abilities. The Lord may call us to do something which does not require the eloquence and ability of a preacher, as was seemingly the case with those who baptized the converts of the Apostle Paul. This does not give preachers the license to look down on those who do other forms of Christian service. God knows what each one is able to do, and He calls him or her to do it. We must make sure, however, that what we hear is His call and not merely our own desire.

An elder of a church was talking to a young mechanic who thought he had a call to give up his shop and go into the ministry. "I feel," said the young enthusiast, "that I have had a call to preach." The elder, knowing his deficiencies as a speaker, shrewdly asked, "Have you noticed whether people seem to have a call to hear you?" Before we subject others to the sound of our voice, we must make sure that preaching comes naturally and that we have a call from God to exercise this ability. Paul knew he was "sent" to preach.

The word for "sent" here is *apésteilen* (649) in Greek, a verb derived from *apóstolos* (652), or "apostle." *Apésteilen* is in the aorist tense, indicating that at a definite time in his life Paul received Christ's call to salvation at a definite time in his life. In 1 Corinthians he repeatedly stresses his claim to apostleship. His first words are, "Paul, called to be an apostle." He also begins chapter 9 with "Am I not an apostle? Am I not free? Have I not seen Jesus Christ our Lord?"

Paul was not commissioned by any group of men, the church or other apostles, but directly by Christ. He says in 1 Corinthians 1:17, "Christ sent me." Christ's call was enough for him.

When he came to Corinth, he did not have the financial or official support of anyone. Instead he accepted the hospitality of Priscilla and Aquila and joined them in their business of tentmaking. Paul's preaching in the sinful city of Corinth was indeed a result of Christ's direct leading, and he did not depend on his preaching to make a living, but made a living plying his trade.

You, too, may be called to preach while making your living at some trade or profession. God forbid that we should reduce the high calling of preaching to a profession for the sake of making a living. One trouble with the Church of Jesus Christ today is that it has too many professional preachers rather than men who have received a direct call from Christ to preach.

Since Paul's call was directly from Christ, he felt he should follow Christ's example and consider himself accountable to Christ. The Lord did not baptize, although the Pharisees accused Him of doing so. "When therefore the Lord knew how the Pharisees had heard that Jesus made and baptized more disciples than John, (though Jesus himself baptized not, but his disciples,) he left Judea, and departed again into Galilee" (John 4:1–3). Baptism is surely placed on a lower level than teaching. The Lord taught and made disciples. The disciples baptized. Baptism did not make a change in the believer registered and proclaimed it.

Paul's interest was to represent and attract people to Christ, not himself. The difference is illustrated in the account of two men who went to hear a certain famous preacher. Coming away from the service they said, "My, what eloquence! He knows how to choose the right words and how to say them! His oratory is simply irresistible!" The next week they went to hear another preacher, equally as famous. They left the service silently and reverently. Finally one said, "My, what a Christ!"

The proper aim of Christian service is to exalt Christ and not self. Whatever Christ's call to us, let us follow it in the spirit of Paul, and of the hymnwriter who said,

The Proper Aim of Christian Service

222
1 CORINTHIANS 1:17

> Not I, but Christ, in lowly, silent labor;
>> Not I, but Christ, in humble, earnest toil;
> Christ, only Christ, no show, no ostentation;
>> Christ, none but Christ, the gatherer of the spoil.

Religious Show-Offs

Years ago it was the custom in a certain theological college for the student who had preached a sermon in class to go into the president's office next morning for a quiet talk about his message. On one such occasion, the revered and saintly old president said to the young man before him, "It was a good sermon you gave us yesterday; the truth you dealt with was well arranged and well presented. But your sermon had one omission, a grave one. There was no word in it for a poor sinner like me."

The Apostle Paul's interest was in reaching the "poor sinners," of whom he acknowledged himself to be chief. The term "to preach the gospel," which Paul indicated was God's special call to him, is the Greek word *euangelízestha* (2097), whose exact meaning is "evangelizing." *Euangélion* (2098) is "the gospel," or "the good news," and *euangelízesthai* (2097) is "to spread the good news." Paul said that God had called him to tell people that the Lord Jesus Christ came to seek and to save the lost.

Paul used the word "evangelizing" to describe his whole activity as an apostle. Like the prophets, he felt under a divine constraint to preach (Jer. 1; 20:9, Amos 3:8; Ezek. 3:17). This was his mission, as he says in 1 Corinthians 9:16: "For though I preach the gospel [*euangelízōmai* {2097}], I have nothing to glory of: for necessity is laid upon me; yea, woe is unto me, if I preach not the gospel [*euangelízōmai*]." *Euangelízōmai*, then, is a missionary term (Acts 14:15; Rom. 1:15, cf. v. 11; 1 Cor. 9:12–18; Gal. 4:13; 2 Tim. 4:5, cf. v. 2). The same gospel is proclaimed in both missionary and congregational preaching. Paul makes no distinction. God Himself speaks through preach-

THE PROPER AIM OF CHRISTIAN SERVICE

ing—not to Christians or to heathen, but to man as such—revealing Himself to him in grace and judgment through the Word. (See Kittel, *Theological Dictionary of the New Testament*, Vol. 2, pp. 719, 720.)

Indeed, every Christian is called to proclaim the gospel. The word *euangelízesthai* (evangelizing) embraces more than preaching from a church pulpit. It involves the proclamation of the gospel by any means—private conversation, teaching, announcing, or even signs and wonders and deeds of charity. Evangelizing is offering salvation, by every possible means.

Paul geared his whole life win people to Christ. His states his philosophy in 1 Corinthians 9:22: "To the weak became I as weak, that I might gain the weak: I am made all things to all men, that I might by all means save some." Do not think you have to preach from a pulpit to evangelize, or be paid by a church or missionary treasurer to be an evangelist. Evangelizing is gearing your whole life to introducing Christ to people, and people to Christ. "Did you ever hear me preach, Charles?" asked someone of a friend. "Never heard you do anything else!" was the unexpected reply. Evidently, this man's whole life was a sermon.

If evangelizing were a way of life for all who bear the name of Christ, we would have the greatest evangelistic movement of the ages. I am afraid too many of us belong to the "silent majority" of Christians. "Well, I never knew before that you were a Christian," said one man to another in a Michigan logging camp, "though we've been on the job together here for two years. When the sky pilot was here last winter and talked with me about my soul, I told him if so clean a chap as you could get along without religion, I believed I could take a chance on it myself." Evangelizing means letting others know what Christ has done for you and what He can do for them.

You may feel you need special wisdom to evangelize. This is not so. Observe what Paul says: "Not with wisdom of words, lest the cross of Christ should be made of none effect." Telling the good news of salvation does not require elaborate rhetoric. The use of words is a very tempting exercise for man. He will use words to show how wise and well educated he is, instead of to help others. Man, deep in his soul, is not an altruistic creature but a very selfish one. Certainly the Lord knew what He was doing when He commanded us to love our neighbor as ourselves. He knew how deep self-love is. Using words to show off is both an enslavement for the unbeliever and a temptation for the Christian who witnesses.

One problem Paul faced in Corinth was the shadow cast on the love Corinthian believers had for the Lord Jesus Christ. This shadow resulted from the Corinthian's undue attachment to Paul and other apostles. Paul gave these Corinthian believers two reasons for not becoming attached to him. First, he did not baptize most of them. Second, he did not evangelize with words of wisdom, not bending the gospel to fit their intellectualism or materialism. He did not believe in a special gospel for a special people.

This brings to mind a preacher who was deeply concerned for the salvation of a Christ-rejecting lawyer. To reach him, he prepared a special sermon for him and urged that he attend a designated service. The lawyer accepted the invitation with thanks. He was unmoved by the sermon. However, as he left church, an illiterate woman, whose heart was filled with the love and compassion of Christ, stopped him and, with tears streaming down her face, said, "I sure love my Jesus, and won't you love my Jesus, too?" The earnest plea went directly to the lawyer's heart, who presently began to rejoice in the Savior's love and forgiveness. We can never over-emphasize the futility of trying to win people to Christ by "wise words," nor the effectiveness of the personal pleas to win people to Christ.

THE PROPER AIM OF CHRISTIAN SERVICE

Paul was a wise man. He could use words effectively. He used all the innate wisdom and oratorical power God had given him, but his motive was never to attract people to himself. In speaking to the Corinthians he was deep but clear.

"Isn't Reverend So-and-So a deep preacher?" asked a friend. "Eh!" replied the other smiling. "I'll tell you a story. When I was a boy I was amusing myself with some other boys in a pool. Some of them were going farther out than I was disposed to go, and I was frightened. To a man who was passing by I called out, 'Is the pool deep?' 'No, young man,' he replied, 'it's only muddy.'"

Some sermons are deep in the estimation of the preachers, but muddy to those who listen to them. Let us give our testimony for Christ with simplicity and sincerity, "not with wisdom of words, lest the cross of Christ should be made of none effect."

The Secret of Preaching With Power

What did the Apostle Paul mean when he said that he was not called to preach "with wisdom of words"? The Greek preposition *en* (1722), translated "with" in this phrase, could better be rendered "by means of." The gospel is a message that God has already delivered to us. It does not appeal to mere human reason in that it does not depend on reason to be intelligible to people. Dressing the gospel up with human wisdom may make it more acceptable to people, but it will not necessarily cause people to receive the offer of salvation in Christ.

"Wisdom of words" is *sophía* ([4678], wisdom) *lógou* (genitive form of *logos* [3056], word in Greek). (Note that *lógou* is singular and should be translated "word" here, not "words" as the King James Version has it.) *Lógos* means both word and intelligence . It is the basic word from which we derive our English word "logic." It is reason. And words are intelligence expressed. *Sophía lógou*, then, means natural wisdom expressed in words. Human wisdom expressed in words can never be adequate to communicate the good news of salvation in Christ. It is good news, but to the natural man it seems humanly unreasonable that God would send His son to die for us while we rebelled against Him. Paul seems to be telling us here to use our natural gifts, but not depend on them totally.

Only the power of the cross of Christ can cause sinful man to accept the good news. Paul would not rely on words of human wisdom, "lest the cross of Christ should be made of none effect." You may cause people to admire you when you speak, but that is not why Christ died. He went to the cross to reconcile sinners to a holy God. Are sinners reconciled to God when you preach or speak? In whatever you do, consider the results. The Greek word *hína* (2443), translated "lest," is telic in meaning, *télos* (5056) being "the goal." Whenever you speak, consider your aim. Is it to make converts, which is the basis of the crucifixion, or is it to gain admiration for yourself, even in the realm of theology?

The verb translated "be made of none effect" is *mḗ* (3361) *kenōthḗ* (2758), which literally means "be not emptied out." There is a simple truth in the gospel—Christ died for our sins so that we might not have to die. By accepting His death in our stead, we receive His life. We are born again. This is so simple that words of human wisdom may obscure it. We must be careful that people get the clear-cut message of the gospel when we preach or testify.

We learn from this verb also that we are not to attribute any success that we may have in preaching the gospel to our eloquence, the charms of language, or the force of human argumentation. Instead we are to attribute it to the preaching of Christ crucified. The success of the preaching of the gospel depends on the simple power of its truths, as attested by the Holy Spirit to the hearts of men, and not on the power of argumentation or the effect of eloquence. If Paul had adorned the

THE PROPER AIM OF CHRISTIAN SERVICE

gospel with the charms of Grecian rhetoric, he would have obscured its wisdom and efficacy, just like the gilding of a diamond would destroy its brilliance. True eloquence, real learning, and sound sense are valuable when they convey the truth with plainness. Certainly these qualities aid in fixing the mind on the pure gospel, and to leaving hearts convicted of God's power. Paul's design here cannot be to condemn true eloquence and just reasoning, but to rebuke the vain parade, the glittering ornaments, and the dazzling rhetoric that the Greeks held in such esteem. (See Albert Barnes, *Notes on 1 Corinthians.*)

Do not shy away from the cross of Christ and the blood that He shed there for sinners. This is the distinctiveness of the Christian gospel. Because it is distinctive, do not neglect it for the sake of ecumenical agreement. At the close of a worship service, a gentleman accosted a preacher and, after conceding that the sermon possessed certain commendable features, added, "But it had one damning defect!" Upon inquiring what this defect was, the startled minister received the following reply: "I am a Jew. I have only recently been born again. Up to that time I attended the synagogue. But there was really nothing in your sermon that I could not have heard in the synagogue, nothing that a Jewish rabbi might not have preached." "That," said the preacher in later years, "was the greatest lesson in homiletics I was ever taught." Be careful lest your words hide the cross, for it is there that sinners can lay down their burden of sin.

When you present the gospel, fruit is what you want. One friend asked another who had heard a moving sermon what he remembered of it. "Truly," he answered, "I remember nothing at all, but I am a different man as a result of it." Contrast this with another man's answer to what he thought of a sermon that had produced a great sensation among the congregation. His reply may hold an important lesson for some of us. "Very fine, sir, but a man cannot live upon flowers."

THE PROPER AIM OF CHRISTIAN SERVICE

Remember philosophy deals with abstract ideas, whereas the cross of Christ is a historical event and as such it can neither be doubted nor neglected. It is no theory of thought; it is a fact and should be presented as such. "How is it," a bishop asked a dramatist, "that I, in expounding divine doctrines, produce so little effect upon my congregation, while you can so easily rouse the passions of your audience by the representation of fiction?" "Because I recite falsehoods as if they were true, while you deliver truths as if they were fiction!" he replied. This indeed is the reason for the weakness of most preaching in our day. The truth of the cross is a fact must be related to the need of men everywhere.

> Whoever receiveth the Crucified One,
> Whoever believeth on God's only Son,
> A free and a perfect salvation shall have,
> For He is abundantly able to save.

The Meaning of the Cross

A woman who went to hear a well-educated preacher took her Bible so that she could refer to any passages he mentioned. Coming away from the worship service she said to a friend, "I should have left my Bible home today and brought my dictionary. The doctor does not deal in Scripture but in such learned words and phrases that you need the help of an interpreter to render them intelligible."

When preachers depend on philosophy, or the wisdom of reason to lead souls to Christ—which is what the term "evangelizing" means—they are in danger of robbing the cross of Christ of its power. That is what the expression, "lest the cross of Christ should be made of none effect," means.

It noteworthy that Paul begins this verse using the first person singular and ends it by using the third person. He says, "For Christ did not send me to baptize, but to evangelize; not in the wisdom of words." Now observe how he continues. He does not say, "lest I render the cross of Christ ineffective," because he would never do that purposely. No true Christian preacher would intentionally weaken the content of the cross of Christ, or relegate it to an inferior position. It is unthinkable that one should ever use human wisdom, reason, and expression intentionally to obscure the simple message of the cross—that Christ died for our sins. Paul uses the third person here to indicate that obscuring the message can happen without our volition: "lest the cross of Christ should be made of none effect." He reverts from the direct first person (implied in the infinitives *baptízein* [907] and *euangelízesthai*) to the indirect form—"lest the cross of Christ be made ineffective." People praising our oratory instead of being saved so easily, happen even as we faithfully preach the gospel, and even to the best and most faithful of us.

I knew a preacher who used to stay up all night memorizing and practicing the delivery of his sermons and prayers. I wondered what for—to show off, to dress the gospel in the wisdom of words? Paul was conscious of how easy it was to cause those who listened to him to say, "What a preacher!" instead of "Lord, be merciful to me, a sinner!" The temptation to show off our human wisdom through words, especially in the pulpit, is a subtle thing. Let us be on our guard against it!

A man who continued to lead an immoral life, despite the fact that he went to church, urged his sister to go with him to hear his minister. She looked at him and tartly asked, "Brother, what good has his preaching ever done you?" Preaching is empty of the message of the cross if those who hear it regularly continue in their sin because the cross of Christ has power to cleanse from sin. "Lest the cross of Christ be emptied out" is the literal translation of this phrase. This implies a fullness in the cross. The content of the cross meets a need in man and is a fountain full to overflowing. What is this content? It is neither the piece of wood on which men nailed the Son of God, nor the idea of sacrifice, but Christ Himself hung on that cross and shed His blood for the remission of our sins. You can wear a cross on a chain around your neck, fasten one to your lapel, or place a lighted one on your church building, but they will mean absolutely nothing to your soul unless by faith you appropriate the blood that Christ shed on the cross for the cleansing of your sinful soul.

There are many today, as there undoubtedly were in Paul's day, who object to using the words "death" and "blood." One should not think of death, they say. Think of the pleasant things of life. Such is the advice of much modern psychology. Paul knew that only Christ's death offers real, abundant life, as we avail ourselves of its benefits for pardon and cleansing and consequent resurrection to newness of life. Notice that Paul does not say the death of Jesus, but the death of Christ—the appointed One, the Anointed of God, the One who existed before He became man, and who became man for the express purpose of dying. Christ is the only person who ever died to accomplish His life's purpose. Those who object to hearing about the blood of the cross, as though the thought were too repugnant for our modern sensibilities, entirely miss the point of Scripture, which teaches that "the life . . . is in the blood" (Lev. 17:11). We do not find it repugnant to accept a blood transfusion to save our lives; why should we find it distasteful to contemplate that Christ shed His blood to save us eternally?

A preacher who announced that he was going to deliver a series of sermons on the blood of Christ was approached by a committee and asked to change his topic to "the death of Christ," because "the word 'blood' is not very popular with many of the people in this university town." The preacher replied, "Jesus might have died in bed without shedding His blood, but 'without the shedding of blood there is no remission' [Heb. 9:22]. I expect to keep the blood as my theme." Indeed, Paul does not speak here merely of "the death of Christ" but of "the cross of Christ" because the cross involves the shedding of the blood of the Son of God for the forgiveness of our sins.

A minister was preaching from the text, "The blood of Jesus Christ his Son cleanseth us from all sin" (1 John 1:7), when suddenly he was interrupted by an atheist who asked, "How can blood cleanse sin?" For a moment the preacher was silent; then he continued, "How can water quench thirst?" "I don't know," replied the infidel, "but I know it does." "Neither do I know how the blood of Jesus cleanses sin," answered the preacher, "but I know that it does."

Paul knew this from personal experience. Had you asked him to explain it, I doubt whether he could. Nor can I, but I have experienced it. Have you? The only way to quench your thirst is to drink water. If you waited for an explanation of how this happens, you could die of thirst. You accept so many mysteries of life because you find that they work. How about giving the blood of Christ, which is shed on the cross for you, a chance to cleanse your soul? Faith in His atoning sacrifice can work this miracle in your life, as it has done for countless multitudes down through the ages to this very day and hour. For "Jesus Christ [is] the same yesterday, and today, and forever" (Heb. 13:8).

LESSONS:

1. The proper aim of Christian service is to exalt Christ, not self.
2. God Himself speaks through preaching—not to Christians or to heathen, but to man as such—revealing Himself to him in grace and judgment through the Word.
3. The word *euangelízesthai* ([2097], evangelizing) embraces more than preaching from a church pulpit. It involves the proclamation of the gospel by any means—private conversation, teaching, announcing, or even signs and wonders and deeds of charity. Evangelizing is offering salvation, by any means available.
4. What God has done to win us back to Himself is humanly unreasonable. No matter how wise our words may be, we may not necessarily

cause people to receive the offer of salvation in Christ. Acceptance of the gospel is dependent upon a power other than human wisdom. Only the power of the cross of Christ can cause sinful man to accept the good news.

5. Wisdom of words, which can be equated with philosophy, deals with abstract ideas, whereas the cross of Christ is a historical event and as such it can neither be doubted nor neglected. It is neither theory nor thought; it is a fact and should be presented as such.

1 Cor. 1:18 | *The Foolishness and the Power of the Cross*

For the preaching of the cross is to them that perish foolishness, but unto us which are saved it is the power of God.

A Bible-believing Christian was assailed by an infidel who said, "I don't understand how the blood of Jesus Christ can wash away my sin, nor do I believe it." "You and Saint Paul agree on that," answered the Bible student. "How so?" "Turn to the first chapter of 1 Corinthians and read verse 18: 'For the preaching of the cross is to them that perish foolishness, but unto us which are saved it is the power of God.'" The infidel looked startled and began to study the Bible, which he soon found to be the power of God unto salvation.

In the 17th verse Paul said that the gospel, or good news, is the cross of Christ. However, human wisdom may empty the cross of its meaning for the sinner. One cannot really make the cross appear more beautiful than it is. As Spurgeon said, "They would paint the rose and enamel the lily, add whiteness to snow and brightness to the sun. With their wretched candles they would help us to see the stars. The cross of Christ is sublimely simple; to adorn it is to dishonor it" (*Sermons on the Blood and the Cross of Christ*, p. 217).

Some people see in the cross a mere act of altruism instead of God's appointed means for the redemption of the sinner. Having this view of the cross empties it of its meaning and power. When Paul said, "Christ sent me not to baptize, but to evangelize, not in wisdom of word so that the cross of Christ may not be without effect," it was tantamount to saying that evangelizing is the cross of Christ. Without the cross, we take evangelism to mean something else; it is not the gospel.

Why Can't You Believe?

In verse 18, Paul explains why he thinks some leave out the cross of Christ and consequently render it ineffective. "For the word of the cross is to them that perish foolishness." The Authorized and other versions inaccurately translate the Greek Word *lógos* as "preaching." The Greek word for "preaching" is *kḗrugma* (2782). From studying verse 17 we have already learned the meaning of *lógos* (3056), for here Paul uses its genitive form *lógou* which we translated "wisdom of word." John 1:1, 14 also uses *lógos* to designate the pre-existent Christ. "In the beginning was the Word, and the Word was with God, and the Word was God . . . And the Word was made flesh."

As I have pointed out previously, *lógos* means two things: "intelligence" and "expression or word." To Paul the cross of Christ, which he called "the good news" (*euangelízōmai* [2097]) in the previous verse, was no longer foolishness now that he was saved. To him and to all believers it the logical way by which God saves people. *Lógos* is that which is not contrary to reason. The logic of the cross is foolishness to those who perish. The word for foolishness in Greek is *mōría* (3472), from which we derive our English word "moron." A moron has limited ability to think logically. *Lógos* is the opposite of *mōría*; a logical person is the opposite of a moron.

Paul is declaring something very significant here. In verse 17 he has cautioned that depending on the wisdom of logic or expression, reasonableness or rhetorical presentation will empty the cross of Christ of its meaning or content. Now in verse 18 he cautions not to think that the gospel, that is the cross of Christ, lacks its own proper logic. While some people think and say that it is only fit for morons, it is in itself the most logical thing there is—"the *lógos* of the cross."

There is often a vast difference between what something is and what it appears to be. If beauty is in the eye of the beholder, so is an appreciation of spiritual truths. The appearance of something is always colored by the eyes that behold it, or the glasses through which they view it. In itself the gospel is *lógos*, "logic." It makes sense in spite of the fact that to the lost it seems just the opposite—foolishness.

A minister who faithfully proclaimed the gospel in an open-air meeting was challenged at the close by an unbeliever who stepped from the crowd and said, "I don't believe in heaven or hell. I don't believe in God or Christ. I haven't seen them." Then a man wearing dark glasses came forward and said, "You say there is a river near this place? There is no such thing. You say there are people standing here, but it cannot be true. I haven't seen them. I was born blind. Only a blind man could say what I have said. And only a spiritually blind man can say what you have said! Does not the Word of God say, 'The fool hath said in his heart, There is no God'?" (Ps. 14:1).

What one person takes as reality, the other takes as absurdity, a figment of the imagination. *Lógos*, "reason," and *mōría*, "foolishness," are what you have when two classes of people view the cross of Christ. It is the antithesis between the true and the apparent, between the divine unseen reality and the public judgment of men. The patients in a hospital might vote upon the agreeableness of the medicines offered them, but they would not be competent to judge their effectiveness. The cross appeals to primary truths that are not at once obvious nor striking to the

THE FOOLISHNESS AND THE POWER OF THE CROSS

popular eye and prescribes duties not welcome to the natural instincts of man.

It is related of Napoleon that when Marshal Duroc, an avowed infidel, was once telling an improbable story, giving his opinion that it was true, the Emperor remarked, "There are some men who are capable of believing everything but the Bible." What a true statement. There are some who say they cannot believe the Bible, yet their capacities for believing anything that opposes it are enormous.

Such people find it easier to believe that this complex universe emerged from the sudden appearance of a bit of brainless slime coming from nowhere rather than by an Intelligence that created it. They avidly read their paper's daily horoscopes as though these were divinely inspired yet reject the sound wisdom and wholesome counsel of God's Word. They observe groundless superstitions, such as refusing to do anything important on Friday the 13th, yet proclaim themselves too enlightened to believe the Bible because they think it unscientific. Thus, we see that unbelief for the vast majority lies in the perverted will and not in the head.

The Logic of the Cross

The other day I tried to explain something to my cat. That may sound foolish, but I was very sorry for her because it was winter and I was obliged to put her out of the house. You see, one of my children had developed an ailment untraceable to physical or psychological causes despite exhaustive tests, and we were now considering allergy as a cause. The cat was the first suspect. "Cat," I said as I took her in my arms, "I wish I could make you understand why I am doing this." Yet she lacked the faculty that could make her understand human reasoning; and even if I became a cat I doubt that I could have explained to her the logic of my action, since a cat has no such logic. If it had, then I could.

God became a man through His incarnation in the Lord Jesus Christ to reveal His mind and His character to us. He endowed us with a logical mind so that we could understand Him through Christ who is called the *Lógos* (Word, Intelligence). It is evident when reading the story of my cat that I am limited in my ability to explain things to her because she does not have a mind like mine. Even so, God limits how much He reveals to us because our minds are limited and attached to their environment.

For instance, God does not describe in detail His reasons for allowing pain and suffering in our lives—no doubt because we could not comprehend His over-all purposes or see the end from the beginning, as He can. Nor does He fully describe life after death, for it is so different from what we know that, even if He did, we would not have the capacity to comprehend it.

This brings us to a consideration of the Apostle Paul's statement in 1 Corinthians 1:18, "The preaching of the cross is to them that perish foolishness, but unto us which are saved it is the power of God."

Why does Paul speak of the cross as being so logical an act of God that shows not His foolishness but His wisdom? Before answering this, I would point out that Paul is not seeking to prove the fact of the resurrection here. He does that later, in the 15th chapter of this epistle. Why does he not prove the resurrection as he is proving the crucifixion? Well, as far as Jesus' enemies were concerned, His death on the cross was a victory for them. Although they agreed the crucifixion was a fact, they did not consider it good news for anyone, and tried to disprove the good news of the resurrection because they could not tolerate its "power."

The cross, any cross at that time, meant a dishonorable death. It was the end of a useless life, the consequence of sin.

THE FOOLISHNESS AND THE POWER OF THE CROSS

However, Paul does not refer to crosses as such, but to a specific cross, the cross of Christ, in verse 17. He does not refer to the wooden object on which criminals were hung, but to Christ Himself who died on such an object. There were three crosses on Calvary, but Paul kept only the central one always in his thoughts.

"We preach Christ crucified," he says in verse 23. And in Galatians 6:14 he exclaims, "God forbid that I should glory, save in the cross of our Lord Jesus Christ." It was not simply a cross in which he gloried, it was *the* cross—the cross of the Son of God. (See "The Word of the Cross," by W. Ridley Chesterton, the *Christian World Pulpit,* Vol. 116, pp. 138-140.)

Since Christ was God—the Word (*Lógos*) made flesh—Paul was speaking about the crucified God. Did it make sense for God to die on the cross? True, if a mere human being were to act in this way, it would be foolish, but when we understand that He who died on the cross was God incarnate it makes sense. It is logical because the action agrees with the nature of God.

In Roman Catholic churches a crucifix is often fastened to the side of the pulpit. It is so placed as to be turned toward the preacher, not the people. It is the first thing he sees when he comes into the pulpit and is always there to remind him who and what should be the great subject of his preaching. The carved image of the Lord, the head crowned with thorns, the feet and hands and side pierced, are all presented as if making an appeal to the preacher to present Christ crucified. If there is one good use of the crucifix that is helpful, it is this, for it reminds the preacher of his proper subject matter, as if Christ were saying, "Remember Me; tell them about Me. Do not preach yourself. Tell them of My love, and of how I came to earth and died, suffering unto death for them. Tell them of Me and of My resurrection." Apart from Christ, the cross has no significance. (See "The Message of the Cross," by Donald MacLeod, in the *Christian World Pulpit,* Vol. 61, p. 282.)

Before pronouncing the cross of Christ as foolishness, take a good look at who the Crucified One is. First, He is a perfectly sinless being. He "did no sin, neither was guile found in his mouth" (1 Pet. 2:22). He was "holy, harmless, undefiled, separate from sinners" (Heb. 7:26), and, hence, He did not have to die. Second, He is the representative of the race, the second Adam, who by His death canceled out the sin brought upon us by the first Adam. In the cross we see the overwhelming love of God for the sinful. "Herein is love, not that we loved God, but that he loved us, and sent his Son to be the propitiation for our sins" (1 John 4:10).

The Cross as a Revelation of God's Love

Under the stress of modern living, man may be forgiven if he sometimes wonders whether the world has gone crazy or he has. But as long as he is able to think and act logically and cope with his circumstances in a realistic manner, he may be considered sane.

When is a person illogical? When he acts in a manner contrary to the reality of his situation. If a man throws himself out of an airplane without realizing that he will be killed, he is insane. But if he jumps from a plane wearing a parachute, and knows how to use it, he is sane.

Let us apply logic to Christ's claim that He was the Son of God, the promised Messiah and Redeemer of mankind. For a mere man to make such claims and to die on a cross thinking that he is able to redeem mankind is nonsensical. That is why the cross seems foolishness to lost men and women: first because they do not believe that the One who died there is Christ, God incarnate; and second because they lack the Spirit of God within them that would enable them to recognize the significance of the cross.

THE FOOLISHNESS AND THE POWER OF THE CROSS

The cross makes sense to the believer because in it he finds full agreement between the act of voluntary crucifixion and the character of Christ. If you view Jesus as a mere man dying on the cross, you cannot make sense out of His voluntary death but will see in it only a forced execution. However, He Himself claimed that no one could kill Him unless He voluntarily laid down His life. Listen to Christ Himself speaking of the voluntary character of His sacrifice: "I lay down my life for the sheep . . . I lay down my life, that I might take it again. No man taketh it from me, but I lay it down of myself. I have power to lay it down, and I have power to take it again" (John 10:15, 17, 18).

These are the words either of a demented man or of God. The actual occurrence of the resurrection proved them to be of God. Therefore, they are not foolish but logical in the most ultimate sense. Take away the deity of the crucified One, and His crucifixion is an example of a man gone completely mad. Unless we see the crucifixion as a sensible act of God on our behalf, His voluntary sacrifice that avails for the cleansing of all who accept it by faith, we never can be saved. We are among those of whom Paul declares, "The preaching of the cross is to them that perish foolishness."

How, then, can we view Christ's death on the cross as a sensible act? By realizing that He was God, acting out His nature, which is first of all Love. "God is love" (1 John 4:8), and if there is anywhere that He proved it absolutely it was on the cross.

Examine natural law and you cannot help but reach the conclusion that He who put it all together and makes it function so perfectly must be all-wise. Dr. A. Cressy Morrison, former president of the New York Academy of Sciences, in his book *Man Does Not Stand Alone*, was absolutely right when he pointed out that one of the reasons he believes in the existence of God is that, by unwavering mathematical law, we can prove that our universe was designed and executed by a great engineering Intelligence (*Lógos*):

> Suppose you put ten pennies, marked from one to ten, into your pocket and give them a good shuffle. Now try to take them out in sequence from one to ten, putting back the coin each time and shaking them all again. Mathematically, we know that your chance of first drawing number one is one in ten; of drawing one and two in succession one in 100; of drawing one, two, and three in succession, one in 1,000, and so on; your chance of drawing them all, from number one to number ten in succession, would reach the unbelievable figure of one in ten billion.
>
> By the same reasoning, so many exacting conditions are necessary for life on the earth that they could not possibly exist in proper relationship by chance. The earth rotates on its axis 1,000 miles an hour at the equator; if it turned at 100 miles an hour, our days and nights would be ten times as long as now, and the hot sun would likely burn up our vegetation each long day, while in the long night any surviving sprout might well freeze. [As condensed in "The Reader's Digest" from *Man Does Not Stand Alone*, New York: Fleming H. Revell Co., 1944.]

By looking at nature and examining the laws under which it operates and is sustained, we are moved to shout, "How great Thou art!" But by looking at the cross of Christ we are moved to confess, "How loving Thou art!" You may look for evidences of God's love in nature, but though His handiwork is marvelous and breathtaking and speaks of an omnipotent Creator, it does not necessarily reveal a loving God.

Some people find it hard to think of God as a God of love. When you think of the sins and sorrows and sufferings of this life, do you ever ask, "What does God think of all this? Does He see it? Does He care about it?" You enter the dark room where death has struck down the breadwinner, or a child, or a mother, and you find souls crushed in sorrow. Can you realize the goodness of God at such a time? Or when you face the mystery of pain as you walk through a hospital, do you wonder, "Why is it, in

THE FOOLISHNESS AND THE POWER OF THE CROSS

God's world, if He is love, that we see such suffering as this—sights of agony and unrelieved pain?" Go down to the slums. Gaze there on the coarseness and horror of the tired mothers with little babies; the children brought up amid curses from their infancy. Listen to the language; see the sights, the squalor, the horror. As you catch sight of the blue sky, will you not be forced to say, "O living God, do You see all this? How can this sin and suffering be permitted in Your universe of mathematical order?"

You will hear explanations, such as, "Well, it is not God's doing; it is the result of sin," but that will not really satisfy you. You want to know what God feels. It is then that you should look at Jesus Christ on the cross. You cannot look in that face and say, "I am not sure whether You care or not. I am not sure whether it is not all the same to You whether I am a saint or a devil. I am not sure whether You understand my suffering, pain, and sin." No, gaze up into the face of your Lord and you cannot doubt His love. Whatever else is true, He knew all this, He felt it as no one else did. He cares. He gave Himself for our deliverance. So if at any time you begin to wonder, look there and doubt no more. That is the heart of God, and it is revealed toward this sinful, sorrowing world of ours. What more could God have done to prove His love to mankind than to commend "His love toward us, in that, while we were yet sinners, Christ died for us" (Rom. 5:8)?

The cross is a proposal to convert pain into precious moral capital, making it an instrument of the highest spiritual refinement. Apart from the cross as God's identification with human suffering, as we find it in Hebrews 12, such suffering would be simply a mockery of our woes. It is foolishness to try to see blessing in suffering if the Christ of the cross is not our God and Savior. Thus, when we as Christians consider Him who endured the contradiction of sinners and the cross, thinking nothing of the shame connected with it, we understand that to suffer is to gain, to triumph. Knowing this, we see how triumphant we would be if we were willing to undergo suffering. Jesus Christ crucified has put high honor upon human pain. He has infused into it such heavenly virtue that it is no longer a foe to the Christian but a friend. Its empire over life is no longer darkness but light.

The Cross as a Revelation of God's Holiness

Men often ask whether a holy God could not have redeemed the world without the death of His Son. Although we dare not set limits on His omnipotence, we have no sufficient reason to answer this tremendous question affirmatively. Had the apostles preached God's forgiveness of human sin without the cross, would the conscience of man have believed them? And if not, why not? Because the conscience of man, whatever else it has lost, still believes in its depths that God's sanctity requires some reparation for sin.

Animal sacrifices in the Old Testament declared the truth that God requires satisfaction for sin. Sin introduced a state of things before God which needed reversal by an act as definite as that which introduced it. God did not consider it compatible with His character of holiness to dispense with the moral laws that govern Himself or that were His essential being, but required reparation for violation of them.

As we reflect on this tremendous and unyielding law, His voluntary offering to undergo anguish and death in the person of the Eternal Son becomes intelligible. He stands, the sinless One, in the forefront of sinful humanity, and offers to the Divine Sanctity, on behalf of a race that He represents, the highest expression of an obedient will. Henceforth, each one who by faith and love on one side, and by divine gifts on the other, is united to the self-sacrificing Christ, has assured confidence when facing the awe-inspiring sanctity of God.

This statement of Christian doctrine appeals to the deepest and most legitimate instincts of conscience. It is also justified in a ratio exactly proportioned to the soul's perception of the existence of a perfectly holy Being and of the demands of His sanctity. Man is worthy of punishment for his evil deeds, if God is still to be, in the moral sense, God. If you do not believe in the holiness of God with its consequent necessity for punishing sin, then the cross of Christ will be foolishness to you.

Man in his unregenerate and sinful state replaces the holiness of God with a social standard of propriety, believing in the socially acceptable instead of in the divinely required. He replaces the idea of sin with the idea of anti-social vice, not considering evil that which offends God, but that which threatens society with ruin or inconvenience. He believes that human effort can avoid the ruin of social order and sees no reason for a holy God to exact compensation for sin as long as the social order is preserved. Having a distorted view of evil, he cannot understand the necessity of satisfying the holiness of God with the punishment of sin. The cross is foolishness to him.(See "The Message of the Cross," by Donald MacLeod, in the *Christian World Pulpit*, Vol. 61, pp. 28–24; and H. P. Liddon, *Sermons on Some Words of St. Paul*, pp. 27–34.)

Now let us look a little further into who these people are to whom the cross of Christ is foolishness. Paul says it is "to them that perish." The Greek word used here is *apolluménois* (622), the present participle of the verb *apóllumi*. Since it is in the intransitive middle voice, it means "to perish, to lose oneself." Of course, the sense is figurative. It describes the condition of the person who is far away from God, who is lost and needs the salvation that Christ provided on the cross. "For the Son of man is come to seek and to save that which was lost [*apolōlós* {622}]"

(Luke 19:10). The New Testament recognizes only two classes of people, the lost and the saved. You cannot be saved unless you first recognize that you are lost. If you do not realize that you are sick, you will not seek medical help. One of the greatest obstacles to salvation is that most of those who need it do not realize it.

A mother attended a worship service in a large, crowded auditorium with her little daughter Mary. Somehow the two became separated. The mother sent a note to the platform which was read aloud: "If there is a little girl named Mary Moore in the audience, who is lost, will she please raise her hand so that her mother can find her." No little girl raised her hand, so the mother had the police searching the city for the child. Still not finding her, the mother came back and as the people filed out, she stood at the door of the auditorium. Among the last of them was Mary. Her mother snatched her up, crying, "Where were you, Mary?" "On the front seat," replied the little one. "Didn't you hear the man read the notice, 'If there is a little girl named Mary Moore in the audience, who is lost, will she please raise her hand so that her mother can find her'?" "Yes," said Mary, "I heard it." "Then why didn't you raise your hand?" "Why, Mother, it couldn't have meant me," said Mary, "because I wasn't lost. I knew where I was."

This is a perfect illustration of the lost. Since they do not realize their plight, they will not respond to the call of the One who came to seek and to find that which was lost. They may brand His way of saving men through His death on the cross as foolishness.

You will rarely find an unsaved person who recognizes his lost condition. Being lost means being separated from God. God, not mankind, deeply feels this separation. God's concept of the sinner is that he is lost, not knowing where he is, and not recognizing his environment for what it is, nor realizing where the road he follows will lead him.

The Foolishness and the Power of the Cross

In a letter to his friend Lucilius, Seneca, the ancient Roman philosopher and statesman, wrote: "My wife's idiot girl Harpaste has suddenly become blind. Now, incredible as the story seems, it is really true that she is unconscious of her blindness, and consequently begs her attendant to go elsewhere because she says the house is dark. But you may be sure that this, at which we laugh at her, happens to us all; no one understands that he is avaricious or covetous. The blind seek for a guide; we wander about without a guide."

How many men are blind spiritually without knowing it! They are blinded by sin and do not know they are sinners. And how often in such cases they refuse the skill of the Divine Physician, who alone can open their eyes that they may see their need of salvation. When men are conscious of their blindness, they seek a guide, but these spiritually blind men wander through life without one.

What Does It Mean to Be Lost?

Although this is an age of great frankness when people boast that they are no longer afraid to call a spade a spade, in fact, they develop a sudden squeamishness when confronted by the blunt question, Are you saved? They might react with even greater distaste to the question, Are you lost? Nevertheless, these questions point up the most fundamental concern of the whole human race, affecting them not only in their few brief years of earthly life, but in the countless ages of their conscious existence hereafter.

The word "lost" (*apolōlós*) is used in two ways in Scripture. Failure to distinguish between these two uses will result in great confusion.

One use is in its referral to a person who knows the Lord, who is a child of God, but who is separated temporarily from God because of sin. As Lewis Sperry Chafer says,

This use of the word does not imply that a change in the structure or character of the lost object is indicated by its being found. It is lost only to the extent that it is out of its rightful place. Israel wandering from their covenants were styled by Christ as "the lost sheep of the house of Israel" (Matt. 10:6). In like manner, a Christian who is out of fellowship with God because of sin is misplaced; yet he remains unchanged with respect to the essential realities which make him a child of God—eternal life, imputed righteousness, and union with God. The God-given illustration of this wonderful truth is declared in the threefold parable of Luke 15: A sheep is lost and "found." It was a sheep all the time, but was out of its place. A coin is lost from its place in the woman's headdress and is "found." It was the same coin all the time. A son was lost and is "found." And he was a son in every step of his wanderings [*Systematic Theology*, Vol. 3, p. 230].

The opposite of being lost in this sense is not salvation but restoration. The believer may return to unhindered communion with the Father. The restoration is complete, for we are told, "If we confess our sins, he is faithful and just to forgive us our sins, and to cleanse us from all unrighteousness" (1 John 1:9). However, it is putting the cart before the horse to tell the unsaved to confess their sins that they may be forgiven and cleansed. Their responsibility is first to believe unto the saving of their souls. Similarly, it is wrong to indicate to a Christian who is out of fellowship with God that he needs to believe on Christ and be saved again. The word "confess" belongs to the child of God; the word "believe" belongs to the unsaved. The wandering son returns to a position which was his before he wandered away. However, when the unregenerate soul is saved, he enters a relationship with God into which he has never come before.

The other use of the word "lost" applies primarily in the New Testament to a state of complete alienation from God. It is the opposite of being saved. The "finding" of such a "lost" one does not merely involve restoration but complete transformation through the power of the blood of Christ. This is the meaning of the word "lost" or "them that perish" in 1 Corinthians 1:18, as well as in Luke 19:10, "The Son of man is come to seek and to save that which was lost." In this instance the lost are the unsaved.

Man is lost when he is without Christ (Eph. 2:12). He is in a fallen state and possessed of a sinful human nature. He inherited this from Adam. When Adam sinned he experienced a conversion downward; he became an entirely different kind of being. Adam—in whom Eve is reckoned as one—is the only human being who became a sinner by sinning. All others are born sinners and commit sin in consequence (Rom. 3:23). Because of this, man is unable to judge the dispositions and acts of God for what they are. Instead of looking at the cross of Christ as a marvelous manifestation of undeserved mercy, he looks on it as "foolishness." He cannot help it. He is unable to perceive spiritual realities, and in that sense is insane. Therefore, he can see no logic in the cross and concludes that God cannot be sane.

When a man is "found" by Christ, he is not simply restored but is changed in his essential nature—and this by the very act of God that he considered foolishness, the cross of Christ. Romans 6:10, 11 tells us, "For in that he died, he died unto sin once: but in that he liveth, he liveth unto God. Likewise reckon ye also yourselves to be dead indeed unto sin, but alive unto God through Jesus Christ our Lord." A lost person looks at suffering as a curse, but a found (saved) person learns to look at it as a blessing. A characteristic of the lost is to consider God's dealings with man as foolishness, while a basic characteristic of the saved is to consider them as wise and benevolent, even when they may not appear so to human reason or judgment. (See Lewis Sperry Chafer, *Systematic Theology*, Vol. 3, pp. 230–32; and "What Does It Mean to Be Lost?" in *Good News From a Far Country*, Wm. B. Eerdmans, 1934, pp. 35–54.)

THE FOOLISHNESS AND THE POWER OF THE CROSS

In 1 Corinthians 1:18, the contrast is very clear between those who perish and those who are being saved. It is interesting to note that here we have two present participles. It would be more accurate to translate *apolluménois* as "those being lost" or "those perishing"; and *sōzoménois* (from *sōzō* [4982]) as "those who are in the process of being saved."

Why are these two classes of people presented in this way as they view the cross of Christ? Because their condition is not static. If you are without Christ you are lost. But your condition of alienation from God need not be permanent. God views your condition as it is now, before He tells you what it will ultimately be. You need not despair of being lost eternally if you are still in this life. When you die, you will have finally and irrevocably sealed your destiny. But now it is in a state of flux; by God's grace and your acquiescence it can change at any time. You are in the process of being lost, but at the same time Christ is in the process of seeking you to find you. He will not pronounce your eternal doom until such time as you finally reject the cross as foolishness. And that will be the last foolish act on your part, from which there can be no repentance (*metánoia* [3341], "change of opinion)". But now, if you are in the process of being lost, God's mercy is still extended to you, and you can change at any moment you wish. You can change in your attitude and estimate of something that is permanently fixed forever—the cross of Christ.

Has God Predestined Anyone to Be Lost?

Every Easter for many years I have been privileged to conduct a tour of the Holy Land where I have retraced the steps of our Lord on the way to Calvary. There in my mind's eye I see the cross on which He hung in agony, and my heart melts with love, awe, and gratitude as I contemplate the fact that "God so loved the world" that He came down to earth in the person of His Son to die for it.

I realize that not everyone feels the same as he gazes on that sacred spot. To some it is just another tourist attraction to check off on their itinerary. Such people regard it as a matter of indifference whether the cross is a myth or a fact of history, a purely human event or a divine transaction.

The Apostle Paul tells us, however, in 1 Corinthians 1:18, that our view of the cross determines whether we are on the way of those who are perishing or those who are being saved. What you permit or do not permit the cross to do in your life determines your state. You may be full of good works, but they will not save you; only Christ through His sacrifice on the cross can do that. If, however, you have permitted His cross to manifest its power in your life, then you are truly Christian, truly saved.

What is the actual meaning of the word "perish" or "lose" (*apóllumi*) in this verse as contrasted with the word "save" (*sōzō*)? Some people who do not believe that there will be eternal suffering for the unrighteous say that it means total destruction or annihilation. Because of the prevalence of this doctrine among many aggressive sects such as the Jehovah's Witnesses, we should carefully examine the meaning of the word in the Greek New Testament. This is the same word found in John 3:16, "For God so loved the world, that he gave his only begotten Son, that whosoever believeth in him should not perish [*apóletai* {622}], but have everlasting life." If the word here means physical extinction, then the expression "everlasting life" must mean physical existence, which obviously is not the meaning here.

The word *apóllumi*, "to perish or become lost," means to be separated from, to be destroyed, to become useless, to be unable to accomplish that for which one is destined. Take as an example Matthew 9:17 which speaks of the wine skins or leather bags used in biblical times. "Neither do men put new wine into old bottles [wine skins]: else the bottles [or leather bags] break, and the wine runneth out, and the bottles perish [*apólluntai*]." This is the same word that we find in John 3:16, 1 Corinthians 1:18, and Mark 2:21. What are we to understand by the expression, "the leather bags shall perish"—that they will cease to exist, or simply that they will be torn and thus rendered useless as far as accomplishing the purpose for which they are intended, that is, to hold wine?

Here are some other examples that demonstrate conclusively that the word *apóllumi*, "to perish," does not mean to become extinct or to cease to exist. Luke 15:17 says, "And when he [the prodigal son] came to himself, he said, How many hired servants of my father's have bread enough and to spare, and I perish [*apóllumai*] with hunger!" Certainly *apóllumai* does not mean to cease to exist in this context, rather it means to suffer deterioration of health and acute distress as a result of hunger. Referring to the cataclysmic destruction of the earth by the flood, 2 Peter 3:6 states: "Whereby the world that then was, being overflowed with water, perished [*apóleto*]." The word "perished" here cannot possibly mean "ceased to exist," because the world is still with us. In Hebrews 1:11 we read that the earth and the heavens "shall perish [*apoloúntai*], but thou [the Lord] remainest." Does this mean that the heavens and the earth shall cease to exist? The rest of the verse gives the explanation: "and they all shall wax old as doth a garment." To perish here means to grow old, to deteriorate, to change.

We may thus conclude that in 1 Corinthians 1:18 "them that perish" does not mean those who are moving toward extinction but those who are moving toward a change for the worse, those who are not accomplishing the purpose for which they were originally created. A person who is lost is unable to find his way home, but he has not ceased to exist. And the home to which God calls every man is His very presence, in heaven.

THE FOOLISHNESS AND THE POWER OF THE CROSS

Is God to be blamed because a man has lost the way? Did God predestine him to be lost and reject the cross of Christ, or is he alone responsible for this? The participle *apolluménois*, "them that perish," is in the middle voice, which indicates that this state is brought about by sinful man himself. God is always setting before us a choice. He gave Adam the choice of obedience or disobedience. Adam chose disobedience and had to reap the consequence of his choice—estrangement from God, expulsion from paradise. Thus, man became a wandering and lost sinner.

Then God provided a second choice for man, the acceptance or rejection of Christ's death for man's sins on the cross. If anyone rejects Christ, he is marching toward his final doom— not extinction but permanent separation from God, which is misery, the opposite of eternal life. If he accepts Him, he is on the road that leads to eternal life, beginning here and continuing with God in heaven.

These two states, perdition and salvation, begin here as a result of one's conscious choice. If people are perishing, it is because that has been and is their choice, whether through deliberate rejection or culpable neglect of God's offer of salvation in Christ. By God's grace they can change their state at any time by believing and receiving the One who died for them. Notice in the Scriptures that though God does predestine, it is always for good and never for evil. "For whom He did foreknow, He also did predestinate to be conformed to the image of His Son . . ." (Rom. 8:29). Nowhere in the Bible is there a verse that states that God predestined anyone to perish or to keep on perishing. The lost have only themselves to blame if they are wandering sinners. "For God sent not his Son into the world to condemn the world, but that the world through him might be saved" (John 3:17).

THE FOOLISHNESS AND THE POWER OF THE CROSS

There Is Life for a Look

A deacon asked a young man presenting himself as a candidate for baptism when he had found Christ as his Savior. "I didn't find Him; He found me," was his reply. Truly, God is constantly seeking the wandering sinner, confronting him with the cross of Christ at every turn.

However, we are not to take advantage of God's mercy. God has already done His part by sending His Son to die for us, and He will continue to seek us even as we may be calling Christ's sacrifice foolish and are continuing to perish. Nevertheless, His continual seeking does not give us the freedom to continually reject the gospel. The more we reject the gospel, the more natural our lost condition becomes and the easier it becomes to reject it the next time because we become confirmed in our choice.

An old man once said to a preacher, "When I was seventeen, I began to feel deeply about settling my soul's estate at times, and this continued for two or three years. But I determined to put it off until I was settled in life. After I was married, I reflected that the time had come when I had promised to attend to religion. But I had bought a farm, and I thought it would not be convenient for me to become religious until it was paid for, as I would have to spend some time and money in attending church. I then resolved to put it off ten years, but when the ten years came around, I thought no more about it. I sometimes try to think about it, but I cannot keep my mind on the subject one moment." The preacher urged him, by all the terrors of dying as an enemy of God, to repent, but he said, "It is too late; I believe my doom is sealed; and it is just that it should be so, for the Holy Spirit strove with me, but I refused."

As with this man, the danger is that we may reach the point where our soul becomes calloused and insensitive to the cross of

Christ, our only hope. Or we may become hardened in our pride, and brush aside all attempts to make us change our mind and repent. Why not give in to the Spirit's pleading now, and bow before the cross of Christ, instead of waiting for some more convenient tomorrow when it will be much more difficult, or even forever too late? After all, until you take your last breath, you have a chance.

Why does the unconverted, unsaved, perishing sinner consider the cross of Christ nonsense? Note that the Apostle Paul, who stated that the cross is foolishness to those who are perishing, was no fool himself. He was a highly-educated man, a university graduate, a world traveler, logician, psychologist, and linguist. He was an intellectual giant among men, yet he proclaimed an unswerving faith in Jesus Christ.

Of course, Paul had not always held the same high opinion of Christ. There was a time when he considered Christ to be an affront to man's intelligence and His cross the most stupid act of history. He felt so strongly about the foolishness of the cross that he even thought it his God-given duty to persecute the Christians and to silence their testimony by putting them in jail. Paul was speaking from personal past experience when he said that the cross of Christ was foolishness to those who were perishing. That is the way it had been with him. Thus, Paul is not really condemning the judgment of the world here so much as he is accurately registering it.

We must be realistic about what the world thinks of Christ. Only then can we face unbelievers adequately with the *lógos*, the "reasonableness" of the cross. Paul seems to imply that it is not at all unnatural for the world to hold such a low opinion of the cross. They are not capable of anything else. What they are determines what they think. Moreover, it is not really man's thoughts that need changing, but man himself. That can be accomplished only through the power of the cross which we should never cease proclaiming, even when our hearers consider it foolish.

Man is not against religion as conceived by himself. Recent polls indicate that almost everyone feels the necessity of a Power higher than themselves. One point at which they balk is that men can be changed by placing their confidence in a historical person, Jesus Christ, who some 2000 years ago died on a cross in Jerusalem. To them, that is not religion but narrow-mindedness. Such people may consider both Paul and all others who have had this experience of complete and radical transformation through the cross of Christ to be fools. In their present spiritual condition the unsaved are incapable of making a different judgment.

If you were to gaze at the noonday sun on a clear summer's day and tell me that it was not dazzling in its brilliance, I could only conclude that you were blind. Will you not come now and look at the cross of Christ? If you submit yourself to its saving power, your view of it will automatically change. Then you will be able to confess with the hymn-writer,

> I must needs go home by the way of the cross;
>   There's no other way but this.
> I shall ne'er get sight of the gates of light,
>   If the way of the cross I miss.
>   The way of the cross leads home,
>   The way of the cross leads home;
>   It is sweet to know, as I onward go,
>   The way of the cross leads home.
>   —Jessie Pounds

What Is Your Greatest Need?

In the Apostle Paul's day, those in Corinth who considered the cross of Christ foolishness included intellectually-minded Greeks, ceremonially-minded Jews, politically-minded Romans, and others.

Although the Greeks were seekers after truth as the product of thought, they found it difficult to admire the gospel or believe it contained any practical value. Instead they saw in the gospel, not a proposition of the human mind extending into the realm beyond, but a person, a poor person at that, dying a shameful death on a cross. To the Greek mind this was a repulsive, physical act. Indeed they thought more highly of their Socrates, who for the sake of his ideals drank the deadly hemlock, making no spectacle of his death. His ideals were independent of his life and continued to live after his death.

Christ, on the other hand, connected the value of what He said to His person. One could not accept His teachings apart from accepting Him. This was unique to the Greek mind. Socrates never said "for my sake," but Christ did. Christ did not come to earth primarily to teach, but to die for sinners. The Greeks would have been willing to accept His ethical teachings, but they could not accept His ignominious death. To accept another's death as payment for their own sins was utter nonsense to the Greek mind. Spiritual change, as far as they were concerned, should depend upon the acceptance of ideas, not upon historical facts such as the death of Christ.

Furthermore, the Greeks believed in justice—that punishment belonged to the offender, not the offended. What justice was there in the offended One giving up his life to offer forgiveness to the offender? What human reason could ever justify such action? Human justice and reason demanded the crushing of the offender. Certainly, dying for the offender, which is what the cross of Christ indicates, was absurd. This case was even more nonsensical since the offended One was omnipotent rather than weak.

THE FOOLISHNESS AND THE POWER OF THE CROSS

"But," says Peter Eldersveld in his sermon on "The Folly of Our Faith," "if the gospel of the Cross were reasonable to us, it could not be the power of God unto salvation. It would then be too much like the wisdom of the world, which has not only failed to lift us out of our sin, but has plunged us deeper into it."

The Jews also considered the cross of Christ foolishness. They reasoned that Christ had the Law, but that He was crucified because as they thought, He acted contrary to the Law, especially by breaking the sabbath. In their estimation He died because He deserved it. How could due punishment be a remedy for man's sins? Had Christ adhered to the Law, He would not have suffered. So thought the Jews; and they looked at His death as the merited death of a fanatic instead of the atoning sacrifice of a Redeemer.

The Romans deified law and order. A kingdom over which they could rule was to them the ultimate in life. Therefore when Christ came, proclaiming his desire to establish an unseen, spiritual kingdom within the human spirit for which He was willing to die, the Romans thought Him divisive. Eventually they put Him to death for the sake of the social and political disorders that He was causing. How could a Roman attribute redemptive power to the cross? Certainly they were so secure in their pride as a powerful ruler over Corinth that they could not possibly depend upon the power of the cross.

There were also reasons which mankind in general would agree upon as a basis for calling the cross of Christ foolishness. Foremost among them was a perverted sense of values. What is forgiveness of sins compared to the need for food, clothes, social life, and order? Dr. William Temple was right when he said to a group of university students, "The world, as we live in it, is like a shop window which some mischievous person has broken into during the night to change all the price labels so that the cheap things have the high price on them, and the really precious things are marked very low."

What we think constitutes our greatest need and God thinks are far apart. We value things that satisfy the senses but starve the soul. We are at the same time full and miserable. We value health of body over peace of soul. Remember how the people objected when Christ forgave a paralytic man's sins before healing his body (Mark 2)? This demonstrated what Christ considered more valuable. To Him who is our Creator, the most important and valuable possession we can have is peace with Him. Because He puts it first, we should seek it above everything else. However most do not. Therefore when we preach that the greatest need of man is reconciliation with God through the blood of the cross, we are considered fools. I chose to become a preacher because I believe that the forgiveness of sins provided by the cross of Christ constitutes man's primary need. I am sure more people would listen to me if I were to tell them how to make money, instead of telling them how to have their sins forgiven. People are certain that they have bodies and appetites, but they are not so sure about their souls and eternal life.

A brilliant young man with a magnetic personality went out to the mission field. His salary was just a pittance. A large commercial firm was so eager to obtain his services that they offered him ten times the salary, but he refused. They offered to make it even larger if he would accept. "Oh, the salary is big enough," he told them, "but the job isn't!" Precisely. Those who meet the greatest need of others fill the greatest jobs. Also the greatest jobs do not always pay the greatest salaries, but they provide the greatest satisfaction.

> I am happy in the service of the King,
>   I am happy, oh, so happy!
> All to Him that I possess I gladly bring,
>   In the service of the King.

THE FOOLISHNESS AND THE POWER OF THE CROSS

In the service of the King,
    Every talent I would bring.
There is joy, and peace, and blessing
    In the service of the King.

The Negative and Positive Results of Salvation

A skeptic once set out to prove that a man's habits could be changed without recourse to religion. He determined to save a drunkard friend of his. He gave him continual comradeship, taking him for walks in his leisure time and sitting up with him nights. He admitted that it was a miserable job, that the man was so weak he could not pass by a tavern. "I dare not leave him alone," he said, "but I am resolved to stick to him."

Some months later a preacher friend asked him how he was making out with the drunkard. "I was getting on fairly well, though it was desperately slow work," he replied, "when a lot of uniformed people arrived with an atrocious band. They invited him to kneel down and ask Christ to come into his heart—a crazy thing to do as far as I am concerned. But you know what? Now he can walk by the tavern and he doesn't need anybody's help. He just passes it by. It's crazy, but apparently it works!"

To some the cross of Christ with its power to save seems foolishness because it is so simple that even a child can understand it. People tend to think that something must be complex to be worthwhile. However, an ignorant savage and a doctor of philosophy have the same common need—salvation from sin. Therefore, salvation must come in a way that both can comprehend and appropriate. That is why our Lord said that unless we become as little children, we cannot enter the kingdom of heaven (Matt. 18:3). The most valuable things in life are common to all. The high and low, the rich and poor, all breathe the same air, and all must bow at the cross if they are to have their sins forgiven. Prideful man sees that as a humiliating act and so brushes it aside as foolishness. He also looks down on the cross of Christ because it is a leveler and he is class conscious.

In the second place, the cross of Christ is foolishness to man because he thinks it belittles him. It tells him he cannot save himself, and therefore God had to act to save him. He sees the cross in the same category as charity; it is mercy. Man, proud as he is, would rather "do it himself" than be helped by someone else.

True, there are the perishing ones who consider the cross of Christ foolishness, but there are also the saved who believe and to whom the cross of Christ is the power of God. Both the verb for "the perishing ones," and its contrasting verb, *sōzoménois*, "those that are being saved" are present participles.

Now which comes first, salvation or the acceptance of the cross of Christ as the power of God? The two are simultaneous. The moment that you realize you are sinking, you cry out for salvation, and the power to lift you up is right there. As you open the eyes of your soul to see what happened, you realize it has been the power of the cross of Christ. You cannot be saved without that power. Salvation completely transforms your nature, and only with this transformation can you recognize that there is power in the blood of Christ.

Alexander Maclaren correctly says that salvation starts from a double metaphorical meaning. It means either "being healed" (Mark 5:23), or "being made safe" (Mark 15:30), and is used in both senses. In one sense the gospel narratives of our Lord's miracles often employ it as the metaphor of a sick man and his cure. In the other sense it involves the metaphor of a man in peril and his deliverance and security.

Indeed, this aspect of salvation shows its dealings with negative occurrences such as disease and danger. Salvation removes from each of us our sin, sickness, and the danger of reaping the fruits and consequences of sin. Some examples of sin's fruits and consequences include guilt, remorse, enslavement to evil habits, a perverted relation to God, and the penal consequences in the hereafter. A person who is sick with sin blurs his spiritual understanding, not being able to see the cross as anything but foolishness. A sinful man cannot be a judge of God, just as a blind man cannot be a judge of colors, or a deaf man of music.

Salvation also deals with positive and more glorious events. One such event is the endowment of the saved man with throbbing spiritual health and strength that comes from a divine life within. As Alexander Maclaren says, "When God saves, He does not only bar up the iron gate through which the hosts of evil rush out upon the defenseless soul, but He also flings wide the golden gate through which the glad troops of blessings and graces flock around the delivered spirit, and enrich it with all joys and all beauties."

It means much to have the negative results of salvation accomplished in our lives, but it is little in comparison with the rich fullness of the positive endowments of happiness and holiness that are an integral part of the salvation of God.

If this, then, is salvation, its precise opposite is "perishing," as mentioned in 1 Corinthians 1:18. Utter ruin lies in that word, the entire failure to be what God meant man to be. If salvation is the cure of the soul's sickness, perishing is the fatal end of the unchecked disease. If salvation is the deliverance from the outstretched claws of the predatory evils that crowd about the trembling soul, then perishing is the fixing of their poisoned talons into their prey and rending it into fragments. It means the disease running its course. It does not mean the cessation of conscious existence any more than salvation means the bestowal of conscious existence.

As perishing is a progressive state, so is salvation. Paul speaks of the perishing ones and of those who are being saved. These are states of heart which increase by the very fact of continuance. Neither perishing nor being saved are static states. To put it simply, the longer you are saved, the more saved you are; and the longer you are lost, the more lost you are.

> O God, not like a stagnant pool
>   With tepid depths, let my life be;
> But like a stream, undaunted, cool,
>   That plunges, surges, toward the sea.
> —J. Gordon Howard

And that sea is the fullness of salvation in Christ!

The Three Tenses of Salvation

Salvation has three tenses in the life of the Christian—past, present, and future. The moment God spoke to your soul and you looked to Christ and were saved, you were delivered from the penalty of sin. This was an instantaneous experience, a passing from death unto life, from the realm of the perishing to the realm of the saved. It was a change from having the devil as your father to relating to God as your Father. If this has not already occurred in your life, it can come to you instantly, through a look of faith. "Look unto me, and be ye saved" (Is. 45:22).

Salvation in the present tense is the power that rescues you from the power of sin. Paul clearly states this in 1 Corinthians 15:1, 2: "I declare unto you the gospel which I preached unto you, which also ye have received, and wherein ye stand; by which also ye are saved [*sōzesthe* {4982}, 'being saved'], if ye keep [hold fast] in memory what I preached unto you."

Salvation in the future tense involves the time when the Lord will save you from the very presence of sin as a ruler of your life. God gives you power to overcome it as it is all around you. Nevertheless, there will be a time when there will be no sin either in you or around you. Romans 13:11 tells us, "Now is our salvation nearer than when we believed." (See *The Sufficiency of the Cross*, by W. W. Martin, pp. 87—110.)

Salvation, however, is presented in 1 Corinthians 1:18 as something that God is continually accomplishing for us. "To them being saved, the word of the cross is the power of God." As Alexander Maclaren says,

> It is not the work of any one moment, but is a continuous operation running through life, not a point either in the past, present, or future, but a continued life. So the process of being saved is going on as long as a Christian man lives in this world; and everyone who professes to be Christ's follower ought, day by day, to be growing more and more saved, more fully filled with that Divine Spirit, more entirely the conqueror of his own lusts and passions and evil, more and more invested with all the gifts of holiness and of blessedness which Jesus Christ is ready to bestow upon him.

Do not be shocked, then, if when you ask me if I am saved, I answer you, "I am being saved." That is the way it should be. There was a moment when I received life from Christ. I was saved then. That is the past tense of my salvation. But I would be an immature Christian if I had not grown from that moment until now. The trouble with many Christians is that they are content to remain spiritual babies.

Someone has said, "Conversion is only five percent of the Christian life. Ninety-five percent is going on with Christ." Dr. Russell Conwell said at the close of his life, "Always remember that when you take a step toward God, God takes a step toward you." There is progressive deterioration for the perishing ones, and progressive growth for those who are being saved. If one is not more of a Christian than he was a year ago, he is less. If one is not more saved—for there is a degree of comparison—he is less saved. This does not mean that our salvation can ever vanish, but that our soul will be lean or flourishing to the extent that we grow or cease to grow in the Christian life. (See *Expositions of Holy Scripture*, by Alexander Maclaren, 1 and 2 Corinthians, pp. 10–19.)

THE FOOLISHNESS AND THE POWER OF THE CROSS

The Greek participle *sōzoménois*, "them that are being saved," is in the passive voice, indicating that this continuous process of salvation is the work of God Himself, and not of you and me. We have no power to save ourselves or anyone else. Our continuing salvation comes to us solely through the initiative of God. Man in his sinful state considers God's whole rescue operation absurd. How could such a man ever take the initiative to approach God and ask Him to save him? Once the change of heart has occurred, however, man's desire is toward God because God within man seeks his Lord in His objective reality. If this does not happen, then man runs away from God. That was the first reaction of Adam and Eve after their fall. They did not want to come into the presence of God, but actually hid from Him.

There is a sense in which, even in our regenerated state, God still has to act as a magnet drawing us constantly to Himself. That is why we must give God the credit for every victory; it is His power that continues to save us, and not our own. Dr. Horatius Bonar once said that he could tell when a Christian was growing. In proportion to his growth in grace he would elevate his Master. He would talk less of what he was doing, becoming smaller and smaller in his own esteem, until, like the morning star, he faded away before the rising sun.

The Apostle Paul does not deny his personal experience of this power. He is not ashamed for those who are perishing to call him a fool. That is why he adds the personal pronoun *humín* (5213), "unto us," immediately after the participle *sōzoménois*, "them that are being saved." This is not only true in the lives of others but also in our own lives. Paul uses the plural pronoun here, not simply "unto me" but "unto us." He could present any number of people in Corinth who could testify of the power of the cross in their salvation.

The Foolishness and the Power of the Cross

Samuel Taylor Coleridge said that he believed the Bible to be God's inspired Word "because it touches me at every point in my nature." Paul and others in Corinth could personally testify of the power of God in their lives. Furthermore, the use of the plural pronoun reminds us that we should always include our brethren in Christ as we speak of His power to save. Paul did so, in spite of the fact that he had just finished rebuking them for their divisiveness and party spirit.

But does it not seem strange to connect the cross on which Christ died with power? The word power in Greek is *dúnamis* (1411), from which we derive the English word "dynamite." It denotes overpowering strength with explosive capabilities. It is a force that causes a change—in this case a constructive change rather than a destructive one. It can change you in spite of yourself. This is the same word we find in Romans 1:16, "I am not ashamed of the gospel of Christ: for it is the power of God unto salvation to every one that believeth." In 1 Corinthians 1:18 Paul states that the "word of the cross" is this power. The good news (the gospel) is the same thing as the word of the cross.

What Kind of Belief Saves You?

When the Christian system was being introduced, an old Roman said, "This system cannot stand because it is founded upon a cross, upon the death of its own Leader, upon a catastrophe; it cannot stand." Not only has the cross stood the test of time, but it is the only way God continues to demonstrate His ability to shake man up and make him into a new creature.

In 1 Corinthians 1:18 Paul indicates that the power of the gospel originates in a historical act, not merely in an idea born in man's mind. At the same time that the cross demonstrated the power of God in favor of man, it satisfied His justice. He allowed His Son to die so that all who believe and accept this death for them may live.

Truly the cross seemed the climax of weakness and despair
even to Christ's disciples. Had Calvary been an isolated event,
it would have been a terrible catastrophe. Nevertheless Easter did
succeed Good Friday when Christ raised Himself from death.
This had to be God's power. Another term for God's power is
His omnipotence. In 1 Corinthians 15 Paul speaks convinc-
ingly of God's omnipotence that is powerful enough to resurrect
the dead.

Think of the characteristics of this divine power. It is in-
vincible. It is also irrefutable, not able to be challenged. Think
of God's power within you, and you will begin to realize that
there is no condition, or circumstance, or opposition, or experience in your life that cannot be rectified. The full realization
of this will enable you to live every moment of your life with the
air of victory.

This power is available and even necessary for all the children of God. "Tarry . . . until ye be endued with power from on
high" (Luke 24:49). This power of God largely works through
man's faculties. It is an energy, a force working within man's personality. It is not a blind, irresistible force, something like the
wind, but rather a dynamic urge, creatively impelling men to do
God's will, and to refuse the wrong. It never destroys man's
personality or suppresses his character and gifts, but rather ful-
fills them.

Paul links the power of God to the cross of Christ or to the
Christ of the cross. In doing this he shows that Christ alone
grants this power. It is not impersonal. God does not hire out
His attributes or rent His power. It is not power like electricity. It cannot be detached from His presence. He strengthens
us by indwelling us. He is not a Giver of power but the Gift of
power itself. Christ is power in a person. We need Him, not "it."

The participle *sōzoménois*, "those that are being saved," speaking as it does of constant salvation, indicates that the power of

God is constantly being manifested in and through us. This power is never stored within us as a reservoir. It is given to us as the need requires. For instance, it is not like a gasoline engine which carries a supply of energy for the day. It is rather like an electric motor which, through its vital connection with the source of power, ever abundantly receives supply each moment it is required.

Material power is one manifestation of God's omnipotence. God can and does exercise power over the material universe. He keeps it going because He made it. For instance, He sends rain to keep us alive. He also sets fast the mountains and the motions of the stars. From this we know that He has the power to subdue every human who resists Him. He could stop rebels from perishing by imposing salvation on them. Just as God said in the beginning, "Let there be light," and there was light, so He might have said at the incarnation, "Let all men know and love and worship the Incarnate Word," and it would have been so. He could crush the human conscience down to a purely passive obedience to the truth of the gospel. However this power would be solely material and an exercise of divine might verses a moral one of divine right. Such power would not save human beings from the guilt and power of sin. Moreover, God preferred to reign over creatures whom He had endowed with moral freedom, and who, in the exercise of that freedom, would choose Him for their King.

Another manifestation of God's omnipotence is mental power—that power which changes the opinions of people. A belief that is mere intellectual conviction has never saved a man; only a belief that means the surrender of the whole life to Christ brings life and salvation. The Lord never told us to go into all the world and argue on behalf of the gospel. I may be able to persuade a person of the reasonableness of Christianity, but even if he were to give intellectual assent to Christianity this

THE FOOLISHNESS AND THE POWER OF THE CROSS

would not necessarily make him a Christian. In fact, Paul himself considered the gospel foolishness up to the very moment that Christ confronted him on the road to Damascus. He did not have a changed mind before his salvation. Paul had to be saved before he could speak of the *lógos* (the reasonableness or logic, the expression or word) of the cross.

A third power by which God manifests His omnipotence is moral or spiritual power. Clearly Paul uses this meaning of the power of the cross to emphasize its effect upon every human spirit. Besides, many believe in the historical event of the crucifixion of Christ. However, what good does belief in Christ's death in Jerusalem 2000 years ago do for a person's salvation? Although the fact of the cross is necessary, agreeing the event took place is not enough for one's salvation. If the historical event by itself was enough, then all men would automatically be saved. No, you have to believe that the death of Christ was the death of God's Son for you personally, and accept His atonement for your sin. "As many as received him, to them gave he power to become the sons of God" (John 1:12).

LESSONS:

1. Although the logic of the cross is foolishness to those who perish, without it, evangelism is ineffective because it no longer includes the heart of the gospel.
2. Believers and unbelievers alike accept the death of Christ on the cross as a historical fact, but their views about it are diametrically opposed. To those who are "lost," that is, those who do not have "the mind" to understand it, it is foolishness, but to those who have the mind of God, who is responsible for the fact, it has a logical explanation.
3. In the cross we see the overwhelming love of God for sinners.
4. Any explanations for the existence of evil fall short if they do not point us to the cross. On the cross Christ has identified with human suffering. He has infused into it such heavenly virtue that it is no longer a foe to the Christian, but is a friend. Its empire over life is no longer darkness but light.

THE FOOLISHNESS AND THE POWER OF THE CROSS

5. Animal sacrifices in the Old Testament declared the truth that God re-
    quires satisfaction for sin. Sin introduced a state of things before God
    which needed to be reversed by an act as definite as that which intro-
    duced it. God did not consider it compatible with His character of ho-
    liness to dispense with the moral laws that govern Himself, or that were
    His essential being, but required reparation if for violation of them. As
    we reflect on this tremendous and unyielding law, His voluntary of-
    fering to undergo anguish and death in the person of the eternal Son
    becomes intelligible.

6. Man in his unregenerate and sinful state replaces God's holiness with
    a social standard of propriety, believing in the socially acceptable instead
    of the divinely required. He replaces the idea of sin with the idea of
    anti-social vice, not considering evil that which offends God, but that
    which threatens society with ruin or inconvenience.

7. The New Testament recognizes only two classes of people, the lost and
    the saved. No one can be saved unless he first recognizes that he is lost.

8. Nowhere in the Bible can a verse be found that states that God pre-
    destined anyone to perish or to keep on perishing. The lost have only
    themselves to blame if they are wandering sinners.

9. Christ connected the value of what He said to His person. One could
    not accept His teachings apart from accepting Him.

10. To be saved is to be healed from the sickness of sin and to be set in
    safety. The saved person is endowed with throbbing spiritual health and
    the strength that comes from a divine life within.

11. Neither perishing nor being saved are static states. To put it simply, the
    longer a person is saved, the more saved he is; and the longer he is lost,
    the more lost he is.

12. Salvation has three tenses in the life of the Christian—past, present,
    and future. Salvation in the past tense is the moment when the Chris-
    tian received life from Christ. Salvation in the present tense is the power
    that rescues us from the power of sin. Salvation in the future tense in-
    volves the time when the Lord will save us from the very presence of
    sin as ruler of our lives.

13. In 1 Corinthians 1:18 Paul indicates that the power of the gospel
    originates in a historical act, not merely in an idea born in man's
    mind. At the same time that the cross demonstrated the power of God
    in favor of man, it satisfied His justice.

THE FOOLISHNESS AND THE POWER OF THE CROSS

1 Cor. 1:19
The Wisdom of the Wise

For it is written, I will destroy the wisdom of the wise, and will bring to nothing the understanding of the prudent.

Two boys stood at the edge of a frozen pond. One of them said to the other, "Billy, I believe it will bear our weight." "Do you?" asked the other. "Yes." "Then get on it." "No," said he, "I don't want to." "Then," said the other, "you don't believe it will bear you." He was right. In the same manner, if a man stands outside the finished work of Christ on the cross and says, "I believe that; I believe it is a valid philosophy; I believe that it is enough to save a man," that man is not saved. He must step out on his belief, or it is merely a worthless profession on his part.

Peter Eldersveld illustrates it this way. He says there was a rich Christian who had a large company of employees, many of whom owed him money. He was constantly trying to teach them something about Christianity, and one day he hit upon a plan. He posted a notice on his property that said, "All those who will come to my office between 11 and 12 o'clock on Thursday morning to present an honest statement of their debts will have them canceled at once." The debtors read the notice with a great deal of skepticism, and on Thursday morning, although they gathered in the street in front of his office, not one of them went to the door. Instead, they murmured and gossiped and complained about their employer, and ridiculed the notice he had posted. They said it did not make sense.

But finally, at a quarter to 12, one man jumped forward, dashed up the steps into the office, and presented his statement. "Why are you here?" the rich man asked him. "Because you promised to cancel the debts of all those who would come as you instructed," the other replied. "And do you believe the promise?" "Yes, I do." "Why do you believe it?" persisted his employer. "Because, although it was too much for me to understand, I know that you are a good man who would not deceive anyone." The rich man took the bill and marked it "Paid in full." At which the poor man, overcome, cried out. "I knew it! I told them so! They said it couldn't be true, and now I'm going out to show them!"

"Wait," said his benefactor, "it's not quite 12 o'clock. The others are not entitled to any special proof of my sincerity." When the clock struck 12, the forgiven debtor ran out waving his receipt in the face of his fellows. With a mad rush they made for the door, but it was too late. The door was locked!

At the end of the world, with all of its foolishness, when the eyes of all will be opened, there are going to be many self-styled wise men who will discover too late that the word of the cross was not the nonsense that they supposed it to be after all. God forbid that you should be one of them! (See "The Folly of Our Faith," by Peter Eldersveld, The Back to God Hour.)

Whose Word Should You Take?

Unregenerate man's attitude toward God's purposes has always been characterized by pride and rejection. Indeed, this attitude existed long before the historical event of Christ's crucifixion and continues today.

Paul refers to the prophecy of Isaiah 29:14 where God condemned the attitude of the men of Judah when Sennacherib threatened their country. God had told His people that He would deliver them and not to focus their confidence upon their human leaders. Instead, they began talking about an alliance with Egypt and thus incurred the wrath of the Assyrians, bringing about the subsequent destruction of Judah. How prone man has ever been to trust his own wisdom and the help of his fellowman rather than placing confidence in God and His promises! God seems so far away when the enemy is at hand.

Thus in 1 Corinthians 1:19 Paul says, "For it is written, I will destroy the wisdom of the wise, and will bring to nothing the understanding of the prudent." The expression for "it is written" in Greek is *gégraptai* (1125), which is in the perfect tense, indicating finality. God wrote it and it stands forever true. "For whatsoever things were written aforetime were written for our learning, that we through patience and comfort of the Scriptures might have hope" (Rom. 15:4). Whenever we find ourselves being disturbed by the attitude of our contemporaries toward God, we shall always do well to look into the Scriptures, and we will understand our times better.

The thing that impresses me about these constant references to the past in Paul's writings is that they always refer to the written word, never to the oral traditions that have always existed. The Apostle Paul expresses no confidence at all in traditions. His references are always to the Scriptures—those things that were written, not those transmitted by word of mouth. The reason I mention this is that some churches today, when called upon to justify certain of their practices that are not based on the Scriptures, fall back upon oral traditions. This is definitely contrary to the practice of the Apostle Paul. Look up in an exhaustive concordance how many times he says, "it is written." It will amaze you. Romans 1:17; 2:24; 3:4, 10; 1 Corinthians 1:31; 2:9; 3:19; 10:7; 15:45 are just a few instances.

We find in Revelation 2 and 3, that when the Lord wanted to convey messages to the existing seven churches of Asia Minor, He did not direct that they be transmitted by word of mouth. Instead in every instance He said "Write." The written word was safest for immediate use and for accurate transmittal through the ages. Martin Luther has expressed the same feeling in his poem, "God's Unchanging Word":

> For feelings come and feelings go,
> And feelings are deceiving;
> My warrant is the word of God,
> Naught else is worth believing.
>
> I will trust in God's unchanging word
> Till soul and body sever;
> For, though all things shall pass away,
> His word shall stand forever.

Can Wisdom Save You?

In quoting from the Old Testament, the Apostle Paul does not always strive either to translate exactly from the Hebrew or to quote exactly from the Septuagint Greek translation. We shall take Isaiah 29:14, then, as he wrote it in 1 Corinthians 1:19. Literally translated it reads: "I shall destroy the wisdom of the wise [plural], and the prudence of the prudent I shall reject."

In verse 18, where Paul said that to those who perish the word of the cross is foolishness, the Greek word for "perish" is *apolluménois* (622). Now, in his quotation from Isaiah 29:14, the first word is *apolō*, meaning "to cause to perish," exactly the same verb in the first person singular future indicative. In the participle *apolluménoi*, which is in the middle voice, we see man causing his own destruction, his own perishing. He is responsible for this. As a result of man's fall he cannot see the value of Christ dying for him on the cross. Man himself destroys his ability to see God's reconciliation through the cross.

God never sends any man to hell. Those who reject His offer of salvation have chosen to go there themselves. How could God force any man to be with Him eternally in heaven if on earth he chose to call God a fool for loving him enough to die for him? We may say that we never went that far. Let us not fool ourselves. All who have not accepted Christ's invitation to come to Him by way of the cross, have in effect called it a foolish notion, not worthy of their serious consideration.

Though *apolluménoi* in verse 18 speaks of man as the agent of his own perishing, *apolō*, "I shall destroy or cause to perish," in verse 19 makes God the active subject of that which is going to take place. In effect, God says, I am going to do this. What is He going to do? In verse 18 we read that to those who are being saved the word of the cross is the power [*dúnamis* {1411}], of God. In verse 19 Paul goes on to show how God is able to apply this power. His basic purpose is to save people. To save them God has to do something about what makes them take the attitude they do toward the cross of His Son. That is their wisdom—human wisdom. That is what causes them to call the cross "foolishness." When man's wisdom is proud enough to call God a fool for what He did at Calvary, then God is going to use His power to destroy what hinders man from believing and being saved. He is going to smash man's wisdom to pieces.

The ensuing verses clarify that Paul is speaking of human wisdom here: "Hath not God made foolish the wisdom of this world? For after that in the wisdom of God the world by wisdom knew not God, it pleased God by the foolishness of preaching to save them that believe" (1 Cor. 1:20, 21). This points to a definite distinction between the wisdom of man and the wisdom of God. In Isaiah's day the men of Judah thought aligning themselves with the Egyptians would bring them safety. Indeed, self-sufficient man has ever thought that by depending on his strength and the assistance of his fellowmen he, too, could be safe.

Human wisdom is the wisdom of the senses. It is the wisdom of physical strength and military might instead of dependence upon God's promise of deliverance. If that is our attitude, then the first thing the Lord must do to save us is to destroy our know-it-all confidence and our dependence on self and others to take care of our salvation.

Wisdom or the faculty of thinking is what distinguishes man from all other creatures. God gave man wisdom so that he might be able to communicate with his Maker and order his life in harmony with divine wisdom. Man used it however to seek more knowledge. Notice that he did not eat of the tree of life, but of the tree of the knowledge of good and evil. He wanted to be equal with God. Thus, his wisdom degenerated from the divine to the merely human. He chose to disobey God, and from then on he has been separated from God.

When Adam realized the consequence of his choice, he would no doubt have attempted to eat of the Tree of Life, but God would not permit that. "And the Lord God said, Behold, the man is become as one of us, to know good and evil: and now, lest he put forth his hand, and take also of the tree of life, and eat, and live forever: Therefore, the Lord God sent him forth from the garden of Eden, to till the ground from whence he was taken" (Gen. 3:22, 23). Fallen man would have sought to save himself by belatedly eating of the Tree of Life, but God intervened. We cannot by our stratagems undo our sin. Our wisdom may prompt us to believe we can, but God says No! I must deliver you from your idea of self-salvation. I must cause your wisdom to perish.

The first step in salvation, then, is the recognition that we cannot save ourselves. We may think it a foolish act that God sent Christ to die on a tree for us. The tree of life in the garden of Eden was intended for man before his fall. It was not the tree of redemption, but of the perpetuation of life. God had to plant another tree of life, the cross of Christ, for fallen man's redemption. This is essential for each individual's salvation.

Moreover God says, "I . . . will bring to nothing [or set aside] the understanding of the prudent." The meaning of the verb *athetēsō* (114) here is "set aside." It is derived from the privative *a* and the verb *títhēmi* (5087), "to place." "I shall place aside the prudence of the prudent." The word for "prudence" is *súnesis* (4907), which is a particular application of wisdom. It is the faculty of comprehension, intelligence, shrewdness, insight, understanding—the faculty of critical judgment. Before God can save a soul, He has to put aside his faculty of understanding.

"But," you say, "how can I believe without understanding?" No unbeliever can understand the logic of God's salvation. It is beyond him. There is nothing anyone can do to save himself, in spite of what mankind's fallen and corrupt intelligence says to the contrary. The only hope is to be wise enough to recognize this fact, and to accept by faith the word of God that if we are to be saved we must come to the tree of life, the cross of Christ.

Once we are saved, our understanding will be enlightened, and we will surely know God and His plan for our lives. Likewise, before our salvation everything about God is a mystery, but afterward the God of all mysteries becomes our wisdom. Once Christ dwells in our heart by faith, then much that was mysterious and unfathomable about God becomes clear.

> Wisdom of God, we would by Thee be taught;
> Control our minds, direct our ev'ry thought;
> Knowledge alone life's problems cannot meet;
> We learn to live while sitting at Thy feet.
>
> Incarnate Truth, help us Thy truth to learn,
> Prone to embrace the falsehood we would spurn,

THE WISDOM OF THE WISE

Groping in error's maze for verity;
Thou art the Truth we need to make us free.
                              —Bob Jones, Jr.

LESSONS:

1. Unregenerate man's attitude toward God's purposes has always been characterized by pride and rejection.
2. Whenever we find ourselves being disturbed by the attitude of our contemporaries toward God, we shall always do well to look into the Scriptures, and we will understand our own times better.
3. The Apostle Paul expresses confidence in the Scriptures, not in oral traditions.
4. The written word was safest for immediate use and for accurate transmittal through the ages.

| 1 Cor. 1:20 | *Where Is the Wise?* |

Where is the wise? where is the scribe? where is the disputer of this world? hath not God made foolish the wisdom of this world?

"Where is the wise?" the Apostle Paul asked the people of Corinth more than 1900 years ago. In 1 Corinthians 1:20, the Greek word for "wise" is *sophós* (4680). People of the Ancient World called wise Greeks sophists. Today the term "sophist" is no compliment since it means one who extends a false line of argument, sometimes with the purpose of deceitfully reaching his goal. The sophists of old soon became known as philosophers, a word we still use, meaning to be a "friend (*phíloi*, [5384]) of wisdom (*sophías*, 4678)." Of course, Paul here challenges the person who thinks himself wise while rejecting God's plan for man, in particular God's plan of salvation through the cross of Christ. No one is at all wise who refuses to let an almighty God save him in the way that He has deemed necessary.

The Folly of the Wise

Adolf Hitler said, "Nothing will prevent me from tearing up Christianity, root and branch. . . . We are not out against 101 different kinds of Christianity, but against Christianity itself. All people who profess creeds . . . are traitors to the people. Even those Christians who really want to serve the people . . . we have to suppress. I myself am a heathen to the core!" The rate of Hitler's success in making good his boast is obvious from reading the words of a German prisoner camp chaplain. He wrote, "I wish you could have been present to see with what avidity the Bibles were received by the German prisoners of war. I am here to tell you that Hitler has not succeeded in eradicating the hope of the Christian faith from the hearts of his people." "Where is the wise?" Where is Hitler now?

It is said that the famous atheist Tom Paine, who wrote *The Age of Reason,* once asked Benjamin Franklin what he thought of the Bible. The only reply from Franklin was, "Tom, he who spits against the wind spits in his own face!"

In verse 20 Paul still has in mind the quotation from Isaiah he mentioned in verse 19. What resulted when the men of Judah forsook Jehovah's counsel and decided to place their trust in human wisdom? Who liberated them? Not the Egyptians or themselves, but God Himself. Where are the wise leaders who thought safety and salvation from the Assyrians lay in an alliance with Egypt? Events proved otherwise. The Assyrian conqueror with his staff of clerks, accountants, and takers of inventory, who registered the details of the spoil of a captured city, disappeared (see Is. 33:18).

As the *International Critical Commentary* says:

> On the tablet of Shalmaneser in the Assyrian Gallery of the British Museum there is a surprisingly exact picture of the scene described by Isaiah. The marvelous disappearance of the invading host was to Isaiah a signal vindication of Jehovah's power and care, and also a refutation, not so much of the conqueror's "scribes" as of the worldly counselors at Jerusalem, who had first thought to meet the invader by an alliance with Egypt, or other methods of statecraft, and had then relapsed into demoralized despair. St. Paul's use of the passage, therefore, although very free, is not alien to its historical setting. [See 1 Corinthians, p. 19.]

WHERE IS THE WISE?

Look at history, Paul seems to say, and you will not find the one who thought himself so wise proven to be right. In the case of Judah, it was not Egypt that saved her but the Lord. Where, therefore, is the wise who insisted that trusting the Egyptians is better than trusting God? "Woe to them that go down to Egypt for help; and stay on horses, and trust in chariots because they are many; and in horsemen because they are very strong, but they look not unto the Holy One of Israel, neither seek the Lord! . . . Now the Egyptians are men, and not God" (Is. 31:1, 3).

The word "wise" (*sophós*) in 1 Corinthians 1:20 is not preceded by the definite article. This is true of the other two adjectival nouns, "scribe" and "disputer." This indicates that Paul is not ridiculing the really wise, the true men of letters and the true arguer on behalf of God. These three constitute a class of their own. (See A. T. Robertson, *A Grammar of the Greek New Testament*, pp. 757, 764.) Paul is not against those who demonstrate true wisdom, education, and logic. He challenges those fools who think themselves wise, and his generation as well as ours is full of them.

Then Paul directs his challenge to another person he calls *grammateús* (1122), "scribe." Isaiah 33:18 asks the same question, "Where is the scribe?" It refers to the person who has something to do with writing, *graphē* (1124), from which the word "orthography" is derived—referring to correct writing or spelling. He was a man of letters, of education. Acts 19:35 is the only instance in the New Testament which uses this word as the title of an Ephesian official in the ordinary Greek sense of "clerk" or "secretary." In fact, this is the Modern Greek word for "secretary" today.

In the Hebrew sense, however, scribes were the theologians of the time of the Lord Jesus and of Paul. Paul himself seems to have been an ordained scribe, since he had a vote and a part in capital prosecutions (Acts 26:10). Thus we see that before his salvation, Paul was wise in his own eyes. He derived his condemnation of these attitudes against the cross of Christ's saving power from his personal experience. Steeped in his traditional theological training, he fancied himself too smart for the cross of Christ. The Lord Jesus charged these scribes with lacking humility (Matt. 23:5), being selfish (Mark 12:40), and being insincere (Mark 12:40). They did not practice what they demanded in their teaching and preaching (Luke 11:46).

Thus Paul challenges the philosopher and the theologian by saying, "Where [the] wise? where [the] scribe or theologian?" Two sections of learning, philosophy and theology, can be so devoid of the Spirit of God that they consider the central theme of Christianity—the cross of Christ—foolishness. Paul says you can be a philosopher or a theologian and an utter fool as far as God is concerned. The apostle was one himself before his salvation. The poet Cowper was right when he said,

> Knowledge is proud that he has learned so much;
> Wisdom is humble that he knows no more.

Why Some Men Cannot Think Straight

If you were to visit Athens, Greece, you would find on the newsstands a magazine called *Suzḗtēsis* (4803), "Discussion" or "Debate." Interestingly enough, this comes from the same root as the word *suzētētēs*, "disputer," which Paul used in 1 Corinthians 1:20—the only instance in the New Testament where we find this word used to describe man. It comes from the conjunction *sún* (4862), meaning "with" and the verb *zētéō* (2212), meaning "look for or search out."

The word as used by Paul, "disputer or arguer," refers to the person who searches with others to find truth or solutions to stated problems. The Greeks were and are great at that. In ancient times they sat under the market porch or portico (*stoá*, 4745) and argued about everything under the sun. Today they sit in coffee houses and argue about how their own country and the world should be run. It is no wonder that before the military take-over in 1967 Greece had over 121 political parties!

The *suzététés* is the person who by his dialectic method of arguing hopes to arrive at solutions. Of the three classes of persons Paul mentions in this verse, few would claim to be in the class of the wise, and few are theologians, but anyone can be an arguer—be he college professor or bootblack. So Paul includes in the entire spectrum of human minds all those who, apart from God's revelation, seek to arrive at a solution of the human problem.

While still referring to these three kinds of people he has already mentioned, Paul writes *tou* (3588) *aiōnos* (165) *toútou* (5127), translated "of this world" or "of this age." Here Paul emphasizes that no age of history lacked such people. They existed in Paul's day and they exist in ours.

"Has not God rendered foolish the wisdom of this world?" asks Paul. He refers not only to the wisdom of his age but also to the wisdom of the world in every age. The wisdom of the world stands in contrast to the wisdom of God spoken of in verse 21. It is earthly wisdom in contrast to heavenly. It is wisdom that originates with man, not with God.

In what way has God proved such wisdom foolish? The first thing man may say in his foolish wisdom is that there is no God. Psalm 14:1 declares, "The fool hath said in his heart, There is no God." As ironic as it is to our human minds, it is the educated who claim the foolish nonexistence of God. We think educated men should know better than the uneducated. However, Paul's statement in Romans 1:22 makes it clear that our ideas are often wrong. He states, "Professing themselves to be wise, they became fools." One of the great mysteries of our world is how an otherwise intelligent man can deny his Creator. It is curious how he can maintain that this complex universe has no Maker, when he readily admits that every artifact, every mechanism of civilization proclaims an intelligence behind it. What stupidity coexists with human wisdom!

The active verb *emōranen* (3471), "made foolish," found in 1 Corinthians 1:20 implies that God delivered man up to a state of stupidity, of acting as it were like a fool. When man refuses to retain God in his knowledge, God delivers him over to spiritual blindness. In verse 18 Paul said that to those who perish, that is, to sinners who do not have the Spirit of God within them, the logic of the cross appears foolishness. Now in verse 20 he turns to the perishing ones, the wise men of this world, and says, "Do you know why you act like this, why you consider the cross of Christ, which is the only hope of your salvation, foolishness? It is because you are fools. God has rendered your wisdom foolish." He says the same thing in Romans 1:28, "And even as they did not like to retain God in their knowledge, God gave them over to a reprobate mind, to do those things which are not convenient."

In effect, Paul says, "Your mind is warped. You can't think straight. You, in Adam, have disobeyed God, and you have reaped the consequence set by God—a reprobate mind that looks at nature and says, 'There is no God.' "

Certainly those around us would consider us fools if we declared that not only did no one make the shirts we wear or the watches we carry but also that these things gradually came into existence over aeons of time to fill a need. They would say we belonged in a mental institution. However, when we declare that the universe evolved or made itself, many today would call us wise, educated, scientific, philosophers! How inconsistent is the judgment of unregenerate men! Paul was never more right than when he declared such wise men to be fools.

WHERE IS THE WISE?

As Napoleon was blazing the trail to his throne, he sought to conquer Egypt. Along with him as assistants he had some of the most able engineers and scientists of France. Naturally, they talked about the land of the Nile and the part that religion had played in it. They agreed that religion had colored and carved the history of Egypt, but that religion after all was only legend and nonsense.

Indeed, they saw all religions in this legendary way. It could not be otherwise, for in their sight even God was a myth. So they talked beneath the starry heavens, these thinkers of France. They were atheists, as were so many of their fellow countrymen. Napoleon listened and contributed nothing to the conversation, but as he rose to leave, he lifted his hand and pointed to the silent stars that shone so brilliantly through the deep black sky. "Very ingenious, Messieurs," he said, "but who made all that?"

Were I to give an exegetical translation of Romans 1:28, I would put it this way: "And since they did not approve in their experience of having God's superknowledge, God delivered them to a mind that has not been tested as to its ability to discern correctly and to do what they should" (a.t.). To have God is true superknowledge (*epígnōsis* [1922]). When we take God into our experience—which is what the cross of Christ enables us to do—we recognize Him for who and what He is. We cannot do it otherwise. We cannot prove the existence of God in a test-tube. We are unable, in our natural sinful state, to prove God and His wisdom as worthy of acceptance rather than of challenge.

Paul says that the wise person who has been made a fool by God cannot do what he ought to. That is why seemingly intelligent leaders make immoral laws that will one day rob man of his last vestige of decency. A minister received a letter confessing to a disordered life which ended: "It just beats me. A doctor of philosophy and unable to solve my own troubles!" True

WHERE IS THE WISE?

wisdom lies far deeper than intellectual knowledge. It lies in being rightly related to the Source of true knowledge—God.

Why Science Cannot Discover God

Colonel Robert Ingersoll, that well-known avowed atheist of a past generation, was one day thrown into the company of Henry Ward Beecher. Ingersoll began to attack those who believed in a God, and Christians in particular.

Strangely, Beecher remained silent. Someone said to him, "Mr. Beecher, don't you have anything to say?" "Nothing," replied Beecher. "In fact, if you gentlemen will excuse me for changing the conversation, I will say that, while you were talking, my mind was bent on a deplorable spectacle that I witnessed today."

"What was it?" inquired Ingersoll at once, who was noted for his kindness of heart. "Why," said Mr. Beecher, "as I was walking downtown today, I saw a poor lame man with crutches slowly and carefully picking his way through a cesspool of mud in the endeavor to cross the street. He had just reached the middle of the filth when a big burly ruffian, himself all bespattered, rushed up to him, jerked the crutches out from underneath the unfortunate man, and left him sprawling and helpless in the pool of liquid filth."

"What a brute he was!" exclaimed the Colonel. "What a brute he was!" they all echoed. "Yes," said the old man, rising from his chair and brushing back his long white hair, while his eyes glittered with their old-time fire as he bent them on Ingersoll, "yes, Colonel Ingersoll, and you are the man. The human soul is lame, but Christianity gives it crutches to enable it to pass the highway of life. It is your teachings that knock these crutches from under it and leave it a helpless wreck in the slough of despond."

Where Is the Wise?

God was present at creation, not man. Yet presumptuous man disputes God's Word and takes it upon himself to explain life's beginning. The evolutionist says: "Once upon a time, perhaps two and a half billion years ago, under a deadly sun, in an ammoniated ocean topped by a poisonous atmosphere, in the midst of a soup of organic molecules, a nucleic acid molecule came accidentally into being that could somehow bring about the existence of another like itself" (Isaac Asimov, in *The Wellsprings of Life*, 1960).

However, I believe in creation, not chance. "The odds against the right combination of circumstances occurring to evolve intelligent life on earth," as estimated by Sir John Eccles, Nobel Laureate in Neurophysiology, are "about 400,000 trillion to one!" It requires more faith in chance happenings to believe this than it requires faith in God to believe that He created the first life by His almighty power.

Why should Paul attack wisdom, theology, and debate? Most men hold those things to be right and good in seeking after truth. Let us support them if they really are. But how far can we trust them? One of the most brilliant minds of all time, the Apostle Paul, in 1 Corinthians 1:20, unleashes a relentless attack upon them. "Hath not God made foolish the wisdom of this world?" Of course He has. However this does not mean we should cease seeking wisdom, studying theology, or engaging in debate. We must develop our minds and keenly exercise our thoughts. One thing we must yet recognize is that our minds, no matter how intelligent and trained, are still finite and can never fully comprehend infinity. The character of an infinite God must be revealed. God had to come down to earth so that we might know Him. Had He not condescended to our human level, we never would have reached high enough to understand Him. Reason is perhaps the greatest endowment of God to man, but we must never become so wise in our conceits that we let the gift cast out the Giver.

What reason does Paul give for God's making foolish the wisdom of the world? How do we know that unregenerate wise men are fools? Paul tells us in verse 21: "For after that in the wisdom of God the world by wisdom knew not God, it pleased God by the foolishness of preaching to save them that believe." The word translated "for" here is *gár* (1063), meaning in this context "because." God rendered their wisdom foolishness "because since in the wisdom of God the world by wisdom knew not God." The conjunction *epeidĕ* (1894), "since," is causal. It explains why man in his own wisdom did not experience God, in spite of the fact that he dwelt in a world that is in itself a demonstration of God's wisdom.

What does "in the wisdom of God" mean? The preposition "in" is the Greek word *en* (1722). In this context *en* denotes sphere, even as it does in English when we say, "I am in the house, in the air, in the sea. I am amid or in the midst of." God placed man in the midst of His wisdom. That which is within and outside him speaks of God's wisdom. Although that wisdom was apparent everywhere, man nevertheless failed to know God in His own experience.

Our brain is far more intricate than the most complex computer devised by man.

> The brain is enormously more sophisticated in potential pathways and micro-circuitry. (There are upwards of 10,000 to 50,000 independent nerve cells in every cubic millimeter of cerebral cortex—10 to 15 billion altogether; each nerve cell is able to receive simultaneous information from thousands of cells, integrating and then funneling this new information to many other cells; consequently, the permutations and combinations of circuitry and sequences become astronomical.)

Your body is not a product of evolution; it was wonderfully designed by an omniscient Creator.

Where Is the Wise?

There are in the human body 600 muscles, 1,000 miles of blood vessels, and 350 arteries important enough to name. The skin, spread out, would cover 16 square feet. It has 1,500,000 sweat glands which, spread out on one surface, would occupy 10,000 square feet and cover five city lots, 20 x 100 feet. The lungs are composed of 700 million cells, all of which we use in breathing, equal to a flat surface of 2,000 square feet, which would cover a city lot. In 70 years the heart beats 2,500,000,000 times and lifts 500,000 tons of blood.

The nervous system, controlled by the brain, has 3,000,000,000,000 nerve cells, 9,200,000,000 of which are in the cortex of the brain alone. In the blood are 30,000,000 white corpuscles and 180 trillion red ones. It is easy to believe that the very hairs of our heads are numbered—about 250,000. Can anything be more pathetic than for some young freshman, created of God in such intricacy and with such infinite wisdom, to spew his infidelity into the face of the very God who created him, the God who saw his substance before it was in existence and who wrote down in His book all his members and fashioned them when as yet there was none of them? [Quoted from the booklet, The *Theory of Evolution Tested by Mathematics*, by Dr. W. B. Riley.]

Hyman Appelman has commented:

The human heart will beat for 70 or 80 years without faltering. How does it get sufficient rest between beats? A kidney will filter poison from the blood and leave good things alone. How does it know one from the other? Who gave the human tongue flexibility to form words, and a brain to understand them, but denied it to all the animals? Is it all accidental? There is no God? That is what some people say. Yet, with all of this abundant evidence of God, man cannot know God until by faith he comes to know God's Son, the Savior, Jesus Christ.

LESSONS:

1. When Paul asks, "Where (the) wise? where (the) scribe?" he directs a challenge against philosophers and theologians. When philosophers and theologians think themselves so wise and learned that they consider the cross of Christ foolishness, they themselves have become fools.
2. Paul not only challenges the philosopher and the theologian, but he also challenges the garden-variety debater. The wisdom of the world,

represented by all three of these categories, stands in contrast to the wisdom of God spoken of in verse 21. It is wisdom that originates with man, not with God.

3. When man refuses to retain God in his knowledge, God delivers him over to spiritual blindness.

1 Cor. 1:21 | *How Can You Know God?*

For after that in the wisdom of God the world by wis-dom knew not God, it pleased God by the foolishness of preaching to save them that believe.

One can see the wisdom of God in nature, in God's creation all around. The best words to express this truth are those of the Puritan Thomas Watson.

> The creation is both a monument of God's power, and a look-ing-glass in which we may see his wisdom. None but a wise God could so curiously contrive the world. Behold the earth decked with variety of flowers, which are both for beauty and fragrance. Behold the heaven be-spangled with lights. We may see the glorious wisdom of God blazing in the sun, twinkling in the stars.
>
> His wisdom is seen in marshalling and ordering everything in its proper place and sphere. If the sun had been set lower, it would have burnt us; if higher, it would not have warmed us with its beams.
>
> God's wisdom is seen in appointing the seasons of the year. "Thou hast made summer and winter" (Ps. 74:17). If it had been all summer, the heat would have scorched us; if all winter, the cold would have killed us. The wisdom of God is seen in checkering the dark and the light. If it had been all night, there had been no labor; if all day, there had been no rest.
>
> Wisdom is seen in mixing the elements, as the earth with the sea. If it had been all sea, we had wanted bread; if it had been all earth, we had wanted water. The wisdom of God is seen in preparing and ripening the

fruits of the earth, in the wind and frost that prepare the fruits, and in the sun and rain that ripen the fruits. God's wisdom is seen in setting bounds to the sea, and so wisely contriving it that though the sea be higher than many parts of the earth, yet it should not overflow the earth; so that we may cry out with the Psalmist, "O Lord, how manifold are thy works! in wisdom hast thou made them all" (Ps. 104:24) [From *A Body of Divinity*, The Banner of Truth Trust, pp. 50, 51].

Can You Know God Through His Creation?

Thomas Watson has pointed out a marvelous demonstration of the wisdom of God to any man who has eyes to see and a mind to think. Nevertheless, Paul says in 1 Corinthians 1:21 that amid God's wisdom the world did not know God by "the" wisdom. What does that mean? By preceding the word "wisdom" here the definite article "the" indicates a particular kind of wisdom. Paul refers to natural wisdom in contrast to revelation. Man discovers natural wisdom instead of accepting it as fact, as *a priori* truth. Natural wisdom is scientific wisdom, and revelation is divine wisdom.

God does not produce observational experiments to persuade us that His laws work. We are the ones who conduct experiments to come up with what we call the laws of nature. These laws that we have been discovering down through the ages declare the wisdom of God. Yet though any thinking man—be he scientist or lay observer—must stand in awe before nature and its laws, comparatively few go beyond that to recognize an intelligent Being, a Creator. They prefer to speak of "nature" rather than "God."

Man's most important and distinctive element is his personality, yet unregenerate man is neither courteous nor intelligent enough to attribute personality to the One who made him and all that exists. Although placed in the midst of the evidences of God's wisdom, Paul tells us, man did not know God.

Furthermore, he did not recognize Him as Creator or even as a Power. What a fool man proved to be!

Instead of speaking of man in his sinful state as the one not knowing God, Paul uses the word "world" in verse 21—*kósmos* (2889) in Greek. Here it means "fallen humanity," just as it does in John 3:16, which tells us "God so loved the world [fallen humanity], that he gave" His Son for its redemption. Christ became man, not for the sake of all creation, animate and inanimate, or even for angels, fallen or good, but solely for fallen man. Only man benefits by His incarnation. Certainly He became man for the sake of sinful man. For this reason Christ commanded us to preach the gospel to the whole world (Mark 16:15)—the world of men hostile to God in spite of the abundant demonstration of His wisdom in His creation. (See G. Kittel, *Theological Dictionary of the New Testament*, Vol. 3, pp. 889, 890.)

Man's intelligence is corrupt because he is sinful. It is not a matter of how much wisdom we need to know God. Human wisdom, says Paul, whether much or little, cannot cause us to know God. It can tell us that there is a God, but it cannot acquaint us with Him intimately and personally. If it could, where was the necessity for the incarnation of God in Christ and His crucifixion for man's redemption?

Even though we may acknowledge the existence of God as a person, and a powerful person at that, we will not experience God Himself through that insight. That is the meaning of the verb *égnō* (from *ginóskō* [1097]), "know." This word comes from *gnósis* (1108) from which the Gnostics of Paul's day derived their name. Their emphasis in the first and second centuries A.D. was on speculative knowledge. In the New Testament this verb *ginóskō* frequently denotes a personal relationship between the persons knowing and the objects known. This is the meaning in 1 Corinthians 1:21. (See Hermann Cremer's *Biblico-Theological Lexicon of New Testament Greek*, p. 154.) As Dr. George Getty says:

HOW CAN YOU KNOW GOD?

A man may read and study the evidences of the existence of God . . . and be able to put into logical form the arguments and theories of the Christian religion, but he will never have a satisfying faith until he has put the doctrine of Jesus Christ to the test of practical experience. . . . To him who seeks the Lord in the name of Jesus Christ, God imparts His Holy Spirit under whose gracious influence there springs up in the heart a faith that glows with radiant light, illuminating the pathway of human life, transforming character, producing a rich fruitage of virtues and blessings. He who has within himself the Spirit of Christ has the crowning evidence of Christianity [*Foundations of Faith*, pp. 86–90].

Can You Know God Through Reason?

Pagan philosophy has never done more than search after God and guess what He may be like. By the confession of some of its more reverent adherents, modern science has brought to light the principle of design in nature. This design gives evidence of an all-wise, all-powerful Creator. If we want to do more than guess what this Creator is like, we will seek to know Him through His certain means of revelation of Himself—the Bible. In the Bible we learn what His thoughts of us and His personal dealings with us entail. We also find all we need to know for our salvation and daily walk. Moreover, we learn who God is and what He requires of us.

Paul uses the verb *ginōskō*, "to know," in 1 Corinthians 1:21 a little differently from the way he uses it in Romans 1:21. The passage in Romans reads, "Because that, when they knew God, they glorified him not as God, neither were thankful, but became vain in their imaginations, and their foolish heart was darkened." In context Paul is speaking of creation, pointing to the conclusion that God exists. In this passage, "knowing" God did not involve a transformation of the nature of man so that he could properly worship God. Moreover acknowledging the existence of God is as far as man's observation can take him.

HOW CAN YOU KNOW GOD?

In 1 Corinthians 1:18 Paul says that the lost or unsaved ones rejected the cross of Christ, the only means of salvation. From this we conclude that the expression in verse 21, "Did not know God," is tantamount to saying, "was not saved." Moreover Paul is saying in verse 21 that the world, unsaved man, did not become personally acquainted with God, did not know Him in such a way as to restore fellowship with Him. Knowing God here does not refer to mere intellectual conclusions about Him, but to actual restoration and fellowship through Christ's vicarious death on the cross.

What a lively and interesting discussion the Lord Jesus had with some of His countrymen who were claiming knowledge of God! They were religious leaders and yet they were not spiritually related to God. The Lord said to them, "Ye neither know me, nor my Father: if ye had known me, ye should have known my Father also" (John 8:19). Though they were looking right at Jesus, He said, "You do not know Me." Then He continued to make it clear that the only way to become truly acquainted with and related to God the Father is through knowing—being saved by—God the Son.

Ask yourself if you simply have intellectual knowledge of God, or do you really know Him through His Son, the Lord Jesus Christ, having accepted His sacrifice for you on the cross? No amount of human wisdom will lead a man to believe that he needs to be changed, and that this change can come about through the cross of Christ. If God's wisdom, originally planted in man, had not become foolishness to him through Adam's disobedience and fall, then you and I would never have been lost and in need of salvation. As wise fools, men cannot see God's wisdom in crucifying Christ for their salvation. We must accept God's sacrifice to experience its power. "For as many as received him [Christ]," John 1:12 tells us, "to them gave he authority to become the children of God." Note that it does not say, "For as many as reasoned their way to Him." One cannot do this.

What characterizes man in his fallen state, then, is the utter inability to save himself. The expression *ouk* (3756) *égnō*, "knew not," is in the second aorist tense, which here refers to any time in the past and also holds true now and forever. There has never been a time when man, through his own wisdom, became personally acquainted with God and became saved.

Immediately after stating this gloomy conclusion about man's state, Paul speaks of God's action in man's favor. It was not, "You asked for it, man, and therefore you deserve to stay where your own actions have placed you. Since you are responsible for losing the way, you can just stay lost." Not at all. God acts, and His action is in favor of man—without, however, violating His justice. Sin deserves punishment, and God did punish it. Instead of punishing each sinner, God sent His Son to die a sinner's death for all sinners.

However, the effectiveness of that act on any individual depends on his acceptance of God's offer. If we refuse to accept it, we remain lost, we stay in the state we have chosen. No one can hold God responsible for this, although He pre-set the consequences of man's disobedience. We disobeyed and fell. In our fallen condition, if we have failed to accept the salvation Christ offers, there will be no more change in our condition. As I have said before, God in one sense sends no man to hell; He ordains it only because of man's choice if he refuses deliverance by rejecting God's offer of salvation.

God was kind to fallen man, although under no obligation to be so. This is what Paul indicates by the verb *eudókēsen* (2106), "it pleased God," in the second part of verse 21. This verb, "to take pleasure," when used with an infinitive, *sōsai* (the first infinitive active of *sōzō* [4982], "save"), conveys a clear hint of choice, resolve, or decree. (See Kittel's *Theological Dictionary of the New Testament*, Vol. 2, pp. 741, 742.) God gave man a choice in the Garden of Eden. Man chose to disobey God. He reaped the God-predetermined consequence of his choice.

Certainly God's kindness was in line with His Character, for He is mercy, love, and truth. Some say God was a fool to save man at His great expense, suffering death on a cross. They called Him a fool for being so good that He chose to save sinners instead of allowing them to reap the consequence of their sin. God could by rights have hated man for what he did. Instead, He exercised *eudokía* (2107), "good pleasure," in providing for his salvation. He went the way of the divinely chosen, not the humanly natural.

> Was it for crimes that I have done
>   He groaned upon the tree?
> Amazing pity! grace unknown!
>   And love beyond degree!
>
> Well might the sun in darkness hide,
>   And shut his glories in,
> When Christ, the mighty Maker, died
>   For man, the creature's sin.
>   —Isaac Watts

What Does It Mean to Believe in God?

The mystery of suffering has caused more people to question God's love than any other problem. Yet, if we understand our relationship with God, it should occasion no insuperable difficulty. All men suffer, and the ultimate of suffering is death. But why? Is it because God is cruel and has ordained evil as man's lot? No, the sad truth is that man chose it himself, first in Eden, then, having fallen into sin, always thereafter. He has what he asked for—what God fixed because of disobedience to His definite directive. We must regard sickness and suffering as the natural expectation of man. "For all have sinned, and come short of the glory of God" (Rom. 3:23). The word *dóxa* (1391), "glory" in this verse and the word *eudokía*, "good pleasure," in verse 21, are related. Man falls short of the good pleasure of God.

Thus, health is the exception for man, conferred only at God's good pleasure. Happily surprised when He gives it to us, we praise Him for it. Conversely, we should never complain about sickness and suffering due us because of our sinful choice in Adam. Understanding we do not deserve it, our total philosophy of life changes the moment of our salvation; for it is all of grace. Just comprehend God's good pleasure in saving you, and you will have nothing but praise in your heart for that and all other good things.

Paul delineates the means by which this good pleasure, the good disposition of God providing for our salvation, comes to man. He can never attain it through his wisdom, but he can receive it by faith, which preaching the gospel communicates. God saves. But whom does He save? "Them that believe," says Paul. God does not arbitrarily save anyone. His salvation is not a rubber stamp that He affixes on all, or on some, without the consent of those who want salvation.

Christ died for all, but saves only those who believe. The words "them that believe" are actually *toús pisteúontas* (4100), "the believing ones," a Greek participial noun. Man's part is to believe—and not just once but continuously. Belief must have a beginning, but it should have no end. The tense of the verb *sósai*, "to save," is aorist, which indicates God's once-and-for-all action. He rescues us from the kingdom of death and darkness and places us in the kingdom of life and light.

Conversion manifests this saving. It is the transformation of our being in the new birth, resulting in an outward change in our lives. God snatches us out of the devil's hand and keeps us from being re-taken by him. As I pointed out in the exegesis of the participle *sōzoménois* (4982) in verse 18, salvation is in three tenses: past, present, and future. Christ's vicarious death on the cross saved us, for "He was wounded for our transgressions" (Is. 53:5). Salvation from sin's power is a continual process by Christ's intercession on high: "He ever liveth to make intercession for them" (Heb. 7:25). Moreover, salvation from sin's presence and influence will occur when we go to be with Him: "And there shall in no wise enter into it any thing that defileth" (Rev. 21:27). The *sōsai* of verse 21, "to save the believing ones," refers to the once-and-for-all salvation that man experiences when he begins to believe in Christ.

What does it mean to believe? Believing is a faculty of the heart: "For with the heart man believeth" (Rom. 10:10). Belief stands in contrast to mental wisdom and is more than mental admiration of universe's Creator. A person can admire God and be totally unsaved. Belief is equivalent to receiving. Faith never stands around with its hands in its pockets. As Dr. Samuel Zwemer said, "Faith is the outstretched hand of the soul taking what Christ offers."

This faith is not abstract, but it receives what Christ offers through the cross. In the phrase "to save the believing ones," Paul does not mention the object of belief. However, in verse 18 he clearly speaks of "the word of the cross," and in verse 23 he speaks of "Christ crucified." Simply to have faith that God merely exists like anything else cannot save you. Salvation only comes to you when you receive Christ as God's substitute for you on the cross. In other words, your faith per se does not save you, but it is the instrument through which you are saved. Faith alone links you to the One of whom the Bible says, "Neither is there salvation in any other: for there is none other name under heaven given among men, whereby we must be saved" (Acts 4:12).

Begging a famous preacher to visit her dying mother, a little girl pleaded, "Come and get my mother in." Having followed

HOW CAN YOU KNOW GOD?

the girl to a slum tenement he sat by the mother's bed and began to speak of the beautiful example of Christ. However the woman interrupted him saying, "That's no good, mister, no good for the likes of me. I'm a poor sinner and I'm dying!" Being a preacher who thought speaking of the cross and the blood of Christ improper, he struggled to remember his mother's simple story of Jesus dying on the cross and explained it to the woman. "Now," she cried, "you're getting at it! That's the story for me!" Afterward the preacher said, "I got her in, and I got myself in, too!" That is the message that can bring salvation—the cross of Christ.

What is the means of making known to lost man this one way of salvation? It is "through the foolishness of preaching." Not that preaching as a means of communicating a message is foolish. *Kērugma* (2782), "preaching," may mean the heralding or proclaiming of a message, or it may mean the message itself. In the ancient world, as well as today, it meant proclaiming something by word of mouth. Undoubtedly, what Paul means here by *kērugma* is the content of the message of the gospel, not the method of delivering it.

Second Corinthians 10:10 mentions that Paul's *lógos* (3056), "utterance or message," was "contemptible." In this instance Paul, no doubt, was struggling with his physical infirmity—which can cause even the best of speakers difficulty. Besides this possible exception, people never considered the delivery of Paul's preaching foolish. At Lystra and Derbe the excellent preaching of Paul and Barnabas made the people say, "The gods are come down to us in the likeness of men" (Acts 14:11). Moreover, the eloquence and power of Paul's speaking caused Festus to say, "Paul, thou art beside thyself; much learning doth make thee mad." These words of Festus drew from King Agrippa the confession, "Almost thou persuadest me to be a Christian" (Acts 26:24, 28). Even those who mocked Paul's gospel were eager to hear him preach. It is the subject of Christian preaching that men have deemed foolishness.

LESSONS:

1. Although placed in the midst of the evidences of God's wisdom, Paul tells us that man did not know God. Furthermore, he did not recognize Him as Creator or even as a Power.
2. Even though we may acknowledge the existence of God as a personality, and a powerful personality at that, through that insight alone we cannot experience God Himself.
3. There has never been a time when man, through his wisdom, became personally acquainted with God and became saved.
4. By rights, God could have hated man for his rebellion, but He chose to save man from his sin through the sacrifice of Christ because He is mercy, love, and truth.
5. Our total philosophy of life changes the moment we are saved because we understand that we do not deserve God's salvation; for it is all of grace.
6. Believing in Christ is a faculty of the heart. It stands in contrast to mental wisdom.

1 Cor. 1:22, 23 | *Preaching Christ Crucified*

For the Jews require a sign, and the Greeks seek after wis-dom:but we preach Christ crucified, unto the Jews a stumblingblock, and unto the Greeks foolishness.

R. S. Tuttle says, "The deepest thirst of the human soul is for God." He continues, "To try to satisfy it with mere things or sensations is like trying to comfort the motherless child with a beautiful doll." The doll may divert the little one for awhile, but in the night you will hear her sobbing for her mother. Tuttle concludes that "The world is full of orphan souls that are crying in the night. In the face of it all, how utterly heart-sickening to witness the effort of some pulpits to offer sensational toys to attract and soothe dying men." Indeed speakers from these pulpits never mention that the only way to have peace of heart is to come to God by way of the cross.

What Should the Church Preach Today?

The Apostle Paul had a reason for using the word *kērugmatos* (2782), "preaching" in verse 21. *Kērugmatos* can mean the content of the message (Christ crucified, see v. 23) and the method of delivering it (preaching). He wanted to make it very plain that preaching is the God-decreed agency for making known the crucified Savior. Preaching as an ordinance is part of God's good pleasure, of His saving attitude toward man.

Of all acts of worship, preaching is the most necessary. How sad when Christian churches re-enact the crucifixion instead of preaching Christ crucified once-for-all to save those who believe. The lack of such preaching explains the barrenness of many churches. In the Christian Church, the pulpit should always be more important than the altar because it is the proclaiming of Christ's once-for-all sacrifice and finished work on the cross that is the Church's mission today. If you are a minister of the gospel, never allow any other activity to overshadow the ministry of preaching. "How then shall they call on him in whom they have not believed? and how shall they believe in him of whom they have not heard? and how shall they hear without a preacher?" (Rom. 10:14). (See Dinsdale T. Young's *The Crimson Book*, pp. 173–189.)

The objection of the natural man is not to preaching per se but to the preaching of the cross of Christ, which involves an acknowledgment of man's lost condition. To tell a man who thinks himself wise that he needs salvation by someone other than himself is an affront to his pride; therefore he dismisses it as foolishness. In such a situation, what should the preacher do? Should he quit preaching this message which offends a man, even though it is his greatest need?

A young preacher said to his older preacher friend, "I always write my sermons, and then carefully revise them so that, if anything is written that might offend any of my hearers, I may erase it immediately!" His friend replied, "Do you mean that you either tone down or avoid forcible statements, either of your own or from Scripture, concerning sin, the cross, and the judgment to come?" "Yes," replied the novice clergyman. "If I think they will offend anyone, I do so."

That is a good recipe for powerless preaching. Take the cross out of preaching and you have deprived it of its soul. No preaching that ignores Christ crucified and risen again can save a sinner. What does it matter if some consider it foolishness, as long as it can save the lost?

The great preacher, Robert Murray M'Cheyne, never took preaching lightly. In truth two of his motives for visiting the sick and dying on Saturday afternoons had an impact on his preaching. First, he wanted to have before him the picture of dying men while he preached. Second, he wanted to bring the gospel of the crucified Christ to men as if they would never have another chance.

Why did God choose to save man through the crucifixion of His Son? The first reason, as we have seen in 1 Corinthians 1:21, is "Since the world through wisdom did not know God." The word for "since" here is the Greek conjunction *epeidē* (1894). Moreover, verse 22, which gives the second reason, begins with the same conjunction. "Since both Jews ask for signs and Greeks seek after wisdom, we preach Christ crucified," says Paul. "We are not yielding to their demands," he seems to say, "for we know that is not what they need."

Paul, like a good spiritual parent, does not give his children what they clamor for but what they need. Man does not need the increase and exercise of wisdom nor more visible proofs of the existence of God. Man can reach the height of wisdom and live in the midst of proofs about God and yet not know God. "We preach Christ crucified," says Paul uncompromisingly. He is the One who can give us the one thing we really need, salvation from sin.

Is It Right to Ask God to Prove Himself?

One of Gustave Dore's best known and most remarkable pictures is the one entitled "Christ Leaving the Praetorium." The guidebook to the Dore Gallery in London suggests the best place from which to view the picture. Certainly the position which shows it from the standpoint of the artist is to the best possible advantage. From other positions in the gallery the effect is quite different and not at all as good. Though the picture does not change, the different standpoints give it different effects. In like manner, two persons may view the same landscape or read the same book with very different results, although the landscape and book remain the same.

This is precisely what happens when men view Christ crucified. The fact is eternal and unchangeable, but people will appreciate its value and importance in exact proportion to the standpoint from which they consider it. Paul suggests that there is a threefold diversity of viewpoint and conclusion. There is the physical, represented by the Jew; the intellectual, represented by the Greek; and the spiritual, represented by the saved among both Jew and Gentile.

The Jews as they view Christ crucified "require" or look for signs. The word translated "require" in this verse is *aitoúsi(n)* (154) in Greek. Its actual meaning is a little stronger, amounting to demand. The Jews demand signs in proof of Jesus. There is an absoluteness about their demand: "Either we are given signs or we will not believe."

It is interesting to note that, with regard to the Greeks, the verb used by Paul is *zētoúsin* (2212), which does not have the sense of demanding, but denotes man's general philosophical search or quest. It refers to philosophical investigation. It is also noteworthy that this is the basic verb from which *suzētētēs* (4804), "disputer or arguer," is derived in verse 20. The philosophical search for truth brings about arguments or discussions among men. It is the search on the human level that includes the opinions of yourself and others who are men like you.

PREACHING CHRIST CRUCIFIED

Philosophy is different from faith. Philosophy is the search for truth by means of human reasoning, whereas "belief" is the acceptance of a declaration of truth made by someone. One can never discover God's plan of salvation through discussion or dialogue. We share thoughts, but must preach the gospel. There is a "maybe I'm right" about human philosophy, but there is a categorical "Thus saith the Lord, and thus hath the Lord done" about God's declarations and actions. For this reason Paul uses the straightforward *kērússomen* (2784) concerning Christ crucified, meaning "we herald, we declare, we preach." The apostles preached experiential, not probable truth.

What is the meaning of the Greek word *sēméia* (from *sēméion* [4592]), "signs," that the Jews demanded from Christ before they would acknowledge His Messiahship? This is one of the many words that the Scriptures use to indicate miracles (*sēméion*, See John 2:11; Acts 2:19; *téras* [5059], John 4:48; Acts 2:22; *dúnamis* [1411], Mark 6:2; Acts 2:22; *megaleíon* [3167], Luke 1:49; *endokson* [1741], Luke 13:17; *parádoxon* [3861], Luke 5:26; *thaumásion* [2297], Matt. 21:15). However, the word *sēméion*, "sign," sharply contrasts with the meaning of *téras*, "wonder." For "sign" has a distinct ethical end and purpose whereas "wonder" has the least ethical and unyielding connotation.

The prime object and end of the miracle involved and declared in the very word *sēméion* is to lead us to something out of and beyond itself. It is a fingerpost of God, as if God were saying, "I do this in order for you to see and understand." The miracle is not valuable so much for what it is as for what it indicates of the grace and power of the doer, or of his immediate connection with a higher spiritual world (Ex. 7:9, 10; 1 Kgs. 13:3; Mark 16:20; Acts 14:3; Heb. 2:4). (See R. C. Trench, *Synonyms of the New Testament*, Eerdmans, 1953, pp. 339–44.)

Thus, the Jews were demanding miracles performed by God, not for the sake of the miracles, but as the finger and voice of God indicating "This is my beloved Son in whom I am well pleased" (Matt. 3:17). The Jews expected physical miracles. Accustomed to such manifestations under the economy of the Law, they expected God to work that way in the economy of grace.

God delivered the Jews from Egypt's bondage of physical slavery through physical signs and wonders wrought by His mighty hand (Deut. 4:34; 5:15). Although He could have dropped the plates of the Law from heaven, God made a glorious physical appearance (or theophany) on Mt. Sinai to give the Jews their Law. His visible presence had dwelt with them, first in the Tabernacle, then in the Temple. His miraculous interpositions had given, preserved, and restored the land of Canaan with much earthly prosperity. The physical blessings of God were so abundant that the Jews lost discernment or desire of spiritual blessings.

Therefore, whenever their prophets foretold the coming of the promised Redeemer they expected Him to be great in earthly power. Of course, there are such descriptions in the Bible, but they refer not to the first coming of the Lord, but to His Second Coming. The Jews, however, being materialistic in their viewpoint, confused the two comings of the Lord. "The Lord shall send the rod of thy strength out of Zion: rule thou in the midst of thine enemies. . . . he shall judge among the heathen, he shall fill the places with the dead bodies; he shall wound the heads over many countries" (Ps. 110:2, 6). "I will make my firstborn, higher than the kings of the earth" (Ps. 89:27). This has not yet come to pass, but the Jews expected Christ to fulfill it during His first coming, and they would not acknowledge Him as Messiah unless He did. They expected Him to be a mighty conqueror who would establish Himself by sheer supernatural strength. Since He did not establish a visible Jewish empire, He could not be the One whom they were expecting. Only such a sign would satisfy them.

Consider the risen Savior's words to Thomas: "Because thou hast seen me, thou hast believed: blessed are they that have not seen, and yet have believed" (John 20:29).

Why So Few Miracles Today?

"A wicked and adulterous generation seeketh after a sign," declared the Lord Jesus to the Pharisees who came tempting Him to show them a sign from heaven (Matt. 16:4). In reality the Lord had shown plenty of signs. However these signs had not satisfied the Pharisees. They wanted a manifestation of physical power directly from heaven (Matt. 16:1; Mark 8:11; Luke 11:16). Of course they should have known that every miracle that Christ performed was a sign from heaven.

Nevertheless, the Jews they expected to see the prophecies of Daniel concerning Christ's Second Coming fulfilled at his first coming. In Daniel 7:13 and 14 we read:

> I saw in the night visions, and, behold, one like the Son of man came with the clouds of heaven, and came to the Ancient of days, and they brought Him near before him. And there was given Him dominion, and glory, and a kingdom, that all people, nations, and languages, should serve Him: his dominion is an everlasting dominion, which shall not pass away, and His kingdom that which shall not be destroyed.

The Lord observed their mistake and told them that the sign they desired should indeed be given, but not to their generation. He added that the principle evidence to be given them was the sign of the prophet Jonah. And what was that? "For as Jonah was three days and three nights in the whale's belly; so shall the Son of man be three days and three nights in the heart of the earth" (Matt. 12:40).

If no other sign could persuade the Jews of Jesus' Messiahship, His resurrection from the dead should have, for it was certainly a physical sign. The day will come, of course, when "The kingdoms of this world . . . become the kingdoms of our

Lord, and of His Christ; and He shall reign forever and ever" (Rev. 11:15), but all things must come in their rightful order in the plan of God. There is a day coming when those who sought and seek a sign "shall see the Son of man coming in the clouds of heaven with power and great glory" (Matt. 24:30). Still the sign-seekers of Jesus' day wanted this sign immediately. Even His disciples expressed this thought and desire when they asked the Lord after His resurrection, "Lord, wilt thou at this time restore again the kingdom to Israel?" (Acts 1:6).

Instead of a King, the multitudes saw One who had nowhere to lay His head, who was born in a stable, and who died on a cross! He had opportunities in His adult life to seize the power of an earthly kingdom, but He purposely and meticulously avoided them. Moreover when He died, the hopes of His followers died with Him. "But we trusted," said two of them, "that it had been he which should have redeemed Israel" (Luke 24:21) from the oppressive power of Rome.

As a result of His resurrection, the disciples (all Jews) comprehended the mission of Christ, but the greater part of the Jews did not; and a crucified Redeemer continued to be a stumbling block to them, or, in the words of Simeon, "set for the fall and rising again of many in Israel; and for a sign which shall be spoken against" (Luke 2:34). Indeed, the fall of Israel occurred, and its rise is inseparably connected with the coming again of the despised Redeemer. But this time they will accept Him, for He will come in power. The Jews still remain a distinct people, as indeed they must, for the prophet Zechariah predicted that by looking on Him "whom they have pierced" and by mourning they shall rise again and be as "life from the dead" (Zech. 12:10; Rom. 11:15). (See *The Works of Thomas Secker*, Vol. 1, third edition, pp. 87–94.)

From this we come to the basic conclusion that God will not alter His plan to please the demands of men. "The Jews demand a sign"—saying that, if they receive it, they will believe. The Lord could have ruled supreme over the world then, as He will one day, but He chose to await the right time. God follows an order and a plan which He will execute in His own time. If we do not understand this fact, we will have trouble making sense out of God's dealings with men. We will expect Him to act today in the same manner that He acted in past ages, and our faith in Him will suffer if He does not. We must not blame ourselves as having little faith, or God as being indifferent if our prayers are not answered according to our wish or timing. In His character and essence He is the same yesterday, today, and forever. We, on the other hand, are not the same people as those in past ages, and He chooses to work differently at different periods of time to accomplish specific purposes.

Take the matter of miracles, for instance. Why did Christ perform miracles when He was on earth, and His disciples also, yet He no longer does so, nor do we—at least not in the same manner and to the same extent? The Lord indeed promised that His followers should do greater things than He did (John 14:12). However, greater does not necessarily mean of the same kind. His miracles, especially meant to persuade the physically oriented Jews, were of a physical nature, but spiritual works are greater, for the soul is greater and more important than the body. The greatest power manifests against the greatest evil which is not ill health or earthquakes or any other physical calamity, but sin, the cause of all suffering.

You remember when four men brought the paralyzed man to Christ for healing. These men were quite naturally expecting a manifestation or proof of His power over the physical world, but the first thing He did was something quite remote from their minds. He simply said, "Thy sins be forgiven thee" (Mark 2:5). There before Him was a practical work to do, a man needing help, yet Christ seemed to take no notice. Then, seeing no outward power, no miracle wrought, some of the spectators began to reason about His words and attribute blasphemy to Him.

Still Christ knew which was the greatest force and power. He knew that the divine word of forgiveness was the greater work to this man. Moreover when He had forgiven him, the lesser work followed quite naturally: "Arise, and take up thy bed, and go thy way into thine house" (Mark 2:11). The Lord Jesus does exactly this with the whole nature of man. He first cleanses the inner nature giving it fresh life before making the outward power visible. This inward cleansing, this new life, comes through the cross. This is how the cross becomes the power of God to our souls. (See W. H. Griffith Thomas, *The Essentials of Life*, pp. 124, 125.)

Walking by Faith and Not by Sight

Were the Jews of Christ's day justified in demanding a sign which would prove the Messiahship of the Lord Jesus Christ? Dr. M. R. De Haan comments:

It is very significant that there are few, if any miracles, signs and wonders recorded during the first two thousand years of human [recorded] history. It is not until we come to the history of Israel, two thousand years after Adam, that signs and wonders began to appear. The first great miracle was the birth of Isaac supernaturally conceived by a miracle which God performed upon Abraham and Sarah. This marked the beginning of the nation of Israel, and from there on we have hundreds upon hundreds of miracles.

Israel, therefore, is peculiarly God's miracle nation, and the nation of miracles. . . . All during her history she has been miraculously preserved, fed and kept. When their Messiah, Jesus, came to offer them the kingdom, nineteen hundred years ago, the greatest era of miracles and signs and wonders was ushered in, as recorded in the four gospels, and the book of Acts. Miracles, then, are inseparably associated with God's dealing with the nation of Israel. Paul says, "The Jews require a sign, and the Greeks seek after wisdom." Miracles are peculiar to the nation of Israel and their history, and are related to the kingdom, rather than to the church age. This is also made clear by our Lord when He commissioned His disciples to preach the message of the kingdom. In Matthew 10 we read: "And when he had called unto Him His twelve disciples, He gave them power against unclean spirits, to cast them out, and to heal all manner of sickness and all manner of disease" (Matt. 10:1). . . .

This particular commission . . . was given only to the twelve apostles, and to none other. They in turn could lay hands on others, and impart these gifts, but there is no record that it ever went beyond this. These gifts in Matthew 10 were apostolic gifts given for the apostolic age for an apostolic ministry. To emphasize the exclusiveness of this apostolic commission to the twelve apostles, Matthew then gives the names of these twelve: . . . "Now the names of the twelve apostles are these; . . . Peter, Andrew . . . James . . . John . . . Philip, and Bartholomew; Thomas; and Matthew . . . James . . . Thaddeus; Simon . . . and Judas" (Matt. 10:2–4).

These twelve are the ones whom Jesus definitely sent forth and He calls them by name. In this we see that the Lord emphasizes that this commission was distinctly apostolic, exclusively for the apostles, for these twelve, and then He commands them saying: "Go not into the way of the Gentiles, and into any city of the Samaritans enter ye not. But go rather to the lost sheep of the house of Israel" (Matt. 10:5, 6).

The signs, miracles, and the wonders Jesus and the apostles performed were also for a definite purpose. The only part of the Bible in existence at the time was the Old Testament. Not a single book of the New Testament had been written. These signs, therefore, were the authentication of the ministry of Jesus and the apostles. These gifts were to approve their ministry as being of God, and were to serve as their credentials while the New Testament was still unwritten. Then, when the canon of Scripture was completed, and the New Testament written, there was no more need for these signs and miracles. We are now expected to believe the gospel, and not to seek for signs and wonders. We are to walk by faith in God's Word and not by sight. These signs were for God's miracle nation, primarily, and so Paul says: "The Jews require a sign, and the Greeks seek after wisdom: but we preach Christ crucified."

The Apostle Peter also makes this clear in his sermon at Pentecost. He says . . . "Ye men of Israel, hear these words; Jesus of Nazareth, a man approved of God among you by miracles and wonders and signs, which God did by Him in the midst of you" (Acts 2:22).

Will you notice two things in this particular passage? First of all, Peter is addressing Israel, and speaking only to the children of Israel, and addresses them as "Ye men of Israel." He is not speaking to the Gentiles. Then notice next that the signs and the wonders that Jesus did were God's approval of His authority and His divine mission. By these signs He proved to Israel that He was their Messiah and proved it by never failing once in helping all who came to Him. One single failure on the part of Jesus would have disqualified and disapproved Him immediately. There is no record that Jesus ever attempted to heal anyone, and failed to do so. Every one of His miracles of healing were successful. This was the proof of His divine mission, and that is the test by which the Bible declares we are to judge the ministry. One failure to heal on the part of Christ would have discredited Him as not having been from God . . . .

So too the apostles after Pentecost were approved of God by signs and wonders and these same miracles: "God also bearing them witness, both with signs and wonders, and with diverse miracles, and gifts of the Holy Ghost, according to his own will" (Heb. 2:4). [See M. R. De Haan, *Divine Healing and Divine Healers*, pp. 8–11.]

Thus, the Jews are totally unjustified in demanding more signs that would prove the Messiahship of the Lord Jesus Christ. If they take the trouble to examine the record, they will find that Jesus was the fulfillment of all prophesied of the Messiah. What more could anyone demand? Still only one quality of the Messiah was not yet found in Jesus. He was yet to exercise His physical power to rule, but He will during His Second Coming. Indeed then He will not be a sacrificial lamb slaughtered for our sakes, but a lion. John gives a vivid picture of what the Messiah will yet do and be from chapter 4 to the end of Revelation. Though the Lord has been singularly partial to the Jews, giving them every reason for the exercise of faith, they as a nation—and most of them as individuals—have rejected Him. Even so, the Lord is not going to bend His plan and give them another sign prematurely. For now, only the preaching of the crucified Christ will bring at least some Jews to salvation. Lowell states:

PREACHING CHRIST CRUCIFIED

Once to every man and nation comes the moment to decide,
In the strife of Truth and Falsehood, for the good or evil side;
One great gift, God's true Messiah, offering each the bloom or blight,
Parts the goats upon the left hand and the sheep upon the right,
And the choice goes on forever 'twixt that darkness and that light.

Philosophy of the Gospel—Which?

Scripture tells us that in appraising the claims of Christianity, the Jews sought a sign and the Greeks sought after wisdom. The Greeks were representative of the Gentile world, seeking their own human wisdom. They glorified the intellect. The cross had nothing in it to recommend it to the natural intelligence of man. Philosophy, friendship of wisdom, was the delight of the Greeks. Since no one else had such an advanced culture as they had, they looked down upon the rest of the world and called them Barbarians (Rom. 1:14). Nevertheless, they were superstitious. At least Paul found them so when he visited Athens (Acts 17:22).

In the February 1971 issue of Reader's Digest there was an article entitled "I'm Not Superstitious, but . . ." which began: "An estimated 20 million Americans, in this age of science and sophistication, carry a rabbit's foot or other good-luck charm." Lest we think this is confined to the uneducated, the article goes on to say that even the U. S. Navy will not launch a new ship on a Friday or on the 13th. An encyclopedia of superstitions published in Germany fills up ten volumes. Also a learned doctor collecting American superstitions has already collected more than 400,000 of them and has not halfway finished! In sports and in the theatrical world, many players would feel insecure if they neglected such rituals as avoiding stepping on a foul line or whistling in a dressing room. Many hotels and office buildings will not designate the 13th floor by that number. Moreover because few people would feel comfortable sitting in seat 13 in an airplane, some airlines omit it.

Perhaps you feel you are not superstitious—but do you never knock wood after bragging about good health? Are you apprehensive about walking under a ladder, or opening an umbrella in the house, or spilling salt? When your palm itches, do you remark that you are going to receive money, or when your nose itches that you are going to have a fight? If misfortune overtook you on Friday the 13th, would you consider it more than a coincidence? Would you start a new venture on that day? If you can answer No to all these questions, you are an unusual person indeed.

The Greeks were people of ideas. The cross, on the other hand, was a fact, and, therefore, it was natural for them to reject it. The paradox of Christianity is not only that human wisdom failed to reach its goal, but that God meant it to fail. In spite of all the efforts of the Greeks to discover God by reasoning, they failed. Otherwise, they would not have dedicated an altar "To the Unknown God." The result of all their human wisdom was that God still remained unknown to them.

If man's wisdom had led him to an understanding of the mind and purpose of God, two things would necessarily have followed. First, that only the wise could come to know God, and the unlearned and ignorant would remain in outer darkness. Second, the knowledge of God so acquired would be purely a mental achievement, abstract and speculative. Certainly it would remain unrelated to the moral life, powerless to redeem, lacking an adequate dynamic, cold and passionless, a sun without energy, a moon shining with pallid radiance over a frozen world.

Paul did not preach a philosophical system to the Corinthians, but the central redeeming fact, the cross of Christ. The Greeks in Corinth were traditional worshipers of Minerva, the goddess of wisdom. To these people came the Christian

Paul, who, though he realized the nerve it required to preach a crucified Christ, refused to modify his message. He insisted that the cross was and is the wisdom of God.

In his missionary travels, before going to Corinth, Paul had gone to Athens. There he stood on Mars Hill and preached to the learned Greeks. In that city he felt that he must give an intellectual discourse to the people who "spent their time in nothing else, but either to tell, or to hear some new thing" (Acts 17:21). He preached a wonderfully eloquent sermon, but it was probably the most ineffective sermon he ever preached. The Greeks were very polite, and they said, "Another day." They thought Paul's religion silly, and when he preached about the resurrection, they called it madness. Everyone knew that dead men do not rise. So Paul went to Corinth. Evidently he had learned his lesson because he resolved that from henceforth he would not try to win men by the wisdom of words or noble oratory. He would preach Christ crucified; he would proclaim and exult in that very thing that gave offense. He knew that philosophy would never enable anyone to achieve life's primary need—knowing God.

The story is told of three people who went into a church building. The first was a businessman who had failed and was contemplating suicide. The second was a rebellious youth, deep in sin, who was planning a robbery. The third was a young woman who was tempted to depart from the path of virtue. The worship service started. The choir arose and sang an anthem about building the walls of Zion. The minister addressed an eloquent prayer to the Lord and then preached on the theme, "Is Mars Inhabited?" Afterward, the businessman committed suicide, the boy stole and landed in jail, and the young woman began a life of moral shame. What might have happened if only he had preached the gospel of personal salvation in Christ!

Paul was one of the greatest intellects of his day. Certainly after becoming a Christian, Paul was one of the most enlightened intellects of all time. Yet through his intellectual approach to the Athenians he won only a few. Through his preaching of the cross of Christ to the lost he won multitudes. This is not to decry intellectual content in sermons. The preacher must bring every bit of his capable brainpower to the preparation and delivery of his message. Nonetheless that message must be the gospel of Jesus Christ as set forth in Scripture. He should also make sure the intellectual structure and form of the message is not an obscuring overlay, but a setting in which the gospel can shine forth in purity and simplicity. Just as a jeweler's box ought not to outshine the diamond ring it contains, so we must present the gospel in such a way that it does not exalt our prowess but the Lord's power.

> This mortal life is far too brief,
>   Eternity too vast,
> To follow human sophistries
> And lose the soul at last.
>   —M. D. Clayburn

The Wisdom of Man Versus the Wisdom of God

The Apostle Paul recognized that the two main characteristics of the people of Corinth were the demand for miracles in the name of Christ and the demonstration of human wisdom. Even so, Paul would not adapt his preaching to what they wanted. He determined to preach nothing among them but the Christ of the cross.

Not that Paul could not perform miracles. He did so when he felt the necessity and wisdom of such acts, as is recorded in the following Scriptures: In Acts 13:11 we find him punishing Elymas the sorcerer with blindness. In Acts 14:10 he healed a cripple. In Acts 16:18 he freed a young girl from an evil spirit.

In Acts 19:11 we read that in Ephesus "God wrought special miracles by the hands of Paul." In Acts 20:10 he restored Eutychus to life. In Acts 28:5 he threw off the effects of a venomous snake bite. In Acts 28:8 he healed the father of Publius. In Iconium it was said of Paul and Barnabas, "Long time therefore abode they speaking boldly in the Lord, which gave testimony unto the word of His grace, and granted signs and wonders to be done by their hands" (Acts 14:3). However, in Corinth he did no miracle, nor did he heal himself of the affliction that he called his "thorn in the flesh."

Paul wrote these words to the sign-seeking Corinthians, "And lest I should be exalted above measure through the abundance of the revelations, there was given to me a thorn in the flesh, the messenger of Satan to buffet me, lest I should be exalted above measure" (2 Cor. 12:7). Undoubtedly, the Corinthians expected a sign from Paul as the representative of Christ in Corinth, but he would not grant their request. What if you and I possessed such powers? What a temptation it might be to give people what they wanted! It might further tempt us to follow their way of visible proofs to the knowledge of God, instead of the way of faith prescribed eternally and historically by God Himself.

In the 16th chapter of Luke the Lord gives us a unique account of a sinful rich man who died and went to Hades, the place of torment. A poor man named Lazarus, a believer, died and went to Abraham's bosom, or Paradise, a place of great rejoicing. The rich man was able to see the happy state of the poor man he had refused to help while on earth. He begged permission to go back to earth to warn his brothers, saying, "If one went unto them from the dead, they will repent" (v. 30). Did the Lord take up this challenge? No. Was it because He had no interest in the souls of the living? No. Scripture tells us that He desires salvation for all men (1 Tim. 2:4). Certainly man cannot order God to act as he wants for his salvation. Abraham, speaking as the Lord's representative, answered the rich man, "If they hear not Moses and the prophets, neither will they be persuaded, though one rose from the dead" (v. 31).

Likewise Paul felt that although he could have performed miracles among the Corinthians, the miracles performed by Christ were sufficient to establish his credentials with them. Certainly, he preached about the miracles of Christ to the Corinthians. Paul had demonstrated repeatedly that he had oratorical abilities and a brilliant mind, but he would not parade these gifts midst these Corinthians. He knew the difference in their desire for great oratory and their need to hear of Christ. He would not succumb to their wishes, but would keep himself faithful to God, who calls us, not to be man-pleasers but preachers of the gospel. As learned as Paul is, he boldly declares to the sign-seeking Jews of Corinth, "But we preach Christ crucified." Note that the word "but" (*dé* [1161]) denotes contrast. Clearly he said the same thing to the philosophizing Greeks. Indeed after Paul had defended the gospel before King Agrippa, Festus said to him, "Paul, thou art beside thyself; much learning doth make thee mad" (Acts 26:24).

A young preacher objected to an offer given him as pastorate of a church near a university campus. He explained he would feel reluctant to discourse on science, history, sociology, philosophy, economics, or politics because the professors who taught these subjects might be in the audience. Then, his superior suggested, "Just preach Jesus Christ and Him crucified. Maybe some of those professors don't know that subject so well."

Paul evidently believed that the cross of Christ was God's way of saving men. Of course, he was not implying that the moment you come to the cross your mind stops functioning. God gave your mind the ability to function, and you should use it to the fullest. If you think that Paul did not make full use of his mental capacities when he preached in Corinth, you should read Acts 18:4 in Greek. It tells us the method of Paul's preaching in the synagogue there. The King James Version says, "And he reasoned in the synagogue every Sabbath, and persuaded the Jews and the Greeks." Now the word "reasoned" in Greek is *dielégeto* (1256), from which we derive the English word "dialectics." It comes from *lógos* (3056), meaning "logic, intelligence." In preaching, Paul used his logical and intellectual capacities to the fullest.

In addition, the second significant word in this verse in this connection is "persuaded," *epéithen* (3982). This means that Paul's argumentation, his logic, was so good that it was able to persuade both Jews and Greeks that what he was saying was true. What the Corinthians had considered foolishness, he persuaded them to accept as the wisdom of God. Thus, the first thing we must recognize is that Paul was preaching the cross of Christ as the wisdom of God, capable of saving sinners. Second, we recognize that in preaching he used all the intellectual powers at his command, but he never depended upon them.

Do not despise the preacher who gives the cross the central place in his preaching. He is not stupid. The cross is true wisdom and deserves its central position. Christ's sacrifice for sinners wins human hearts. A young girl once said, "No one shall ever win my hand unless he gives me proof that he would die for me!" Years passed, and one day she heard a Christian speak of what Christ did on the cross. "Here is the One who has died for me!" she exclaimed. "To Him alone shall I devote my heart forever!"

When you sing the words of that hymn, "Love so amazing, so divine, demands my soul, my life, my all," do you really appreciate their significance? Do you fully comprehend that Christ was God in the flesh, who suffered for your sins, the Sinless One for the guilty? If so, you will be able to say with Paul that the

PREACHING CHRIST CRUCIFIED

cross is indeed the wisdom of God that makes men wise unto salvation.

Who Was Responsible for Christ's Death?

Why was the Apostle Paul so single-minded about preaching Christ crucified? Because he realized that God had chosen it to be the means of man's salvation. That is what the Bible teaches from beginning to end. Accordingly, the two ordinances which Christ taught His disciples to observe relate to His death. The ordinance of baptism symbolizes the believer's burial and resurrection with Christ whereas the ordinance of communion, partaking of the bread and wine, symbolizes His broken body and His shed blood.

The Old Testament is full of symbolism and direct prophecies concerning the sacrifice of the Lord. Why was Abel's offering more acceptable to God than Cain's? No doubt because it was a blood offering. What is the significance of the story of Abraham's willingness to sacrifice his son Isaac? Can one adequately explain it except as a foreshadowing of the One who would Himself be sacrificed upon the cross? What was the Passover Feast except a signpost pointing toward Calvary?

Christ Himself spoke of His death, though not as clearly as He would have liked to because as He said to His disciples, "I have yet many things to say unto you, but ye cannot bear them now" (John 16:12). How shocked His disciples were when He mentioned it to them. How little they understood what He meant. In fact, it was not until after the resurrection that they began to comprehend the meaning of the cross.

John the Baptist declared the purpose of Christ's coming right at the outset when he said, "Behold the Lamb of God, which taketh away the sin of the world" (John 1:29). "The Son of man," writes Mark, "came not to be ministered unto, but to minister, and to give His life a ransom for many" (Mark 10:45).

Thus, when Jesus knew the time had come for Him to be offered up, "He steadfastly set his face to go to Jerusalem" (Luke 9:51). He suffered and died as He said, that the Scriptures might be fulfilled.

When we come to the book of the Acts, we find it full of references to the cross. When Peter preached at Jerusalem after Pentecost, he spoke of the Lord's death being the result of "the determinate counsel and foreknowledge of God" (Acts 2:23). In other words, he told the Jews that they were not primarily responsible for the death of Christ, though in handing Him over to the Roman authorities they were the human instruments. Peter hinted that it was something cosmic, something that went right back into eternity. God is in this matter, he declared.

When you study the teaching of Paul in the Book of Acts, you find that he does exactly the same thing. The key verses to the whole understanding of Paul's method are Acts 17:2, 3. Here we find that when he came to the synagogue at Thessalonica he "reasoned with them out of the Scriptures, opening and alleging, that Christ must needs have suffered, and risen again from the dead; and that this Jesus, whom I preach unto you, is Christ." (See "The Preaching of the Cross," by Martyn Lloyd Jones, in *The Christian World Pulpit*, Vol. 139, pp. 232, 233.)

Thus, when Paul came to Corinth, he preached Christ crucified even though he knew the Jews considered this a stumbling block. Observe that the reference is to Christ crucified, and not Jesus. If Paul were preaching Jesus crucified, the Jews would not have objected, for He would be just another man crucified, as were so many in the world's history. However the crucified Christ was the Messiah, God's anointed, the God-Man. Since they rejected the Messiahship of the Lord Jesus, naturally they rejected the idea that His crucifixion held any value for them or anybody else. The Jews expected a victorious Christ, one who would restore the glories of the kingdom of David and Solomon.

Instead He died on a cross. For the Jews the cross was the last stroke against any hope of their accepting Jesus as their Messiah (Matt. 27:42; Luke 24:21).

The Greek word given for "stumbling block" is *skándalon* (4625). Unfortunately this translation is not satisfactory since *skándalon* actually means a trap or snare laid for an enemy (in the Septuagint; Josh. 23:13; 1 Sam. 18:21. Also Rom. 11:9; 1 Pet. 2:7, 8). An older form of the word is *skandaléthron*, which translates as a trap-spring. A trap-spring, also called *pássalos* or *rhóptron*, is a trap's stick which holds bait until by its touch an animal causes it to spring up and shut the trap (Liddell and Scott, *Greek English Lexicon*). Of course its metaphysical meaning is a stumbling block, or that which stands in the way. Think of a rat going after a piece of cheese in a trap. The moment the rat tries to take it, down comes the bar that kills him. That is what Christ crucified is to the Jews, a death trap. Instead of enabling them to see Israel restored to its glory, the would-be Messiah was trapped and died. To them He is now dead and brings no good to the realization of their dreams.

In the expression "Christ crucified" the verb is *estauroménon* (4717) in Greek. Because this verb is a perfect passive participle, it indicates two things. First, Christ's crucifixion is fixed; He will not be crucified again. It was a once-and-for-all act in the world's history. It stands on its merits, whether the Jews like it or not. Second, the passive voice indicates that someone other than Christ crucified Him. Paul believed this other was God, while the unbelieving Jews thought it was man. For God, the cross represented the voluntary sacrifice of His Son; therefore, the atonement for sin. For the Jews, it was the springing of the trap, the death trap placed by man that took Jesus' life and, therefore, prevented Him from proving He was the Messiah and thus saving His people.

A Christian gave a Jewish woman in a large hospital a gospel tract, the title of which was "Knowing Christ as Savior, Lord, and Friend." She accepted the tract graciously, and seeing the title asked, "Do you believe, as some people do, that the Jews crucified Jesus?" The woman who gave her the tract prayed silently for a moment and then gave the right answer to the question: "It was my sins and your sins that put Christ on the cross." Then she quoted Isaiah 53:5, "But He was wounded for our transgressions, He was bruised for our iniquities." If you view the cross as God's voluntary act of sacrifice of the Son for our sins, you can be saved. If you see it as a death trap set and sprung by man, you are lost—that is, eternally separated from God.

Will All Religions Lead You to God?

Some people do not feel that the cross of Jesus—and they usually refer to Him as Jesus instead of Christ—differs much from other crosses. His enemies murdered Him, and He could not help Himself. They do not consider this unique, for how does His death differ from that of many other good men who have suffered for their beliefs? For many people the crucifixion has no significance beyond being a very sad event. Agreeing that the death of Jesus stands out vividly in history, they blame this on the emphasis which Christians have placed on it. So the cross is for many a death trap. Such people stress the life of Jesus rather than His death. This explains why so many people claim to draw their inspiration from Jesus but have little concern for the particular manner of His death.

Remember that the Romans practiced crucifixion. That, in itself, would make the Jews hate a cross. Although the Old Testament mentions punishment by hanging on a tree, the usual Jewish method of execution was to pelt the victim with stones until he or she was dead. To be hung upon a tree was to suffer the most ignominious death that cruel men could devise.

Moreover they considered a cross, being made of wood, a tree. The book of Deuteronomy goes so far as to say, "He that is hanged is accursed of God" (Deut. 21:23).

Even though, to the Jews, the manner of Christ's death was the one shameful event of His amazing life, His crucifixion remains a fact of history. The perfect participle *estauroménon*, "crucified," indicates the unchangeableness of His crucifixion. No view or explanation of man can change its true occurrence. For instance, it made no difference in the sun's power and influence that man once believed it to be a tiny planet dancing around the earth. Though new knowledge convinced all thinking men that the sun was a mighty force in the vast universe and our earth but a tiny speck, the sun remained the same, unaffected by what men thought from age to age.

In 1 Corinthians 1:23, Paul explains that he used the term "Greeks" in verse 22 to refer to the whole Gentile world, the unbelieving non-Jews, among whom the Greeks held intellectual leadership. The word "foolishness" in verse 23 is exactly the same Greek word *moría* (3472) used in verse 18. Again we see that the logic of the cross is foolishness to the lost ones.

Now Paul says the crucified Christ is foolishness to the Gentiles (non-Jews). Therefore, if those who think the cross foolishness are lost, the Gentiles who consider the crucified Christ foolishness are lost. Your view of Him indicates whether you are lost or saved.

The Gentiles did not first make a careful study of the gospel and then reach a verdict. So drunk with their own conceited pride, they did not care to examine any views other than those they already held. To the Greeks, it was either that all religions are equally good, or no religion is good. They would not narrow to one way to God, one way of salvation and therefore would not attribute redemptive uniqueness to Christ's death on the cross. The story of a man crucified, who would redeem all who looked upon Him by faith was just too simple for their minds to accept. It is ridiculous, they said, for such an important matter as man's relationship with God to be resolved so easily. The very simplicity of the cross baffled them. One could not accuse the Greeks of an open rejection so much as of a contemptuous pre-judgment, made without properly hearing and weighing the evidence. In summary, their attitude was "It couldn't be; therefore it isn't."

Applied to the specific fact of the resurrection as Paul so brilliantly examines it in 1 Corinthians 15, they said, "The resurrection is impossible; therefore Christ did not rise." Only a mind so proud of its knowledge that it is sure it could not be wrong would say, "You couldn't be right, so why bother to examine your viewpoint or even your evidences for the fact itself?" This is the attitude of many intellectuals today. There can be no objection to free thought because God gave us freedom to think and choose. But the same God gave us standards of right and wrong. There is an acceptable yardstick against which our views can be measured.

You may complain about narrow-mindedness. Why should God decree the cross as the only means for man's redemption? Surely other religions, other ways, must be equally meritorious. You may argue against oxygen being the only element that will keep breath in your body, but you must still breathe it to stay alive. Why accept God's decree in this matter for keeping you alive physically, and reject His right to establish Christ crucified as the only way for you to obtain eternal life? You have the freedom to reject oxygen, of course, but you will die. And you have the freedom to reject the cross of Christ without even seriously considering it, but you have no voice in what the consequence of your choice will be. God has inexorably set the penalty—spiritual death.

Of course, you may object that some who preach the gospel are not as well educated or intellectual as you. The Greeks also objected to the fact that the preachers of Christianity were mostly ignorant and humble men. These men had no training in the Greek schools, and thus did not even represent the intellectual element in Judaism. Paul, of course, was a notable exception. (See "The Cross a Stumbling Block," by Ralph H. Turner, in *The Christian World Pulpit*, Vol. 142, pp. 14–24.)

However, one need not be a university graduate to report facts accurately. The character of a witness determines his credibility. Certainly a witness that has nothing personal to gain by giving his testimony will have good credibility. The Bible consists of sixty-six books, written by about forty different human authors, some well educated, some not. Regardless of their education, most writers of the Bible had strength of character since they continued to deliver God's message to a sinful world which scorned and persecuted them.

> Whence but from heaven could men unskilled in arts,
> In several ages born, in several parts,
> Weave such agreeing truths? Or how or why
> Should all conspire to cheat us with a lie?
> Unasked their pains, ungrateful their advice,
> Starving their gain, and martyrdom their price!

LESSONS:

1. The objection of the natural man is not to preaching per se, but to the preaching of the cross of Christ which involves an acknowledgment of man's lost condition.
2. There is a threefold diversity when men view Christ crucified: there is the physical, represented by the Jew; the intellectual, represented by the Greek; and the spiritual, represented by those who have been saved through personal acceptance of Christ as Savior among both Jews and Gentiles.
3. In all of His dealings with men, God follows an order and a plan which He will execute in His own time.
4. The greatest evil in the world is not ill health, or earthquakes, or any other physical calamity, but sin, which has caused all suffering.

PREACHING CHRIST CRUCIFIED

5. The paradox of Christianity is not only that human wisdom failed to reach its goal, but that God meant it to fail. In spite of all the efforts of the Greeks to discover God by reasoning, they failed.
6. Philosophy will never enable anyone to achieve life's primary need— knowing God.
7. Man cannot order God to act as he wants for his salvation.
8. Although the Jews were the human instruments who handed Christ over to the Roman authorities to be crucified, it was the sins of all of us that put Christ on the cross.

1 Cor. 1:24

The Power and Wisdom of God

But unto them which are called, both Jews and Greeks, Christ the power of God, and the wisdom of God.

The gospel of forgiveness through faith in Christ's cross may be a stumbling block to the Jews and foolishness to the Greeks—that is, the Gentiles—but there is a third category of men. Besides the materialists and the intellectuals, there are also the spiritually-minded. First Corinthians 1:24 makes reference to these: "But unto them which are called, both Jews and Greeks, Christ the power of God, and the wisdom of God."

Dying To Conquer

"To them which are called" refers to the same class that we find in verse 18, "to those that are being saved." This is the effectual call unto salvation issued to those who will accept the offer of redemption through Christ crucified. These are those who have not only heard the invitation of Christ, "Come unto me," but have responded by coming. Of course, many are called but not all respond and are therefore not saved. Jesus says of them, "For many are called, but few are chosen" (Matt. 22:14).

We see from this that there are two calls. John Bunyan illustrates it this way: "The hen has two calls, the common cluck, which she gives daily and hourly, and the special one which she means for her little chickens." Moreover, Spurgeon says,

> There is a general call, a call made to every man; every man hears it. Many are called by it; you are called . . . in that sense, but very few are chosen. The other is the special call, the children's call. You know how the bell sounds over the workshop to call the men to work—that is a general call. A father goes to the door and calls out, "John, it's dinner time!"—that is the special call. Many are called with the general call, but they are not chosen; the special call is for the children only, and that is what is meant in the text, "Unto them which are called, both Jews and Greeks, Christ the power of God, and the wisdom of God." That call is always a special one. . . . It is an effectual call. There is no resisting it.

It is a roll call, name by name. Christ positively affirmed, "All that the Father giveth me shall come" (John 6:37). Only God can give this special effective call. You may try to resist it, but you will finally surrender. Saul the persecutor was a prime example of trying to resist the effectual call of Christ. He finally succumbed when Christ used his very name saying, "Saul, Saul, why persecutest thou me?" (Acts 9:4). The effectual call of Christ came to Zaccheus in a similar way. Having climbed a tree to see Jesus amidst a crowd, he witnessed the Lord step under the tree and say to him, "Zaccheus, make haste, and come down; for today I must abide at thy house" (Luke 19:5). Spurgeon explains, "Zaccheus was taken in the net; he heard his own name; the call sank into his soul; he could not stay up in the tree, for an Almighty impulse drew him down." (See C. H. Spurgeon, *New Park Street Pulpit*, Vol. 1, p. 56.)

The Jews had no cause to expect military exploits, miraculous victories, and outward splendor in their Messiah. Their prophets had foretold that He was to come to them lowly and meek (Zech. 9:9; Matt. 21:5), to be despised and rejected of men, to pour out His soul unto death an offering for sin, and to make intercession for transgressors (Is. 53). If His death, for want of knowing the Scriptures, appeared an objection, His rising again and ascension into heaven was full proof of His authority. Although He brought them no deliverance from temporal enemies, He freed them from infinitely more formidable ones, from sin and guilt and the wrath of God. Furthermore, rather than instituting a short-lived tyranny over the nations of the earth, He obtained for them an eternal triumph over death and hell, making them kings and priests unto God, to reign with Him forever and ever. Thus Christ was, in this most important sense, the power of God unto salvation. Certainly His real greatness exceeded all that they looked for, unspeakably more.

When Christ crucified is preached, He can become to those who believe "Christ, God's power and God's wisdom." In other words, without Christ all men live in a weak and foolish state called sin. With Christ man has a new inner self and salvation from death. For God had decreed that "The wages of sin is death" (Rom. 6:23). Then He paid the penalty of death through the blood of His Son. God judged sin at the cross and canceled man's debt to Him. If it were not for the cross of Christ, we would all be eternally lost. Christ died in our place, for it should have been our death. If we accept His sacrifice for us, then we are saved. Because Christ paid for our sin, He is the only One who has the power to forgive it.

God will meet us nowhere except at Calvary, and, if we will not meet Him at the cross in grace, we must meet Him at the throne in judgment. The cross is the point of contact between God and the sinner. In the death of Christ we recognize our identification with Him. When Christ died on the cross, we died with Him. We are now in a position where we can be conquerors over everything in and around us that is against God and would hinder us from knowing His power. (See Gordon Watt, *The Cross in Faith and Conduct*, pp. 75–77.)

THE POWER AND WISDOM OF GOD

O help me, Lord, to realize
    That Thou art all in all;
That I am more than conqueror
    In great things and in small.
No need have I but Thou hast met
    Upon the cruel tree.
O precious, dying, risen Lord,
    Thou art my victory!
                —Avis B. Christiansen

Power That Can Change Your Life

Tacitus, that great Roman historian of the First Century, made a wise observation when he said, "The lust for power, for dominating others, inflames the heart more than any other passion." Power is a word of rather terrible significance among men. Of all gifts they crave, it is what they want most. They desire money, of course, but only because it has the power to buy and command.

What suffering the lust for power has caused! The power of kings and tyrants, the power of the mob, the power of armies and navies, the power of wealth, position, and place—this was the power the Jew looked for in his Messiah. However God sent a helpless baby who later became a crucified Jesus. It was the power of love working by attraction rather than compulsion. It was the appeal of a life laid down, the power of service to the uttermost. It was the power to transform a human life so that men might not only know what is right but also acquire the will to do it.

The ancient world had ethical codes in abundance, but not the power to live up to them. What is the use of accumulating knowledge, education, and culture of the mind if they do not help you find an answer to the great questions of life? History shows that the educated man is as liable to moral weakness and even the grosser sins as his more ignorant brother. What men needed then as now is not so much a demonstration of Christ's power and wisdom through miracles, but power that could change their lives. Paul was able to compare the changed lives of Corinth's Christian community with the lives of Corinth's pagans who professed such a great love for wisdom. Christ wrought not the mere illumination of reason, but the redemption of the whole man.

A Korean once came to a missionary and said, "We have a code of morals. We have known what we ought to do, and what we ought not to do, but we have had no power to do what we knew to be right. But when Jesus Christ came into our lives, we had power to do right!" Jesus Christ, the living Word of God, is the power of God that can change men's lives.

This reminds me of the story of a man who was sitting on a pile of planks next to a package on the sidewalk. Two officers passing by noticed the bundle and, ever suspicious of bombs, stopped and asked what it contained. "Dynamite!" said the man. The officers jumped. One officer gingerly seized the package, and the other seized the man, taking both to police headquarters. When they opened the package, they found it contained Bibles! "Where is the dynamite?" inquired the officers. "The Word of God is quick, and powerful, and sharper than any two-edged sword!" replied the Bible distributor.

He was right. Our English word "dynamite" closely relates to the Greek word the sacred writer uses for "powerful." And the *dúnamis* (1411), "power," of 1 Corinthians 1:24 is the cross of Christ. It is the power against sin. Through his presentation of Christ crucified as the power of God Paul implies that a person indulging in sin is weak. There is no other way to become strong in your soul than by coming to the cross.

Paul also implies that the sinner is ignorant from God's point of view. This is spiritual ignorance which is the result of sin. There was never a more striking show of the barrenness and powerlessness of mere intellect than in the altar the Athenians built to "The Unknown God." Then man's extremity was God's opportunity; He Himself revealed that which man's intellect had vainly tried to find; and Christ became the wisdom of God to men. After cleansing our moral nature, He enables us to see things truly and clearly, leaving the Christian with the only true philosophy of life. With Christian holiness and humility, he has the only true means to knowledge. One has well said, "A Christian on his knees sees farther than a philosopher ever will on his tiptoes." With Christ as his wisdom, he can say exultantly through all the light and shadow of earth's journey, "Lord, to whom shall we go? thou hast the words of eternal life" (John 6:68).

The only proof you need that the cross of Christ is the power and wisdom of God is the changed lives of those who have embraced it. Examine how born-again believers behave and think, in contrast to their former life. By doing this you will realize that what people think foolishness is wiser than their wisdom, and what they consider weakness is more powerful than all the strength that they possess. That is the gist of 1 Corinthians 1:25: "Because the foolishness of God is wiser than men; and the weakness of God is stronger than men." God's power and wisdom are far superior to any that man possesses.

It is noteworthy that instead of using the substantive *mōría* (3472), "foolishness" in verse 25, as he did in previous verses, Paul uses the expression *tó* (3588) *mōrón* (3474), "that which seems or is foolish." Furthermore he uses *tó asthenés* (772), "that which is weak," to make "weakness" agree with *tó mōrón*. Of course, both of these, the foolish thing and the weak thing, refer to Christ crucified. Paul does not wish to ascribe the abstract qualities of foolishness and weakness to God, as if they were His attributes. Considering it erroneous to even put the accusation that God is foolish and weak on the lips of a fool, he transfers

the whole argument to man. Look at the saved man. Is he
wiser or more foolish than the sinner? Is he stronger or weaker?
Paul answers categorically that he is wiser and stronger. Indeed the power and wisdom of the cross of Christ find their
proof in human lives.

Consider former teenager Nicky Cruz, gang leader and
troublemaker whose delight was to torment the weak and helpless, and to fight for the sheer love of violence. He went to a
gospel meeting to break it up, and instead the love of Christ
broke him. He became a full-time evangelist with a special
ministry among young people. (See "God's Cure for the Dope
Addict," in *Quest for Reality*, compiled by Merton B. Osborn, pp.
43–50.)

A changed life is an incontrovertible argument. One illustration of this is in the story of a subtle Greek philosopher
Zeno. For when he was once trying to show that there is no such
thing as motion, Diogenes simply got up and walked about!
Therefore when cynics sneer at Christianity and say it is all a lot
of nonsense, the best way to refute them is to produce the evidence of a changed life.

LESSONS:

1. God has two calls. One is a general call, made to every man. Everyone
   is called in this sense, but few are chosen. God also has a special call
   meant only for His children. This special call is an effectual call.
   There is no resisting it.
2. Jesus Christ, the living Word of God, is the power of God that can
   change men's lives—not merely their intellect or reason, but their
   whole lives.
3. The only proof or demonstration anyone needs that the cross of
   Christ is the power and wisdom of God is to look at those whose lives
   have been changed by it.

THE POWER AND WISDOM OF GOD

1 Cor. 1:25, 26	*The Foolishness of God and the Wisdom of Men*

Because the foolishness of God is wiser than men; and the weakness of God is stronger than men. For ye see your calling, brethren, how that not many wise men after the flesh, not many mighty, not many noble, are called.

Most of the perplexity that troubles men's minds in this complex civilization of ours is due to their estrangement from God. Isaiah recognized this long ago when he declared that God's thoughts are not our thoughts, nor our ways God's ways (Is. 55:8).

Take God's thought about the world in which we live. When everything is green and pleasant, we concur that it is a beautiful world. However when tempest and storm visit the earth, we are of a different mind. We look at the devastation caused by earthquake and flood and say, "This is not the kind of world I would have made."

What Kind of World Would You Have Made?

If we had our way in making the world, we would have kept the flowers, the birds, the leafy trees, the blue skies, and the sunshine. Even so, we would have done away with pestilential insects and the wild and savage beasts. The flowers would never wither, the trees would never shed their leaves, the birds would never cease to sing, and June would never give place to January. The blue skies would never weep with blinding rain, and storms and earthquakes would never shake the earth. Ours would be a world without an ugly or painful thing in it. There would be nothing to hurt or destroy.

Moreover, passing to man, we would have arranged human life differently. There would be no suffering, no pain, no disease. We cannot understand them; we cannot fathom why a good God ever allowed them. We think that if we had God's power, we could make a better and happier world than this. Why, for instance, did God make the conditions of life such that we have to work for our daily bread? We prefer leisure to work. And what about temptation, sin, and death? Why should these things be here at all? A world without problems, temptations, pain, and death—a world in which the sky is always blue and the sun always shines—this is our idea of a good world.

In view of all this, how can we regard God's wisdom as higher than ours? How can we consider Him all-powerful? If we had the chance, we would make a better job of things. That is what we are saying when we reject Him as foolish in His creation, providence, and redemption of man.

The truth is that God's wisdom is so much higher than ours, is so eternal in its encompassment, that we lack the ability to comprehend it. As much as a child may try to understand the reasons behind some of his parents' acts, he simply cannot. He considers them foolish, but wise parental actions do not change to accommodate the child. We can trace a great part of society's moral decay to the parental abandonment of wisdom to comply with foolish desires of young, immature minds.

Moreover, when it comes to our Heavenly Father, how can any of us compare His wisdom with ours? He makes a flower, but once we cut it from the stem we cannot even put it together again—though we pride ourselves on being able to take a trip to the moon and back. To the scoffer who looks at the cross and says, "God! What a fool!" I would say, "Just a minute! How would you have redeemed the world?" God's thoughts are so infinitely higher than ours that we fail to appreciate them.

We want a world of ease and comfort. Therefore to us an ideal world would have no temptation, suffering, death, or the need for hard work. However, God had something better and more worthy in mind than this when He made the world—a world in which we must face and endure difficulty, sorrow, toil and pain. After all, comfort and ease are rather ignoble ambitions. If God's ideal for Himself were the same as ours, He would never have allowed the crucifixion of the Lord Jesus Christ for our salvation.

What God had in mind for us was not comfort but character. And character develops best, not in a world of ease, but in a world of conflict and struggle. Man being what he is, such a world as we sometimes dream about would be his ruin. A perfected man is ready for a world without struggle or sorrow, pain or death. Certainly this kind of world is a picture of the life to come. Nevertheless, in his present sinful state, sorrow, pain, loss and temptation are necessary for his moral discipline and development. God aims not for comfort but for an enriched and purified soul.

God's thoughts about values, about the things that are worth possessing, are certainly not ours. Ours gather about temporal and material things like success and wealth, rank and fame. However God does not judge men on that basis. In Luke 18:9–14 the Lord Jesus tells of two men who went to the temple to pray. One was a respectable religious character, the other a sinful publican. Who went home justified? Not the self-righteous Pharisee who thanked God he was not like other men, but the poor repentant sinner.

THE FOOLISHNESS OF GOD AND THE WISDOM OF MEN

We esteem outward appearances and performances, while God esteems a contrite spirit and a humble heart. We measure by size; God measures by quality. Hence for Him the poor widow with her pennies gave more than the rich. God has different standards of values from ours. Whose scale of values is right? We know deep in our hearts that God's is. He does not value wealth, fame or rank, but goodness, truth and love, and a contrite and humble spirit. Our peace and happiness in life depend on making God's power and wisdom ours.

In this entire portion of 1 Corinthians 1 Paul has been primarily addressing God's thoughts and actions concerning man's redemption as indicative of God's foolishness and weakness. How can anyone regard Omnipotence as wise in causing the One in whom dwelt all the fullness of the Godhead bodily to die on a cross? Force was the Jews' method of redeeming the world—and it seems to be ours also. God's method was that of sacrificial love. God's thought clashes with ours. It offends our pride to have to receive salvation as a gift; we would prefer to earn it.

You remember how, when Naaman came to Elisha with hope of being cured of his leprosy, he had formed his own idea of how the prophet would heal him. "He will surely come out to me, and stand, and call on the name of the Lord his God, and strike his hand over the place, and recover the leper" (2 Kgs. 5:11). Instead of coming out to receive him, the prophet sent a message to him saying, "Go and wash in Jordan seven times, and thy flesh shall come again to thee, and thou shalt be clean" (v. 10). Naaman was angry. This message hurt his pride. The demand was too simple, and he was about to turn back to Syria in a rage.

In the same way, God's method of redeeming men hurts their pride. "What shall we do," asked the Jews, "that we might work the works of God?" (John 6:28). That is what we want—to do something, to feel that we can earn our acceptance and redemption. The truth is we can do nothing; we must accept salvation as a gift if we are to have it at all. "I will take the cup of salvation, and call upon the name of the Lord" (Ps. 116:13). There is a fountain opened by God's grace for all sin and uncleanness, and all we have to do is to wash and be clean. God's thoughts about redemption are not our thoughts. "For as the heavens are higher than the earth," so are God's thoughts higher than our thoughts (Is. 55:9). It would have been a hopeless business for us if He had left us to earn our salvation. No, we must say with the hymn-writer:

> Nothing in my hands I bring;
> Simply to Thy cross I cling.
> [See *Morning and Evening*, by
> J. D. Jones, pp. 182–196.]

The Appeal of Jesus to the Universal Heart

If asked what qualifications a ruler should have who would win men's allegiance, would you answer, "Someone like Jesus Christ?" Look at Christ, not only on the cross, but also in the manger. Would you not have said it was foolish for Him to be born in any place except a palace if people were to accept Him as King? Who would ever expect God to come down as a little child, a poor child at that? Why arrange it so that what occurs between His childhood and the time of His public ministry is unknown? Why call poor, unlearned, unknown fishermen to spread His gospel? Is that wisdom?

Yes, there was divine wisdom in the seeming foolishness of the birth and early years of Jesus. He would not have been a complete man if He had not submitted to the weakness and helplessness of real babyhood and childhood. He would not have been "touched with the feeling of our infirmities" (Heb. 4:15), if He had not been born of a woman and grown as we grow. Likewise, He would have been entirely outside the experiences of the great mass of mankind if He had been born in a palace and nurtured in the lap of luxury.

After all, the vast majority of mankind belong to the ranks of the toiling poor. The rich are a tiny minority. Many have but little of this world's goods. When Christ stooped to that lowly birth, when He emptied Himself and took upon Himself the form of a servant, He identified Himself with the bulk of mankind. Yes, it would have been sheer foolishness—that lowly birth and humble upbringing—if God's purpose was to win a temporal kingdom for Jesus in Palestine. However, if His purpose was to win a kingdom in the hearts of men everywhere, we can see now that the foolishness of God was wiser than the wisdom of men.

Jesus made His appeal to the universal heart. The tendency of all religions that address themselves to the intellect—to educated and cultured people—is to become exclusive, to become scornful of the uneducated and the poor. A religion that was only for the philosophical and the learned would have shut out the great mass of mankind. Plato and Socrates are the delight of the few, but Christ is the Savior of the world.

What would have happened if Jesus had yielded to the temptation to come down from the cross and sit on a king's throne? It would have meant the establishment of a temporary earthly kingdom; while through the cross He established His kingdom in the hearts of men forever. "And of His kingdom there shall be no end" (Luke 1:33).

It seemed stupid to suggest that the death of Jesus could really save men from sin, but it did. To rob Christ of His cross is to strip Him of His power to save souls. It was an act of supreme wisdom to die in our place instead of leaving us to try to find our way of salvation and so be lost forever. The wisdom of true love is to do what will promote the highest welfare of the one we love most. Truly God so loved mankind that He could not help giving His Son to die for us. (See *Richmond Hill Sermons*, by J. D. Jones, pp. 23–39.)

In effect, Paul applies this to the believers at Corinth in 1 Corinthians 1:26 when he says, "Look at yourselves and see what happened and how you measure up when compared to your unbelieving neighbors. What I have said about the superiority of God's wisdom over man's wisdom, in connection with the supposed foolishness of Christ's death on the cross for our redemption, is not just an abstract idea. There can be practical proof of it."

The first word of verse 26 is *blépēte* (991), "see." This can be either in the second person present indicative or in the present imperative. If it is the first, it merely means "You see," as the King James Version has it. Nevertheless, I believe it is an imperative, a command, a challenge that Paul throws out to the Corinthians. "See! Look!" This fits in with the heated discussion Paul has been carrying on to prove how wrong man is in thinking that God was a fool, a weakling, in sacrificing His Son on the cross. "Hold on!" bursts Paul. "Look at yourselves and see what that idea has done to you!"

The conjunction *gár* (1063), translated "for," which follows in the Greek text, would carry the emphasis better were it translated "therefore." "Look therefore at your calling, brethren." The word for "calling" is *klēsin* (2821), the substantive of the adjectival noun *klētoís* (2822), "the called ones," which Paul used in verse 24 to indicate those effectually called who believed the gospel. It is equivalent to the word "salvation" in one of its aspects. He uses the word *klēsin*, "call," however, to underline the emphasis of the offer, the provision of salvation rather than the reception of it. In the matter of man's salvation God must receive all the credit, and He stands a better chance to receive all the glory. Our acceptance of God's gift is secondary. Were it not for the offer, there would be no acceptance. "Therefore look at your

THE FOOLISHNESS OF GOD AND THE WISDOM OF MEN

calling" could be paraphrased, "Therefore look at what Christ did for you," not "How wonderfully you responded to His call."

The next clause further explains the word "calling": "how that not many wise men after the flesh, not many mighty, not many noble, are called." The common people composed the great majority of the Christian church in Corinth, as they do everywhere. Of Christ it is written, "And the common people heard Him gladly" (Mark 12:37). In Corinth God honored Paul's preaching so that some dignitaries were also saved, such as the two chief rabbis of the Jewish synagogue, Crispus and Sosthenes (see Acts 18:8, 17), as well as the city treasurer, Erastus (Rom. 16:23).

The bulk of the believers, however, were common people, most probably slaves. "Not many wise . . . mighty . . . noble." Paul repeats the phrase "not many" three times for emphasis. "Not many" means that God did call and save some. "O Father, Lord of heaven and earth . . . thou hast hid these things from the wise and prudent, and hast revealed them unto babes" (Matt. 11:25). For though God does save some wise people (according to the flesh), some mighty, and some of noble birth, He does not save many. We cannot deny this. It was so in the experience of Christ and of Paul, and 1 Corinthians 1:29 gives the reason for it, "That no flesh should glory in his presence."

One Discovery You Cannot Possibly Make

The popular notion of the man on the street is that you have to be "good" to get to heaven. In his mind he argues, "I'm as good as anybody else, so I'll take my chances on getting there." His notion of salvation is that, if you are not a criminal but just an average "good guy," God will not be too hard on you. Just what kind of people does God save? Jesus Christ answered this by saying, "I am not come to call the righteous, but sinners to repentance" (Matt. 9:13).

In 1 Corinthians 6:9–11 the Apostle Paul tells us what kind of people were saved in Corinth. The list is impressive. The worst sinners were effectively called through Christ crucified. "Know ye not that the unrighteous shall not inherit the kingdom of God? Be not deceived: neither fornicators, nor idolaters, nor adulterers, nor effeminate, nor abusers of themselves with mankind, nor thieves, nor covetous, nor drunkards, nor revilers, nor extortioners, shall inherit the kingdom of God." Then he adds, "And such were some of you."

That is the past tense of those whom Christ came to save. What was their present condition? "But ye are washed, but ye are sanctified, but ye are justified in the name of the Lord Jesus, and by the Spirit of our God." That is what the wisdom and power of God did—and still does—through Christ crucified.

Speaking of the "wise men after the flesh," the great majority of whom rejected the gospel, Paul does not attribute to them real wisdom, moral strength, or true nobility. Their "wisdom according to the flesh" (*katá* [2596] *sárka* [from *sárx* {4561}]) was not of God. According to Paul, the flesh (*sárx*) is the willing instrument of sin and is subject to sin to such a degree that wherever flesh is, all forms of sin are likewise present. Paul also declares that no good thing can live in the flesh (Rom. 7:18). Although the expression *katá sárka* occurs only after "the wise," it also qualifies the other two adjectival nouns, "the mighty" and "the noble." Thus, all three classes are characterized by worldliness—worldly wisdom, worldly power, and worldly nobility.

The word for "wise" is *sóphoi* (4680), exactly the same word Paul has used throughout this passage. Using this word he refers to human wisdom. The word for "mighty" is *dúnatoi* (1415) which is the same word as *dúnamis* (1411), "power," the power of God as referred to in verse 24. All three are counterfeit qualities that sinful men exhibit. While they may seem to be wise, strong and powerful, it is not the wisdom and strength of God which results from their salvation, as spoken of in verse 24.

However, verse 26 adds another element that is especially applicable to the Jews. It is the element of ancestry, of noble birth. The word in Greek is *eugeneís* (2104) which literally means "those of good birth" (*eú* [2095], "good"; *génos* [1085], "family, birth, ancestry"). The Jews constantly argued that they were perfect before God because they were the sons of Abraham. John the Baptist denounced their pretensions, however, when he called them "the offspring of vipers" (*gennḗmata* [1081] *échidnōn* [2191]; Matt. 3:7; Luke 3:7).

In the 8th chapter of John we find the Lord Jesus having a lively discussion with the Jews. "I know that ye are Abraham's seed," He said to them (v. 37). That was their noble birth. But of what use was it? They were not following in their Father Abraham's footsteps. "If ye were Abraham's children, ye would do the works of Abraham," Jesus told them. "Ye are of your father the devil" (vv. 39, 44). Scripture represents the devil as a serpent, a snake, a viper. Jesus did not accept the Jew's claim of perfection because they were of the ancestry of Abraham. They were rather despicable snakes because of their pride and arrogance. When it comes to their relationship with God, some people will claim they have no need of repentance because of their ancestry. Few who pride themselves on being righteous because of belonging to a good family will accept Christ's sacrifice for them. It takes much humbling for one of noble birth to kneel at the cross with common people.

That which is of the world is enmity to God. The flesh does not receive the things of the Spirit. The Lord brought this out in the conversation He had with Nicodemus. This Jewish religious leader could not understand the miracle of regeneration. He was wise according to the flesh; he was mighty; he was noble. Nonetheless, the Lord had to say to him, "That which is born of the flesh [*sárkos*] is flesh; and that which is born of the Spirit is spirit" (John 3:6).

Neither Paul nor Christ had anything against true wisdom, understanding wisdom as the God-given ability to think. After all, some of the greatest thinkers of all time, among them Paul himself, accepted the grace of God and believed. One of the most fascinating courses I had in college was the History of Science. What particularly impressed me was how many of the early discoverers of our basic scientific principles, such as Newton, Bacon, Pascal, and Boyle, were Christians—in fact, many of them were theologians. Many do not accept God's provision for their salvation not because they are unable to think, but because sin has perverted their thinking. Moreover if these worldly wise, mighty, and noble are to be saved, they must be saved, not because of their human superiority, but because they are willing to set aside their wisdom, might, and nobility. They must become like children, as our Lord said. This does not mean shedding their intelligence, but their pride of intelligence, position, and birth. Those are wise who recognize that they know so little in comparison with God.

Returning to Paul's statement in 1 Corinthians 1:26, "that not many wise men after the flesh, not many mighty, not many noble, are called"—why was this? Because sin had bound them so inseparably to their environment that they could not envision any other way of life. Christianity was something of a novelty to them. Naturally, it would repel those who had least to gain and most to lose by any change. The worldly wise, the mighty, and the noble were privileged classes. Certainly the changes Christ was introducing would have caused a violent upheaval in their lives. Christ required them to come down from their lofty places and kneel with common folk at the foot of the cross. They could not receive salvation in any other way. The gospel is the leveler of all humans.

THE FOOLISHNESS OF GOD AND THE WISDOM OF MEN

Down with thy pride! With holy vengeance trample
  On each self-flattering fancy that appears;
Did not the Lord Himself, for our example,
  Lie hid in Nazareth for thirty years?

LESSONS:

1. God's wisdom is so much higher than ours, is so eternal in its encompassment, that we lack the ability to comprehend it.
2. The Jews' method of redeeming the world was that of force—and it seems to be ours also. God's method was that of sacrificial love. God's thought clashes with ours. It offends our pride to have to receive salvation as a gift; we would prefer to earn it.
3. Jesus Christ's lowly birth and humble upbringing would have been sheer foolishness if God's purpose was to win a temporal kingdom for Jesus in Palestine. However, if His purpose was to win a kingdom in the hearts of men everywhere, His "foolishness" was wiser than the wisdom of men.
4. In the matter of man's salvation God must receive all the credit. There is no glory we can claim that would make us worthy of it.
5. He is wise when he recognizes that he knows so little in comparison with God that there is one discovery he cannot possibly make—how to save himself from sin.

1 Cor. 1:27–29

What God Has Chosen

But God hath chosen the foolish things of the world to confound the wise; and God hath chosen the weak things of the world to confound the things which are mighty; and base things of the world, and things which are despised, hath God chosen, yea and things which are not, to bring to naught things that are: That no flesh should glory in his presence.

The Bible nowhere intimates that God is against the proper use of human intelligence. When Paul declares that God does not call many wise, mighty, or noble men, it is because they are so proud that they refuse to humble themselves to come to Him. Nevertheless, He certainly uses the intelligent and well informed in the pulpit, on the mission field, and in lay witness.

Among those whom Christ called to preach, Paul was intellectually and educationally in a class all his own. However, it was Paul who made these attacks against worldly wisdom, might, and nobility. He knew that they had hindered rather than helped him to yield to the cross of Christ for salvation. This does not mean that he would have been better off ignorant. True, in the novelty of the introduction of Christianity, the majority of the Pharisees and rulers did not believe in Christ (John 7;48: cf. 12:42). Even so, immediately after the day of Pentecost a great company of the priests became obedient to the faith (Acts 6:7). Also many of those who used sorcery at Ephesus brought their books together and burned them publicly (Acts 19:19, 20).

Look at our world today. Which are the most advanced nations and people of the earth, those who have accepted Christianity or those who are apart from its influence? Where ignorance has prevailed, there infidelity and superstition have abounded. At the introduction of Christianity and its initial influence, many of the wise indeed rejected it, but those whose prejudices in favor of their ancient traditions remained unshaken were even more opposed to it. The benefits of knowledge are Incalculable, but such knowledge becomes dangerous when it rejects the One who gave it. Sin can make the educated more dangerous than the ignorant. That is why gross immorality prevailed and still does among the wise, the mighty, and noble according to the flesh. That is what Paul was trying to prove: that the wisdom of the world, the might and power of the world, cannot change the worldling from a debauched sinner to a saint.

God Never Makes Mistakes

God does not depend upon man's wisdom, strength, or noble birth to accomplish His work. True, it has pleased Him to save and use great minds, strong bodies, and persons of noble background. He is no respecter of persons. He does not discriminate against either the poor or the mighty. He saves all who come to Him, as Christ Himself said: "Him that cometh to Me I will in no wise cast out" (John 6:37). However, it is often true that a person who has a crutch of his own to lean on will not turn to God. It is not God's fault that not many wise, mighty, or noble are saved. As many as will come, the Lord will save—but so few come. In contrast, the humble—for indeed humility is the true opposite of all three categories: the worldly wise, mighty, and noble—come in greater numbers.

A skeptical physician declared he could see no reason why he should have to come to the cross of Christ for salvation. A friend gave him a famous apologetics book containing an irresistible defense of the reasonableness of the gospel. It satisfied the doctor's reason, but it did not move his will. A short time later someone called him to the bedside of a little girl who was dying. She whispered that she had something to say to him and that she hardly had the courage to say it as it was about his peace with God. Thus she added, "Tomorrow morning, when I am stronger, I will tell you." However, in the morning she was dead. This led to the physician's conversion and a subsequent life of dedicated Christian service. God used a child rather than an apologist of the faith to lead a learned man to Christ. Interestingly the word *mōrón* (3474) in Modern Greek has come to mean "child, baby." Thus we could paraphrase 1 Corinthians 1:27 as "But God has chosen the *mōrá*—the foolish things, or those who are like little children—and the weak ones of the world, to confound the wise and mighty ones."

Then Paul goes on in verse 28 to add two more classes of people or things to the foolish and the weak that God uses. They are the ignoble or base in the eyes of the world, the despised things that God has chosen, and the things that are not. With the foolish God puts to shame the wise. With the weak God puts to shame the mighty. With the base God puts down those that are lofty. With the despised God brings down the renowned. With those that are not He brings to nothing those that are.

The word that arrests attention here is the verb *exeléxato* (1586), "chose." What can this mean? Does God pick and choose among men? The Greek verb is compound, made up of the preposition *ek* (1537), "from among or out of," and the verb *légō* (3004), "to say with the expression of thought." *Eklégō* (1586) actually means "to select from among, knowing what one is doing." For instance, from a group of applicants standing before him, an employer "selects" one for the job he has in mind. That is the word *eklégō*. Having in mind the task he needs done, he tries to gather as much information as possible about each person. Then he tests them on the basis of all this and makes his selection (*eklogē* [1589]). It is anything but random picking.

Now of course, when you and I choose, we stand the chance of being mistaken about our evaluation. We are not perfect either in our understanding of people or of what purpose needs achievement. Therefore, we may select the wrong person or set the wrong goal. Our knowledge at best is only in part.

With God it is vastly different. He does not blindly select men for salvation or for the accomplishment of His purposes. There is nothing haphazard, capricious, nor frivolous about any of God's activities. Whatever He does, whomever He chooses, or whatever circumstances He selects for every one of us, He bases on a prior full and unmistakable knowledge of everything. Therefore, He cannot make a mistake. God gives His effectual call to salvation to those He knows will respond to it. One cannot say, however, that He willingly blocks anyone, for He desires that none be lost and that all should come to repentance.

The Men and Women God Chooses and Uses

Nowhere does human wisdom seem to be more fallible than in the choice of marriage partners. The divorce statistics are enough to convince someone of this. This also holds true in the business world. An employer hires a man he thinks will do a good job for him. The events prove otherwise, and he has to let him go.

How different it is with God's choices when He calls a man or woman to salvation or service for Him. Paul uses the verb *exeléxato*, "chose," three times in 1 Corinthians 1:27, 28 to refer to God's choice of men. It is in the first aorist tense which fixes this choice in the mind of God once-and-for-all. There is no trial-and-error process with Him. He is not like us who say, "Well, we'll try this or that individual out and see whether he'll prove worthy of our choice." Nothing of the kind. God chooses once-and-for-all, and nothing or no one can snatch those He chooses away from Him. Otherwise, we would have to attribute limited knowledge and faulty action to Him. He would not be God anymore. He would not be omniscient if He could be mistaken about His choices. He cannot be omnipotent if those He chooses manage to escape from His hand. He is an omnipotent and omniscient God, who has said, "I give unto them eternal life; and they shall never perish, neither shall any man pluck them out of my hand" (John 10:28).

The Apostle Paul is trying to emphasize in 1 Corinthians 1:27, 28 that God's choice of people, things, or circumstances is not discriminatory. He is not partial to the wise according to the flesh, or to the mighty or noble of this world. He can and does choose any individual and any circumstance to accomplish His purpose.

There is a little conjunction in these two verses that, like the verb *exeléxato*, "chose," occurs three times. It is the telic conjunction *hína* (2443) meaning "in order to." The King James Version loses sight of it by hiding it in the verbs "to confound, to bring to naught." It would have been clearer and truer to the emphasis of the Greek to say "to" in each instance. In other words, every time God chooses, it is not for the sake of a choice, but for a purpose.

Is that not what Paul really meant in Romans 8:28 when he said, "And we know that all things work together for good to them that love God, to them who are the called according to his purpose"?

WHAT GOD HAS CHOSEN

The temptation to doubt the goodness of God came to a Christian businessman when he had suffered heavy losses. "Why did He allow these reverses to come to me?" he questioned. One night as he sat dejected and discouraged before the fireplace, his six-year-old son came and sat on his lap. Over the mantle hung a motto that read, "God's works are perfect." "Daddy, what does 'perfect' mean?" asked the boy. Then, before the father could reply, he continued, "Does it mean that God never makes a mistake?" The thought was just what the father needed. Hugging his son to him he said, "Yes, Johnny, that's just what it means!"

The word "perfect" in Greek is *téleios* (5046) which comes from *télos* (5056) meaning "end or goal." When you say that your pen is perfect, for instance, you mean that it can accomplish the purpose you bought it for—it can write. The conjunction *hína* is telic, that is, it has a *télos*, a goal, a purpose. Every choice of God has just that. Moreover, that goal or purpose is always for His glory and the accomplishment of His eternal plan. That is what we as children of God should consider "good." Did you ever notice that Romans 8:28 does not say, "All things work together for *your* good," but "for good"? The good as God sees it, not as we with our limited knowledge would have it.

Take the first statement of 1 Corinthians 1:27, "But God hath chosen the foolish things of the world in order to confound the wise" (a.t.). The word *mōrá*, translated "foolish things," is in the neuter gender. It refers primarily to things. Also, the word translated "wise" is *sophoús*, masculine plural, meaning "wise men." God chose foolish things or circumstances in order to confound those who thought themselves wise according to the flesh, as is clearly stated in the previous verse. Nevertheless, we could take *tá* (3588) *mōrá*, in spite of its neuter gender, as indicating people, since in the immediately preceding verse Paul spoke of the wise men, the mighty men, and the noble men (*sophói* [4680], *dúnatoi* [1415], *eugeneís* [2104]: all in the masculine plural). God chose the circumstances, things or people that the world thought foolish to confound worldly wise or conceited people.

What does the Greek verb *kataischúnē* (2617), "to confound," used twice in verse 27, mean? It is a compound verb made up of *kátō* (2736), meaning "down," and *aischúnō* (153), "to bring to shame." It means to bring disillusionment to those who are full of proud confidence. At the end of verse 28, to avoid repeating this verb, Paul uses *katargḗsē* (2673) which is equivalent in meaning. *Katargḗsē* means "to render inactive." God chooses circumstances and people that the world considers foolish to disillusion or render inactive, the minds of the wise. Although they may consider His agencies foolish and ineffective, these wise people of the world come to a point where they cannot say anything and are dumbfounded by God's activities.

Study history, both sacred and secular, and you will see how God has accomplished His purposes by means of seemingly small and contemptible instruments. He cured the snake-bitten Israelites by looking at a serpent of brass. What virtue could there be in a brazen serpent? It was a mere image and was not even applied to the snakebites. Nevertheless, a man had only to look upon it for it to work a cure. (See Num. 21:8, 9.)

The less probability in the instrument, the more it reveals the wisdom of God. The Lord Jesus took clay and applied it to the eyes of a blind man to make him see. Would this not disillusion any ophthalmologist? God's ways seem paradoxical to man. When God desired to elevate Joseph and make all his brothers bow down to him, what method did He choose? First, Joseph was thrown into a pit, then sold into Egypt, and later put in prison (Gen. 39). Through this imprisonment God made a way for his advancement. For God to save in an ordinary way would not so well display His wisdom. Likewise when He goes about it strangely by saving in the very way men think will bring destruction, His wisdom shines forth in a conspicuous manner.

How God Brings Good Out of Evil

"God moves in a mysterious way, His wonders to perform" is an old hymn's truth evident in the unlikely persons and circumstances He often uses to show forth His wisdom. For instance, when God wanted to make Israel victorious over the enemy, He chose a nobody, Gideon, and then cut down his army to virtually nothing. "The people that are with thee are too many," He said (Judg. 7:2). He reduced the army of 32,000 to 300, and by taking away the means of victory He made Israel victorious.

God had a design to bring His people out of Egypt. Only what a strange course He took to bring it about! He stirred up the hearts of the Egyptians to hate the Israelites. "He turned their heart to hate His people" (Ps. 105:25). The more they hated and oppressed Israel the more God plagued the Egyptians, and the more eager they were to let Israel go. "And the Egyptians were urgent upon the people, that they might send them out of the land in haste" (Ex. 12:33).

Moreover God chose to save Jonah from drowning in the sea by allowing a great fish to swallow him up and so bring him safely to shore. God would also save Paul and all that were in the storm-tossed ship with him by first allowing the ship to break up and its passengers to land upon its broken pieces (Acts 27:44).

God's Church often grows in the midst of persecution. God makes the enemy do His work. He can make a straight stroke with a crooked stick. That persecutor of the Church, the Roman Emperor Julian, said, "The showers of blood have made her more fruitful." The Christian life is like ground in that the more it is harrowed the better crop it bears. Examples of this truth are evident in Scripture. For instance, in Exodus the king of Egypt says to the children of Israel, "Come on, let us deal wisely with them; lest they multiply. . . . But the more they afflicted them, the more they multiplied and grew" (Ex. 1:10, 12). Likewise, the apostles scattered by reason of persecution became like the scattering of seed; they went up and down, preaching the gospel and bringing in converts daily. Even so, Paul was put in prison only to have his bonds become his means for spreading the gospel (Phil. 1:12).

Do you find it hard to believe that God's wisdom makes the most desperate evils turn into good for His children? Just as a pharmacist can mix several ingredients that by themselves are poisonous, to make a life-saving medicine, so God makes the most deadly afflictions cooperate for the good of His children. He purifies them and prepares them for heaven (2 Cor. 4:17). God makes His people profit by losses, and turns their crosses into blessings.

Do you realize that God can cause even the sins of men to carry on His work? He does not approve of sin, but He allows man to have freedom of choice, and through that comes sin. Truly, He could crush out sin by crushing out mankind. If God had not given life and breath to the Jews, they could never have crucified Christ. Nevertheless, God did not abhor this sinful act any less.

When a musician plays an out of tune violin, he causes its sound, but the jarring and discord come from the violin itself. Even so, men's natural motion and wisdom are from God, but their sinful motion and thinking are from themselves. Herein is God's wisdom, that the sins of men carry on His work, yet He has no hand in them.

Men today reject God in spite of the fact that they cannot stand the desperate circumstances in which they find themselves. Still the God's wisdom is evident in these desperate cases. Erudite lawyers love to wrestle with difficulties in the law because these show their skill all the more. God's wisdom is never at a loss. Moreover, the Morning Star of deliverance often appears when providences are darkest. "O give thanks unto the Lord," sang the Psalmist, "who remembered us in our low estate" (Ps. 136:1, 23).

God also shows His wisdom through making fools of wise men as He allows their wisdom to be the means of their overthrow. Ahithophel, King David's traitorous advisor, had deep policy: "And the counsel of Ahithophel, which he counseled in those days, was as if a man had inquired at the oracles of God" (2 Sam. 16:23), but he counseled to his shame. Certainly the Lord answered David's prayer to "turn the counsel of Ahithophel into foolishness" (2 Sam. 15:31; also see 17:14).

God "taketh the wise in their own craftiness" (Job 5:13). When they think they are dealing wisely, He not only disappoints them but also ensnares them. The snares they lay for others entrap themselves. "In the net which they hid is their own foot taken" (Ps. 9:15). God loves to counterplot politicians; He makes use of their wit to undo them, as in the case of Haman, who hanged upon the very gallows his hands had wrought.

Adore the wisdom of God. Rest in it. God sees humility to be better for us than joy. It is better to lack comfort and be humble, than to have it and be proud. When you lack bodily strength, rest in God's wisdom. He sees what is best. Perhaps the less health the more grace, the weaker in body, the stronger in faith. When God shakes the tree of the body, He is gathering the fruits of righteousness. Trust God where you cannot trace Him. It is so often true that God is most in His way when we think He is most out of the way. (See Thomas Watson, *A Body of Divinity*, pp. 52–54.)

WHAT GOD HAS CHOSEN

Judge not the Lord by feeble sense,
    But trust Him for His grace;
Behind a frowning providence
    He hides a smiling face.

His purposes will ripen fast,
    Unfolding every hour;
The bud may have a bitter taste,
    But sweet will be the flower.

Blind unbelief is sure to err,
    And scan His work in vain;
God is His own interpreter,
    And He will make it plain.
         —William Cowper

How God Chooses to Save the World

When the Apostle Paul declared that God had "chosen the foolish things of the world to confound the wise," he was not talking about things that were foolish or stupid in themselves. He referred to things that the world considers stupid and foolish. The expression obviously does not refer to worldly things, but to things, circumstances, or people found in the world yet not tainted by the world. Similarly, the confounded wise are not wise as the world considers them to be.

Man would never have supposed the accomplishment of his salvation in the way God devised—through the crucifixion of Christ. In this first chapter of his Epistle to the Corinthians, Paul is not speaking either of creation or of providence, but of redemption through the cross. It is the cross as a means of redemption that appears foolish to the wise of the world. In truth you often hear unregenerated people speak contemptuously of the idea of a God of love who would "barbarously" slay His own Son to satisfy His vengeance and appease His wrath against fallen man. "Where's the justice in that?" they ask. "Where is the love?" They totally ignore that God as the incarnate Christ Himself paid the penalty He had decreed so that the sinner might go free.

> Well might the sun in darkness hide,
> And shut his glories in,
> When Christ, the mighty Maker died
> For man, the creature's sin.
>   —Isaac Watts

God in His wisdom chose the cross because He foreknew it would be efficacious. It was His method based on His nature, and hence it could not but succeed. The verb *exeléxato*, "chose," involves all of this foreknowledge of God. Certainly He provided the cross in the full and absolute knowledge of its sufficiency to provide release for the sinner from the guilt and power of sin.

To the wise of the world, the crucifixion of Christ was ridiculous. How could it affect the world and disturb the great and indomitable Roman Empire? If mentioned at all in the official records of that state, a Roman officer may have written a few sentences about it in a report. No human being, not even Christ's disciples, could have understood the wise and mighty power that was born in the seemingly foolish and weak cross.

Here was the masterpiece of divine wisdom, to contrive a way out of the sin of man and into the justice of God. God's solution astonished both men and angels. Neither men nor angels could have created a better plan than His. After all, men had not the head to devise nor the heart to desire what God's infinite wisdom designed for us, and the suffering of angels would not atone for the sins of man. In His mercy God had a desire to save sinners, yet without allowing His justice to be wronged.

Must man then forever be lost? In this conflict between mercy and justice the wisdom of God stepped in and said, Let God become man. Let the Second Person in the Trinity be incarnate and suffer. Fitness decreed that He should be a man; and ability required that He be God. In this way justice could be satisfied and mankind saved. Thus, the wisdom of God causes justice and mercy to embrace each other.

It is not just the cross that seems foolish to the wise of the world, but also the means of applying salvation. In his worldly wisdom man seeks salvation by his works. God ordained that it be by faith. Why does God declare there is wisdom in faith? So that, as Paul says in 1 Corinthians 1:29, "no flesh should glory in His presence." If God were to convert men by the ministry of angels, then man would glory in angels and give them the honor which is due God. Instead, God works by weak tools, makes use of men of like passions with ourselves, and by them converts sinners so that all can clearly see that He does all things by His power. "We have this treasure in earthen vessels, that the excellency of the power may be of God, and not of us" (2 Cor. 4:7). In this we see God's wisdom, that no flesh may glory in His presence. (See Thomas Watson, *A Body of Divinity*, p. 51.)

Furthermore, the world not only considers the cross of Christ and faith by which man appropriates salvation foolish (*mōrá* [3474]), but also weak (*asthenē* [772]), ignoble (*agenē* [36]), and despised (*exouthenēména* [1848]). All these Greek adjectival nouns in verse 28 are in the neutral plural and can refer to events in history, to providences of God, or to men and women God may use. Despite the world's view of the means of God's salvation, He accomplishes His purpose of redeeming man.

Why does God choose such means? Some say it is because He wants to display His glory to men in making use of things that others would have found altogether inadequate. Paganini once deliberately broke three strings on his violin, held it up to the audience to see, and then exclaimed, "Paganini and one string!" Paganini with four strings was almost an orchestra in himself. Therefore he sought to limit his resources that he might magnify his powers.

Some people would have us believe God is like Paganini. However, I do not believe it. That is a distinctly human thing to do, but it is too petty and small for God. What would He gain from such a display of His power? The applause of men? What is that to God? No, the suggestion is foolish and unworthy of association with God. Everything that we know of God shows that He is not eager to display His omnipotence in this showy manner. That is why He has entrusted so much of His work to us.

> Go, labor on; spend and be spent—
>   Thy joy to do the Father's will;
> It is the way the Master went;
>   Should not the servant tread it still?

Why Strong-Arm Methods Cannot Save the World

What did the Apostle Paul mean when he spoke of God's choosing the foolish and weak things of the world to confound the wise? To understand what the world considers foolish and weak we must see what it considers wise and strong. What does the world rely on to realize its aims and purposes? Of course, its ultimate goal is happiness.

Watch the pageantry of the world's display and what will you find there? Wealth, temporal power and authority, social position and arrogance, force of arms and compulsion, self-aggression and cruel indifference—these and other things like them will be represented there because these are the strong things of the world. These are the things upon which men rely most for what they call success. Pomp of wealth and military power and force are on constant exhibition.

All of us know what the strong things of the world are and who its strong men are. Now you can probably see more clearly what the weak things of the world are, the things upon which men never rely to carry out their designs and realize their aims. Here are a few of them: meekness, tenderness, humility, pity, mercy, forgiveness, love, self-sacrifice. The world considers these too weak to secure success and attain positions of power and influence. They consider them admirable virtues, but not to promote the ascendancy of man. Secretly they despise them as weak. They are not for a hard, cruel world like ours.

God chose these things for at least two obvious reasons. First, the strong things of the world, such as human wisdom, physical strength, nobility of ancestry, and fame, were useless for His purpose. Second, because the weak things of the world are really the only strong things of life.

Now what was God's purpose? The salvation of the world and the redemption of life. The strong things of the world were useless for this purpose. Here is a human soul in need of redemption and changing. How can you change a man's mind, a man's thought, a man's way of looking at things? That is what conversion means—a change in a man's outlook, his way of thinking, resulting in a change of soul.

How are you going to tackle this problem? Shall we try the strong things of the world and see what they will do? Which of them shall we use? Let us take force, which the world considers the strongest compulsion. What amazing things this has achieved! It has trampled nations beneath its feet, subdued fortresses and armies, and even conquered the world. Your Caesars and Alexanders and Mussolinis and Hitlers and Stalins all knew its power. It has done great things for those who have placed their trust in it. However turn all the compelling power that you have upon a soul, upon a mind, upon a conviction or a way of thinking and you are beating the air. What power do you have over a soul or a mind with these weapons? None at all. Can you compel a man to change his mind by flogging him? He may recant, but you will not have convinced him, only cowed him.

What God Has Chosen

What do history and experience say about the matter? Men have tried to force human thought into an unyielding and fixed mold before. They have done it with almost every man who has broken through the limits of knowledge of his age and proclaimed the discovery of a new world of knowledge. You remember Galileo who declared that the earth revolves around the sun, contrary to the accepted belief of his age? They put him behind prison bars and made him suffer to compel him to change his mind. As his bodily strength began failing, the aged scholar was tempted to say whatever they wanted to hear. Still however much he tried, the mind, the conviction, won. When they thought they had subdued him, the old man would cry, "No, you are wrong; the earth goes around the sun!" You cannot change a man's way of thinking by force, nor can you convert a soul by any strong-arm methods.

Knowing that force does not bring change, Christ rejected the idea of a worldly Messiah. God did well to reject the strong things of the world. He chose the weak things of the world because He knew intrinsically what we have realized by experience, that they are the strong things of life.

If you can see this and believe it, you will have a new vision of some of those things that you despise, and a new relationship to them. The opinions and values of the world influence you more than you care to admit. Much of the trouble in the world occurs when men draw back and refuse to employ what the world has labeled weak. You may be failing to see that the weak things of the world are indeed the strong things of life. God chose what you are rejecting, and in doing so He was laying hold of the levers of power.

Let me take one so-called weak thing, called sentiment, to show you how strong it is. The Lord asked Simon Peter as he stood in the midst of the other disciples, "Simon, son of Jona, lovest thou Me?" (John 21:15–17). He did not ask him how much money or strength he could bring into Christ's service. Love, a mere sentiment. Men would despise it as weak, but Christ, whose knowledge of value far exceeds ours, placed the highest price tag on "love."

He did not ask Peter, "Do you understand Me? Will you fight for Me?" but "Do you love Me?" He repeated the question, going deeper each time, delving down to the heart. He made him admit he loved Him, although he had denied Him. Simon said it before them all. And on that confession the Lord Jesus built His hopes of Simon's impulsive life. He was delving down to the deepest thing within him, the thing that like a rock would never move: sentiment, love, affection for Him. The heart is the only foundation that never gives way. The weak thing of the world is the strong thing of life.

A young man was on the border of nervous collapse as he lay on an operating table. Among the nurses, he noticed one watching him intently. He thought he knew her and called her to him. "Yes," she said, "we have met before." Then he whispered, "Would you mind holding my hand?" She gripped it, and he became calm as he awaited the operation. What a strong thing sentiment is! It can conquer a man's fears even in the face of life's most serious crises.

Foolish and Wise Boasting

A woman who was helping needy individuals find a night's lodging became so concerned over their plight that she burst into tears. Is pity a weak thing? That is what the unbelieving world thinks. But the pity in that woman's heart is the only hope of the outcast and homeless. And God has chosen it to save and redeem human life. His choice was wise.

What is it that holds you to your hard, unwelcome task? It may be the smile on a baby's face or the pain of a husband's or wife's body. The light in the eyes that you love enables you to accept joyfully the difficult and harsh conditions which you would otherwise find unbearable. Despite all you may say to the contrary, you, too, are choosing the weak things of the world as a foundation for your life. Your choice is a wise one.

Keep these things—love, pity, tenderness—as treasures of the heart, as foundation stones of life. Do not be ashamed of them. They are the only hope this wayward, broken life of ours can ever know. There is power in sympathy and redemption in pity. I am glad God chose the weak things of the world and rest my hope of redemption in His choice.

Why does God choose to confound man's wisdom and power through what the world considers weak? Paul tells us in 1 Corinthians 1:29: "That no flesh should glory in his presence." This verse begins with the conjunction *hópōs* (3704), "in order that," followed by the negative *mé* (3361), "not." This conjunction is rarely used and is much stronger than the conjunction *hína* (2443), used in verses 27 and 28. God has so constituted the means of man's salvation that no man can receive the credit. If we could do anything at all to save ourselves, then we would naturally be proud of it. Therefore, God has excluded self-sufficiency to prevent self-glorification.

The verb translated "glory" in the King James Version is *kauchḗsetai* (2744) which means "boast." It expresses self-confidence that seeks glory before God and relies upon self. Paul contrasts this kind of boasting with faith. The Christian has much to be thankful for to the Lord. Likewise, he must remember that everything that he has is a gift from God and not self-acquired.

Paul, who is almost the only one in Scripture who uses this word *kaúchasthai*, tells us that we must glory, we must boast. In Romans 5:11 Paul uses the same Greek word, "We also joy [*kauchōménoi*, 'boast'] in God through our Lord Jesus Christ, by whom we have now received the atonement." Thus we see that the boasting which stems from faith in Christ is good. It is expressing confidence in Christ. Paul also expressed it well in 1 Corinthians 4:7: "For who maketh thee to differ from another? and what hast thou that thou didst not receive? now if thou didst receive it, why dost thou glory [again the Greek word is *kaúchasai*, 'boast'], as if thou hadst not received it?"

Godly boasting springs from a regenerated spirit, but foolish boasting emanates from the flesh. "In order that no flesh may boast." "Flesh" (*sárx* [4561]) stands for the unregenerated carnal man. In verse 26 the people whose wisdom God considers insufficient are called "the wise according to the flesh." Also observe that the boasting is before God. "In order that no flesh may boast before God." When you come before God, do not presume to speak of the things that you have accomplished as a man, but thank Him for what He has given you. Boasting in God through Christ is necessary. In others words, you must praise God for all that Christ did for you, not stand before God and tell Him how wise, strong, and noble you are in yourself. Indeed the latter is utter foolishness. There is no wisdom, strength, or nobility apart from Christ that is worth mentioning before God.

Notice how Paul speaks about these natural carnal endowments. "Yea doubtless, and I count all things but loss for the excellency of the knowledge of Christ Jesus my Lord: for whom I have suffered the loss of all things, and do count them but dung, that I may win Christ" (Phil. 3:8). When you have Christ, all other things are not worth boasting about before God. In truth, they are not even worth mentioning. Oh, yes, men may talk about their wisdom, strength, and nobility to each other, but what are these before God? Nothing!

This is what Paul stresses in verse 30 in continuation of the thought he introduced in verse 26. He said, "See your calling, brethren." You are called; you are saved people. How? He tells the Corinthians in verse 30, "But of him are ye in Christ Jesus."

WHAT GOD HAS CHOSEN

Naturally, we humans want to possess something we can be proud of and that will bring us admiration from others. Truly God recognizes man's ambition to be first among equals. Thus Paul tells us in verse 30 how we can acquire all the things and qualities we need to be proud of without working for them. We become heirs of them through a relationship. It is just like being adopted by royalty. Once you become a member of the royal family, you are given all the privileges of royalty.

God has called you to salvation, Paul told the Corinthians in verses 26 to 28. Take heed to your calling. God did not save you because you were wise or strong or of noble birth. The reason He saved you was to make you become something you were not before and something you could not become by your efforts. Even if you could become wise, strong, and noble on your own, you could not possibly win God's approval or attention in that way. You could not become what it takes to make God proud of you.

Does God want to be proud of you? Yes, just as much as you want to be proud of yourself. In Psalm 149:4 we read, "For the Lord taketh pleasure in His people," and then in verse 9, "This honor have all His saints." The marginal reading of the English Revised Version renders it, "He [God] is the honor of all His saints." In other words, men find their real glory and distinction when God is in them. They become great when they are temples of the Holy Spirit. As born-again believers they have God's life in them which is what He recognizes as His own and can therefore admire. Paul wishes to emphasize the reality of the life we have in Christ that shows in every aspect of a believer's life.

LESSONS:

1. The benefits of knowledge are incalculable, but such knowledge becomes dangerous when it rejects the One who gave it.

WHAT GOD HAS CHOSEN

2. God's choice of people, things, or circumstances is not discriminatory. He is not partial to the wise according to the flesh, or to the mighty or noble of this world. He can and does choose any individual and any circumstances to accomplish His purpose.

3. In 1 Corinthians 1, Paul is not speaking either of creation or of providence, but of redemption through the cross. It is the cross as a means of redemption that appears foolish to the wise of the world.

4. It is not just the cross that seems foolish to the wise of the world, but also the means of applying salvation. Man in his worldly wisdom seeks salvation by his works. God ordained that it be by faith.

5. The strong things of the world are useless for God's purpose in saving the world; the weak things of the world are the strong things of life.

6. Boasting about what God has done for us springs from a regenerated spirit, but boasting about what we have accomplished emanates from the flesh.

What God Has Chosen

1 Cor. 1:30

You Who Are in Christ Jesus

But of him are ye in Christ Jesus, who of God is made unto us wisdom, and righteousness, and sanctification, and redemption.

All men are hungry for recognition and honor. However, most of us seek it in the wrong places. We seek it in external things acting as if wealth, rank and social standing can confer it. Learning these cannot confer the recognition and honor we seek, we become disappointed. There is great difference between "honors" and "honor." Society can confer "honors," but no society in the world can confer that rarer and finer thing "honor" upon a man. Only God can do that. (See "The Glory of God and Man," by J. D. Jones, in *The Christian World Pulpit*, Vol. 82, pp. 161–163.)

What It Means to Be "in Christ"

Observe how 1 Corinthians 1:30 begins: "Of him you are in Christ Jesus." The phrase translated "of him" is *ex* (1537) *autoú* (846) in Greek. The preposition *ek* (or *ex*) means "out of," indicating the originating cause. *Autoú* is the genitive of the intensive pronoun *autós* used here as a personal pronoun. Paul could have expressed this thought with the genitive of the relative pronoun *hós* (3739), *hoú* (*ex hoú*), but this would not have carried the particular emphasis of *ex autoú*. "Out of himself" you are in Christ, says Paul.

To emphasize exactly the same idea negatively, in Ephesians 2:8 Paul says, "For by grace are ye saved by faith; and this not of yourselves [*ex humōn* {5216}]." This salvation did not originate from yourselves. Faith presupposes the object of faith, the offer of salvation. Paul told the Corinthians in verse 27 that God chose the foolish, the weak, and the ignoble—those that are despised—to save them, to make them something they were not, to conform them to His image.

Paul did not flatter the Corinthians by telling them that they had wisdom, strength, and nobility. God is not as concerned with what people have as with what they are. Whatever you have will never cause Him to admire you. Others usually admire you for that, but not God. That is why Paul, in speaking to the Corinthian Christians, did not say, "You have this, that, and the other admirable quality of life," but "You are now what God originally made you to be."

Now the Corinthians were something God could admire. They were His honor. We usually admire those who are like us. In like manner God can only admire those who are what He is. How do we become what He is? Only and entirely as a result of His activity in us. It is "of Himself" that you are in Christ Jesus, says Paul emphatically. He has made you what He is—something you could not have accomplished yourself. Therefore, do not boast of your salvation because of something you have done. He has done it all.

When you are in Christ, you are not merely professors of His name, learners of His doctrine, followers of His example, or sharers of His gifts. You are not merely men and women ransomed by His death or destined for His glory. These external connections exemplify how your individual life relates to Christ's in the same way that one man's life may relate to another's by the effect of what he teaches, gives, or does. Paul says to the Corinthians and to all born-again believers, In your case, your life is not merely external, that is, "just like" His life, parallel to His. You are actually in Christ, and He is in you. This is something unique that Christ does for those who accept Him.

In 1 Corinthians chapter one Paul speaks of the believers as being "in Christ" three times. First in verse 2 he addresses them as those "that are sanctified in Christ Jesus." Second in verse 4 he thanks God for the grace of God which is given them in (not "by" as the King James Version has it) Jesus Christ. Third he says in verse 5, "In everything ye are enriched in [not by] him."

No other religion teaches such a relationship. Many people are followers of Buddha, of Confucius, or of Mohammed. However no one can say he is in Buddha, or in Confucius, or in Mohammed. Simply receive Christ as your Savior, and God places you "in Christ." Your life and His are one. "If any man be in Christ, he is a new creature" (2 Cor. 5:17).

For a brief moment in the early days of Christianity, Nero and Paul were contemporaries. Nero was a man of worldly wisdom, power, and nobility. He was the supreme power of his world. Everything in the shape of wealth and rank and earthly dignity was his. People trembled at his nod. In some cities people worshiped him as a god.

Paul on the other hand seemed to be one of the most humble and insignificant of men in the Roman world. A distant province had sent him as a prisoner to Rome. He was a Jew and an outcast at that, belonging to a small and despised sect. They stoned him at Lystra, imprisoned and scourged him at Philippi, and treated him as the very filth of the world.

One can hardly imagine a greater contrast than that between Nero and Paul. Although initially the world worshiped Nero and persecuted Paul, it has long since decided between the two. Despite his imperial dignities, and his vast, limitless power, the world has cast Nero out into the night of contempt and scorn and has enshrined the humble servant Paul and crowned him with honor.

In other words, even this ordinary world of ours recognizes that honor not spring from the trappings of wealth and rank, but from character. Furthermore, goodness and righteousness are the only real greatness, and it is God who is the honor of His saints.

> I heard the voice of Jesus say,
>   "I am this dark world's light;
> Look unto Me, thy morn shall rise,
>   And all thy day be bright."
>
> I looked to Jesus, and I found
>   In Him my Star, my Sun;
> And in that light of life I will walk,
>   Till trav'ling days are done.
>   —Horatius Bonar

Are You a Member of God's Family?

Speaking to Christians, in 1 Corinthians 1:30 Paul states, "Ye are in Christ Jesus." By this he meant that that was their position. Having already spoken in verse 28 of "things which are not" and "things that are," the Apostle turns to his fellow-believers and says, "but . . . ye are." Even so, from whom did they receive this existence, this life? From God Himself as its immediate origin and continuous author. Where does one find this life? "In Christ Jesus."

To understand how glorious the state of the believer is, we must first understand what this oft-repeated statement, "being in Christ Jesus," implies. Paul wants the believers to understand that they are no longer living a life that is merely external and, as it were, parallel to Christ's life. They are in Christ Jesus, and He also is in them.

If you are a believer, you have a life that is from God, and that life is in Christ Jesus. That is a life connection. Remember what Christ said to His disciples before His crucifixion and resurrection: "At that day ye shall know that I am in my Father, and ye in me, and I in you" (John 14:20). In 1 Corinthians 1:30 Paul simply echoes this promise. His is the voice of those who have entered into predicted knowledge.

One of the first things a believer realizes is that the Lord Jesus is "in the Father." Apart from Christ we cannot become "of God." Thus, before we become "of God" the Lord Jesus must first be "in the Father." Jesus is one with the Father in essence, in eternity, in infinity, although, as John 1:1 tells us, not identical with Him in personality.

The mystical relationship we can have with God through Christ is certainly difficult to believe if we first do not believe in this relationship between God the Father and the Lord Jesus Christ. God the Father and God the Son first had to be "One in the Other" before anyone could be born of the Father—"of him"—and be "in Christ Jesus."

The Lord spoke very distinctly of His relationship with the Father and the Father's relationship with Him, two distinct beings in each other. "Thou Father art in me, and I in Thee" (John 10:38; 14:10; 17:21). That is the kind of relationship that we as believers enjoy with God and in reality with each other as members of the same body: "That they all may be one" (John 17:21). "God was in Christ, reconciling the world unto Himself" (2 Cor. 5:19). Thus our life is "hid with Christ in God" (Col. 3:3).

To be in Christ means to be saved, to be born again, to be a new creature. Unless you believe that "God was in Christ, reconciling the world unto Himself" (2 Cor. 5:19), you cannot be saved. Surely, you cannot understand nor fully accept this relationship of God the Father and God the Son unless you enter the family of God by faith in Christ. Faith precedes knowledge, and knowledge is added to faith. That added knowledge is exactly what Paul speaks of when he tells us that Christ is made unto us "wisdom."

In 2 Peter 1:5 Peter counsels the early Church believers, "Add to your faith virtue; and to virtue knowledge." Faith involves a transformation of one's being and relationship with God, placing him "in Christ" and thus within God's family. Then it gives the believer "virtue" and changes his behavior. Faith first brings about a character change, second a behavior change, and third, knowledge, a capacity to understand that which was incomprehensible to the unbeliever in his unregenerate state.

Oh, if we could only take in all the implications of Paul's statement to the Corinthian believers and to us! "Of him ye are in Christ Jesus." How marvelous to be in Christ and to have Christ in us, even as God the Father is in Him and He in God the Father. Being in Christ Jesus means that we are partakers in all that He does, all that He has, and all that He is. We died with Him and rose with Him and live with Him and are seated in heavenly places with Him.

Oh, the glory of our position in Christ! When the eye of God looks on us and finds us in Christ, He does not condemn us, but pardons and accepts us in the Beloved (Rom. 8:1; Eph. 1:6). We are righteous in His righteousness. He loves us with the love that rests in Him. We are sons of God in His Sonship. We are heirs with Him in His inheritance and will one day be glorified with Him in His glory.

The corollary of believers being in Christ is that He is in us. This means that He associates His presence with our whole inward and outward life. We live, yet not we, but Christ lives in us (Gal. 2:20), and He is our strength and our song (Phil. 4:13). This indwelling of Christ is by the Holy Spirit. Scripture passages speak interchangeably of the Spirit being in us and of

Christ being in us (Rom. 8:9, 10), or of the Holy Spirit being in us, and our members being the members of Christ (1 Cor. 6:15, 19). Thus, in this expression, "I in you," is included the whole life of the Spirit in man, with all its discoveries, impulses, and achievements, its victory over the world, its conversation in heaven, and the earnest of our final inheritance.

In Christ's expression, "Ye in Me, and I in you," we have the declaration of a human life in Christ. Moreover, the still higher mystery of the union of the Father and the Son reveals our life as a life in God. "At that day ye shall know that I am in My Father, and ye in Me, and I in you" (John 14:20). Paul shouts it out to the Corinthians, as the fulfillment of this promise, "Of God ye are in Christ Jesus!" The day is come.

Of course, we realize as Paul said in 1 Corinthians 13:9 that we now know only in part. Even so, we know enough for the present. Certainly we look forward to that day when we shall know more fully, when we shall be conformed to the image of Christ, and shall be clothed with our resurrection body. This will be at the Second Coming of the Lord, of which the 14th chapter of John's gospel speaks. (See Thomas Dehany Bernard, *The Progress of Doctrine in the New Testament*, pp. 177–184.)

The Secret of Being a True Christian

Men have four basic needs that only Jesus Christ can satisfy. These are wisdom, righteousness, sanctification, and redemption. These seemingly abstract theological terms represent our deepest needs. If we are basically unhappy, it is because we are not wise according to God, we are not righteous, sanctified, nor redeemed.

However, do not think these qualities can be acquired by doing certain things. It is only because the eternal Son of God became man—something that He was not from the beginning—that God can restore us to what He originally created us to be. In Genesis 1:27 we learn that God created man in His own image. Man lost that likeness and nature when he disobeyed God and has continued in that state ever since—unwise, unrighteous, unholy, and unredeemed—a sinner. Consequently, not being what God originally created him to be, he is unhappy and miserable. His restoration to God is the only way he can again become happy or blessed.

Just as God gave innocent man the privilege of choice, He now gives sinful man the opportunity to accept or reject the means of restoration and salvation. Though God has provided the means of salvation, it is up to man to appropriate or reject it. God has done His part, and therefore He is not responsible for our final fate. He bases it on our choice regarding His offer of salvation.

Christ states this truth clearly when He says to Nicodemus, "He that believeth on [Me] is not condemned: but he that believeth not is condemned already because he hath not believed in the name of the only begotten Son of God" (John 3:18). Notice the phrase, "the only begotten Son of God." In Greek "only begotten" is *monogenoús* (3439) which means the only one of the same family. The compound word *monogenés* (in the nominative) comes from *mónos* (3441), which means "alone, only," and the word *génos* (1085), which means "family." It is the same word from which we derive the English word "genealogy," the family tree.

Now in 1 Corinthians 1:30 we have the same word as a formal verb, *egenéthē* (1096), "became." Unfortunately the King James Version renders it "is made," instead of its correct translation "was made, or became." It is exactly the same verb as that used in John 1:14, "And the Word became [*egéneto*] flesh." The only difference is that *egenéthē* in 1 Corinthians 1:30 is in the first aorist passive, whereas *egéneto* in John 1:14 is in the second aorist middle. As in first-century Greek, the aorist passive form frequently has the force of the middle, and I believe that *egenéthē* has the force of the middle here. He (Christ) became unto us wisdom from God, righteousness, sanctification, and redemption. The tense and meaning here are historical.

Those to whom the Apostle Paul was writing had not always been Christians. Their Christian life had a beginning, and that epoch occurred when Christ Jesus became to them the God that the Apostle had proclaimed Him to be. The gift of life came from God to the Corinthians on a definite historic occasion. Christ, the eternal *Lógos* (3056) or "Word," became flesh. He became man. Through His incarnation, death, and resurrection, He made it possible for us to move by faith into the family of God and be in Christ.

Upon receiving Christ as Savior we become wise according to God, we become righteous, sanctified, redeemed. Truly Christ became these qualities to us. He satisfied our innermost beings by His incarnation, death, and resurrection. Christ, unlike all other leaders, did not merely teach the wisdom of God, righteousness, holiness, and redemption, but truly became those things to us. Being a Christian is not having these four qualities, but having Christ. Conversely, it is impossible to have these qualities of character unless we are in Christ. Oh, yes, we may demonstrate acts that give the appearance of wisdom, righteousness, holiness, and redemption, but this is not the same as being wise, righteous, holy, and redeemed.

Observe how Paul shifts the pronouns in this 30th verse. He begins by saying, "Of him you are in Christ Jesus." Then he adds, "who [Christ] became unto us [not you] wisdom from God, righteousness and sanctification and redemption." How could he leave out himself? He rejoiced in the possession of these things. He wanted to boast of what Christ had done in him. In effect

YOU WHO ARE IN CHRIST JESUS

he says to the believers of Corinth, The work of Christ can be to you what it is to me as an apostle.

Christ is no respecter of persons. Although He may assign us different work with varying degrees of responsibilities according to our abilities and opportunities, our position in Christ and the results of that position are the same. Certainly in the life of Christ in human beings there are no privileged characters. A layman can have these basic qualities just as much as an apostle or a clergyman. Christ became unto us all wisdom from God, all righteousness and sanctification and redemption. We need these qualities, but they can become ours only as Christ is ours. Christian qualities cannot be separated from the person of Christ Himself.

This is the secret of Christianity. To be a Christian, it is not sufficient that we adopt certain Christian principles, but Christ must actually become ours. We cannot have what He stands for without Him. By receiving Him we become truly wise, truly righteous, truly sanctified, and truly redeemed. This does not mean that we will become fully developed and mature in the expression of these qualities all at once. Instead the germ, the life-seed, will have been implanted in us so that, being born again, we will more and more evidence the fruit of the Spirit as we grow in the Christian life. Christ then indwells the believer and will manifest these qualities through him. These four terms represent very real needs in a man's life which if not met will cause him to be miserable indeed. The poet expressed it well who said,

> O love triumphant over guilt and sin,
> My soul is soiled, but Thou shalt enter in;
> My feet must stumble if I walk alone,
> Lonely my heart, till beating by Thine own.
> My will is weakness till it rest in Thine;
> Cut off, I wither, thirsting for the Vine.

YOU WHO ARE IN CHRIST JESUS

My deeds are dry leaves on a sapless tree,
My life is lifeless till it live in Thee!
                    —Frederic Lawrence Knowles

Where to Find the Answers to Life's Perplexities

Everybody would like to be wise, but not everybody wants to pay the price for wisdom. This wisdom is not the mere accumulation of facts in our minds, facts that have no relation to the regulation of our daily life and conduct. Certainly the wisdom we seek involves the ability to solve the problems of life aright, and to meet temptation and trial without being defeated, to make the utmost and best of the life that God has given us. Still, how shall we do this? We echo the question of Job, "But where shall wisdom be found? and where is the place of understanding?" (Job 28:12).

Although men have been groping for wisdom from the beginning of time, most of them have been unable to find it because what they thought was wisdom failed to meet their fundamental needs. The test of wisdom is in the results produced. Christ became unto us wisdom because in and through Him we found our righteousness, sanctification, and redemption.

Truly, the wisdom that men have so long sought, God Himself has freely given through Christ. All the knowledge we need for the guidance and control of our lives we have in Him. Certainly there are still many things we would like to know that Christ does not reveal to us. Likewise, if we search the gospels diligently, we must admit that some of our questions remain unanswered. There is such a thing as reverent Christian agnosticism, a state of "not knowing" certain things. God does not relieve Christian people from "the burden of the mystery." Moreover life for even the greatest saint is not without its perplexities. The Psalmist was aware of this as he sang, "Thy judgments are a great deep" (Ps. 36:6). He meant they were as unfathomable as the depths of the ocean.

We have spoken of Job, that sorely tried man of God in Old Testament times. Alexander Whyte aptly comments:

> The worst of it was that Job could not find out, with all he could do, why it was that God had so forsaken him. Job had a good and honest heart, and a conscience void of offense both toward God and toward man. With the whole of the Book of Job in our hands, we know what neither Job nor his friends knew. The captivity of Job arose out of God's pure and unchallengeable sovereignty, as we say. God deserted and forsook Job for reasons that were sufficient to Himself, and in which He had no counselor. It was to silence the scoffs and sneers of Satan: it was to produce a shining example of submission and resignation and trust in God, that would stand out to the end of time ["Job Groping," *Lord, Teach Us to Pray*, pp. 78, 79].

The one thing we can be sure of is that God in Christ has given us all the light we really need at the moment. Assuredly, if we sit at His feet and strive to learn His will, we shall find "the peace of God, which passeth all understanding" (Phil. 4:7).

What is the nature of wisdom? The philosophers of ancient Greece, whose names were household words in Corinth and every Greek city, made themselves famous for all time by their efforts to solve the problem of wisdom. They sought after it with an all-consuming passion. Knowing what this wisdom really was will help us understand what they were really seeking.

Men have always asked certain profound questions about life and destiny, about goodness and God. The condition of being unable to answer these most practical and pressing of all questions we call "ignorance" (*agnōsía* [56], from which we get the word agnostic). Additionally, the condition of being indifferent to the necessity of having these questions answered or of being content with trivial, shallow, unsatisfying answers, we call folly (*mōría* [3472], from which we get the word "moron"). Ignorance on the one hand, folly on the other. Contrasting both, the condition of being in the possession of true and satisfying answers is what we call "wisdom."

Where can we find the answers to life's great questions? Paul says that Christ is God's explanation of these questions to us. "He became wisdom unto us" (1 Cor. 1:30), and note that he adds "from God." Verse 30 reads, "But of [*ex*] him are ye in Christ Jesus, who of [*apó* {575}] God is made unto us wisdom." Although the English translation uses "of" for two different Greek prepositions, these prepositions have different meanings. The first preposition here translated "of" is *ek* (or *ex*) and means "from within." The second is *apó* which means the general starting point. Note also that the expression, "of God," referring to wisdom, comes at the end of the phrase, not at the beginning, as the King James Version has it. "Of him [*ex autoú* {846}] then are ye in Christ Jesus, who became wisdom unto us of God [*apó theoú* {2316}]." (See A. T. Robertson, *A Grammar of the Greek New Testament*, p. 577.)

We are in Christ Jesus from within God. That is a more intimate relationship. A Christian is born of God; he is a child of God. He has come from within God Himself. Distinct from this, wisdom, the ability to know the right and satisfying answers to the most perplexing questions of life, is the effect of being born of God. First He gives us new life and then a new mind. We cannot know first, before we are in Christ. It is when we are in Him that we can have the wisdom of God. We are what we are *ek Theoú*, "from within God." We have what we have *apó theoú*, "from God." The one is life and the other the quality of life known as wisdom, the specific ability to know the answers to the why's and wherefore's of life, the source of all things and the destiny of all things as far as God has revealed them. How enriched then our mind becomes when we are in Christ.

You Who Are in Christ Jesus

Wisdom in verse 30 stands by itself. The other three seemingly abstract qualities—righteousness, sanctification, and redemption—are the results of that wisdom. The three things
that Christ became to us are the result of His wisdom. They represent the answers to our greatest needs. Wisdom is the answer
to our intellectual questions. Before we are saved we must understand that we are lost and that only Christ can save us. As
Andrew Murray says, "It was by the tree of knowledge that sin
came; it is through the knowledge that Christ gives that salvation comes. In Him are hid all the treasures of wisdom and
knowledge" (*Abide in Christ*, p. 51).

This wisdom stands in opposition to the boasted "wisdom
of this world" which is often foolish, sometimes scornful, always
incomplete. Christ stands forth as the perfect expression of the
"wisdom of God." He is given to you and me as a sealed gift is
put into the hands of a poor man. On the outside is written,
"Wisdom, the fullness of the blessing of the gospel of Christ."
I open the box and find three priceless jewels are lying in it for
me: righteousness, sanctification, and redemption.

Does God Really Expect Us to Be Perfect?

Wisdom is possessing true and satisfying answers to the fundamental questions that man has always asked of himself. When
the Apostle Paul told the Corinthian Christians that God had
made Christ wisdom, righteousness, sanctification, and redemption to them, he was speaking of a constellation that did not
consist of four stars in a straight line, but one that was triangu-
lar in form, with wisdom reigning in the center. In other words,
righteousness, sanctification, and redemption are explanatory of
wisdom. If we understand the meaning of these three basic
terms, we shall understand the basic questions and human needs
to which they constitute a satisfying answer.

Christ's gift of righteousness, sanctification, and redemption, looked at in the direction of the past, brings pardon. Looked at as affecting the present, it brings holiness. Looked at as regarding the future, it will bring glory—presupposing we are "in Christ" through faith in Him and His atoning work for our salvation.

The Greek word for "righteousness" is *dikaiosúnē* (1343). Perhaps "justice" would express it better. A judge is one who decides what is right and wrong. Justice must deal with sin. It intervenes when there is a deviation from that which is lawful. Logically we must conclude that only an absolute God can render absolute justice. Our judgment at best can be merely relative. His is absolute. No judgment that we render can be altogether objective. We often know what kind of decisions our human justices will grant. Their philosophy of life colors their opinion of what is right and wrong. An immoral judge will likely condone immorality, whereas a moral judge will likely condemn it. What a person is, definitely determines what he thinks. Because God is absolute perfection, He alone can claim perfect righteousness. His judgment is inerrant. Actually, righteousness derives from word for "right" (*dikaíōma* [1345]) which also may mean "regulation, commandment, rule," depending on the context. That is the law. Break the rule, and we are unrighteous. God is the rule as well as the Ruler. What He expects us to be and how He expects us to act are the measuring sticks by which we know whether we are righteous or not.

Since God is the righteous, personal Creator (see James 1:17; 1 John 1:5), perfect in all His ways (Romans 3:25, 26), and is true wisdom, He must have created man with a view to his ultimate perfection and blessedness. God did not create man to be unhappy, restless, and tortured in his conscience. God created man in His own image. By nature of His character, God could not have created man to be forever an imperfect creature, at war

YOU WHO ARE IN CHRIST JESUS

with himself and with the universe where God placed him. God created man with an ultimate perfection and blessedness in view. He created us to be ideal men—God-like men.

Nevertheless we all recognize that in our natural state we are anything but ideal or God-like. In our sinful, unrighteous condition we fail to recognize what God's model is for an ideal, perfect man. By "perfect" here I mean according to God's expectations. Let me illustrate. A shipbuilder enters his yard and looks around him. There are the vast skeletons of ships just begun; there are others advancing to completion. However there is nothing satisfactory in the scene. The big hulls are at present useless. A thousand hammers are tapping in vexatious discord. The miry ground is strewn with wood and metal. Still the owner stands content amid the imperfection. He never even thinks of doubting the process he beholds. In his mind he carries the ideal of a perfect ship, and he justifies the imperfect ships by imputing to them that ideal.

God is like that great shipbuilder. The ideal man exists in His mind. He has the blueprint. Man is like the ship being built. When God looks at it He does not despair because He knows what He can do with the imperfect man. Unfortunately man cannot be that optimistic because of his inherent inability to know what God can do. Man cannot see the glorious destiny that God envisions so clearly.

If into the yard of the shipbuilder we lead a savage who has never seen a sea or a ship, what will he think? He can never conceive the ideal that is in the mind of the shipbuilder. If, however, we bring out a tiny model of a finished vessel and make it float on the water before him, he will get the idea in some way, imperfect though it may be.

Transfer this illustration to the ideal man in the mind of God. Could we know it in an abstract way? In our sinful state we are more ignorant about spiritual truth than the savage.

Hence God brings down a model that we can see—the Lord Jesus in the flesh—the *Lógos* (3056), the Word made physically visible. Christ then becomes bodily the ideal destiny of man always in the mind of God. He brings Him down to the level of our apprehension. Thus God's ideal has become actual for us in Jesus Christ and is what the Bible calls the righteousness of God and is what God originally created man to be.

Now how can we be what Christ is? By receiving Him to live within us (Gal. 2:20) and to live out His life in us. Thus this great perfect Being, the Lord Jesus Christ, becomes the righteousness of unrighteous humans. It would be utterly impossible for us to know what God expects us to be, even as the savage cannot possibly conceive of a ship he has never seen. God, therefore, invites us to cover ourselves with the perfect righteousness of Christ and to believe that in that righteousness He accepts us. That is what the Bible calls imputed righteousness, that is the perfect law-keeping and obedience of Christ put to our credit. It is not human goodness at all. It is not even conformity to the ideal. This is impossible because we lack the knowledge of God's ideal. It is simply that which the believer becomes by being in Christ. "For He hath made him [Christ] to be sin for us, who knew no sin; that we might be made the righteousness of God in him" (2 Cor. 5:21).

Likewise God imputed righteousness to Old Testament saints such as Abraham. We read in Genesis 15:6, "And he believed in the Lord; and he counted it to him for righteousness." (See also Rom. 4:3; Gal. 3:6; James 2:23.) Moreover the Bible calls the result of the imputation of God's righteousness upon the sinner when he believes on the Lord Jesus Christ justification (*dikaíōsis* [1347], akin to *dikaiōsúnē*). The soul sees itself in Christ, pure because God reckons it to be pure. In the concrete form of Jesus Christ the soul has received the great abstract ideal in the mind of God. Certainly, one can then bury the

YOU WHO ARE IN CHRIST JESUS

consciousness of his imperfection in Christ who is the right-eousness of God. (See Wade Robinson, *The Philosophy of the Atonement*, pp. 56–61.)

God's Claim Upon Us

When we accept the Lord Jesus Christ as our Savior, He gives us two kinds of righteousness, imputed and imparted. The moment we accept Him, He imputes His righteousness to us. Then He imparts His righteousness to us through the out-working of our daily conduct. Imparted righteousness must necessarily follow upon the heels of imputed righteousness. Righteousness is dependent upon and springs from that great law of right that pervades all the relations of man to his Maker and to his fellowmen. This great law of right indicates certain rights as existing between ourselves and others with whom we are directly related. God has His rights in us, and our fellowmen have their rights in us. The recognition of these rights and the fulfillment of the claims they carry with them is what we understand as practical righteousness. He is a righteous man who gives to God and to his fellowmen their due.

God has certain rights in us that we are bound to recognize and respect, and these arise out of the nature of our relationship with Him. These rights, furthermore, can have no existence unless God is a personal God and unless He has made some distinct revelation of Himself to us and of His will concerning us. If God is only a vast abstraction, an ultimate incomprehensible force, a mystic universal law, the idea of right at once ceases to exist so far as He is concerned. We could then no more owe Him a debt of right than we could be under any moral obligation to the law of gravitation or any other known form of physical force.

Two friends, meeting after a long time, were discussing the current breakdown in morals, especially among the younger generation. "What do you suppose really causes it?" asked one who in the past had openly declared she felt no need of God in her life. Her Christian friend hesitated, feeling it would be useless to give her own opinion as a believer, since the other had so often rejected her attempts to speak of religious matters in the past. Before she could formulate a reply, however, her friend advanced her theory. "Don't you think the breakdown in religious values has something to do with it?" "Yes, I do," agreed the other quickly. "If young people have turned their backs on religion, and feel that God is dead, they no longer have any absolute standards of right and wrong, no authority to turn to for direction, and the result is anarchy. Everyone does that which is right in his own eyes." Surprisingly, her friend agreed with her. Even unbelievers are coming to see that if God is dead, society has nothing on which to base its ethics. Annihilate God and you can do as you please!

We live righteously before God when we recognize our obligation to respond to His claims upon us. We recognize His purpose for us, and we respond to it. Not to do so is to rob God. Then when we have the righteousness of Christ imputed to us, we are wise to recognize that God's purposes concerning us coincide with our truest and highest interests. Therefore we have no excuse on the grounds of our well-being for opposing or ignoring those purposes. This makes God's claim of right all the stronger. We should therefore accept His will as the law of our conduct. Not to do this is to wrong God Almighty, to defraud Him of His rights in us, thus breaking the first and fundamental commandment of the law of righteousness. To accept and obey His will is to fulfill the first demand of that law.

Never think that God arbitrarily imposes these claims of His. If He did, then He could withdraw them. Indeed to withdraw them would be to resign His proper position in the universe and to give up His original design for calling man into being. Moreover doing this (if such a thing were conceivable) would inflict the greatest possible injury upon the universe at large. Certainly, anarchy and chaos would take over the universe. Within his nature man may give up all claim to sovereignty and cheerfully accept the will of another as the true law of his well-being, but God can make no such surrender. He can permit no compromise because His will is and must be best.

As God's rights now exist in us, He first asks us to make a full and willing surrender of ourselves to Him, to live for His glory according to His will. We are to hold our faculties, powers, and talents as in trust for Him, employing them for His own blessed purposes. This is God's positive claim upon us.

God's second and negative claim to His rights on us is that we should abstain from anything opposed to His proper relationship with us and His will concerning us. In response to His claims, let us say with the poet,

> It is Thy right to choose, my blessed Lord;
>   All that I have is Thine, and Thine alone;
> Whatever Thou wilt ask, at Thy dear word,
>   That will I give, to be indeed Thine own.
>
> If Thou wouldst take from out my weary life
>   Something on which I lean for peace and rest,
> Accept it, Lord; my heart will know no strife;
>   I leave with Thee to judge the right and best.
>
> Or, if Thou think'st my joys too much of earth,
>   And Thou wouldst have them found more oft in heaven;
> Take from me, Lord, pleasures of lesser worth,
>   And to my soul let holier joys be given.
>
> And if, perchance, some precious gift of Thine
>   Needs to be lifted from my clinging love,
> Take even this, and fix this heart of mine
>   For e'er and only on Thyself above!
>
> Ah, Lord, I trust Thee! Thou wilt never take
>   Aught from my life but what my life should give;

Choose what Thou wilt; that choice I too will make,
And in my death to self learn how to live.

—Henry W. Frost

Does Society Have a Claim on Your Life?

We have learned that because God has rights in us, He makes positive and negative claims upon His children. Even so, it is not only God who has rights in us, but also our fellow human beings. We owe a debt to society. None of us lives unto himself. From our earliest years we have been dependent upon our fellowmen for all the necessities and amenities of life. Human hands supported us in our helpless infancy and supplied our wants while we were utterly incapable of doing anything for ourselves. We owe society for feeding, clothing, housing, educating, training, and surrounding us with all the comforts of civilized existence.

The efforts and sacrifices of those who went before us purchased our national liberty for us. In reality, next to God, man has been our greatest benefactor, and therefore man has certain rights upon us. To recognize and respect these is to fulfill the law of righteousness. To ignore these is to break the law of righteousness; it is to go contrary to all Christ was and taught.

This duty to our fellowman is first positive. We should help and benefit him as occasion may offer. We should pay back the debt we owe society by seeking to live in such a way to make the world a better place. Certainly, the second great commandment is "Thou shalt love thy neighbor as thyself" (Matt. 19:19). Nevertheless, the priest and the Levite did not fulfill this commandment in their conduct toward the man who lay wounded between Jerusalem and Jericho. Suppose that man had died of his wounds and of exhaustion because no one helped him; who would have been his murderers? The robbers, you say? And yet they left him only half-dead. With proper care and attention he might have recovered. Others besides the robbers would be answerable for his death. Positively, the robbers would have been guilty of murder and violence, but negatively the priest and Levite would have murdered him by denying him the brotherly help he so urgently needed.

"To him that knoweth to do good, and doeth it not, to him it is sin" (James 4:17). When we lead a selfish life, not going out of our way to benefit and help our fellowmen, we fall short of the highest type of human conduct. This selfishness is also sin against the claims and rights of society in us and a flagrant breach of the law of righteousness, of being in Christ.

Lastly follows that which all are ready to a greater or lesser extent to admit—the negative rights of society in the individual. The rights of my fellowman bind me to abstain from injuring him in any way, either morally, intellectually, or physically; either by fraud or violence, by word or deed, or even by thought. Not to recognize these rights and claims of my fellowman and not to respect and fulfill them also flagrantly violates the law of righteousness.

Therefore, when we are in Christ, the law of righteousness binds us. This law provides a positive duty toward God—what we should do as a result of your relationship with Him—and also a negative duty, that from which we should abstain. Furthermore we have a positive and negative duty to our fellowman as well.

Unfortunately, most people do not commonly acknowledge and adhere to this fourfold obligation of the law of righteousness. They only recognize one part. Were you to inquire about their spiritual condition they would answer, "Well, I've never done any harm to anyone; I can't see that I'm very bad." The Pharisees had this kind of righteousness. Though I think it is rarely true in any full sense of the words, suppose that you have not harmed anyone, then how much does this assertion refer to the law of righteousness?

YOU WHO ARE IN CHRIST JESUS

We may say we have done no harm to anyone. However, does that mean that we have performed our positive duty toward God? Certainly not. We were not even thinking of Him when we said the words. Does it mean that we have performed our negative duty to God or that we have performed our positive duty toward our fellowman? The priest and the Levite in the account of the Good Samaritan did no positive harm to the man lying half-dead. They inflicted no fresh wounds on him, but they failed to do him any good.

In other words by claiming, "I have done no harm to my fellowman" we are claiming to have kept one-fourth of the law of righteousness. Suppose we owed a debt of $200, and paid back only $50. Would that mean we had fully settled our obligation? Of course not. No one would consider us righteous if we defaulted on the other $150. Of course, if that $50 were not even genuine money, our unrighteousness would compound our debt.

None of us can really claim to have never harmed anyone. Are there no companions whom we, by our example or conversation, have led into sin? Men, are there no women you have helped to degrade? Women, are there no men you have tempted to lust by your immodest behavior or dress? Have you never used language, or told stories, that encouraged others to profanity or unclean conversation? Fathers, are you sure that, by your example of worldliness and godlessness, you have done no harm to your children? Brothers, have you never misled your younger brothers who were so ready to imitate you since you seemed a hero in their eyes, and who, alas, have learned to imitate your sins?

Why have I brought up all of this? So that we can understand what righteousness to judge for ourselves whether we are righteous or not. Does our heart condemn us? Are we saying within ourselves, "If the claims of the law of righteousness are so comprehensive and strict, who can hope to fulfill them?" After knowing what true righteousness is, we can judge for ourselves whether it is possible to either modify or withdraw these claims. If not, then we will begin to feel our need of what Paul found in Christ. Once his eyes had been opened—and that takes the wisdom that is from God—to see the true claims of righteousness and to discover his unrighteousness, he had no rest until he found a new and better righteousness in Christ. Neither had he rest until he cast away the filthy rags of his insufficient and unsatisfactory righteousness and clothed himself in the righteousness of God appropriated by faith. Do you have that garment of righteousness found in Christ? (See W. H. M. H. Aitken, *The Glory of the gospel*, pp. 198–206.)

When Is a Christian Sanctified?

So far in our studies we have seen that the Lord Jesus Christ becomes righteousness to those who receive Him as Savior from sin. That is, He justifies us. He paid the penalty for our sin through His death, to count us as righteous, not guilty, before God the Father. We are in Christ and in Him God accepts us. Thus we are righteous in Christ.

Moreover righteousness in 1 Corinthians 1:30 is linked with her twin sister, sanctification. "But of him are ye in Christ Jesus, who of God is made unto us wisdom, and righteousness, and sanctification, and redemption." Two Greek words appear between righteousness and sanctification, the particle *te* (5037) and the conjunction *kaí* (2532). When used together they mean "and also," as if there were a special relationship between the two things that they join.

Although righteousness and sanctification must always go together, they are different qualities, otherwise they would not have different names. Even so, they blend into each other. That which proves to be holy in us is the new life we received when we believed in Christ. It is impossible for life to be holy unless it is the life of Christ in us. Sanctification is the fruit, whereas righteousness is the tree itself. There can be no fruit without the root being grounded and settled.

One can also render these two Greek particles, *te kaí*, as "and then." First, our legal position is righteousness, a total renovation of the whole man by the righteousness of Christ. That is our legal position. Christ places our past on Himself, and God declares us righteous. On the other hand, sanctification has to do with what happens after that declaration of our righteousness in the court of God's justice. We go out, not to continue our past sinful life, but as new creatures. "Old things are passed away . . . all things are become new" (2 Cor. 5:17). Our past is justified and our present is purified. Sin no longer has dominion over us. We are freed from its power, though not from its indwelling presence. We are holy both in heart and in every aspect of our life. We are made partakers of the divine nature. Led by the Holy Spirit, we become His living temples.

What is our sanctification as believers? Some view sanctification as an experience the believer must seek after salvation. In this view, first we are saved and then sanctified through a decision that we make to consecrate ourselves fully to the Lord. It is as if some believers were merely justified and made righteous in the sight of God, and some were also sanctified. Certainly some misunderstand sanctification. Though they believe that Christ in and through us makes us righteous, they think that we can sanctify ourselves by our endeavor to lead a holy life.

Now "sanctification" in Greek is *hagiasmós* (38). Words derived from the same root are the verb *hagiázō* (37), "to sanctify," and *hágios* (40), "holy or saint," used as an adjective describing a person or thing that is said to be holy, or as an adjectival noun referring to a holy person. Essentially the word means to set apart or to separate. "To sanctify," with its various forms, is used 106 times in the Old Testament and 31 times in the New Testament. Of course, he or it that is set apart is said to be holy.

It indicates classification in matters of position and relationship. God's activity in our lives separates us from the rest of the world that is unholy, sinful, and does not care about God.

The saints, therefore, are separate people, separated from the world unto God. That is what Paul means in 1 Corinthians 1:30 when he declares, "Christ became unto us righteousness." God tried us in His legal court and found us guilty. However, because we accepted Christ's voluntary payment for our sin, His death on Calvary's cross, God pronounced us righteous or justified. We did not have to die for our sins, since Christ died for them. If having been found guilty we had also rejected the offer of Christ's death, we would remain unregenerate sinners, still in our lost estate. We would still be in the prison in which we were born, in sin and iniquity (Ps. 51:5).

Our faith in Christ's sacrifice separates us from the world that we have known thus far and places us in Him. Being in Christ we are in this sense sanctified or set apart. We call this "positional sanctification." Truthfully, we did nothing meritorious to attain this position; we received this sanctification in receiving Christ, that is accepting Him as our Savior. This acceptance results in our being pronounced not guilty and removes us from the sphere of the world to the sphere of the sanctified, the separated ones, the holy men of God, the saints. Thus there are only these two classes of people: the sinners who have not been declared righteous and the sinners who have become saints. Righteousness, then, is the gateway to sainthood.

There is a perfection in this positional sanctification. Either we are in Christ or we are not. If we are in Him, we are set apart. As L. S. Chafer says: "Positional sanctification is as perfect as He is perfect. It is as complete for the weakest saint as it is for the strongest. It depends only on one's union with and position in Christ. All believers, not only some, are classified as 'the saints.' So, also, they are classed as the 'sanctified' " (Acts 20:32; 1 Cor.

1:2; 6:11; Heb. 10:10, 14; Jude 1). (See Chafer's *Systematic Theology*, "Doctrinal Summarization," Vol. 7, p. 280.)

The Corinthian believers were far from being perfect in their Christian behavior. In fact Paul had just finished admonishing them for their divisiveness and their devotion to men instead of to Christ (1 Cor. 1:10–13). Now in verse 30 he tells them that Christ became their sanctification. Moreover, in chapter 3:1–3 he says to them, "And I, brethren, could not speak unto you as unto spiritual, but as unto carnal, even as unto babes in Christ. I have fed you with milk, and not with meat: for hitherto ye were not able to bear it, neither yet are ye able. For ye are yet carnal: for whereas there is among you envying, and strife, and divisions, are ye not carnal, and walk as men?"

Yet in 1 Corinthians 1:2 Paul had addressed the Corinthians as "them that are sanctified in Christ Jesus, called to be saints." (See also 1 Cor. 6:11.) Though they were far from perfect and sinless in practice, the believers in Corinth were saints, or sanctified ones because they were in Christ.

Thus we conclude that you and I do not have to be perfectly sinless to be sanctified or a saint in the eyes of God, though the full implications of our sanctification still have to be worked out in our daily lives.

"Freedom Now"

The believer's position in Christ is due entirely to the work of Christ, and He never does anything imperfectly. Therefore, we cannot improve upon the work of Christ for us. God is holy or sanctified. This could never mean that there has been an improvement in God's state, since He has been perfectly holy from the beginning. Neither can our positional sanctification be improved upon, either by God or by us. Whatever God does shall be forever. Nothing can be taken from it and nothing added to it.

YOU WHO ARE IN CHRIST JESUS

Even so, the outworking of our sanctification is always subject to improvement. God constantly calls upon us to improve our manner of life, conforming it with the His character in Christ. That is growth, maturing, experimental or practical holiness.

A good analogy is that of a child born into this world. Through physical birth he moved from one world, that of his mother's womb (the "water" referred to in John 3:5), to the world of air (the "wind," symbolizing the Holy Spirit, in John 3:5). In this connection it is noteworthy that *pnoē* (4157), "breath," and *pneúma* (4151), "spirit," come from the same root word in Greek. A little baby is a perfect creature from the moment he is born. He had nothing to do with achieving this perfection, of course. He is in the world of air, of breath, just as much as a wise, mature old man. Both are perfect in this respect, although there is a tremendous difference between them in their growth and maturity. God places everything in the environment of each that they need for their growth. The actual practical growth and maturity will depend on the assimilation of those elements necessary for growth. Both the child and those around him will play a big role in determining how far he will advance in achieving goals within the sphere of Christ.

This growth of the saints, the babes in Christ, is experimental or practical sanctification, and Christians possess it according to their willingness to obey the commands of Christ. In truth, most of the Scriptures are admonitions indicating how a child of God can achieve the highest possible degree of this experiential holiness. Heaven is the portion of all saints, of all believers, but one determines how much each he will enjoy it by the degree of experimental holiness he achieves. The Scriptures call this our "work of faith" (1 Thess. 1:3). In heaven God will reward us according to our faithfulness, whereas our basic enjoyment of heaven will depend on our positional sanctification.

YOU WHO ARE IN CHRIST JESUS

Positional sainthood, therefore, is not subject to progression. Every born-again person is as much a saint the moment he is saved as he ever will be in time or eternity. The Spirit has chosen to give believers the title of "saints" more often than any other designation except one. They are called "brethren" 184 times, "saints" 62 times, and "Christians" 3 times. [L. S. Chafer, *Systematic Theology*, "Doctrinal Summarization," Vol. 7, p. 277.]

God the Father, the Son, and the Holy Spirit (1 Thess. 5:23; Eph. 5:26; Heb. 2:11; 9:13, 14; 13:12; Rom. 15:16; 2 Thess. 2:13) sanctifies men, places, and things positionally. Moreover, because sinful man can never justify or render himself righteous by his works (Rom. 3:20; Gal. 2:16; 5:4; Eph. 2:8, 9; Titus 3:4, 5), he can never positionally sanctify himself.

However, once saved or made righteous in Christ and separated unto Him, God actually commands him to sanctify himself. God constantly commanded Israel to sanctify themselves, to live up to their calling as His chosen people. Similarly, He says to believers in Christ, His chosen ones, that they are to be holy as He is holy. Thus the believer depending on God can sanctify himself by separating himself from sinful practices. That is holiness of life, not of position.

In 2 Timothy 2:21 we read, "If a man therefore purge himself from these [vessels of dishonor, to depart from iniquity], he shall be a vessel unto honor, sanctified, and meet for the master's use." "Present your bodies a living sacrifice, holy, acceptable unto God" (Rom. 12:1). "Come out from among them, and be ye separate" (2 Cor. 6:17). "Let us cleanse ourselves from all filthiness of the flesh and spirit, perfecting holiness in the fear of God" (2 Cor. 7:1). "Walk in the Spirit, and ye shall not fulfill the lust of the flesh" (Gal. 5:16). (*Ibid.* pp. 274–284; and H. A. Ironside, *Great Words of the Gospel*, pp. 53–62.)

Paul now adds a fourth word to describe the privilege that is ours because of our position in Christ. We acquire His wisdom,

YOU WHO ARE IN CHRIST JESUS

His righteousness, His sanctification—and finally His redemption. What is redemption? The word used in 1 Corinthians 1:30 is *apolútrōsis* (629) which occurs ten times in the New Testament (Luke 21:28; Rom. 3:24; 8:23; 1 Cor. 1:30; Eph. 1:7, 14; 4:30; Col. 1:14; Heb. 9:12, 15). In most of these instances it refers to a full deliverance of the soul from sin and particularly of the body from the grave. It is a compound word made up of the preposition *apó*, meaning "from or away from," and *lútrōsis* (3085), "ransoming." The verb is *lutróō* (3084), "to redeem," and the payment for redemption is *lútron* (3083), "a ransom." Two words synonymous with *lutróō*, "redeem," are *agorázō* (59), "to buy" (Rev. 5:9) and *exagorázō* (1805), "to buy out of the market and not to return" (Gal. 3:13). Modern Greek commonly uses the verbs *agorázō* and *exagorázō*. In Modern Greek *agorá* (58) is still the market place where shoppers go to buy what they need.

The Bible presents man in his sinful state as a prisoner, a slave of sin (Rom. 7:14; 1 Cor. 12:2; Eph. 2:2). He is helplessly condemned to die (Ezek. 18:4; John 3:18; Rom. 3:19; Gal. 3:10). Someone had to pay a price to buy off or redeem mankind from the slavery of sin. That price was death. The sinner himself had to pay for that, for "The wages of sin is death" (Rom. 6:23). However, God would accept a proper substitute (Heb. 9:27, 28). That Substitute who was able and willing to redeem all mankind potentially, and all who would accept His offer of redemption, was Christ.

When we are in Christ, that means the blood of Christ paid for us. That is our spiritual redemption. Our souls are first freed from the judgment and guilt of sin. Redemption thus is the means of our justification. We also experience freedom from the dominion or power of sin. That is our sanctification. Again the means of our sanctification is our redemption. It is through the blood of Christ that we transferred from the sphere of sin and Satan to the sphere of Christ and a holy life (1 John 1:9). Those seeking a political and social utopia cry out the slogan "Freedom Now." Yet only when mankind seeks first the true freedom from sin found in Christ will legitimate freedoms be granted to their fellowmen, for only as men are right with God can they be right with their neighbor.

LESSONS:

1. Paul says to the Corinthians and to all born-again believers that their lives are not merely external, that is, "just like" His life, parallel to His. They are actually in Christ, and He is in them. This is something unique that Christ does for those who accept Him.

2. To be in Christ means to be saved, to be born again, to be a new creature. Unless you believe that "God was in Christ, reconciling the world unto Himself" (2 Cor. 5:19), you cannot be saved.

3. Men have four basic needs that only Jesus Christ can satisfy. These are wisdom, righteousness, sanctification, and redemption. If men are basically unhappy, it is usually because they are not wise according to God; they are not righteous or sanctified or redeemed.

4. Christ, unlike all other leaders, did not merely teach the wisdom of God, righteousness, holiness, and redemption but truly became those things to us. We all need these qualities, but they can become ours only as Christ is ours. We cannot separate Christian qualities from the person of Christ Himself.

5. The wisest saint still has many questions about God. Despite this, Christians can be assured that God in Christ has given us all the understanding we need at the moment.

6. Wisdom is possessing true and satisfying answers to the fundamental questions that man has always asked of himself.

7. Righteousness, sanctification, and redemption are the three aspects of wisdom.

8. Christ's gift of righteousness, sanctification, and redemption, looked at in the direction of the past, brings pardon. Looked at as affecting the present, it brings holiness. Looked at as regarding the future, it will bring glory.

9. Imputed righteousness is the righteousness we have in Christ as a result of His work for us. When this imputed righteousness is worked out in our day to day conduct, it is known as imparted righteousness.

YOU WHO ARE IN CHRIST JESUS

10. We live righteously before God when we recognize our obligation to respond to His rights in us. We recognize His purpose for us, and we respond to it. Not to do so is to rob God.

11. When we are in Christ, the law of righteousness binds us. This law provides a positive duty toward God—what we should do as a result of our relationship with Him—and a negative duty, that from which we should abstain. Furthermore we have a positive and negative duty to our fellowman as well.

12. There are only two classes of people: the sinners who have not been declared righteous and the sinners who have become saints.

13. Positional sanctification means that every born-again person is as much a saint the moment he is saved as he ever will be in time or eternity. Positional sanctification is not subject to progression. However once saved or made righteous in Christ, he is also commanded to sanctify himself. This sanctification refers to holiness of life, not of position.

14. When we are in Christ, that means the blood of Christ has paid to redeem us. That is our spiritual redemption.

YOU WHO ARE IN CHRIST JESUS

1 Cor. 1:31 — *Glory in the Lord*

That, according as it is written, He that glorieth, let him glory in the Lord.

Is it enough for the believer in Christ to have redemption and sanctification? There is a third aspect of our redemption to which the Greek word *apolútrōsis* (629) sometimes refers. It is the redemption of our bodies (Rom. 8:21–23; Eph. 1:14; 4:30). Our practical holiness, or experiential sanctification as we call it, is incomplete because in this life we are still in the body with its carnal desires and appetites. As long as we are in the body, even as believers in Christ, justified saints, we shall struggle with it.

Paul himself said to the Corinthians, "I keep under my body, and bring it into subjection: lest that by any means, when I have preached to others, I myself should be a castaway" (1 Cor. 9:27). In Romans 6:12, 13 he says, "Let not sin therefore reign in your mortal body, that ye should obey it in the lusts thereof. Neither yield ye your members as instruments of unrighteousness unto sin: but yield yourselves unto God, as those that are alive from the dead, and your members as instruments of righteousness unto God." Because the body still seeks to dominate us, we are commanded to live a holy life.

Something to Boast About

In 1 Corinthians chapter one Paul repeatedly speaks of our
position in Christ: our wisdom, righteousness, and positional
sanctification that come to us from being in Him. Naturally the
Corinthians became disturbed and dismayed every time they suffered defeat in their struggle for a holy life commensurate with
their position in Christ. Thus Paul seeks to comfort them by assuring them that the day is coming when believers will receive
redemption from their sinful bodies. Certainly the day is coming when my body and yours will experience redemption, being
made into the likeness of the glorious body of our Lord Jesus
Christ. As now we experience redemption from the very power
and dominion of sin, but not without a personal struggle, so
then, after our physical death, we shall experience redemption
from the very presence of sin. Every believer, because he is in
Christ, has assurance of this freedom no matter how much
practical or experiential sanctification he attains.

In the past through the work of Christ we became clothed
with His wisdom, righteousness and sanctification or holiness.
However the last privilege, the redemption of our bodies, is yet
to come. God has reserved it for our enjoyment in the future, not
in the past or present. Because we accept Christ's death as a sacrifice for us and because God has accepted us in the Beloved, we
now have wisdom from God so that we can make proper eval-
uations. Likewise we have righteousness, that is, God no longer
condemns us as guilty sinners, and we have His holiness. Because
He died, we are what we are and where we are in Christ.

Still this cannot be compared to that which awaits us because
of our position in Christ. "Beloved, now are we the sons of
God, and it doth not yet appear what we shall be: but we know
that, when he shall appear, we shall be like him; for we shall see
him as he is" (1 John 3:2). No wonder Paul bursts out in joyful

anticipation, "Eye hath not seen, nor ear heard, neither have entered into the heart of man, the things which God hath prepared for them that love him" (1 Cor. 2:9). That is you. That is me. That is all of us who are in Christ. Is that not a wonderful thing to anticipate?

Which of our possessions in Christ result from our efforts? Absolutely none. His wisdom, righteousness, sanctification, and redemption of our bodies come to us simply by our being in Him. Our being in Him is also God's doing. We have absolutely no reason for pride except in that Christ has made us what we are. Such pride as this should certainly promote the deepest feelings of humility.

Verse 29 gives us a definite warning not to boast of our human attainments, for they are not really worth bragging about. "That no flesh should glory in His [God's] presence." When you talk to God, do not seek credit for what you have done. Moreover it would be more becoming if you also observed this in talking to others.

Now in verse 31 we have a more or less positive command to boast about or glory in what God did for us through Christ. Glorying and boasting seem to be instinctive with every man. All of us have something of which we are proud and about which we like to talk. Paul recognized this to be a natural human trait. Those out of Christ speak of their achievements, while those in Christ are to speak of the things that they enjoy in Him.

Glorying in this case is not pride of self but gratitude for gifts received. Boasting in the Lord is praising the Lord. In Psalm 34:1, 2, we read, "I will bless the Lord at all times: His praise shall continually be in my mouth. My soul shall make her boast in the Lord." Then again in Psalm 44:8 we read, "In God we boast all the day long, and praise thy name forever."

Paul probably summarily quotes Jeremiah 9:23, 24 here: "Thus saith the Lord, Let not the wise man glory in his wisdom, neither let the mighty man glory in his might, let not the rich man glory in his riches: but let him that glorieth glory in this, that He understandeth and knoweth me, that I am the Lord which exercise lovingkindness, judgment, and righteousness in the earth: for in these I delight, saith the Lord."

Thus the Lord wants us to boast, to praise, but to change the subject of our praise from self to God. Whereas in our unregenerate state we may have talked about our own wisdom, strength, and nobility, now we are to talk about Christ and what He has become to us: wisdom from God, righteousness, sanctification, and redemption. God thus does not suppress the instinct to boast but ennobles the area of its fulfillment. That is the glory of the Christian life.

Indeed Flavel said, "When God intends to fill a soul, He first makes it empty. When He intends to enrich a soul, He first makes it sensible to its miseries, wants, and nothingness." Likewise Charles Fox stipulated the following requisites for those who would serve in God's army: "Foolish enough to depend on God for wisdom; weak enough to have no honor but God's honor; despised enough to be kept in the dust at His feet; and being nothing enough for God to be everything."

Giving All Glory to God

Recently I read some wise advice from Bishop Wilberforce that deeply impressed me:

> Think as little as possible about yourself. Turn your eyes resolutely from any view of your influence, your success, your following. Above all, speak as little as possible about yourself. Guard especially against those little tricks by which a vain man seeks to bring around the conversation to himself and gain the praise or notice which his thirsty ears drink in so greedily. Let the Master's words ever ring in your ears: "How can ye believe, which receive honor one of another, and seek not the honor that cometh from God only?" (John 5:44).

The naturalist William Beebe told of an exercise in humility practiced during visits he made to Theodore Roosevelt at Sagamore Hill. Often, after an evening's talk, the two men would stroll over the wide-spreading lawn and look up into the night sky. They would see who could first find the pale bit of light near the upper left-hand corner of the Great Square of Pegasus. Then either Beebe or Roosevelt would exclaim, "That is the spiral galaxy of Andromeda! It is as large as our Milky Way. It is one of a hundred million galaxies. It is two and a half million light-years away. It consists of one hundred billion suns, many of them larger than our own sun!" After a moment of awesome silence, Roosevelt would grin and say, "Now I think we are small enough. Let's go to bed!"

"He that glorieth, let him glory in the Lord." Actually what is rendered as "he that glorieth" is a present participle in Greek, *ho* (3588) *kauchōménos* (2744), "he that is glorying." It is as if this glorying is inevitable and unavoidable. Of course, "glorying" is not the exact translation. The more accurate equivalent of "glory" in Greek would be *dóxa* (1391). The verb here is *kaúchōmai*, meaning "to boast with pride."

Since you are going to boast, you should boast in the Lord. Paul does not say "God" or "Jesus Christ," but "Lord," a title attributed to both God the Father and God the Son. *Kúrios* (2962), "Lord," means "the strong one." Through God's power through Jesus Christ you as a believer have become what you are. He is the Creator; you are merely the creature. Shakespeare said, "But man, proud man! drest in a little authority plays such fantastic tricks before high heaven as to make angels weep!" Never assume that you are what you are because of your strength of character. Realize that God in Christ is the source of all that you are and have.

The sovereignty of God, of the Lord Jesus Christ, should make us realize that we have no other object in which we can boast than that we are in Christ. Riches, power, position—all are from Him. He is Lord. Recognize the fleeting nature of everything that is in the world. When General Charles DeGaulle learned of the fall of Khrushchev, he exclaimed, "Sic transit gloria mundi!" "Thus passes away the glory of the world."

Peter said, "For all flesh [is] as grass, and all the glory of man as the flower of grass" (1 Pet. 1:24). How quickly a "Who's Who" becomes a "Who Was"! To understand the fleeting nature of one's greatness is to ascribe all power and glory to the Lord. Napoleon epitomized his fading fame thus: "I am doing now what will fill thousands of volumes in this generation. In the next, one volume will contain it all. In the third, a paragraph, in the fourth, a single line." Let your glory be in what will last as long as your being; let it be in the Lord. That is what the wisdom of God will lead the believer to do.

Let us human beings align our boasting with the rest of the created universe: "The heavens declare the glory of God" (Ps. 19:1). Let us align it with providence: "For of him, and through him, and to him, are all things: to whom be glory forever" (Rom. 11:36). Let us align it with the song of the angels: "Glory to God in the highest" (Luke 2:14). Even the individual personalities of the Godhead glory in each other. The Father glorifies the Son, as shown by Jesus' prayer in John 17:1, "Father, glorify thy Son, that thy Son also may glorify Thee." Also, when the Holy Spirit takes the things of Christ, and shows them to us, Jesus says, "He shall glorify Me" (John 16:14).

Now how can you, as a child of God, put this command of Paul's to "boast in the Lord" into practical operation? By taking advantage of every opportunity, and even in a sense creating opportunities, to show in word and deed that you belong to Him. If you really are proud of something, you cannot hide it. If you really are proud of the Lord, you will not be able to hide Him from view. Stand up for Him when you hear others oppose

Him and His principles. If you hear the proud ridicule His gospel and despise His people, put in a strong word for Him. He is Lord. He will give you the wisdom, courage, and strength to do it. Show that you belong to Him by the calmness and faith you demonstrate in troubled times. Let your boast in the Lord be shown through wise contempt for those material things and honors that others value so much but which you now to be worth so little. (See *The Biblical Illustrator*, 1 Corinthians, Vol. 1, p. 116.)

The praise of men is dear to the human heart. Yet some of the greatest of men have been the most humble, acknowledging their debt of gratitude to God. One of his friends asked the inventor of the telegraph, Professor Samuel F. B. Morse, "Professor Morse, when you were making your experiments in your rooms at the university, did you ever come to a standstill, not knowing what to do next?"

"Oh, yes, more than once."

"At such times what did you do next?"

"Whenever I could not see my way clearly, I prayed for more light."

"And the light generally came?"

"Yes. And may I tell you that, when flattering honors came to me from the invention which bears my name, I never felt I deserved them. I had made a valuable application of electricity, not because I was superior to other men, but solely because God, who meant it for mankind, must reveal it to someone, and was pleased to reveal it to me."

The first message sent by the inventor of the Morse code was, "What hath God wrought!" God grant us the grace when some accomplishment of ours brings praise, to acknowledge in our hearts and with our lips that all glory belongs to Him.

Glory in the Lord

LESSONS:

1. Those out of Christ speak of their achievements, but those in Christ are to speak of the things that they enjoy in Christ.
2. Glorying in this case is not pride of self but gratitude for gifts received. Boasting in the Lord is praising the Lord.

Bibliography

Aitken, W. H. M. H. *The Glory of the Gospel.* London: John F. Shaw and Co., n.d.

Asimov, Isaac. *The Wellsprings of Life.* Greenville, SC: Adon Books, 1960.

Barnes, Albert. *Notes on the New Testament (1 Corinthians).* Grand Rapids, MI: Baker Book House, 1949.

Bernard, Thomas Dehany. *The Progress of Doctrine in the New Testament.* Grand Rapids, MI: Wm. B. Eerdmans Publishing Co., 1949.

Blackstone, W. E. *Jesus Is Coming.* Old Tappan, NJ: Fleming H. Revell Co., 1908.

Bowran, J. G. "The Family Church." *Christian World Pulpit* 75 (1909): 55.

Castles, Norman. "Partnership." *Christian World Pulpit* 148 (1945): 52, 53.

Chafer, Lewis Sperry. *Systematic Theology.* Vol. 3. Dallas, TX: Dallas Seminary Press, 1948.

_____. "Doctrinal Summarization." *Systematic Theology.* Vol. 7. Dallas, TX: Dallas Seminary Press, 1948.

Charlton, J. M. "Fellowship With Christ." *Christian World Pulpit* 14 (1878): 337–39.

Chesterton, W. Ridley. "The Word of the Cross." *Christian World Pulpit* 116 (1929): 138–40.

Crago, T. Howard. *Real Discipleship.* London: Marshall, Morgan & Scott, n.d.

Craig, Clarence Tucker. *A Reader's Notebook.* Compiled by Gerald Kennedy. New York: Harper & Brothers, 1953.

Cremer, Hermann. *Biblico-Theological Lexicon of New Testament Greek.* Edinburgh: T. & T. Clark, 1954.

Cruz, Nicky. "God's Cure for the Dope Addict." In *Quest for Reality,* compiled by Merton B. Osborn. Chicago: Moody Press, 1967.

Cumming, John. *The Great Preparation.* 1st ser. New York: Rudd & Carleton, 1860.

De Haan, M. R. *Divine Healing and Divine Healers (pamphlet).* Grand Rapids, MI: Radio Bible Class.

Eldersveld, Peter. *The Folly of Our Faith (pamphlet).* Chicago: The Back to

God Hour.

Elliott, W. H. *Day by Day*. London: Nicholson and Watson, Ltd., 1940.

Getty, George A. *Foundations of Faith*. Philadelphia, PA: The United Lutheran Publication House, 1925.

Griffith, Thomas, W. H. *The Essentials of Life*. London: Pickering & Inglis, n.d.

Hastings, James, ed. *The Great Texts of the Bible, 2 Corinthians and Galatians*. London: T. & T. Clark, 1913.

_____, ed. *A Dictionary of the Bible*. Vol. 4. Edinburgh: T. & T. Clark, 1923.

Ironside, H. A. *Great Words of the Gospel*. Chicago: Moody Press, 1944.

Jones, J. D. "The Glory of God and Man." *Christian World Pulpit* 82 (1912): 161–63.

_____. *The Hope of the Gospel*. London: Hodder and Stoughton, 1926.

_____. *Morning and Evening*. London: Hodder and Stoughton, 1934.

Jowett, J. H. "Even unto the Clouds." *Christian World Pulpit* 81 (1912): 291, 292.

Kittel, Gerhard, ed. *Theological Dictionary of the New Testament*. Vol. 1. Grand Rapids, MI: Wm. B. Eerdmans Publishing Co., 1964.

_____. *Ibid*. Vol. 2. 1964.

_____. *Ibid*. Vol. 3. 1965.

_____. *Ibid*. Vol. 5. 1967.

Ladd, George E. *The Blessed Hope*. Grand Rapids, MI: Wm. B. Eerdmans Publishing Co., 1966.

Lenski, R. C. H. *The Interpretation of St. Paul's First and Second Epistles to the Corinthians*. Minneapolis, MN: Augsburg Publishing House, 1961.

Liddell, H. G. & Scott, R. A. *Greek-English Lexicon*. Oxford: Clarendon Press, 1958.

Liddon, H. P. *Liddon's Advent Sermons*. Vol. 1. London: Rivingtons, 1889.

_____. *Easter Sermons*. Vol. 2. New York: E. P. Dutton and Co., 1885.

_____. *Passiontide Sermons*. London: Longmans, Green, and Co., 1891.

_____. *Sermons on Some Words of St. Paul*. London: Longmans, Green, and Co., 1898.

Lloyd-Jones, Martyn. "The Preaching of the Cross." *Christian World Pulpit* 139: 232, 233.

Maclaren, Alexander. *Expositions of Holy Scripture, St. Paul's Epistles to the*

Corinthians (*to 2 Cor., ch. 5*). New York: A. C. Armstrong and Son, 1910.

_____. "The Unsearchable Riches of Christ." *The Contemporary Pulpit* 5 (1886): 15–25.

MacLeod, Donald. "The Message of the Cross." *Christian World Pulpit* 61 (1902): 282–84.

Martin W. W. *The Sufficiency of the Cross.* London: Pickering & Inglis, n.d.

Miller, J. R. *The Garden of the Heart.* London: Hodder & Stoughton, 1906.

Morgan, G. Clampbell. *The Corinthian Letters of Paul.* London: Oliphants Ltd., 1954.

Morrison, A. Cressy. *Man Does Not Stand Alone.* Old Tappan, NJ: Fleming H. Revell Co., 1944.

Murray, Andrew. *Abide in Christ.* New York: Grosset & Dunlap, n.d.

Olver, G. W. *The Biblical Illustrator, 1 Corinthians.* Vol. 1. Edited by J. S. Exell. Grand Rapids, MI: Baker Book House, 1964.

Passmore, T. H. "Grace." *Lenten Sermons.* Edited by Frederick J. North. Garden City, NY: Doubleday, Doran & Co., 1928.

Pentecost, J. Dwight. *Things to Come.* Findlay, Ohio: Dunham Publishing Co., 1958.

Riley, W. B. *The Theory of Evolution Tested by Mathematics.* N.p., n.d.

Robertson, A. T. *A Grammar of the Greek New Testament in the Light of Historical Research.* New York: George H. Doran Co., 1923.

Robertson, Archibald, and Plummer, Alfred. "A Critical and Exegetical Commentary on the Epistle of St. Paul to the Corinthians." In *International Critical Commentary* (1956):10, 19.

Robertson, F. W. *The Biblical Illustrator, 1 Corinthians.* Vol. 1. Edited by J. S. Exell. Grand Rapids, MI: Baker Book House, 1964.

Robinson, Wade. *The Philosophy of the Atonement.* New York: E. P. Dutton & Co., 1912.

Secker, Thomas. *The Works of Thomas Secker.* Vol. 1. Dublin: Beilby Porteus & George Stinton, 1775.

Smith, Wilbur M. *The Biblical Doctrine of Heaven.* Chicago: Moody Press, 1968.

Smyth, Newman. "God's Faithfulness." *Christian World Pulpit* 50 (1896): 43–45.

Spurgeon, C. H. *Sermons on the Blood and Cross of Christ.* Edited by C. T.

Cook. London: Marshall, Morgan & Scott, 1965.

————. *The New Park Street Pulpit.* Vol. 1. Grand Rapids, MI: Zonder-van Publishing House, 1963.

Trench, Richard C. *Synonyms of the New Testament.* Grand Rapids, MI: Wm. B. Eerdmans Publishing Co., 1953.

Turner, Ralph H. "The Cross—A Stumbling Block." *Christian World Pulpit* 142 (1942): 142–44.

Vance, Joseph A. "Unconscious Saintliness." *Christian World Pulpit* 109 (1926): 84.

Watson, Thomas. *A Body of Divinity.* London: The Banner of Truth Trust, 1960.

Watt, Gordon. *The Cross in Faith and Conduct.* Parkstone, Dorset, England: The Overcomer Literature Trust, n.d.

"What Does It Mean to Be Lost?" *Good News from a Far Country.* Grand Rapids, MI: Wm. B. Eerdmans Publishing Co., 1934.

Whyte, Alexander. "Job Groping." *Lord, Teach Us to Pray.* Garden City, NY: Doubleday, Doran and Co., 1929.

Young, Dinsdale T. *The Crimson Book.* Cincinnati, Ohio: Jennings and Graham, 1903.

Lexicons, Encyclopedias, and References for Greek Readers, from Classical and Koine Greek to Modern Greek

Byzantiou, S. D. *Lexikon tēs Hellēnikēs Glōssēs* (*Lexicon of the Hellenic Language*). Athens: Koromēla, A., 1852.

Dēmētrakou, D. *Lexikon tēs Hellēnikēs Glōssēs* (*Lexicon of the Hellenic Language*). Athens: Dēmētrakou, 1954.

Enkuklopaidikon Glōssologikon Lexikon (*Encyclopedic Glossological Lexicon*). Athens: Morfōtikē Hetaireia.

Enkuklopaidikon Lexikon Eleutheroudaki (*Eleutheroudaki Encyclopedic Lexicon*). Athens: Eleutheroudakis, 1927.

Kalaraki, Michael and Nikolas Galanos. *Iōannou tou Chrusostomou Ta Hapanta* (*Complete Works of John Chrysostom*), 1899.

Liddell, Henry George, and Robert Scott. *Greek–English Lexicon*, as Translated and Enriched by Xenophōn P. Moschos and Michael Kōnstantinides. Athens: John Sideris.

Megalē Helēnikē Enkuklopaideia (*Great Hellenic Encyclopedia*). Pursos (Pyrsos), Athens: Hēlios.

Neōteron Enkuklopaidikon Lexikon Hēliou (*New Encyclopedic Lexicon "Hēlios"*). Athens: Hēlios.

Papaoikonomou, George L. *Lexikon Anōmalōn Rhēmatōn* (*Lexicon of Irregular Verbs*). Athens: Kagiaphas.

Stamatakou, J. D., *Lexikon Archaias Hellēnikēs Glōssēs* (*Lexicon of the Ancient Hellenic Language*). Athens: Petrou Dēmētrakou, 1949.

Works by Spiros Zodhiates

Repent (*booklet*). Ridgefield, NJ: AMG Publishers, n.d.

Was Christ God? Grand Rapids, MI: Wm. B. Eerdmans Publishing Company, 1970.

Which Saves? Baptism, Repentance, Faith? (*booklet*). Ridgefield, NJ: AMG Publishers, 1961.

Scripture Index

10:7	274
11:19	159
12	172
12:2	402
12:4, 9	88
12:11	69, 86
12:13	201
12:28, 30, 31	88
13:9	172, 379
14:7	63
15	116, 266, 327
15:1, 2	262
15:13–19	191
15:23	93
15:25	6
15:24–28	45
15:45	196, 274
15:51, 52	97
16:15	215
16:17	xii

2 Corinthians

1:1	3, 7
1:11	88
1:14	115
3:5	86, 102
4:7	363
4:17	154, 359
5:9, 10	110
5:17	79, 375, 397
5:18–21	194
5:21	196, 399
5:19	377, 403
6:10, 11	59
6:17	401
7:1	23, 401
8:1–5	146
12:7	319
12:9	43

Galatians

2:7–9, 11–14	187
2:16	401
2:20	151, 378, 389
3:1	194
3:2, 3, 11	188
3:6	389
3:10	402
3:13	402
3:26	60
3:27	203
4:7	51, 59
4:13	222
5:16	182, 401
5:17, 19	182
5:19–21	181
6:14	194, 238

Ephesians

1:1	3
1:6	378
1:7	194, 402
1:11	11, 110
1:14	402, 405
1:22	18
2:2	402
2:8	138, 210, 374, 401
2:12	248
2:20	3
3:5	3
4:30	402
5:23	18
5:26	401

Philippians

1:10	115
1:12	359
2:14, 15	107